Open Secrets

OXFORD STUDIES IN WESTERN ESOTERIꓳ

Series Editor
Henrik Bogdan, University of Gothenburg

Editorial Board
Jean-Pierre Brach, École Pratique des Hautes Études
Carole Cusack, University of Sydney
Christine Ferguson, University of Stirling
Olav Hammer, University of Southern Denmark
Wouter Hanegraaff, University of Amsterdam
Ronald Hutton, University of Bristol
Orion Klautau, Tohoku University
Jeffrey J. Kripal, Rice University
Michael Stausberg, University of Bergen
Egil Asprem, Stockholm University
Gordan Djurdjevic, Independent scholar
Peter Forshaw, University of Amsterdam
Jesper Aa. Petersen, Norwegian University of Science and Technology
Manon Hedenborg White, Malmö University

CHILDREN OF LUCIFER
The Origins of Modern Religious
Satanism
Ruben van Luijk

SATANIC FEMINISM
Lucifer as the Liberator of Woman in
Nineteenth-Century Culture
Per Faxneld

THE SIBYLS OF LONDON
A Family on the Esoteric Fringes of
Georgian England
Susan Sommers

WHAT IS IT LIKE TO BE DEAD?
Near-Death Experiences, Christianity,
and the Occult
Jens Schlieter

AMONG THE SCIENTOLOGISTS
History, Theology, and Praxis
Donald A. Westbrook

RECYCLED LIVES
A History of Reincarnation in
Blavatsky's Theosophy
Julie Chajes

THE ELOQUENT BLOOD
The Goddess Babalon and the
Construction of Femininities in Wes
Esotericism
Manon Hedenborg White

GURDJIEFF
Mysticism, Contemplation, and
Exercises
Joseph Azize

INITIATING THE MILLENIUM
The Avignon Society and Illuminisn
in Europe
Robert Collis and Natalie Bayer

IMAGINING THE EAST
The Early Theosophical Society
Tim Rudbog and Erik Sand

MYSTIFYING KABBALAH
Academic Scholarship, Nation
Theology, and New Age
Boaz Huss

SPIRITUAL ALCHEMY
From Jacob Boehme to
Mary Anne Atwood
Mike A. Zuber

THE SUBTLE BODY
A Genealogy
Simon Cox

OCCULT IMPERIUM
Arturo Reghini, Roman Traditionalism,
and the Anti-Modern Reaction in
Fascist Italy
Christian Giudice

VESTIGES OF A PHILOSOPHY
Matter, the Meta-Spiritual, and the
Forgotten Bergson
John Ó Maoilearca

PROPHECY, MADNESS, AND HOLY
WAR IN EARLY MODERN EUROPE
A Life of Ludwig Friedrich Gifftheil
Leigh T.I. Penman

HÉLÈNE SMITH
Occultism and the Discovery of the
Unconscious
Claudie Massicotte

LIKE A TREE UNIVERSALLY SPREAD
Sri Sabhapati Swami and Śivarājayoga
Keith Edward Cantú

FRIENDSHIP IN DOUBT
Aleister Crowley, J. F. C. Fuler, Victoria B.
Neuburg, and British Agnosticism
Richard Kaczynski

THE UNKNOWN GOD
W. T. Smith and the Thelemites
Martin P. Starr

AMERICAN AURORA
Environment and Apocalypse in the Life
of Johannes Kelpius
Timothy Grieve-Carlson

THE LADY AND THE BEAST
The Extraordinary Partnership between
Frieda Harris and Aleister Crowley
Deja Whitehouse

THE MAGICAL DIARIES OF
LEAH HIRSIG 1923–1925
Aleister Crowley, Magick, and the New
Occult Woman
Manon Hedenborg White and
Henrik Bogdan

LIGHT IS SOWN
On the Cultivation of Kabbalah in
Medieval Castile
Avishai Bar-Asher and Jeremy
Phillip Brown

OPEN SECRETS
The Popular Fiction of Britain's Occult
Revival, 1842–1936
Christine Ferguson

Open Secrets

The Popular Fiction of Britain's Occult Revival, 1842–1936

CHRISTINE FERGUSON

OXFORD
UNIVERSITY PRESS

Oxford University Press is a department of the University of Oxford.
It furthers the University's objective of excellence in research, scholarship,
and education by publishing worldwide. Oxford is a registered trade mark of
Oxford University Press in the UK and certain other countries.

Published in the United States of America by Oxford University Press
198 Madison Avenue, New York, NY 10016, United States of America.

© Oxford University Press 2025

All rights reserved. No part of this publication may be reproduced, stored in a retrieval system, transmitted, used for text and data mining, or used for training artificial intelligence, in any form or by any means, without the prior permission in writing of Oxford University Press, or as expressly permitted by law, by license or under terms agreed with the appropriate reprographics rights organization. Inquiries concerning reproduction outside the scope of the above should be sent to the Rights Department, Oxford University Press, at the address above.

You must not circulate this work in any other form
and you must impose this same condition on any acquirer.

Library of Congress Cataloging-in-Publication Data
Names: Ferguson, Christine, author.
Title: Open secrets : the popular fiction of Britain's occult revival, 1842–1936 / Christine Ferguson.
Identifiers: LCCN 2025002001 (print) | LCCN 2025002002 (ebook) |
ISBN 9780197651599 (hardback) | ISBN 9780197651612 (epub) |
ISBN 9780197651629 | ISBN 9780197651605
Subjects: LCSH: Paranormal fiction, English—History and criticism. |
English fiction—19th century—History and criticism. | Popular
literature—Great Britain—History and criticism. | English
fiction—20th century—History and criticism. | LCGFT: Literary criticism.
Classification: LCC PR830.O33 F47 2025 (print) | LCC PR830.O33 (ebook) |
DDC 823/.809—dc23/eng/20250305
LC record available at https://lccn.loc.gov/2025002001
LC ebook record available at hhttps://lccn.loc.gov/2025002002

DOI: 10.1093/oso/9780197651599.001.0001

Printed by Marquis Book Printing, Canada

The manufacturer's authorized representative in the EU for product safety is
Oxford University Press España S.A., Parque Empresarial San Fernando de Henares,
Avenida de Castilla, 2 – 28830 Madrid (www.oup.es/en).

To Patricia Merivale, for opening the door

"I withhold no lesson from the pure aspirant; I am a dark enigma to the general seeker."

Edward Bulwer Lytton, *Zanoni* (1842)

"When people start talking about the danger posed by making psychic knowledge available to the masses, they are generally trying to monopolize the knowledge for themselves. In my opinion, the best safeguard against such abuse of knowledge is widespread dissemination."

William S. Burroughs, *The Adding Machine: Selected Essays* (1985)

"I think that nothing can be communicated by the art of writing."

Jorge Luis Borges, "The House of Asterion" (1947)

Contents

Acknowledgments	xi
1. Introduction: In Bulwer's Bookshop	1
2. Magical Meisters: The Problem of Progress in the Occult *Bildungsroman*	40
3. Self, Sex, and Liberation in the Female Reincarnation Romance	72
4. Journoccultism: Numinous News and the Mantic Fragment	103
5. Occult Detection in the Aeon of Horus	138
6. Conclusion: Forming Occult Fiction in the Secular Age	170
Notes	183
Bibliography	209
Index	225

Acknowledgments

This book was a long time in the making and could not have been completed without the generous support of many institutions, funders, and individuals. A Carnegie Small Research Grant in 2014 allowed me to immerse myself in the work of the incredible and, at the time, still relatively little-known Victorian occultist and novelist Mabel Collins, whose writing helped me to formulate the research questions that lie at the heart of *Open Secrets*. A subsequent Princeton University Library Fellowship (in 2015) and Alfred A. and Blanche W. Knopf Travel Stipend to the Harry Ransom Center (in 2018) allowed me to access key archives dedicated to my focal authors. In these archives, and at the Warburg Institute, Senate House Library, and the British Library, I was supported by expert librarians who helped me to make the most of my time and identify crucial sources within their holdings. Special mention is due to Mr X of *The Fortean Web Site of Mr X*, who magnanimously provided me with important publication details for Charles Fort's early periodical fiction and sent me a pen drive full of very rare Forteana that I very much hope will seed a future project.

My approach to popular fictional occulture has been enriched by the feedback I received from the wonderful audiences at, and organizers of, the conferences where I presented early versions of this research. For their generous invitations to deliver plenary lectures, I thank the European Popular Culture Association, the International Gothic Association, the British Women Writers Association, the Donner Institute for Research in Religious and Cultural History, and Åbo Akademi University.

For their intellectual inspiration, encouragement, invaluable subject knowledge, and friendship, I thank my colleagues within Gothic, Esotericism, and Victorian Studies who are themselves producing groundbreaking scholarship on the interface between spirituality, cultural history, and literature: Aren Roukema, Giuliano D'Amico, Liana Saif, Julia Strube, Egil Asprem, Kateryna Zorya, Per Faxneld, Manon Hedenborg White, Justine Bakker, Tanya Cheadle, Roger Luckhurst, Darryl Jones, Nick Daly, and Andrew Radford.

xii ACKNOWLEDGMENTS

Two semesters of research leave funded by the University of Stirling allowed me to start and finish the writing of the manuscript. I am particularly grateful also to my colleagues in Stirling's Division of Literature and Languages who made it possible for me to take the time away. Special thanks are due to Tim Jones and Michael Shaw, brilliant scholars of Victorian and Gothic literature, respectively, whom I am privileged to work alongside and call friends.

For their confidence in *Open Secrets* and support in its production, I thank my series editor, Henrik Bogdan; the expert staff at Oxford University Press; and my reviewers. Finally, for their humor, patience, solidarity, and love as I wrote *Open Secrets*, I thank my sisters, Annette Ferguson and Heather Ferguson, and my partner, Angus Mackay.

1

Introduction

In Bulwer's Bookshop

1.1 Threshold Fictions

We stand on the threshold of a shadowy interior space that simultaneously beckons and repels. The alluring contents within are guarded jealously by a stern gatekeeper who seems to have forgotten that we are here, after all, by invitation. Here are said to lie treasures of inestimable value to seekers sufficiently pure and bold of heart to face the potentially fatal risks of their acquisition.[1] Yet even if won, their possession may prove fleeting. Some who cross this border suffer immediate and rude expulsion; others, initially more successful, find the riches gained within stolen away in the night, never to be regained. Better, perhaps, to stay away in the face of such prospective disappointment, heartbreak, even death. Yet still, the threshold beckons, its risks and dangers only heightening its irresistible attraction for those who would grasp the secrets undiscernible by mundane perception and hidden from the common ranks of humanity.

The scenario I have just described is one with which scholars and aficionados of literary occulture will be deeply familiar. It is replayed again and again in the popular fictional texts on which this study will focus, perhaps nowhere more famously than in that grandfather of modern British occult novels: Edward Bulwer Lytton's *Zanoni* (1842).[2] Although rarely read by non-specialist readers today, *Zanoni*'s influence on the literary and new religious scenes of mid-Victorian Britain was immense and unparalleled, inspiring imitation and praise from writers of such diverse reputations, readerships, and affiliations as Charles Dickens, Emma Hardinge Britten, and H. P. Blavatsky. Indeed, "as far as esotericism in Victorian Britain is concerned," Joscelyn Godwin has remarked, "there is no more important literary work than *Zanoni*, and . . . no more important figure than Bulwer-Lytton."[3] A key source of the novel's renown lay in its origination of the Dweller on the Threshold archetype, a horrifying and erotically provocative wraith who

Open Secrets. Christine Ferguson, Oxford University Press. © Oxford University Press 2025.
DOI: 10.1093/oso/9780197651599.003.0001

2 OPEN SECRETS

appears in Book Four to repel the premature initiation attempt of the insufficiently prepared neophyte Clarence Glyndon, taunting him with calls to "kiss me, my mortal lover."[4] For wanting to know too much, too soon, and for the wrong reasons, Glyndon is left a broken man, destined to be dogged by the Dweller until he can learn the courage to face and resist it. In many respects, the Dweller's fame as spiritual gatekeeper has surpassed that of his creator; while Bulwer's literary reputation fell at the end of the nineteenth century into a marked decline from which it has never fully recovered,[5] the Dweller, granted new currency in the works of high-profile twentieth-century occult practitioners such as Rudolf Steiner and Dion Fortune, continues to exert an influence on the modern occultural imagination.[6]

The Dweller may be *Zanoni's* best-known guardian of the threshold, but it is not the landmark novel's only, first, or necessarily, as this study will suggest, most important one. *Open Secrets* examines the popular genre fiction produced by participants within and adjacent to Britain's modern occult revival in relation to another, earlier gatekeeper: the suspicious and calculating bookseller whose caginess about his stock becomes a vital literary and spiritual marketing strategy, and who thinks as much about the popular narrative forms of this world as he does the exalted conditions of the next. We encounter him in *Zanoni's* introductory paratext, where Bulwer invokes the found manuscript trope of the Gothic tradition that he knew so well to produce a sensational pre-history for the story about to unfold. Here, an unnamed, spiritually aspirational narrator—perhaps, readers are led to suspect, Bulwer himself—describes his visit to the dusty Covent Garden book shop run by the surly Mr. D__, whose truncated name functions both as allusion to the real-life London occult bookseller John Denley (1764–1842) and consonantal forerunner of the more formidable guardian we will encounter later on, when D__ becomes Dweller.[7] Although the historical Denley was, in R. A. Gilbert's words "only too willing to sell his books,"[8] Bulwer's Mr. D__ is a much more reticent figure who deliberately and self-defeatingly dissuades buyers from purchasing his hard-won and beloved arcane stock. "It went absolutely to his heart when a customer entered his shop," our narrator remarks; "he watched the movements of the presumptuous intruder with a vindictive glare, he fluttered around him with uneasy vigilance; he frowned; he groaned."[9] On those rare occasions when he reluctantly fulfils the commercial function of his shop, Mr. D__ is immediately struck by seller's remorse, "not infrequently" appearing at the homes of successful customers to beg them to "sell him back, at [their] own terms, what [they] had so egregiously

INTRODUCTION 3

bought from him."[10] Given these propensities, it is unsurprising that what will turn out to be the main text of *Zanoni*, a tale of an elite and ancient two-man occult brotherhood operating in late eighteenth-century Europe, was not purchased from Mr. D__. Rather, his shop simply offers a stage for our narrator to encounter the mysterious "old gentleman"[11]—perhaps the now-aged Clarence Glyndon himself—who bequeaths to him the two cipher manuscripts that inform the narrative of *Zanoni*, along with a substantial financial inheritance. The money, we learn, is no simple gift; it comes with formidable conditions. Although, like Mr. D__ and Zanoni himself, the old gentleman has a horror of the common masses, he nonetheless desires that his young protégé "prepare" these cipher manuscripts "for the public."[12] The existence of the ensuing narrative signals that this venture has been successful, at least in part. At the introduction's close, our narrator explains that he only discovered the second cipher manuscript two years into the translation of the first, and remains uncertain as to whether his synthesis and translation of the two is correct: "with all my pains, I am by no means sure that I have invariably given the true meaning of the cipher."[13] By refusing to return to the frame narrative at the novel's close, Bulwer denies readers any final clue as to the authenticity of what they have just read. Secrets of some kind have spilled across the threshold, but of what nature, credibility, or coherence, we must remain deeply uncertain.

What does this opening interlude in Mr. D__'s shop contribute to our understanding of Bulwer's germinal occult novel, and how might it yield new interpretive vistas for the emergent field of literary esotericism studies within which *Open Secrets* is situated? Perhaps most immediately, it reminds us that the vehemently elitist and restrictive philosophy of knowledge acquisition that runs through *Zanoni*'s highly conservative central plot, with its repeated attacks on republicanism, political egalitarianism, and scientific materialism, is not the whole story.[14] No matter how much Mr. D__ may loathe the prospect of his hard-won textual pearls falling into the hands of unruly swine, he never shuts up shop; similarly, Bulwer's old Rosicrucian gentleman cannot bear the prospect of his secret cipher story being available only to an audience of spiritually vetted initiates, even as he acknowledges that it is unlikely to find mass favor. In this, fascinatingly, he is wrong; our narrator explains that the first partial publication of the text in a periodical "excite[d] more curiosity than I had presumed to anticipate."[15] Despite, or perhaps more accurately, *because*, of its anti-commercial, elitist window-dressing, the occult novel remains closely attuned to the rhythms and requirements of the

4 OPEN SECRETS

popular literary market, using the conceits of secrecy and inaccessibility to render itself all the more attractive to the mass reading public it has always courted, no matter how much it might sometimes protest the opposite.

Further, this scene establishes reading, reception, and commercial textual circulation as central preoccupations of modern occult fiction, dramatizing its reliance, no less than that of its secular counterparts, upon the always unstable and expanding community of readers in which they circulate, one whose interests, interpretive practices, identities, and beliefs are far from homogeneous. The scene compels us to abandon any fantasy of achieving interpretive totality, transparency, or supremacy, reminding us that there is no guarantee that the text we are reading is indeed the right or final version, and raising the possibility that its spiritual message, if accessible at all, might be better told or sold in another way, or through a different formula.

As such, the episode in Bulwer's bookshop can usefully prevent us from relegating the incredibly rich range of popular genre fiction produced by high-profile practitioners, proselytizers, and seekers within Britain's occult revival to the status of simple content-delivery vehicle, a corpus which adopts the trappings of fiction only to unreflexively or cynically share esoteric teachings or to document in thinly veiled form the real-life spiritual experiences of its creators. Instead, it reorients us toward the aesthetic ambition, reach, and formal variety of a body of fiction whose considerable genre innovation has too often been lost within what we will come to recognize as the largely biographical and literalist priorities of literary esotericism studies. The diverse popular literary genres adopted and expanded by Britain's fiction-writing occult revivalists—including the *Bildungsroman*, the romance, the eclectic New Journalistic periodical story, the detective tale—were never just arbitrary receptacles for authorial belief or experience. Instead, they were crucial sites for interlinked projects of spiritual and aesthetic innovation. *Open Secrets* focuses less on the always elusive content of the mysteries, whether actual or simply rhetorical, that occult fiction promises to expose than on the genre forms, conventions, and histories through which such alleged secrets are installed and partially revealed. The concept of the paradoxical secret, one that is both jealously guarded and also widely advertised, has, as Hugh Urban has recently argued, long been central to the social organization, public status, and authorizing strategies of modern occultism;[16] in its prioritization of wonder, mystery, narrative *telos*, and the suspenseful "dialectic of veiling and unveiling . . . lure and withdrawal,"[17] popular fiction offered a perfect site through which to dramatize

INTRODUCTION 5

not just the content but the typical structure of occult knowledge, to play with its logical, narrative, and experiential contradictions, and to explore its creative, philosophical, and political capacities in ways not available to emic works of occult non-fiction addressed exclusively to committed spiritual seekers. We will examine these capacities through a series of chronologically arranged case studies focused on select genres in which some of the best-known modern esoteric seekers, British-born and, or, based for much of their writing careers, made their name during the occult revival, that period of renewed scientific, religious, and cultural interest in ceremonial magic, hidden forces, and spiritual survival trigged by the widespread promulgation of mesmerism at the turn of the nineteenth century and the emergence of modern spiritualism and then psychical research several decades later. The early twentieth century brought not an end to, but a dramatic transformation of the revival, with the near total abandonment of psychical research by the scientific mainstream and the widespread tabloid moral panic targeted at controversial Thelemite Aleister Crowley (1875–1947) changing the way in which occult and spiritualist pursuits were publicly perceived,[18] and paving the way to counter-cultural and New Age forms of esotericism. *Open Secrets* focuses primarily on the period from publication date of Bulwer's *Zanoni* (1842) to that of Fortune's *The Goat Foot God* (1936), a novel that pays homage to Bulwerian precedent by returning us to the threshold of a closely located but now much more accessible central London occult bookshop. Its goal is both to recognize the fascinating contribution of the revival's fiction, some of which receives its first ever sustained scholarly analysis here, to the emergence, development, and religious reception of key genres of popular literature, and to place in closer dialogue the two main disciplinary sites—Gothic studies and esotericism studies—within which emically authored occult fiction has hitherto been studied, whenever this much-misunderstood body of writing has been examined at all.

1.2 Esotericism Studies and the Gothic: Toward a Rapprochement

Since the turn of millennium, Gothic studies and esotericism studies have served as central investigative sites for the analysis of occult fiction. United by their willingness to take seriously non-canonical imaginative literary works that represent or deploy unorthodox spiritual beliefs and practices, they

6 OPEN SECRETS

have approached this territory from different directions: Gothic studies, by contextualizing the supernaturalism of this corpus within the tradition of the dark fantastic and through psychoanalytic concepts of repression and abjection, and esotericism studies, by connecting it, either via authorship, narrative content, or reception, to historical iterations of specific esoteric traditions and movements, including Kabbalah, Rosicrucianism, Theosophy, alchemy, and spiritualism. In terms of disciplinary formation, esotericism studies is younger than Gothic studies, establishing the majority of its research centers, degree programs, scholarly societies, and dedicated academic journals in the first decade of the twenty-first century. Although increasingly interdisciplinary in scope, its early membership was largely, if not exclusively, composed of historians and sociologists of religion.[19] Gothic studies, by contrast, took off within Anglo American literary studies in the 1970s and 1980s, fostered and catalyzed by feminist challenges to, and expansions of, the European literary canon, by the rise of psychoanalytic and post-structuralist theory, and by the growth of cultural studies. These different histories, approaches, and agendas have complicated and, in some cases, impeded the relationship between the two sub-disciplines, rendering it thus far less productive than their shared seriousness of purpose and overlapping primary source base promises. A closer and more dynamic relationship between the two is both possible and necessary for the future development of occult fiction studies; to forge it, we must first recognize and address the blind spots that have hitherto kept these fields apart.

1.2.1 Rethinking Rejection: Three Challenges for Literary Esotericism Studies

Although esotericism studies may be a relatively new formation (or academic "brand"), the history of magic and its representation within art and culture have long been established as legitimate subjects of scholarly research across a broad spectrum of humanities disciplines, including philosophy, art history, religious studies, and literary studies, even if not always packaged in readily identifiable terms. Rather than originating the study of occult history and art within the academy, then, the "comparatively recent phenomenon" of esotericism studies, as Michael Bergunder describes it, has worked to consolidate and "for the first time . . . conceptualiz[e] esotericism as a consistent phenomenon of European cultural and religious history since the fifteenth century."[20] Under its aegis can be studied and historically connected the figures, practices, and traditions of what Wouter Hanegraaff has influentially termed "rejected knowledge:" ceremonial magic, mesmerism, hermeticism, clairvoyance, entheogenic ritual, spirit contact, and so forth.[21] In this purview, esotericism studies can rightly be said not just to describe, but also to invent, the subjects it studies: as Kocku Von Stuckrad observes, "'Esotericism' as object matter does not exist; 'esotericism' is a construction of scholars who order phenomena in a way that they find suitable to analyse processes of Western history of culture."[22]

Disciplinary formation is a dynamic enterprise that at its best can reveal, connect, and create scholarly momentum around previously siloed fields of knowledge. It also inevitably produces casualties along the way. One such loss within literary esotericism studies has been an awareness of the substantial precedents for the study of occult-themed, authored, and inflected imaginative literature within literary studies in general, and Gothic studies in particular.[23] This problem has been fueled in part by the massive influence of Hanegraaff's rejection or "waste-basket" paradigm on the constitution of the field, which holds that Western esotericism can be understood as a knowledge discourse or "grand narrative of ancient wisdom" given coherence through its *rejection* [my emphasis], first by seventeenth-century Protestant polemicists and then by the academy.[24] As a result, many esotericism studies scholars have been primed to associate the topics they study with rejection and marginalization, sometimes with just cause, but also sometimes in cases where only a difference of categorization and conceptualization exists. As I have previously discussed, this latter tendency is particularly evident within the field's apperception of literary studies.[25] We detect it, for example, in Hanegraaff's 2013 claim that, "So far, scholars of literature have seldom noticed the presence of esotericism in modern and contemporary literature, but it is in fact one of its core dimensions."[26] It surfaces also in the work of literary scholars such as Miriam Wallraven, whose important analysis of female-authored occult fiction has been informed by both the secularization thesis and Hanegraaff's framing of esotericism as rejected knowledge; she opens her compelling *Women Writers and the Occult in Literature and Culture* (2015) by declaring that "[d]espite the proliferation of spiritual and occult fiction in the twentieth century, academia suffers from a distinct 'occultophobia' . . . A spiritual phobia in general can be diagnosed as well, devaluing or ignoring literary texts revolving around many forms of 'the human search for direction and meaning, for wholeness

8   OPEN SECRETS

and transcendence.'"[27] This suggestion that modern literary study reflects a particular (and now much-contested) understanding of secularization as a process of religious withdrawal or rejection is one we will return to in our conclusion; let me simply observe here that Wallraven's indictment of literary studies as a whole for sidelining textual engagements, not just with particular forms of religiosity, whether new or old, but with the search for meaning in general, seems highly exaggerated and almost impossible to sustain. As a current generation of esotericism studies scholars seeks to reappraise what Egil Asprem and Julian Strube describe as "long-standing assumptions and biases about esotericism as 'Western,' 'rejected,' 'oppositional,' and 'elite,'"[28] the secularist framing of literary studies as enduringly, even foundationally, hostile toward the spiritual, whether it be levied by those inside or outside the discipline, warrants closer scrutiny and greater skepticism, particularly as it pertains to the critical corpus on occultism and literature.

We must interrogate, rather than mutely accept, the truism that literary scholars have consistently neglected or anxiously rejected the presence of esotericism and the occult in the texts they study. On close inspection, it proves to have little historical basis. Indeed, academic monographs on these topics started to appear in the nineteen-fifties, with Pierre Georges Castex's *Le conte fantastique en France: de Nodier à Maupassant* (1951) leading the way. Here Castex argues for the substantial influence of the early nineteenth-century occult revival, or as he calls it, the "Renaissance de l'Irrational,"[29] on the French fantastic tale of Nodier, Balzac, Nerval, Gautier, Lautreamont, and others. Whatever one may feel about Castex's equation of occultism with irrationality, there can be no doubt that his study, which pays considerable attention to the literary influence of Allan Kardec and Éliphas Lévi, takes its subject very seriously indeed. On its heels came John Senior's *The Way Down and Out: The Occult in Symbolist Literature* (1959), followed by a series of studies that would approach the relationship between occultism and literature through the lens of a single author, period, or esoteric tradition: David R. Clark's "'Metaphors for Poetry': W. B. Yeats and the Occult" (1965); Robert Lee Wolff's *Strange Stories and Other Explorations in Victorian Fiction* (1971); Martha Banta's *Henry James and the Occult: The Great Extension* (1972); Katherine H. Porter's *Through a Glass Darkly: Spiritualism in the Browning Circle* (1972); George Mills Harper's edited collection, *Yeats and the Occult* (1975); Sally Ortiz Aponte's *La esoteria en la narrativa hispanoamericana* (1977); and Barbara diBernard's *Alchemy and Finnegan's Wake* (1980). These studies laid the groundwork for the explosion of occult-focused works

INTRODUCTION 9

of literary scholarship that appeared in the run up to, and first decade of, the millennium: in terms of major academic monographs alone, this includes Marie Roberts's *Gothic Immortals: The Fiction of the Brotherhood of the Rosy Cross* (1990); Diana Basham's *The Trial of Woman: Feminism and the Occult Sciences in Victorian Literature and Society* (1992); Leon Surette's *The Birth of Modernism: Ezra Pound, T. S. Eliot, W. B. Yeats, and the Occult* (1993); Helen Sword's *Ghostwriting Modernism* (2002); Pamela Thurschwell's *Literature, Technology, and Magical Thinking, 1880–1920* (2001); Roger Luckhurst's *The Invention of Telepathy: 1870–1901* (2002); and Dorothea E. von Mücke's *The Seduction of the Occult and the Rise of the Fantastic Tale* (2003), to name just a few of many. Considering this demonstrable precedent, it should have been impossible in the 2010s to declare that literary scholars had been uniformly negligent of, or wholly hostile to, the presence of esotericism in the works they study, even if the occultural literary-critical corpus is admittedly not as large as that dedicated to the relationship between literature and orthodox religiosity. The persistence of this myth of critical silence within some areas of esotericism studies has no doubt complex and manifold reasons. One of its undeniable effects, however, has been to shore up an aggrandizing self-positioning of esotericism studies as a program of radical recovery work that daringly defies a larger academic field of "literary studies" imagined to be homogenously opposed to the recognition of occultism as either a set of historical traditions or a potent source of artistic inspiration. Neither of these characterizations are true.

Beyond straightforward minimization, another problematic tendency within the critiques of literary studies circulated by some contemporary esotericism studies scholars is misconstrual. It is particularly detectable in the dismissal of the methodologies and critical perspectives ascendent within literary studies as ideologically partisan, fashionably post-modern, or, contrastingly, wholly empirical and descriptive. Consider, for example, Nicholas Goodrick-Clarke's complaint in *The Western Esoteric Traditions* (2008) against those "extreme etic" scholarly approaches which "involv[e] a reductionism that privileges present-day academic interpretive fashions or political preoccupations such as social equality, race, or gender."[30] The term *fashions* seems intended to perform a significant amount of heavy lifting here, working in this framing to tar the current with the stamp of the trivial and the ephemeral. Goodrick-Clarke's claim also implies that emic occult practitioners and scholars, both past and present, have somehow *not* been preoccupied by issues of social equality, race, or gender, and that

10 OPEN SECRETS

discussions of their work in such contexts now represents an unjustifiable form of presentism. Again, this is claim is immediately contestable, as the careers of key nineteenth-century occultists and activists such as Britten, Victoria Woodhull, Paschal Beverly Randolph, Henry Louis Rey, and Annie Besant, among many, many others, demonstrate. Far from representing edgy contemporary impositions, questions of power, human equality, and justice have lain at the heart of the Western esoteric traditions throughout their long histories, so much so that they simply cannot be studied comprehensively without reference to these coordinates. By deeming such concerns "fashionable," Goodrick-Clarke sidesteps the need to offer any evidence-based rebuttal of the relevance of politics or social activism to the history of esotericism; it is enough simply to deem such scholarly recognitions to be of fashion, and hence, implicitly, of limited critical import.

Other esotericism studies scholars who have been more willing to recognize the significance of the political concerns that Goodrick-Clarke dismisses as tendentiously presentist nonetheless evince a similar suspicion of contemporary literary studies for abandoning the scholarly objectivity they claim for their own approaches. Per Faxneld's excellent *Satanic Feminism: Lucifer as the Liberator of Woman in Nineteenth-Century Culture* (2017) takes a position that in many respects could not be further apart from Goodrick-Clarke's. Here Faxneld insists on the centrality of gender politics and feminist discourse to the cultural history of Satanism in nineteenth-century Europe. Yet Faxneld, too, rails against those "highly politicized professors" who "interpret, or rather counter-read, clearly patriarchal, misogynist works (that they too agree have this attitude) as subversive manifestoes,"[31] condemning as "superficial and careless" feminist literary analyses of *Carmilla* and *Dracula* that "carry out counter-readings that interpret the literary texts in a way contrary to their surface meaning as well as the authorial intent and historical context."[32] The correct approach, he counsels, is "always to respect the integrity of the sources and resist any temptation to remake what one finds displeasing. A scholar must naturally never intentionally misrepresent . . . the content of the source material in order to make it a tool for political struggle."[33] While I share Faxneld's impatience with the knee-jerk subversivism that pervades some veins of Gothic studies—as indeed, do many Gothic Studies scholars themselves[34]—his distinction between "politicized," counter-intuitive, depth-based (and hence false) and presumably neutral, apolitical, biographically based, surface-focused (and hence true) readings is questionable. What standard

INTRODUCTION 11

of judgment will serve to distinguish those critical approaches that are "ide-ological" from those which are not—or is ideology, as Terry Eagleton writes, "like halitosis ... what the other person has?"[35] Do literary texts have only single, correct meanings, easily and accurately locatable on their surfaces? Social and cultural anthropologists have long recognized that there is no such thing as a value-free, wholly objective description that represents the sole and best possible choice; "description," writes Adam Drazin, "is not in-tellectually neutral; it is a purposeful act."[36] Is the authorial self, furthermore, always coherent, fixed, and accessible to the scholar, even at significant his-torical distance? And does "respecting the integrity" of one's sources simply mean confirming their author's stated intentions for them, as evidenced in diary entries, memoirs, advertising materials, interviews, or other paratexts? Such a requirement would substantially impoverish the ever-expanding crit-ical methodological range of literary studies; it would also strip away the aesthetic complexity of the literary works it studies by making it possible to declare their meaning without reading them closely, or even at all. Moreover, as Strube points out in a recent discussion of anti-post-modernist sentiment within esotericism studies, such an idealized standard of scholarly objec-tivity is simply impracticable; all acts of interpretation require some form of critical mediation, if only to determine their subjects as appropriate for and amenable to academic study. "Surely," he writes, "one does not have to be lost in 'postmodern' theory to maintain the impossibility of simply 'lis-tening' to what the sources have to tell."[37] This is not to insist that all modes of textual interpretation are necessarily equivalent, or that it is impossible to distinguish between persuasive and flawed readings (or indeed, rigorous or unsound methodologies). Rather, it is to challenge the naïve conviction that there is such a thing as a value-free and purely objective methodology to be found beyond the so-called fashionable stylings—whether post-modern or feminist—of the contemporary literary academy.

I have thus far identified two limitations within esotericism studies-based approaches to occult fiction; first, a tendency to ignore or down-play precedents within literary studies, and second, a resistance to critical methods that push beyond textual surface and authorial intention to adopt an self-consciously political lens, no matter how appropriate such an ap-proach might be to the works under discussion, as in, for example, the foregrounding of gender and race in an analysis of the literary output of nineteenth-century female Theosophists or spiritualist abolitionists. Before closing this discussion, I want to address one more: an inclination toward

12   OPEN SECRETS

essentialist interpretation that simultaneously de-aestheticizes occult literary works while, and by, assessing them primarily as symptoms of an alternative religiosity presupposed to be universally repressed in the either the "West" and/or the modern era. We see this tendency, for example, in Victoria Nelson's ambitious two-volume study of the religious affordance of Western popular culture from antiquity through to the present day: *The Secret Life of Puppets* (2001) and *Gothicka* (2012).[38] Composed in an engaging, novelistic style, these books offer a pleasurably engaging and tightly plotted account of a sudden ontological shift in the West—dated with perhaps suspicious precision to the year 1700[39]—which forced the longing for the sacred into the collective unconscious, from whence forward it would be sublimated through art. The possibility that such a massive and abrupt shift, granting it happened at all, might have been experienced differently by diverse groups of people, or indeed, by some not at all, is not countenanced in Nelson's duology. Instead, she refers continually to a collective "we" and "our," implicating her reader in the undifferentiated mass of Western secularists, or "superstition-free rationalists," whose sole remaining escape from "our materialist worldview" lies in cultural inscriptions of the supernatural.[40] "[O]utside the purview of organized religion," she writes in *Gothicka*, "the genre of supernatural horror has been the preferred mode, or even the only one allowed one, a predominantly secular-scientific culture as ours has had for imagining and encountering the sacred, albeit in unconscious ways."[41] But exactly whose "ours" is being encultured here? As historians of religion and science have routinely pointed out, the extent to which secularization (if understood merely as the decline of faith), or indeed scientific rationality has gained absolute settlement in any modern national or regional context, never mind the entire "West," remains very much in question, even if, as Nelson does here, one excludes the continued presence of organized religion from this conversation.[42] Equally puzzling is Nelson's suggestion that those secular popular culture practitioners who turn to the supernatural to encounter the sacred are necessarily doing so in a covert, subconscious way. As the case studies in *Open Secrets* will show, it is entirely possible, and indeed, common, for occult writers and heterodox seekers operating outwith traditional religious structures to be highly self-aware of their complex artistic and spiritual intentions in producing popular supernatural literary works. While *The Secret Lives of Puppets* and *Gothika* aim to elevate the popular cultural aesthetics of the supernatural by linking them to an innate human longing for the sacred, they ultimately diminish the creativity of horror by

INTRODUCTION   13

reading it as the reflex of a universal psychological impulse that Nelson cavalierly refuses to evidence. Thus, in *Gothika*, Nelson states: "it may be overgeneralizing to see these works . . . as early warning signs of a growing tide of religiosity . . . but I leave that determination to the *disputandum* of the scholars to whose work I am indebted."[43]

While Nelson's use of the word *warning* in the statement above puts an implicitly negative spin on the impending religious revival she argues popular horror fiction to augur,[44] other essentialist interpreters of occult fiction have welcomed the spiritual renaissance they too find anticipated in their source base. Writing from a far more explicitly religionist position than Nelson, Arthur Versluis celebrates the capacity of literary works to cure the longstanding spiritual malaise that modern Westerners—here also presented as a homogenous demographic—are now beginning to challenge: "for the first time in several hundred years, many people have realized that despite all the material comforts made possible by our machinery, their inner lives have become progressively more barren."[45] Literature and art, he posits, can offer the experience of union long sought by mystics, thus operating, through "a means of initiation," to heal the psychic wounds inflicted by modernity.[46] In *Authors of the Impossible* (2010), Jeffrey J. Kripal adopts a similarly esoteric critical meta-language to describe, not just the reception, but rather the *production* of what he calls "paranormal" writing, arguing that the authors he takes as subjects (Frederic Myers, Charles Fort, Jacques Vallee, and Bertrand Méheust) "make impossible things possible through their writing practices. They do not simply write about the impossible. They give us plausible reasons to consider the impossible possible. Thus, they both author and author-ize it."[47] For Kripal, occult literature becomes a form of magic that necessarily compels readers, again, imagined as a mass, to change their view of reality. Pleasurably provocative as such framings may be, they remain extremely difficult to evidence. For Versluis, at least, who takes a very dim view of what he imagines to be the evidentiary processes typical within contemporary literary scholarship, this elusiveness is undoubtedly a great advantage: "Those studying the humanities, and especially literature, have often turned more and more to quasi-scientific approaches, as if catalogic, quantitative, or reductive explanations or investigations would somehow, finally, validate literature or the humanities in the face of scientism's obvious and total victory."[48] Fascinatingly, Versluis here accuses literary scholars of exactly the opposite tendencies charged by Faxneld: rather than being disrespectful and subversion-seeking ideologues who go *off piste* to deliberately

14   OPEN SECRETS

skew textual meaning, they are imagined as soulless, mechanical empiricists who simply list and categorize data.[49] Read together, their comments offer an intriguing snapshot of how literary studies can be understood—and misunderstood—by religious studies scholars who share an interest in the fiction inspired by and about alternative spiritual belief.

If religious and literary studies-based scholars of esotericism are to work more closely together, as indeed they must for the future of their common inter-discipline, it will be essential to move beyond the erasures, generalizations, and straw man characterizations that I have briefly discussed here. *Open Secrets* is driven by the conviction that esotericism studies has much to gain by engaging with, rather than downplaying or dismissing, the substantial and long-standing literary-critical corpus on occultism in literature, and with the expansive methodological toolkit—including but not limited to close reading, historicist, genre-based, political, theoretical, creative, and formalist approaches—that literary studies scholars wield. It is time to move beyond interpretive methods that automatically default to immediate surface denotation, to perceptions of authorial intent, whether evidenced or surmised, or to hazy, essentialist assumptions about the psychological needs of a mass cultural collective.

1.2.2 Gothic Studies and the Problem of the Religio-Historical Real

Well before the rise of Gothic studies in the 1970s and 1980s,[50] literature with occult and supernatural themes was widely taught in British and American literature departments, even if its esoteric content was rarely treated literally or offered as primary focus of study. After all, even the most canonical of approaches to English literary study would necessitate at least some contact with characters and concepts such as Shakespeare's Prospero, Marlowe's Dr. Faustus, or Yeats's second coming. As such, it would be impossible to claim that occult motifs, traditions, and practices, in their fictional representation at least, have been rejected in either the academic teaching of or scholarship on English literature. Following the canon wars of the late twentieth century, in whose aftermath, observes Talia Schaffer, "the vast mass of English professors and their students marched steadily towards inclusivity,"[51] this content has gained greater curricular presence, most notably through the growth of Gothic literary studies. It is important here to stipulate that Gothic

INTRODUCTION 15

fiction and occult literature are by no means synonymous; occult themes, ideas, tropes, and authors can, as this book will demonstrate, occupy a wide variety of genres, and the Gothic literary imagination has proved perfectly capable of pursuing its critically assigned fascination with irrationality, transgression, terror, and trauma in mundane, material contexts. Nonetheless, the representation of occult motifs and esoteric practices—spirit contact, magical ritual, clairvoyance, alchemical experiment, necromancy—within fictional works has often worked to badge them as Gothic, or at least to open them up for investigation by Gothic studies scholars. It is unsurprising, then, that some of the most sustained engagements with occult fiction in literary studies scholarship thus far have happened within this field.

Gothic studies does have its own dedicated research centers, degree programs, societies, and journals, but its pursuit is by no means confined to these sites;[52] at the time of writing, it would require considerable effort for an undergraduate student of English literature in Britain or North America to navigate their degree program without at least some contact with Gothic texts, in the form, say, of Horace Walpole's *The Castle of Otranto* (1764), Jane Austen's *Northanger Abbey* (1817), Mary Shelley's *Frankenstein; or the Modern Prometheus* (1818), or Bram Stoker's *Dracula* (1897). Given this ubiquity, Gothic studies scholars by no means view occultural tropes as minor, rejected, embarrassing, or inconsequential aspects of their source base; on the contrary, they are much more likely to assert, as Jarlath Killeen does of nineteenth-century Britain, that "the occult was everywhere . . . and it was far from a marginal concern."[53] As such, their outlook naturally aligns more readily with Christopher Partridge's concept of occulture, which sees occult ideas, beliefs, and practices as increasingly "ordinary" parts of popular culture,[54] than it does with Hanegraaff's rejection hypothesis.

Yet the prevalence of occultural plots, tropes, characters, authors, and reception communities within the sources they study has not automatically led Gothic studies scholars toward a historically nuanced understanding of the heterodox religious dimensions of this territory.[55] On the one hand, they have been quick to recognize and center this material in their analyses. But too often, as reflex of their field's debts to psychoanalytic theory and Derridean hauntology, they have extracted and segregated such content from the history of actual occult practice and heterodox belief, if not from history per se; the occult is figured as a metaphor for a shifting panoply of cultural anxieties, as a manifestation of certain essential human psychological reflexes, or as a catalyst for the forms

16 OPEN SECRETS

of readerly affect privileged by readers of the Gothic: terror, shock, intrigue, and arousal.[56] As Sam Hirst shrewdly observes in their recent analysis of the influence of Anglican and Dissenting theologies on first-wave Gothic, "it has . . . become a critical commonplace that the Gothic was a reflection of wider secularization, that the supernatural became increasingly untethered from a 'traditional religious framework' (Geary 1992, 16), and that its use became tied almost exclusively to the aesthetic production of fear and a theologically empty experience of the numinous."[57] In such an interpretive paradigm, the occult as encountered in Gothic studies is rarely tracked precisely back to historical occulture, but more often identified as a stand-in for other sociocultural concerns, anxieties, or subconscious yearnings. Patrick Brantlinger provides an apposite example of this deflective tendency in *The Reading Lesson*, observing that "the Gothic often cloaks its transgressive themes in medieval superstition and the 'marvellous.' The supernatural in Gothic tends to function like an aspect of dreamwork, partially—but only partially—displacing or disguising the sexual energies that lie at the heart of its nightmarish fantasies."[58] This suggestion that magic and the supernatural typically stand in for a non-esoteric *something else* when they surface in the Gothic will be of limited use as we seek to understand the occult fiction produced, sometimes for the express purpose of readerly conversion, by heterodox spiritual seekers. Writing of this "unexpectedly pervasive" literary-critical tendency to consign spirits and magical manifestations within Gothic writing to the realm of psycho-sexual or deconstructive figuration, Nicola Bown, Carolyn Burdett, and Thurschwell ask, "Where is the supernatural to be found in this kind of haunting?"[59]

This interpretive drift only intensifies when the language of metaphoric haunting spills over—as it so often has—into the Gothic scholar's own critical lexis and rhetorical toolkit. In an important critique of this tendency, Alexandra Warwick examines Julian Wolfreys's equation of the Gothic with the same primary mechanism through which, from the vantage of Derridean post-structuralism, *all* texts produce meaning. She writes:

> [E]verything becomes possibly identifiable as Gothic, because what is there that is not meaning or text, criticism or literature? Describing or using Gothic in this way becomes little more than the assertion that there is textuality at work, and it becomes useless as an interpretive gesture, simply because it is so large as to be meaningless.[60]

The fact that these problems have now long been recognized within Gothic studies has not led to their abatement. If anything, the mass proliferation and popularization of new, often quite light-hearted Gothic forms in the post-millennial period, referred to by Catherine Spooner as "happy gothic," has only made it easier to dissociate supernaturally inflected writing from actual esoteric traditions and beliefs.[61] In the Gothic studies of the early 2020s, psychoanalytic, hauntological, and anxiety thesis-based historicist readings of occult motifs continue to outweigh those that engage with specific new religious or esoteric traditions.

It is not my argument that such figurative, deconstructive, or psychoanalytic interpretations of occult fiction are never warranted, nor indeed that occult-themed novels, particularly when authored by verified magical practitioners or spiritual seekers, should be approached within Gothic studies in an exclusively earnest or po-faced manner that reifies their relationship to specific occult movements. On the contrary, I critiqued this very tendency within some veins of literary esotericism studies in the previous section. Rather, I argue that the avoidance of religio-historicist approaches constitutes a critical blind spot deeply out of step with the historicism that Gothic studies elsewhere embraces. After all, as Tim Jones points out, the field has since its beginnings embraced a deeply historicized approach to its focal genre as a means of self-authorization, championing Gothic texts by asserting that they "engaged . . . with the pressures of history, and held real political relevance, in much the same way that other, more 'respectable' forms of literature are expected to."[62] It is not history itself that scholars of the Gothic have neglected, repressed, or mishandled in their study of the occult fantastic, but more specifically the *history of occultism*. Consider the clear irritation with which Chris Baldick and Robert Mighall dismiss the claims of those early Gothic critics, including Montague Summers and Devendra P. Varma, who "present the Gothic as a healthy revival of medieval modes of spirituality" or suggest that "the value of Gothic fiction lay in its reassertion of the *truths* the supernatural against the blinkered atheism of the Augustans."[63] According to Baldick and Mighall, Summers and Varma let their own personal religious convictions—"the former was an ardent Roman Catholic convert, the latter a Hindu mystic"[64]—blind them to what they present as the clear anti-religiosity of first-wave Gothic, evident in its "thoroughly modern distrust of past centuries as ages of superstition and tyranny."[65] Yet a distrust of the spiritual stylings and practices of the past, ones recast as "superstition," is not the same thing as anti-religiosity; on the contrary, it was precisely this

18   OPEN SECRETS

distrust, and dissatisfaction, that spurred the growth of the occult revival in the nineteenth century. Surely it is just as misguided to deny the presence of spiritual yearnings or ontologies in the work of *some*, new religiously inclined or affiliated authors of occult Gothic, as it is to project such qualities onto the entirety of the genre's first wave. We find another example of this impatience with the prospect of genuine occult conviction in Norman Paige's contention that "the gothic and the fantastic" should not be "considered through reference to real beliefs, as if somehow readers of these new genres were less sceptical than readers of fairy tales, or more critical of hegemonic reason."[66] Of attempts to analyze Jacques Cazotte's *Le Diable amoreux* (1772) in relationship to eighteenth-century French Luciferianism, he writes, "The appeal to the state of actual beliefs in late eighteenth-century Europe, though a tempting recourse, is in fact of little relevance to a question that is fundamentally aesthetic in nature."[67] Here Paige overreaches: it is perfectly possible, as *Open Secrets* will demonstrate, to recognize belief as a potential context for the production and reception of occult fiction without insisting that its readers or writers—even when spiritual practitioners themselves—believed naively and identically in everything such works depict. No less does an acknowledgment of the social and cultural significance of Christianity for Victorian literature compel us to conclude that works like Elizabeth Gaskell's *Mary Barton* (1848) or Alfred Tennyson's *In Memoriam, A.H.H* (1850) were popular only because their audiences had a shared, unquestioning faith in a particular version of the Christian God. Surely scholars of the Gothic and the literary fantastic can pay attention to belief without discounting the aesthetic, just as scholars of esotericism studies and religion studies can recognize the formal and aesthetic qualities of occult fiction without sacrificing their attention to its theological, philosophical, and biographical concerns.

Another disjunction between Gothic and esotericism studies perspectives on occult fiction has been the former's preoccupation with the transgressive, the deviant, and the dark, one that does not always easily map onto the emically authored works that *Open Secrets* will consider. This framing is summarized usefully in Fred Botting's definition of Gothic as a form of "negative aesthetics:"[68]

> Darkness...characterizes the looks, moods, atmospheres and connotations
> of the genre. Gothic texts are ... not rational, depicting disturbances of
> sanity and security, from superstitious belief in ghosts and demons, displays
> of uncontrolled passion, violent emotion or flights of fancy to portrayals

INTRODUCTION 19

of perversion and obsession. Moreover, if knowledge is associated with rational procedures of enquiry and understanding based on natural, empirical reality, then gothic styles disturb the borders of knowing and conjure up obscure otherworldly phenomena or the "dark arts," alchemical, arcane and occult forms normally characterized as delusion, apparition, deception.[69]

As will become evident over the course of our chapters, Botting's construal of the occult as a form of deliberate, transgressive, and atavistic anti-rationalism would have been unrecognizable, and deeply offensive, to those nineteenth- and twentieth-century esoteric seekers who insisted on the modernity and scientific compatibility of their systems; so, too, does this framing have limited applicability to the fictional works they produced to explore, cultivate, and test the numinous world. The "negative epistemology" of occult seekership foregrounded in Gothic studies has little in common with the largely optimistic model of knowledge production championed by historical students of the occult sciences, one lodged, as Marco Pasi writes, in "a positive confidence both in the human capacity of knowing the other [supernatural] reality and in the desirability of such knowledge."[70] While the writers of the occult revival were certainly capable of exploiting the supernatural for scare purposes, they also, as we will see, emphasized its redemptive qualities and progressive effects, flooding the alchemist's study and the séance room with light rather than darkness. Bulwer's *Zanoni*, for example, declared occultism to be an advanced form of natural science which would ultimately be recognized as wholly compatible with as-yet undiscovered scientific principles and methods;[71] far from championing deviance and violating "borders and norms,"[72] its deeply anti-revolutionary *ethos* uses occultism to buttress the aristocratic *status quo*. Of course, not all works of Victorian occult fiction share *Zanoni*'s politics, which are, we will soon see, by no means consistent. But its example is enough to warn us against any premature or automatic equation of popular fictional occultism with social or sexual transgression. A closer engagement with esotericism studies research has the potential to substantially inflect and expand the range of affective responses, political valences, and social positions that Gothic studies scholars assign to occult fiction.

Finally, one further, substantial benefit that Gothic studies might gain from a closer engagement with esotericism studies is a greater historical precision. The devaluation of "real" occult movements and practices within

20 OPEN SECRETS

the latter has meant that even when these contexts have been regarded as interpretively significant within Gothic scholarship, they are sometimes handled with a lightness of touch that borders on the cavalier. If, after all, occultism is imagined as always already irrationalist, *qua* Botting, then there might seem to be little need to examine or distinguish between its currents in much depth, or to interrogate dubious if well-worn claims about their membership and origins. Thus Roberts's *Gothic Immortals*, a study of early nineteenth-century Rosicrucian fiction, repeats the rumor that "Bulwer was a member of the Rosy Cross" and speculates that "his achievements in the arcane terrains of occult fiction may be attributable to first-hand evidence."[73] Historians of modern British occultism, and Bulwer's own biographers, have been far more skeptical of such allegations; Godwin, for example, points out that there is no evidence to suggest that Bulwer ever "attended a single meeting" of the *S.R.I.A* (Societas Rosicruciana in Anglia), an order to which he was honorarily, and without his consent, appointed in the 1860s.[74] Roberts acknowledges this evidential dearth, but nonetheless allows the speculation to stand. A similar imprecision spills into Killeen's *Gothic Literature 1825–1914* (2009), which describes the work of the "Society for the Investigation of Psychic Phenomena" as an attempt to "provide a certain scientific validation for occult phenomena."[75] If by this title Killeen intends the late-Victorian Cambridge-based Society for the Psychical Research (SPR) (there was no Society for the Investigation of Psychic Phenomena), this is an inaccurate description of its mission; far from aiming to validate purported occult manifestations in any a priori sense, the SPR had the distinctly more modest goal of simply testing with a view to settling the question of their putative reality once and for all.[76] As historians of the society has shown, its late nineteenth-century members were unanimous neither in their initial belief positions nor in the conclusions to their investigations.[77] Rather than buttressing and confirming the worldviews of their occultist and spiritualist contemporaries, the SPR more frequently antagonized them, with high-profile believers like Arthur Conan Doyle ultimately resigning their membership in disgust over what they saw as its unjustified and stubborn agnosticism in the face of convincing proofs as to the existence of the spiritual world.[78] Killeen brushes over the complexity of this history when he declares that "[t]he members of the Society for Psychical Research"—now accurately named—"all felt that they were investigating some of the more occluded aspects of Nature, but Nature nonetheless, and their publications all point towards the same conclusion."[79] Without wishing to be ungenerous to

INTRODUCTION   21

an otherwise excellent study of the long nineteenth-century evolution of the literary Gothic, such reductive simplifications of the period's heterogeneous occultural and psychical research networks risk similarly impoverishing our understanding of the supernatural fictions they inspired or directly produced.

The problems I have identified within approaches to occult fiction across esotericism studies and Gothic studies alike are not offered in a spirit of hostile censure. After all, no single discipline—indeed, not even all of them collectively—can occupy the space of Borges's Aleph, or boast the capacity of his library of Babel, encompassing every possible vantage at once. Inevitably, my own scholarship does in places undoubtedly demonstrate the same faults I here diagnose. Rather, my aim is to suggest what might be achieved if the perspectives, methods, and emphases of these two sub-disciplines vital to the study of occult fiction could be brought into closer dialogue. Gothic scholarship offers to esotericism studies a means of more closely appraising considerations of genre, narration, figuration, and style within the literature of the occult, and an alternative to a rejection hypothesis ill-suited to explain the popular fictional works that *Open Secrets* will analyze. Even if only a few won commercial success or wide audiences,[80] they earn this designation as "popular" through their embrace of recognizable literary genres that unashamedly sought a mass audience. As Ken Gelder writes, "a writer produces popular fiction because he or she intends (or would prefer) to reach a large number of readers. Whether that intention is realized depends upon the case—since not every work of popular fiction is a bestseller—but even so, a choice has been made and a particular kind of career grinds into motion."[81] Whatever their sales figures or respective literary legacies, all of the occultural writers considered in this study made the conscious decision to "inhabit the field of popular fiction," a milieu that, in the words of David M. Earle, requires its entrants to "make a series of strategic decisions about their own practices. They think about the kind of popular genre they will take up, the extent to which they will distinguish that genre from others . . . the difference they might make to that genre, and the kinds of readerships they will write for. These things all involve investment and risk."[82] Esotericism studies has much to gain by paying closer attention to these choices and the sometimes-competing investments—spiritual, political, philosophical, formal, and aesthetic—they entail.

Similarly, Gothic studies can only be enriched by grappling with, rather than looking through, the historical traditions, practices, and movements

22   OPEN SECRETS

that inspired the never exclusively figurative occult tropes and beliefs embedded within the literature of the supernatural. Authors directly affiliated with or networked to the occult revival offer ideal subjects for such a closer engagement with the history of alternative spirituality, not because their fictional productions offer examples of "pure" or "authentic" heterodox belief in any naïve sense, but rather because they are the figures most in need of this kind of careful genre-focused analysis. Too often, the biographical coordinates and personal spiritual convictions of figures such as Crowley or Fortune have been treated as the only things worth knowing about their popular genre writing, as if their creative ambitions were always necessarily subordinate to their occult personae. A critical methodology which more closely interlinks literary and esotericism studies will show us that this was not the case.

1.3 Occult Fiction in the Faustian Forties

In this second half of the chapter, I want to return to Bulwer's *Zanoni*, the novel that, as we have seen, is often accorded foundational status within the fictional corpus of Britain's occult revival. Its influence on the later occult collectives and fiction we will encounter in *Open Secrets* was virtually unrivalled, although Marie Corelli's *A Romance of Two Worlds* (1886) surely came in as a close second; in it we find ample evidence of Bulwer's fascination with occult philosophy and heterodox spiritual systems, even if the full extent of his involvement in and commitment to particular occult traditions is likely to remain indeterminable.[83] Certainly, Bulwer would not have needed to be an actual occult initiate or secret society member to pursue his interest in the unseen world. In the years immediately leading up to and following *Zanoni*'s publication, the occult had become a strong, nearly ubiquitous presence, in British popular fiction. In acknowledging this textual proliferation, we can recognize the novel not (just) as the foundational fictional *Ur*-text of the occult revival, but also as a canny respondent to the changing market for occult-themed fiction in the second quarter of the nineteenth century, one into which Bulwer had by the 1840s already made many different entries.

A key driver of the transition from first-wave to early Victorian Gothic in this period was Charles Maturin's landmark *Melmoth the Wanderer* (1820), a sprawling opus that fueled the growing vogue for Faustiana which *Zanoni* would later exploit. Its labyrinthine plot tells—or perhaps more accurately, alludes to, through a series of torturously interlinked and incomplete fragments—the story of a seventeenth-century English man named John Melmoth who enters an infernal compact to supernaturally extend his life for 150 years. While the terms of the agreement are never explicitly detailed, they seem to involve a requirement to tempt others away from God's path, as we see Melmoth repeatedly attempt and fail to do. "It has been reported of me," the eponymous anti-hero somewhat evasively declares:

> That I obtained from the enemy of souls a range of existence beyond the period allotted to mortality—a power to pass over space without disturbance or delay, and visit remote regions with the swiftness of thought— to encounter tempests without the hope of their blasting me, and penetrate into dungeons, whose bolts were as of flax and tow to my touch. It has been said that this power enabled me to tempt wretches in their fearful hour of extremity with the promise of deliverance and immunity, on condition of their exchanging situations with me. If this be true, it bears attestation to a truth uttered by the lips of one I may not name, and echoed by every human heart in the habitable world.
>
> No one has ever exchanged destinies with Melmoth the Wanderer. *I have traversed the world in the search, and no one, to gain that world, would lose his own soul!*[84]

In this disappointing, temptational track record, Melmoth surpasses even Stoker's Dracula in the failure of his infernal designs; while the Count only manages to create one-and-a-half vampires during his three months in Britain, Maturin's tortured immortal manages not a single conquest in over 150 years. Even the most desperate of Melmoth's targets, including the Spaniard Alonzo Moncado, who is incarcerated in a monastery, and the beautiful former castaway Donna Isidora, facing death in an inquisitorial prison, reject his enticements; his skills of spatial penetration do not, alas, seem to have been accompanied by any rhetorical advantage. Like Christopher Marlowe's Doctor Faustus (1604) and Matthew Lewis's Alonzo in *The Monk* (1795), Melmoth pays the price for aspiring to acquire forbidden knowledge and is, at the novel's end, dragged off to hell.

Melmoth the Wanderer sets the sets the stage for *Zanoni* in several crucial ways. First, it details and exemplifies at exhaustive, even exhausting, length the supernatural powers that Bulwer, among many other authors in this study,

24   OPEN SECRETS

would attribute to occult adepts: the ability to read minds, to bilocate, to produce unearthly music in the minds of percipients, to control the weather, and to extend youth and life alike beyond their natural limits, if not quite forever. Second, in its lurid violence, anti-clericalism, frequent airing of atheistic sentiment, and insistence on the diabolic, misanthropic, and ultimately futile nature of occult seekership, it cemented the popular presentation of occultism as a negative epistemological formation that is dismantled in *Zanoni*, where esoteric wisdom secretly serves the wider *demos* even if it is not fully open to them. In this project of moral and social rebranding, Bulwer would be something of a minority among his literary contemporaries. Within the substantial corpus of Faustian and Rosicrucian fiction produced by British writers in the first half of the nineteenth century—including key works such as P. B. Shelley's *St. Irvynne; or, The Rosicrucian* (1810), William Harrison Ainsworth's *Auriol; or the Elixir of Life* (1844), and G. W. M. Reynolds's *Wagner the Wehr-Wolf* (1846-1847)—occult study and initiation are commonly figured as dangerous, irreligious, and malevolent enterprises with tragic consequences for all involved. *Zanoni* is a fascinating rarity in this respect, insisting both on the purity of its two adepts Zanoni and Mejnour and of the spiritually improving and beneficial effects of initiation, even if few seekers—we see none do so—are equipped to pass its tests. While, like Maturin's *Melmoth the Wanderer*, the novel ends with the death of its eponymous immortal, this resolution is here depicted as an act of pious sacrifice rather than a consequence of divine punishment. Having learned to love the beautiful singer Viola di Pisani, Zanoni takes her place at the guillotine, confident that they will be able to resume their loving relationship when reunited on a higher spiritual plane. Willingly abandoning, for Viola's sake, the physical immortality to which he had so long clung, Zanoni declares, "I go with my free-will into the land of darkness . . . I go where the souls of those for whom I resign the clay shall be my co-mates through eternal youth. At least, I recognize the true ordeal and the real victory . . . Wherever the soul can wander the Eternal Soul of all things protects it still!"[85] The true subject of the novel's initiatory plot, these words imply, has been Zanoni not Glyndon; his true test, not to face down the Dweller, but to embrace mortality and its inevitable consequence. Some forty years later, Theosophical novelist Mabel Collins would, in *The Blossom and the Fruit* (1888), stage the spiritual progress of her initiate-heroine Fleta in a similar manner, with her death serving to continue rather than culminate her magical career.

INTRODUCTION 25

Although hedged round with cautions and conditions, occult seekership in *Zanoni* is a positive enterprise whose benefits are not solely individual, but, as is suggested by the linkage of Zanoni's sacrifice to Robespierre's death, social and political, working to redeem Europe from the threat of revolutionary terror. Esoteric study both *in*, and, as the opening paratext suggests, *of* the novel—even if necessarily partial and potentially unreliable—is imagined as an improving activity for the self and the collective; open secrecy might enrich us all. This is a message well suited for, and enabled by, an 1840s climate in which British literary and publishing markets, as Mark Turner explains, were undergoing mass expansion and unprecedented diversification. "By the 1840s," he writes:

> an explosion in print had come to define print culture in Britain, enabled by such technological and institutional developments as the railways and postal system, and by the rise of cheap print and politics. All of these modern phenomena offered new possibilities for circulation, dissemination, and innovation when it came to forms and formats of print media.[86]

Following closely in the wake of the 1832 Reform Bill, these transformations powered Britain's popular occultural landscape in two key ways: first, they provided new, cheaper means of producing and disseminating works of lurid literary occulture, including penny bloods with Faustian themes and satanic plots; second, they stoked conservative anxieties about the insurrectionary consequences of mass literacy and knowledge democratization that the occult novel would often exploit.[87] Moreover, they established the popular print ecology that enabled the discourse of Modern Spiritualism to spread so rapidly across the country when news of the inaugural 1848 Hydesville rappings first hit British shores, and without which this popular movement may have been stillborn.[88] These conditions would in the same decade allow the novel as genre to attain its prevailing status as the most popular and widely consumed of all literary forms.[89] *Zanoni* thus emerges as a combined product of the historical expansion of both occultism and the novel, a process that it is also, in its cagy paratextual framing, simultaneously *about*.

Yet although Bulwer had prefaced *Zanoni* as a work explicitly prepared for wide public consumption, he notably eschewed the new, more accessible formats made available by the early nineteenth-century print renaissance when he came to publish it. The author was then at the peak of a

26   OPEN SECRETS

hard-earned literary reputation just about to enter a period of long decline, fading in tandem with the fortunes of the popular genres through which he had launched his career: the silver-fork novel and the Newgate novel.[90] As biographer Leslie Mitchell points out, Bulwer only permitted the serial publication of his novels on a handful of occasions, feeling on the whole that "the serialization of novels in reviews and journals was impossibly vulgar."[91] This reluctance reflects what Brantlinger identifies as Bulwer's pointed and paradoxical ambivalence about the spread of mass literacy in this period,[92] a mood that would only intensify as he abandoned the political radicalism of his youth for the conservatism that would dominate his late-life political career.[93] Notably, and with no small irony, those surrounding works of occultural fiction that *did* embrace the cheaper new formats eschewed by Bulwer evidenced a far more antagonistic stance to the dispersal of esoteric knowledge, even if adopted largely for the purposes of producing thrilling effect rather than from orthodox religious conviction. Indicative here is Harrison Ainsworth's chaotic and unfinished *Auriol; or the Elixir of Life* (1844), first serialized as *The Revelations of London* in the author's own *Ainsworth's Magazine* between October 1844 and January 1845. It dramatizes the fate of its eponymous protagonist Auriol after he drinks an alchemical elixir in 1599 and retains his youth through to the 1830s, at the unfortunate cost of having to perform regular human sacrifices. He falls in love with the beautiful and innocent London merchant's daughter Ebba who, in the novel's final instalments, is abducted and confined in a mysterious house full of magical books, Zoroastrian tapestries, hidden passages, and cunningly-designed confinement chairs which trap their occupants via mechanized diving helmets that drop down from the ceiling and then flip their trapped victims into an underground prison. As a final insult to his readers' tortured patience, Ainsworth's narrator then hints that the immortality story might all just be a delusion on Auriol's part, who could in fact be an incarcerated lunatic who never left his sixteenth-century time frame. After airing this possibility, the serial then breaks off abruptly without conclusion, preventing readers from determining the truth either way.

A similarly adverse—and bewildering—representation of occult study can be found in Reynolds's *Wagner: The Wehr-Wolf*, serialized in *Reynolds's Miscellany* between November 1846 and July 1847. Like *Auriol*, it traces the fate of an eponymous protagonist in early modern continental Europe, in this case, a starving and abandoned old man living in the Black Forest who strikes an infernal bargain for extended life, renewed youth, and great

INTRODUCTION 27

wealth. Wagner too pays a dark price for these boons, transforming into a wolf on every full moon. Reynolds, who clearly sought readerly sympathy for his protagonist, never shows him spilling human blood, although he does depict Wagner as brutal victor in what is surely the finest werewolf versus boa constrictor fight scene in Victorian literature. The novel's complicated, perfervid, and salacious plot, typical of the penny blood format it adopts,[94] follows Wagner as he falls in love with the beautiful but psychopathic Nisida, daughter of the Count of Riverola. Ultimately, he is delivered from the curse by Christian Rosencreutz himself, and then undergoes a sensational process of accelerated aging and decay which anticipates the similar demise of later fictional occult adept Ayesha in H. Rider Haggard's *She: A History of Adventure* (1887). If Rosicrucianism is ennobled here, it is because it quite literally brings occult over-reachers down to earth, rather than, as in *Zanoni*, elevating them upward into a higher sphere.

1.4 Bulwer, Occultural Fiction, and the Question of Genre

In comparison to the eccentric occultural fantasies and serial publication routes of Ainsworth and Reynolds, we can see *Zanoni* as both in and out of step with it surrounding fictional milieu, at once tentative and deeply enthusiastic about engaging a real or imagined public with occult philosophy. These tensions reflect the writer's long-standing struggle with the question of how—and for whom—the supernatural might best be represented in fiction, one underway for at least a decade by the time of *Zanoni*'s advent, and in no way concluded by it. Revenants, demons, premonitions, and magi permeate Bulwer's fictional *oeuvre* from its beginnings. In his first novel, the epistolary romance *Falkland* (1827), the supernatural surfaces to seal the enduring romantic affection between the misanthropic recluse Erasmus Falkland— an ardent reader, we learn, of Maturin's *Melmoth the Wanderer*[95]—and the beautiful married woman Lady Emily Mandeville. On the night of their intended elopement, her husband discovers their plot; in shock, she dies of a brain hemorrhage and then appears before her thwarted lover in spectral form to wish him farewell. Heartbroken, the young Falkland goes off to fight for Spain in the Peninsular war, where he sustains a fatal wound and dies with a lock of Lady Emily's hair clasped to his chest.

After this fairly superficial deployment of haunting as romantic device in *Falkland*, the supernatural would gain more ground and gravity in

28 OPEN SECRETS

the occultural works that Bulwer produced in its wake. Most notable, and certainly the oddest, of these was the eclectic monthly periodical serial *Asmodeus at Large*, published between January 1832 and February 1833 in the *New Monthly Magazine*, which Bulwer was then editing.[96] A sort of political gossip column, literary review, morality tale and occult fantasy all in one, *Asmodeus* is best known, where known at all, for its 1832 instalment "The Tale of Kosem Kesamim the Magician," which is sometimes incorrectly read as a stand-alone story rather than as part of a miscellaneous running series.[97] This act of extraction has encouraged some scholars, such as Godwin and Roberts, to position the tale as a discrete and internally coherent precursor to *Zanoni*; it has the considerable disadvantage, however, of concealing the entrenched messiness of Bulwer's occult fictional practice in this period.[98] In fact, Kosem's inset tale is simply one part of a sprawling urban occultural picaresque in which an unnamed, ennui-stricken Londoner liberates the demon Asmodeus from a bottle, allowing the two to strike out on a series of adventures, both otherworldly and mundane, together. They sup at a witches Sabbath; attend the theatre and complain about its contemporary debasement; debate the First Reform Bill; gamble in Paris; and visit a magical undersea lair where sits "the Cavern of Wind," and in which "all the tidings of the million tribes of mankind" are transmitted to the mysterious nameless deity who rules man's fate.[99] Amidst such otherworldly excursions, the serial remains profoundly worldly and of its moment, with a considerable amount of the conversation between Asmodeus and our narrator consisting of gossip about contemporary Members of Parliament. For the most part, Asmodeus seems less interested in leading our narrator to damnation than in reading the daily newspapers. Thus we learn that, during their sojourn in the subterranean city of the witches, Asmodeus arrives "every morning to breakfast . . . full of the news of the upper world, laden, laden with books and, journals, reports and truths—and making me as much conversant with the little squabbles on the world's surface, as if I were, as heretofore, a partner of them!"[100] The serial swerves throughout between registers of high seriousness and profound silliness, settling in its conclusion on a tragic note when our narrator learns that Julia, the seventeen-year old girl he has courted and then abandoned because of her insufficiently high social status, has leapt off a London bridge to her death. In remorse, he pledges to spend the rest of his life in penitential solitude.

Asmodeus at Large reads like the work of an author desperately seeking to exploit occultism as a resource for his writing, but unable to commit to any particular genre pattern or tone for its development. Sometimes it seems merely to offer a pretext for light-hearted fantasy, following in the vein of its clearly signposted intertext, Alain-René Le Sage's *Le Diable boiteux* (1707). In one of the serial's first instalments, Bulwer identifies his Asmodeus with the "Devil ... whose adventures with Don Cleofas you know well."[101] This allusion to Le Sage's protagonist Don Cleophas Leandro Perez Zambullo establishes two potential connections between the novels. First, it might lead us to expect in Bulwer's work a ribald mood of non-seriousness similar to that of the earlier work;[102] second, if more obliquely, it links Bulwer's work to the discourse of a literary proto-realism that it itself fails to practice. In a pivotal scene in which the friendly devil Asmodée lifts the roofs of Parisian houses so that his companion may see the foibles within, Le Sage's novel has been recognized for establishing a key epistemological priority of the canonical literary realism that was to come. "[R]emoving housetops in order to see the private lives play out beneath them," observes Peter Brooks in his classic study *Realist Vision* (2005), "suggests how centrally realist literature is attached to the visual, to looking at things, registering their presence in the world through sight."[103] Bulwer clearly had this moment in mind when he had his Asmodeus make a similar offer to his narrator, proposing "Let us look down ... what a wilderness of houses! Shall I uncover the roofs for you ... or rather, for it is an easier method, shall I touch your eyes with my salve of penetration, and enable you to see through walls?"[104] If we were to prioritize this scene, we might build a similar case for *Asmodeus at Large* as a work that harnesses diablery for the rationalist epistemology, if not quite the practice, of literary realism, insisting that all parts of the world, including its supernatural realms, can be accessed through empirical data and visual perception.

Yet the anarchic eclecticism of Bulwer's approach to the serial form, in which the magical and mundane seem constantly vying for priority, and different genre aspirations are advanced in each new instalment, renders such a coherent interpretation difficult. How are we to reconcile these parts? Is *Asmodeus at Large* a work of high-toned supernatural fantasy? An eclectic and disorienting compendium of gossip and rumor that anticipates, in its defiant fragmentation, the journoccultural modes of numinous contact to be discussed in Chapter 4? Or should we prioritize its conclusion to recognize it as a somewhat belated version of the popular libertine tragedy? Can its differing genre trajectories, registers, and formal gambits successfully combine? Even Bulwer seems to have recognized that they did not, as evidenced

30   OPEN SECRETS

by the heavy-handed "moral" he appended to the final instalment in an attempt to corral reader response:[105]

> The more ingenious reader may, perhaps, already have perceived, that, while adapted to this miscellany by constant allusions to real and temporary events, a metaphysical meaning runs throughout the characters and the story. In the narrator is embodied the SATIETY which is of the world; in Asmodeus is the principle of vague EXCITEMENT in which Satiety always seeks for relief. . . A fervid, though hasty, PASSION, succeeds at last, and Asmodeus appears no more, because in LOVE, all vague excitement is merged in absorbing and earnest emotion. The passion is ill-fated; but in its progress it is attempted to be shown, that, however it might have terminated, it could not have been productive of happiness. It was begun without prudence, and continued without foresight . . . The doom of Satiety is to hate self, but be forever alone.[106]

Even had *Asmodeus's* original audience consumed its monthly parts in entirety and in chronological sequence—and there is no guarantee that they did—it would, one suspects, have been very difficult for them to recognize the overarching metaphysical coherence imputed to the text here. His characters have been too precisely anchored within the specific social milieu of the 1832 London *bon ton* to be purely allegorical, and, if our narrator's budding relationship with Julia is doomed from the start, the narrative does very little to foreshadow such an outcome. One senses that Bulwer himself was not convinced by this *post hoc* explanation.

Captured vividly in *Asmodeus at Large*, Bulwer's deep uncertainty as to how to form, frame, and leverage occultural subject matter continued as he came to compose *Zanoni*. He had been tinkering with the novel's central immortal magus figure for quite some time, creating a prototype of him in the earlier occult romance *Zicci* that appeared, as one of Bulwer's few serialized novels, in the *Monthly Chronicle* in 1838. Like the "The Tale of Kosem Kesamim," *Zicci* too is sometimes critically misidentified, presented simply as the same novel as *Zanoni* under a different name—Mitchell describes it as being "later republished as *Zanoni*"[107]—or as simply a truncated version of it.[108] Far from being a straightforward republication or expansion of *Zicci*, *Zanoni* is in fact a radical reworking of it, one that, despite considerable instances of duplication, transforms the former's moral assessment of magical practice. *Zicci* is notably shorter than *Zanoni*, corresponding only to

INTRODUCTION   31

the mid-sections of the later novel in which the titular magus (here Corsican rather than Chaldean) courts and rescues a beautiful young Neapolitan soprano (here named Isabel rather than Viola), and where the young English seeker Clarence Glyndon pledges himself to the occult adept Mejnour after being rejected by Zicci. Absent here is the framing encounter in Mr. D_'s bookshop, the entire French revolutionary plot, and the famous Dweller in the Threshold figure who made *Zanoni*'s fame in the occult milieu. *Zicci* instead terminates just before Mejnour rejects Glyndon's first premature demand for initiation, leaving readers poised tantalizingly on the threshold.[109] When Bulwer elected to usher them further through it in *Zanoni*, he ethically upscaled and ennobled his eponymous magician. Zicci is not the double, but a dissolute version, of Zanoni, his motives for pursuing immortality more narcissistic and his worldview more jaded. Thus when Isabel begs him to return her love, he explains: "I am a man, Isabel, in whom there are some good impulses yet left, but whose life is, on the whole, devoted to a systematic and selfish desire to enjoy whatever life can afford."[110] Later, alone in his chambers, he complains of his world weariness: "One sand more out of the mighty hour-glass . . . one more nearer to the last! I am weary of humanity."[111] As treatment for this dejection, Zicci then drinks a potation of dried herbs that produces an immediate and visible physical rejuvenation, something that Zanoni never does; the later text has far too lofty a view of occult science to show it in the service of such a vulgarly material act of magical beautification. Zicci is ultimately a far less idealized, and hence more fully human, magus figure than his successor, admitting to Glyndon his deep loneliness: "I sicken for human companionship, sympathy, and friendship; yet I dread to share them, for bold must be the man who can partake my existence and enjoy my confidence."[112] As these substantial textual variations make clear, *Zicci* is neither a direct microcosmic precursor or, as it is sometimes deemed, a "prequel" to *Zanoni*;[113] rather, it is an experiment in occultural story-telling that casts its adept protagonist in a morally questionable light and cuts off before reaching any affirmative consequence can be tied to heterodox religiosity and the dissemination of esoteric lore.

Zanoni works less to shut down the false starts, misdirections, and ambivalences about the entrance into occult seekership expressed in *Asmodeus at Large* and *Zicci* than to redirect them into questions about the goals, achievement, and consequences of true initiation. How do we know when it has been attained, and what happens after the threshold has been crossed? Is Glyndon, it asks us to consider, a failed initiate rightly punished

32 OPEN SECRETS

for his egotistical desire to penetrate the secrets of nature in order to "surpass my kind" and gain "unearthly power"?[114] Or is his seeming failure—and the horrifying encounter with the Dweller in the Threshold it produces—simply a mechanism of ultimate spiritual success, as it would be in so many of the subsequent occult novels it inspired, from *The Blossom and the Fruit* to *The Goat Foot God*? If we equate Glyndon with the old man in Mr. D__'s shop, and thus recognize him as the author of the cipher manuscript bequeathed to the frame narrator, then it seems he has eventually entered the ancient Brotherhood after all. The fifth chapter of *Zanoni*'s third book opens with a paean to the Brotherhood's many virtues, accompanied by a footnote which reminds us that these words are written "by the author of the original MS, not by the editor."[115] And this author here clearly identifies himself as a successful initiate:

> Venerable Brotherhood, so sacred and so little known, from whose secret and precious archives the materials for this history have been drawn ... Thanks to you, if now, for the first time, some record of the thoughts and actions of no false and self-styled luminary of your Order be given, however imperfectly, to the world ... if I, the only one of my country, in this age, admitted with a profane footstep, into your mysterious Academe, have been by you empowered and instructed to adapt to the comprehension of the uninitiated, some few of the starry truths which shone on the great Shemaia of the Chaldean Lore, and gleamed dimly through the darkened knowledge of later disciples, labouring like Psellus and Iamblichus, to revive the embers of the fire which burned in the *Hamaria* of the East.[116]

The elder Glyndon's ultimate admission into the "the mysterious Academe" renders its membership status less dire than it appears at the end of *Zanoni*'s main text, where only the "passionless and calm" Mejnour is left, "indifferent whether his knowledge produces weal or woe."[117]

The passage above also raises questions about the ongoing *necessity* of initiation, given its pronouncement that at least some of the knowledge hitherto only available to learned sages in the ancient Near East is now being opened to all and sundry, albeit in coded form. Why should uninitiated readers risk facing the Dweller if they can access occult wisdom sufficient for their purposes through the old man's partially translated manuscript? The new form of open occulture is not only more accessible, but also, the novel moots, potentially more ethical than the old, which restricted the manifold benefits

INTRODUCTION   33

of its secrets—protection from diseases, indefinite extension of life—to only a handful of literate, elite male seekers. Glyndon raises this inequity with Mejnour as he prepares for his first initiatory trial:

> if possessed of these great secrets, why so churlish in withholding their diffusion. Does not the false or charlatanic science differ in this from the true and indisputable—that the last communicates to the world the process by which it attains its discoveries; the first boasts of marvellous results, and refuses to explain the causes?[118]

Mejnour responds with what would become a default defense for esoteric secrecy and conspiratorial knowledge control alike: namely, that the unvetted *demos* cannot be trusted to deploy arcane knowledge and magical powers in a non-destructive way. "Imagine the tyrant, the sensualist, the evil and corrupted being possessed of these tremendous powers;" he urges. "[W]ould he not be a demon let loose on earth?[119] Nonetheless, the case for secrecy is far from closed. Later, in one of his final communiqués with Mejnour before his death, Zanoni admits that "of late I have sometimes asked myself, 'Is there no guilt in the knowledge that has so divided us from our race?' . . . how many virtues must lie dead in those, who live in the world of death and refuse to die?"[120] Far from acting as trusted stewards of nature's hidden secrets, equipped with the skill and insight to apply them where most needed, initiates might simply serve to entomb them; dammed up and prevented from flowing outward, esoteric knowledge corrupts and rots those adepts who, like Zanoni's precursive shadow Zicci, selfishly cling to life. Articulated in the run up to his self-sacrifice, these doubts create the possibility that Zanoni's act may be as much a protest against occult elitism and hierarchy—against the refusal to share wisdom, and bodily experience, with other men—as a testament to his love for Viola Pisani.

As these prospects demonstrate, the closer we examine the epistemological and ethical claims made for initiation in *Zanoni*, the less coherent they become, aligning neither with the negative aesthetics of the Gothic tradition—although sometimes invoking them through the terrors of the Dweller—nor with the positive positioning of occult seekership within the exclusive and sometimes exclusionary esoteric cadres which *Zanoni* inspired. A similar instability manifests through the novel's hybrid form, which fuses elements of the two genres—idealist romance and historical realism—that Bulwer would throughout the novel present as necessarily distinct and unequal, with the

34   OPEN SECRETS

former far superior to the latter. In the introductory episode, for example, we hear the old man, an artistic connoisseur as well as adept, counsel our narrator that "all works of imagination, whether expressed by words or by colours, the artist of the higher schools must make the broadest distinction between the Real and the True,—in other words, between the imitation of actual life, and the exaltation of Nature into the Ideal."[121] Yet this is a distinction that *Zanoni* itself patently refuses to uphold. Real-life French revolutionary figures, such as Cazotte, Nicolas de Condorcet, Georges Couthon, and Maximilien Robespierre, spill into the plot, their introduction accompanied by explanatory authorial footnotes that establish the accuracy of the reported dates and identify archival sources for the recorded dialogue.[122] Amidst these acts of careful historical portraiture and earnest documentation are episodes of delirious supernatural fantasy and frequent blasts at the inadequacy, not to mention turpitude, of realist representational strategies.[123] *Zanoni* combines different, sometimes even seemingly opposed, genre conventions—invoking the Gothic sublime, for example, in its interlude in the volcanic, banditti-ridden landscapes of Southern Italy, or domestic realism in its light-hearted enumeration of the household rituals of the English middle-classes[124]—while steering audiences to read and rank particular genres in ways contradicted by its own formal practice. A work of open occulture *Zanoni* may be, but it is far from being a lucid one; attentive audiences must have found themselves perplexed as to how to read its contrasting injunctions and modes.

Bulwer was alert enough to this conundrum to include an explanatory appendix entitled "Zanoni Explained," one not unlike the concluding key to *Asmodeus at Large*, to all new editions of the novel published from 1853 onward.[125] This supplement, however, is more puckish than definitive, and should be approached with some caution. It was written in 1842, not by Bulwer himself but by his friend, Harriet Martineau, although its authorship in the print editions is only anonymously signified through the phrase "By —."[126] As David Huckvale explains, Bulwer did not solicit this contribution, which Martineau had sent to him with a cover note apologizing for her presumption in writing it. He did, however, "[think] highly enough of her interpretation to have it inserted at the end of future editions."[127] For Anna Maria Jones, this decision speaks less to Bulwer's assent to the key's accuracy than it does of his commitment to a "suggestive system" which "privileges eclectic collections of facts, texts, and ideas over some more 'systematic' pursuit of knowledge."[128] In other words, Bulwer included Martineau's key not as *the final*, but rather as *a next*, word on the novel it appended, serving as a contribution to a system of philosophical eclecticism about which readers were expected to form their own conclusions. The key's equation, for example, of Mejnour with "Science," Zanoni with "Idealness," and Viola with "Human Instinct" were to be taken,[129] Jones writes, as prompts for thinking, not as fixed allegorical connections. Bulwer may well, she suggests, have included Martineau's key "as an example of misreading... the product of one too much wedded to her system to discern whether truths may lie in the 'minute and near' details."[130] Whether Bulwer published the key as a red herring or not, there is little evidence that *Zanoni*'s diverse readers adhered to its instructions. Perhaps the most influential of these within the later nineteenth-century occult milieu was the foundational Theosophist Blavatsky, whose own esoteric treatises, as Huckvale notes, "are peppered with references to Bulwer-Lytton in general and *Zanoni* in particular," and who names Bulwer over fifteen times in her magnum opus, *Isis Unveiled: A Master Key to the Mysteries of Ancient and Modern Science and Theology* (1877). The latter completely overrides Martineau's allegorical interpretations of the novel's supernatural entities—in which Adon-Ai was made to represent the principle of Faith, and the Dweller on the Threshold that of Fear[131]—to argue for them as authentic depictions of actual elementary spirits.[132] Secular literary critics, writing both before and after the publication of Martineau's Key, demonstrated an equal independence—and substantial divergence—of thought in their interpretation of its content and respective accomplishments. Some hailed it as a work of dramatic profundity which evidenced Bulwer's mature moral vision and admirable "spiritual mission" to elevate his readers;[133] others praised what they saw as its only redeeming aspect, namely a beautiful prose style that leavened the otherwise impenetrable incoherence of its metaphysical speculation;[134] yet more lampooned it as an ill-conceived mashup of cod-philosophy and grandiose posturing,[135] which, as one critic lamented in 1884, was directly responsible for the tide of "esoteric bosh" then flooding the literary market.[136]

It is this very multiplicity, evident in its infusion and confusion of different genre positions, philosophical stances, ethical claims, that represents *Zanoni*'s most important legacy for *Open Secrets*. The novel can be deemed a work of *open* occulture both in the sense that it aims to disseminate esoteric ideas and lore widely, if partially, among its uninitiated readerships, and that it leaves the question of what and how occult content should mean in fiction—should it reflect attested authorial belief, adopt a consistent affective

36   OPEN SECRETS

or political stance, provide an easily interpretable "surface" from which critical readings must not depart—firmly and thoroughly open. The open occultural fictions that this book will examine were written in popular genre modes that deliberately if not always successfully courted wide audiences; they are provocative, complex works that attempt to fuse aesthetic, philosophical, and spiritual innovation in a non-hierarchal way, and that resist the narrowly deterministic modes of interpretation—whether biographical, political, affective, psychoanalytic, or religious—often applied to literary supernaturalism in both esotericism and Gothic studies scholarship. They deserve recognition, not simply as the instruments, vehicles, or symptoms of the pre-ascertained spiritual commitments of their occultural authors, but as spaces of dynamic genre making in which heterodox ideas are subject to play and test rather than dutiful application. *Open Secrets* asks us to linger awhile in Bulwer's bookshop and consider how some of the most important works of occult fiction produced in Britain between the 1840s and 1930s imagine their place within its unashamedly commercial premises; how they speak to audiences, each other, and the new religious and paranormal ideas from which they took their cue; how they enter, debate, and transform the mass literary genres whose goal was to let readers in rather than keep them out. Distinguished by period, authorship, and genre, the texts examined in the chapters ahead are united in their shared rejection of the claim, offered surely with some irony in Bulwer's dedicatory epistle to John Gibson in the 1845 edition of *Zanoni*, that works of occult fiction such as his are "not meant" for "the common herd."[137]

Our next chapter examines one of, if not *the*, most durable forms of the Victorian occult novel: the *Bildungsroman*. In its focus on the development of youthful innocence into mature experience, the genre seemed ideally suited to narrate and confirm the promises of progressive spiritual evolution advertised by the period's leading occult practitioners. Yet as examples of its uptake by occult seekers and practitioners reveal, the secular and the occult male *Bildungsheld* became increasingly irreconcilable figures in the mid-nineteenth century, their relationships to development, maturation, knowledge acquisition, and temporality distinctly at odds. Chapter 2 discusses these tensions, and their implications for the gender history of Victorian occultism, through an analysis of two key examples of the nineteenth-century occult male *Bildungsroman*: Edward Bulwer Lytton's *A Strange Story* (1862) and the Chevalier Louis de B__'s *Ghost Land; Or Researches into the Mysteries of Occultism* (1876). Far from replicating the genre's traditional endorsement of liberal individualism, these novels imagine occult seekership as a form of learned and enduring self-subjection to paternal and patriarchal authority, one in which male occult students ultimately become far more passive, receptive, and developmentally arrested than the contemporary female spiritualist mediums with whom they have often been contrasted as foil. In this process, they require us to rethink the gender coordinates typically assigned to both their host genre and to the mid-nineteenth-century occult milieu in which they circulated.

Continuing this focus on occultural gender politics, Chapter 3 examines one of the most commercially successful and prolific forms of the *fin de siècle* popular occult novel: the woman's reincarnation romance. Following the Theosophical Society's successful introduction of reincarnationism into British popular consciousness, rebirth became a staple of romances produced by women writers who either occupied central positions within, or were substantively inspired by, the late Victorian occult revival: Marie Corelli and Mabel Collins. Here we will see how these figures feminized reincarnation and its mechanism of karmic justice to contest the patriarchal lens of the male-dominated imperial romance genre with which their work is sometimes—mistakenly, I argue—conflated. Eschewing the prurient sensationalism of later pulp black magic stories, reincarnation romances such as Collins's *The Blossom and the Fruit: A True Story of a Black Magician* (1888) and Corelli's *Ziska: The Problem of a Wicked Soul* (1897), emplot and seek justice for female victims of sexual and gender-based violence across the extended scope of reincarnative time, questioning, in the process, whether the gendered body might be best understood as a vehicle of liberation or site of entrapment. My chapter positions such novels as expressions of a potent but under-recognized vein of occult feminism which adopted the popular romance as both stage and rehabilitative target.

Diurnal, ephemeral, and accessible, the newspaper might seem antithetical to the types of texts (ancient, singular, obscure) and forms of literacy (cryptic, rarefied) privileged within the rhetoric of the occult revival. Yet the latter was considerably indebted to the former, and not only because so many late Victorian and early twentieth-century magical practitioners and occult students made their living as men and women of the press. Chapter 4 examines the significance of the new journalism, not simply for the dissemination of new religious and esoteric beliefs, but also for the textual poetics and visionary techniques of late nineteenth and early twentieth-century occultism. I use the work of W. T. Stead, Hannen Swaffer, Arthur Machen, and

38   OPEN SECRETS

Fort to demonstrate the emergence of what I term "journoccultism," namely the processes and reading techniques through which esoteric thinkers have used news media to transact their dealings with the numinous world and to represent mystical epiphany. We trace the development, first, of an informational vein of journoccultism that deployed the technical and practical techniques of the press to report on life in the otherworldly spheres in an accessible way, and second, of a more mystical strand that aimed to represent— or even induce—altered forms of readerly consciousness in which magical connections and paranormal phenomena might be more readily perceived. Together, these modes worked to break down oppositions between popular and elite forms of esoteric writing and to assert the importance of deliberately disposable, fragmentary, terse, commercial, and shallow textual forms to alternative spiritual seekership.

Chapter 5 turns to the figure of the occult detective, arguably the most enduringly popular fictional archetype produced by the occult revival. Introduced to the Victorian public through characters such as Sheridan Le Fanu's Dr. Martin Hesselius, this spirituo-scientific crime fighter deploys his knowledge of unseen entities and spiritual laws to bring miscreants to justice and explain, if only partially, the occult significance of their acts. By the *fin de siècle*, he had become a ubiquitous presence in the pulp and weird fiction press, manifesting in Stoker's Van Helsing, Machen's Dyson, and Algernon Blackwood's John Silence. When British occultist Aleister Crowley came to produce his own version of this popular archetype in *The Scrutinies of Simon Iff* (1917–1918), he was thus entering a well-established literary sub-genre that he would use as testing site for his nascent Thelemic philosophy. Here we will read the Iff stories in dialogue with *The Book of the Law* (1904), the controversial received text foundational to the new religious movement of Thelema, observing how Crowley uses occult detection to shape, articulate, and probe the questions about secular and spiritual law raised therein. In its practical and theoretical solutions to crime, we will see, *The Scrutinies* served as outlet for the most radical and reactionary of Crowley's political impulses, hailing sexual transgression while buttressing the precincts of an exclusive white, male elite against incursions by deviant outsiders imagined as biologically and racially impure, even inhuman.

The Conclusion returns us to the space of the occult bookshop, this time entering the premises of T. Jelkes's antiquarian bookstore as featured in Fortune's novel *The Goat Foot God* (1936). Separated from Mr. D__'s bookshop by almost one hundred years if only a few city blocks, this

INTRODUCTION 39

imaginary location embodies the changes in occultism's popular fictional practices and purview of which my conclusion will take stock. The playful mode of readerly seekership practiced in Jelkes's shop belies the sometimes top-down, rigidly instrumentalist theories of textual initiation that Fortune would endorse elsewhere, attributing to occult fiction a far more dynamic range of spiritual and aesthetic affordances than that of knowledge transmission alone. We finish by considering what the new religious capacities and formal complexities that *Open Secrets* has identified in the genre fiction of leading occult revivalists might have to tell us about the endurance, place, and work of alternative spirituality in the literature of the secular age.

2

Magical Meisters

The Problem of Progress in the Occult *Bildungsroman*

For many nineteenth-century occult and spiritualist believers, the *Bildungsroman* seemed the ideal vehicle through which to proselytize the public. What better way to stage the seeker's journey from callow innocence to initiatory experience, and to banish stigmatizing associations between supernaturalism and primitive retrogression, than through a genre that had, since its popularization in Johann Wilhelm von Goethe's *Wilhelm Meisters Lehrjahre* (1795–1796), been associated with the progressive development of a single, youthful protagonist?[1] Its narrative logic appealed to and inspired the efforts of some of the era's most active and influential occultural writers, even if their prolific contributions to the genre remain almost entirely unrecognized within histories of the genre—Paschal Beverly Randolph, Mabel Collins, David Duguid, Marie Corelli, and the two figures who form the focus of this chapter, Edward Bulwer Lytton and Emma Hardinge Britten.[2] Among the many potential causes for their neglect within this literary-critical context, perhaps the strongest of all is a prevailing association between the *Bildungsroman* and an emergent secular realism in which occult heterodoxy has no place. Yet there are important gains to be made by situating and amplifying the presence of occult fiction within the expansive and contested terrain of the Victorian *Bildungsroman*. First, such a recovery will allow us to rethink this secularist bias and recognize how the genre has from its origins engaged with, and even relied upon, esoteric tropes and structures of education to construct its familiar plots of socialization. Second, this move will also reveal, not just the affinities, but also the contradictions and tensions, between the different models of progress, maturation, and time on offer within the genre and the mid-Victorian esoteric milieu, ones that the occult *Bildungsroman* is particularly well-equipped to show.

This chapter will show how the *Bildungsroman* formed an alluring yet distinctly uneasy formal fit with the counter-intuitively static temporality and paternalistic tendencies of male seekership novels such as Bulwer's

Open Secrets. Christine Ferguson, Oxford University Press. © Oxford University Press 2025.
DOI: 10.1093/oso/9780197651599.003.0002

A Strange Story (1862) and Britten's *Ghost Land* (1876). As we will see, stasis and arrested development are more frequently the outcomes for the *Bildungshelden* in these landmark occult novels than maturation and individuation; furthermore, their stalled trajectory is depicted as an inevitable, sometimes even desirable, consequence of the alternative temporality and the dominating patriarch figures—predecessors of Theosophy's Mahatmas—that their surrounding occult networks were coming to favor. The problem of progress that we will encounter in this chapter's focal texts is, I will argue, primarily a paternal one, and as such has important implications for our understanding of the gender dynamics of occult identity formation in nineteenth-century Britain. Esotericism studies scholars and historians of spiritualism have long recognized that the forms of empowerment and agency available to women within the Victorian occult milieu were deeply compromised; the male occult *Bildungsroman*, as we will see, shows that the forms of identity modeled for men in this context were no less ambivalent in their approach to agential individualism.

2.1 Politics and Progress in the *Bildungsroman*

The *Bildungsroman* is, as Sara Lyons correctly observes, "one of the most controversial terms in literary study," and narrowing it down for the purpose of incorporating new examples is no straightforward feat.[3] Critics continue to debate its origin point and destinations, ideological tenor, differing national iterations, and generic boundaries, sometimes policing these tightly, and at others, notes Richard Salmon, "so capaciously that virtually any novel, especially of the nineteenth century, can fit within the rubric."[4] Perhaps the most consistent point of critical consensus is that *Bildungsromane* are "preeminently the novels of youth," long-form prose narratives in which a young, still unformed protagonist sets out of a course of self-development and education and ultimately reaches a mature reconciliation between personal desire and the demands of the wider community.[5] While the young *Bildungsheld* may be either male or female, the gendered opportunities for independent growth and the expectations of social compliance they face within their fictional worlds are often very different, as they are too in the female reincarnative romances, such as Collins's *The Blossom and the Fruit* and Corelli's *Ziska*, which we will encounter in the next chapter.[6] Often, the *Bildungsroman*, like the golden age detective tale to be discussed in

42   OPEN SECRETS

Chapter 5, has been read as an innately conservative form, in the former's case because of its equation of individual maturity with social conformity via a process in which "the Romantic youth progressively adjusts his or her desire for freedom and creative fulfilment to the demands of society."[7] So, too, however, has it been increasingly celebrated for invoking this politically simplistic narrative arc only to expose its contradictions. Thus, in his highly influential study of the European *Bildungsroman*, Franco Moretti argues that:

> the success of the *Bildungsroman* suggests that in fact the truly central ideologies of our world are not in the least . . . intolerant, normative, monologic; to be wholly submitted or rejected. When we remember that the *Bildungsroman*—the symbolic form that more than any other has portrayed and promoted modern socialization—is also the *most contradictory* of modern symbolic forms, we realize that in our world socialization itself consists first of all in the *interiorization of contradiction*.[8]

As the social world that the *Bildungsheld* ultimately accepts is by no means a static, fixed, or coherent one, claims Moretti, then it would be a mistake to dismiss such conclusions as simply traditionalist or even authoritarian. His point—that the political orientation of particular *Bildungsromane* must be calibrated in relation to the dynamism of the social milieu they end up accommodating—will be one to which we return.

The *Bildungsroman*'s ability to expose the pace, transformative effects, and ideological contradictions of modernity derives, for Moretti and others, from its emergence within the specific historical conditions of eighteenth and nineteenth-century Europe, ones which fostered the new form of temporality that the genre encodes. To put this more simply, it is a form both *of* and *about* a particular experience of time associated with modernity. For Mikhail Bakhtin, a crucial early theorist of the genre, the *Bildungsroman* connects "man's individual emergence . . . to historical emergence . . . He emerges *along with the world* and he reflects the historical emergence of the world itself. He is no longer within an epoch, but on the border between two epochs, at the transition point from one to the other."[9] Importantly, *Bildungshelden* do not inhabit the atemporal space of mythical quest; rather, they are depicted as operating within a period of precise historical transition whose conditions make their own concerted self-development from youth to adulthood newly possible. As many commentators point out, the idea that adult selfhood might be something to deliberately cultivate and attain through trial is of fairly recent origin in the West. Julia Prewitt Brown, for example, observes:

> Seeing youth as the most decisive phase of life is a relatively new phenomenon in history. Social historians tell us that it began in the late eighteenth century, when traditional, agrarian society gave way and the new generation had to contend with a far more uncertain life in the city. Before then, being young simply meant not yet being an adult.[10]

Only in a social structure where personal vocation—for white, bourgeois, male subjects at least, if few others—had become partially subject to choice, rather than a pre-determined necessity or fated destination, did the *Bildungsroman* come into its own. As we will see, this historico-temporal dimension of the form would come to pose a significant ontological challenge to its nineteenth-century occult interlocutors, even while serving as a key source of its attractiveness; after all, what better way to assert the contemporary relevance and progressive outlook of an esoteric spiritual philosophy than by allying with what was rapidly becoming recognized as modernity's primary novelistic mode?

2.2 A Magical Counter-History of Wilhelm Meister

We can find this modernizing *ethos* at the heart of the novel long asserted, if no longer without challenge, to be the inaugural European *Bildungsroman*: Goethe's *Wilhelm Meister's Apprenticeship*. "Concerned," as Sarah Vandegrift Eldrige and C. Allen Speight write, "with the location and development of the subject within . . . modernity,"[11] it follows the progress of a romantically inclined burgher's son who temporarily sets aside the mercantile career bestowed on him by his father to pursue a life of artistic and sexual freedom amidst a company of itinerant actors. By the novel's close, and via the intervention of the mysterious Tower Society that has been watching and guiding his actions from afar, he is ready to embrace his adult role as husband and father within an expanding imperial milieu. While the novel's originary status within the secular *Bildungsroman* tradition has become increasingly disputed,[12] there are good reasons to continue to assign it this position within the reception community of the British occult revival. First and foremost, Goethe appears to have been a favorite author of British

44   OPEN SECRETS

spiritualists and occultists, who regularly ransacked his epigrammatic prose and putative biography for quotations to adorn their publications and defiantly read his work against the common-sensical, Presbyterian grain established by *Wilhelm Meister*'s first English translator, Thomas Carlyle.[13] Thus, from its 1882 launch onward, the London-based spiritualist periodical *Light* positioned the German polymath's alleged dying words—"Light, more light!" on its masthead,[14] placing them alongside St. Paul's scriptural assertion to the Ephesians that "whatsoever doth [make] manifest is light"[15] as if to grant these utterances implicit spiritual equivalence. This was by no means the first time that spiritualists had co-opted Goethe for their cause; indeed, two decades earlier, pioneering British spiritualist William Howitt had identified the entire Goethe family as spirit believers in an 1866 article for the *Spiritualist Magazine*.[16] The German writer's influence would only intensify within the Theosophical and Anthroposophical circles that emerged at the *fin de siècle*, largely through his championship by Austrian occultist Rudolf Steiner, who edited Goethe's scientific writings between 1883 and 1897 and used them as the basis for his anthroposophical principles.[17] Later, when Steiner designed the movement's headquarters in Dornach, Switzerland, he bestowed on them the title of the Goethenanum. As Edward Lingan writes, "Steiner viewed Goethe as an occult adept who possessed supersensible perception, and he viewed some of Goethe's writing as revealed texts with occult meaning."[18] Steiner's appropriation of Goethe was anticipated, if not directly catalyzed, by the occulturally inclined popular fiction writers in late Victorian Britain who regularly turned to Goethe for inspiration, including Corelli whose sardonic, sneering Lucio Rîmanez, in the best-selling supernatural thriller *The Sorrows of Satan* (1895), clearly owes a debt to the Mephistopheles of *Faust: Part One* (1808) among other landmark literary Lucifers. The full extent of Goethe's considerable influence on the Victorian occult revival is yet to be comprehensively mapped and exceeds the remit of the current chapter. For our purposes, it is enough to recognize that the German sage was a frequent touchstone and intertextual source for our focal writers Bulwer and Britten, even if their own fictional re-imaginings of male *Bildung* would take a dramatically different path than *Wilhelm Meister's Apprenticeship*.

We can recognize this divergence by revisiting *Wilhelm Meister*'s treatment of two subjects of immense importance to the Victorian occult revival and its textual production: supernatural phenomena and filial relationships. Goethe's novel takes each very seriously indeed; its plot is pervaded by

MAGICAL MEISTERS 45

ghosts, fathers, and, in Wilhelm's fixation with Shakespeare's *Hamlet* (1599–1601), whose lead role he eventually performs, ghostly fathers. The young burgher's journey of self-discovery is precipitated through and against the will of his money-minded and staunchly practical father, who sees no value in the dramatic performances beloved by his son—"How can any one waste his time so?"[19]—and thus sends him out on the business trip that will allow young Meister, neglecting his commercial duties, to dally and play amongst theatre folk. This sojourn is riven through with what Jesse Rosenthal terms a "genre-bending supernaturalism" that we might more readily equate with the German *Schauerroman* than the realist *Bildungsroman* tradition.[20] Meister anticipates his first lover Mariana's betrayal in a portentous dream; later, seeing the as-yet unidentified figure of his rival Norberg at her door, he starts as if seeing "a spirit of midnight, which awakens unutterable terror" and "leaves doubts without end behind it in the soul."[21] In Book Three, it will be Meister's time to play the specter as he disguises himself as the Countess's husband to meet her for a secret tryst; when, by accident, the Count sees him in this dress, the older man becomes convinced that he has been visited by an otherworldly *doppelgänger* who presages his own death. Eager to conceal his illicit liaison, Meister and his new associate, Jarno, encourage this belief, "talking, in the presence of the count, about warnings, visions, apparitions, and the like."[22]

This ghostly performance precedes another, far more momentous one in the young artistic amateur's self-directed education. With Serlo's company, he decides to stage a performance of *Hamlet* in which he will play the lead. Meister's experience of reading the works of the English dramatist is described in terms of bewitchment—the narrator remarks that:

> we have heard of some Enchanter, summoning, by magic formulas, a vast multitude of spiritual shapes into his cell. The conjurations are so powerful that the whole space of the apartment is quickly full; and the spirits, crowding on to the verge of the little circle which they must not pass, around this, and above the master's head, keep increasing in number, and ever whirling in perpetual transformation . . . So sat Wilhelm in his privacy: with unknown movements, a thousand feelings and capacities awoke in him, of which he formerly had neither notion nor anticipation.[23]

Given this enchanted figuration of Shakespearean reading, it is unsurprising that, when Wilhelm attempts to cast the role of Old Hamlet's ghost,

46   OPEN SECRETS

he should proceed along supernatural lines. Unable to settle on a candidate, he receives an anonymous letter announcing that "the Ghost shall arise at the proper hour!"[24] Indeed, at the debut performance, a mailed and visored figure appears on stage to play the role with *gravitas* before disappearing without a trace. Who was this mysterious figure? Was he of this world or the next? Could he have been the apparition of Wilhelm's own recently departed father, returned from the dead to recall him to his filial duties? Only near the end of the novel does the theatrical ghost's identity become clear; it has been played by the Abbé, the benevolent emissary of the Tower Society who has secretly monitored and directed Wilhelm's development from afar and will ultimately serve him with the apprenticeship scroll that marks his readiness to become a responsible citizen and father.

The Tower Society episode represents the simultaneous peak and deflation of the novel's esoteric impulses. Secret societies and hidden forms of knowledge seem to have been much on Goethe's mind in the period of *Meister*'s composition; in 1794, he had embarked on the composition of a new libretto that would continue Wolfgang Amadeus Mozart's *Die Zauberflöte* and show that "Mozart's works elevated the use of the supernatural and magical plots, taking them out of the realm of farce and making them elevated and serious."[25] But in *Wilhelm Meister*, as Theodore Ziolkowski suggests, the occult is treated with a far greater degree of irony and distance than in Goethe's project of Mozartian exegesis.[26] The initiates of the Tower Society—Jarno, Lothario, and the Abbé—are not mysterious sages equipped with magical powers and hidden knowledge, but flawed mortals whose ambitions are practical and secular; they are men of business who plan, at the novel's close, to travel around the globe and "work nonpolitically behind the scenes on behalf of anti-Jacobin liberalism, the protection of private ownership, and therefore the encouragement of scientific and commercial enterprise."[27] Their adoption of a secret society structure to enact these goals, and to monitor Meister's development, has more to do with its pedagogical impact than on a genuine commitment to a secret knowledge tradition. Thus, after Meister receives his scroll of apprenticeship—a curious text combining lofty apothegms with covertly observed and inscribed incidences from his life— during the Tower Society's quasi-Masonic ceremony, Jarno explains:

> The taste of youth for secrecy, for ceremonies, for imposing words, is extraordinary; and frequently bespeaks a certain depth of character. In those years, we wish to feel our whole nature seized and moved, even though it

be but vague and darkly. The youth who happens to have lofty aspirations and forecastings, thinks that secrets, and effects much by means of them. It was with such views that the Abbé favoured a certain Society of young men; partly according to his principle of aiding every tendency of nature, partly out of habit and inclination; for in former times, he had himself been joined to an association, which appears to have accomplished many things in secret.[28]

Secrecy is thus adopted by the Society for the purely pragmatic purpose of teaching the romantically inclined Wilhelm to be his own guide, and, by indulging his passion for the theatre, to "let him quaff his error in deep, satiating draughts" and hence learn the folly of seeking "cultivation where it was not to be found."[29] The Tower Society has no particular set of universal precepts or teachings to pass onto Wilhelm, and to which he must adhere; on the contrary, he dismisses the contents of his apprenticeship scroll as "wise saws" which provide "but a sorry balsam for a wounded heart."[30] Writing of this Tower Society episode, Michael Bell observes that although "Goethe is a great lover of mystification," but "typically when you get there the cupboard is usually bare."[31] What matters is not pedagogical content but rather outcome, and the final product of *Wilhelm Meister's Apprenticeship*—if not the narrative terminus of the character himself[32]—is a mature, civic-minded *pater familias* no longer determined to kick against the pricks of the social milieu into which he was born. As Wilhelm declares in the novel's final line, his restless, revolutionary days are over: "I know not the worth of a kingdom ... but I know I have attained a happiness which I have not deserved, and which I would not change with anything in my life."[33]

Thus, while uncanny encounters, seemingly supernatural occurrences, and the machinations of a secret knowledge society often take center stage in *Wilhelm Meister's Apprenticeship*, they are invoked only to be ultimately abandoned; like vestigial organs, they are necessary to the early stages of Wilhelm's self-culture but can be safely left behind once he has come into his own. As in the rationalist Gothic tales of his English contemporary, Ann Radcliffe, there are no real ghosts in Goethe's *Wilhelm Meister's Apprenticeship*, and the covert operations and rituals of the Tower Society, once explained, can never again strike terrified awe in their unsuspecting subject. Yet when the narrative structure of this prototypal, implicitly secularizing *Bildungsroman* was appropriated within a firmly occultural ontology, one where unseen spiritual forces and arcane, initiatory cadres were

48 OPEN SECRETS

no juvenile paraphernalia to be discarded on maturation, but rather realities whose recognition is the very goal to which *Bildung* arcs, this outcome would be very different. Having established *Meister*'s sublimation of the esoteric, we will now turn toward two such acts of genre recoding as produced by the Goethean occult writers Bulwer and Britten.

An analysis of Bulwer's and Britten's defiantly occult *Bildungsromane* allows us to push back against and complicate Moretti's famous disparagement of the genre's Victorian iterations as childishly anti-realist, naively moralistic, and beggared, both artistically and intellectually, by their recourse to rote happy endings. The contradictions between individualism and conformity that the European *Bildungsroman* exposes, Moretti claims, are in its British counterparts smoothed over: "from Fielding to Dickens . . . we have but one long fairy-tale with a happy ending, far more elementary and limited than its continental counterparts."[34] Thus Pip in Charles Dickens's *Great Expectations* (1861) gains and then loses a fortune, not as the result of his own self-conscious efforts, but through a bizarre coincidental encounter; the novel's conclusion, in Moretti's reading, simply endorses Pip's childhood values and affiliations rather than equipping him with new ones. One might extrapolate from Moretti's reading that the further one drifts from the representational structures of social realism—the more one fixates on the Manichean struggle between good and evil, rather than on the complexity of moral choice in modern life—the more difficult it will be to produce a *Bildungsroman* that is anything other than a simplistic fairy story. As we will now see, such logic does not apply to the logic of the occult *Bildungsroman*. Instead, *A Strange Story* and *Ghost Land* expose the profound challenges to, even the impossibility of, progress at the individual, social, and cosmic level precisely in the way they pursue an anti-realist esoteric worldview.

2.3 Arrested Development in *A Strange Story*

The first example of the occult *Bildungsroman*'s problem of progress that I will discuss features in Bulwer's *A Strange Story*, a novel serialized in Dickens's periodical *All the Year Round* between August 10, 1861, and March 8, 1862, before appearing later that year in a single volume published by Sampson, Low, Son & Co. Much had changed for the author in the twenty years since he had written *Zanoni*. No longer a radical literary lion in his prime, Bulwer was now very much an establishment figure who had forged an eminent political career on Britain's imperial stage while changing his affiliation from Whig to Conservative. Both the moralistic strain and high-falutin style of his prose fiction were coming to seem increasingly out of fashion in a mid-century literary environment that favored realist novels; while his books still sold, critics took an increasingly dim view of them. Two particularly pertinent features of Bulwer's early career, however, remained constant: he retained both his interest in occult science and seekership—while not publicly claiming any affiliation with the Societas Rosicruciana in Anglia (SRIA) or adherence to modern spiritualism[35]—and his artistic allegiance to Goethe. Both exerted a formative influence on *A Strange Story*, the idea for which had, as Andrew Brown notes, come to the writer oneirically in a dream.[36]

Literary critics have long recognized Bulwer's respective contributions to the traditions of the *Bildungsroman* and of supernatural fiction in Britain while almost never linking the two, a fact that seems clearly to reflect the secularist bias within the genre's critical reception. Thus, while Suzanne Howe, in her landmark early study of *Wilhelm Meister*'s influence in Britain, identifies Bulwer as one of the genre's most active and prolific British "follower[s],"[37] she does not include any of his major occult novels in her analysis of his contribution to the *Bildungsroman* genre: *Falkland* (1827), *Pelham* (1828), *The Disowned* (1829), *Godolphin* (1833), *Ernest Maltravers* (1837), *Alice; or the Mysteries* (1838), and *Kenelm Chillingly* (1873) appear here, but not *Zanoni* or *A Strange Story*. Writing some seventy years after Howe, Salmon makes the same omission in his account of Bulwer as a "decidedly neglected exponent[t] of the genre" whose "contribution to the establishment of the *Bildungsroman* should not be underestimated, whatever our response to his novels as such"[38]—like Howe, he evidences this influence through *The Disowned, Godolphin, Ernest Maltravers*, and *Alice; or, The Mysteries* rather than any of the major occult novels. This omission seems more remarkable when we consider that Bulwer's reception of Goethe and *Wilhelm Meister* was consistently inflected by the supernatural. One of his earliest published references to *Wilhelm Meister* appears in the Mephistophelean miscellany discussed in our last chapter, *Asmodeus at Large*. In the work's 1833 single volume edition, we find our narrator and Asmodeus discussing the German sage's death over the morning paper. While the former enthuses over his *oeuvre*, Asmodeus dismisses *Wilhelm Meister* as "a wonderfully stupid novel,"[39] a sure sign, perhaps, of his untrustworthy judgment. This provokes a robust defense from our narrator, who exclaims "What an effect it produced on me!—what a new

50 OPEN SECRETS

world it opens now. You read the book, and you wonder why you admire it. When you have finished it, you find yourself enriched; it is like a quiet stream that carries gold with it—the stream passes away insensibly, but the gold remains to tell where it has been."[40] Lest we remain in any doubt as to who to believe, Bulwer has his narrator then call Goethe "the man who changed the whole literature of Germany, perhaps Europe" and *Wilhelm Meister* "the mature work of a very stupendous, brooding mind, that worked out the block of nature from the most artificial, recondite tools."[41]

A Strange Story epitomizes Bulwer's distinctly occult interpretation of Goethe's *Wilhelm Meister*, replacing the burgher's son with Allan Fenwick, a newly qualified and myopically materialistic graduate of the Edinburgh Medical School who learns, through a tortured love affair with the ethereal and vulnerable clairvoyant Lilian Ashleigh, that the soul and the supernatural world are no mere fictions. In this plot trajectory, and in its publication history, the novel acts as an uncanny occult mirror of the better-known English *Bildungsroman* whose serialization it followed in *All the Year Round: Great Expectations*. Like Dickens's Pip, Fenwick too sets off on his fictional course with false illusions about how the world works; he also temporarily accesses riches from Australia,[42] and falls in love with a beautiful if elusive woman who, unbeknownst to him, is being controlled by a malicious agent—the vengeful spurned woman Miss Havisham in *Great Expectations*, who has groomed the young Estella to act as an instrument of misandrist sexual revenge, and the soulless occult vampire Margrave, formerly Louis Grayle, in *A Strange Story*, who seeks to further extend his already preternaturally lengthened youth by exploiting and draining Lilian. Following many struggles, the two *Bildungshelden* ultimately end up with the women of their choice after abandoning their naïve beliefs in, on Pip's part, the value of unearned riches, or, on Fenwick's, the non-existence of the soul. Fascinatingly, both conclusions are attributable to Bulwer. As Brown explains, Bulwer and Dickens were actively reading and exchanging feedback on their *All the Year Round* serial novels in 1861; it was at Bulwer's urgence that Dickens revised the original draft ending of *Great Expectations* to feature a reunion between Pip and Estella. "In this, as in most matters of literary taste," remarks Brown, "the judgement of history has rarely coincided with that of Bulwer, and it is ironic that in many quarters today Bulwer's claim to fame should rest on his thus 'meddling' with the conclusion to a greater novel than he himself ever penned."[43] Leaving value judgments aside, we might observe that Bulwer's contribution to the development of the British *Bildungsroman* tradition was certainly no less sincere or sustained than Dickens's, and is arguably far more ambitious in its extension of the temporal span in which growth might occur well beyond the typical limits of human life.

To say that such prolonged development *might* occur is not, however, to suggest that it actually *does*, in *A Strange Story* at least. For as much as the narrating Fenwick styles his tale as a retrospective account of growth from ignorance into spiritual knowledge, his narrative overwhelmingly depicts the identities produced by occult contact—whether of a malign or benevolent nature—as arrested, adolescent, or, at best, perpetually beholden to paternal authority. This set of connections is forged first, and most horrifyingly, through the text's antagonist Margrave, the evil, soulless adept who Bulwer enlists as foil to Fenwick's nascent atheism. Fenwick first encounters Margrave in the provincial town of L__,[44] where he has set up a medical practice and started work on an ambitious treatise of philosophical empiricism with which he aims "to take a rank and leave a name as one of the great pathologists to whom humanity accords a grateful, if calm, renown."[45] At a garden party hosted by the local *bon ton*, he meets a stunning young Adonis newly returned from travels in the East who captivates the company with his wit and learning even as the children who flock around him seem strangely drained by his presence. "Never before have I seen a face so radiant," Fenwick recalls:

> There was in the aspect an indescribable something that literally dazzled. As one continued to gaze it was with surprise; one was forced to acknowledge that in the features themselves there was no faultless regularity; nor was the young man's stature imposing, about the middle height. But the effect of the whole was not less transcendent.[46]

This, of course, is Margrave, the famous fictional prototype for Bram Stoker's Dracula who, in this scene, also suggests the seeds of Robert Louis Stevenson's Mr. Hyde in his evocation of a corporeal strangeness that lies beyond the sum of his physical parts.[47]

Like Dracula, Margrave is, in fact, a false-faced fiend who levies his occult powers to command lunatics to do his bidding, to defy death, and to pollute local girls. His specific target is Fenwick's dreamy fiancée, Lilian, who, under his mesmeric control, steals away from her home to join him at a remote seaside location. While Margrave's motives are magical rather than sexual—he seeks in her the pure clairvoyance that will permit "he who knows how to direct and to profit by it . . . to discover all that he desires to know for the guidance and preservation of his own life"[48]—Lilian's reputation is nonetheless left in tatters by this coerced liaison. It is far easier for the residents of L__ to imagine her a woman seduced than a woman entranced. To protect her from the near fatal opprobrium of L__, Fenwick quickly marries Lilian and emigrates with her to the Australian outback, where he will continue his physiological research while overseeing a sheep farm. Here, the cunning if now vastly depleted Margrave tracks the pair down and compels Fenwick's participation in an alchemical ritual that will, if successful, rejuvenate his own magical longevity and save the life of the now dying Lilian. In a move that suggests the character's influence on yet another late Victorian gothic villain, H. Rider Haggard's Ayesha in *She: A History of Adventure* (1887), Margrave drinks too much of the elixir of life and dies, leaving Lilian and Fenwick to thrive in their colonial pastoral idyll, assured in their renewed conviction of spiritual immortality.

This is an extremely abridged version of *A Strange Story*'s immensely complicated narrative, one which ranges wildly in tone from gentle Austenian social satire in its depiction of the bourgeois mores of L__, to abstruse philosophical treatise in the endless lectures exchanged between Fenwick and his mentor, Julius Faber, and hair-raising horror in its account of the bloody murder of Sir Philip Derval and the ghastly spectral manifestations of the Scin-Laeca, a skeletal apparition of the still-living Margrave that visits Fenwick after dark. What connects all these threads is a persistent focus on a progress that is, in many ways, no progress at all. Prior to his renegade occult immortalization, Margrave has been Louis Grayle, the "haughty quarrelsome, reckless, handsome, aspiring, brave" son of a local usurer with upward aspirations for his offspring.[49] Unfortunately, his father's ambitions are never realized. After killing a man in a duel, the young Grayle flees England in disgrace and spends decades travelling in the East, becoming "an orientalised Englishman" who gains "a terrible knowledge in those branches of the art which, even in the East, are condemned as instrumental to evil."[50] At Aleppo, he murders local magus Haroun in order acquire the secret to the Elixir of Life. This act is both pragmatic and sensual; Grayle kills to gain what Haroun will not freely give, and to stoke his insatiable desire for new pleasures and experiences. Thus, in his new guise of Margrave, he quizzes Fenwick with the rhetorical question: "Do you not pity the fool who prefers to lie a bed, and to dream rather than to live? . . . Do you not long for a rush through the green of the fields, a bath in the blue of the river?"[51]

MAGICAL MEISTERS 53

This constant impulsion forward drives Grayle into his homicidal encounter with Haroun which, once concluded, propels him into a perpetual, hollow present where he is no longer *in time* with his fellow humans, or stirred by their suffering. While others change and age, Margrave stays firmly the same, unmoved and unmovable through what Fenwick recognizes as his "main moral defect ... a want of sympathy."[52] So it happens that when a small child he has been playfully carrying on his shoulders fall off and injures himself, Margrave's only reaction is to protect his ears from the sound of its pitiful cries: "Oh, nothing so discordant as a child's wail. I hate discords. I am pleased with the company of children; but they must be children who laugh and play."[53] When the child subsequently sickens and dies, he registers no emotional response whatsoever. In this position, he emerges as a more sinister version of Mejnour, the aloof adept in Bulwer's earlier *Zanoni* whose millennia-long tenure on earth has distanced him from the concerns of the living, even if, unlike Margrave, he does not inflict on them actual harm. Margrave's commitment to an eternal present equips him with a counterintuitively anti-occult stance, even though his powers were acquired by magical means. Thus, in conversation with Fenwick, he mocks astrology for its inapplicability to a being such as himself. "Astrologers? No!" he declares. "They deal with the future. I live for the day; only I wish the day never had a morrow."[54] When, in response, Fenwick suggests that he must surely share "that vague desire for something beyond—that not unhappy, but grand discontent with the limits of the immediate Present, from which man takes his passion for improvement and progress,"[55] Margrave reacts with perplexed confusion: "What a farrago of words is this? I do not comprehend you."[56]

Margrave's trajectory of occult knowledge acquisition then, brings him not to self-knowledge, but to nonsense, and, by the novel's finale, produces a complete collapse of both his identity and corresponding sense of personal past. In Australia, Fenwick questions Margrave about Louis Grayle, hoping to force from him a confession that they are one and the same. But Margrave seems confused about his own past, saying only that "I remember [Grayle] ... as one remembers a nightmare."[57] The fact that he became the beneficiary of Grayle's legal will provides no conclusive evidence of the nature of their connection one way or another; perhaps Louis Grayle willed the fortune to his new alter-ego after faking his own death, or perhaps Margrave is Grayle's illegitimate, and mentally disordered son. Bulwer's narration refuses to authorize either of these scenarios as true. After asking Fenwick, "May I not be the love-son of Louis Grayle?," Margrave's expression becomes

54   OPEN SECRETS

"very troubled, the tone of his voice very irresolute—the face and the voice of a man who is either blundering his way through an intricate falsehood, or obscure reminiscences."[58] The more he struggles to remember, the more elusive his past history and previous identities become, until Margrave eventually if tentatively opts for a rationalist—and hence in the logic of the novel, false—solution. "Louis Grayle!" he exclaims:

> Louis Grayle! All my earlier memories go back to Louis Grayle! All my arts and powers, all that I have learned of the languages spoken in Europe, of the sciences taught in her schools, I owe to Louis Grayle. But am I one and the same with him? No—I am but a pale reflection of his giant intellect. He stands apart from me, as a rock from the trees that grows out from its chasms. Yes, the gossip was right. I must be his son.[59]

The figurative language employed here makes it clear that Margrave's conclusion is no product of rationalist deduction. On the contrary, having magically stepped outside the logic of developmental time, he can no longer recognize any connection between his younger and present self. It is ultimately easier to think of the former as a separate entity entirely, not as a root to his branch, but as a rock from which a tree flourishes by mere happenstance.

Thus far, I have shown how Margrave, as *A Strange Story*'s most developed portrait of an occult adept, functions as a figure of anti-*Bildung*, a seeker whose esoteric education has produced, not experience or social settlement, but stasis and a narcissistic indifference to others. Of course, such a representation need not necessarily compromise the novel's overarching narrative of occult meliorism, one that insists on the improving effects of heterodox spiritual instruction. After all, Margrave is the novel's antagonist, not its *Bildungsheld*; it is not to him we should look for a depiction of the beneficial effects of occult pedagogy. That role belongs instead to Fenwick, Bulwer's magical version of Goethe's Meister, who learns to abandon his scientific hubris and become a capable husband through his battle with Margrave. But in this character, too, we find signs of arrested development and stalled maturation that seem only more positive than those exhibited by Margrave in their affirmation of traditional forms of patriarchal and paternal authority. For, far more than *Wilhelm Meister*, or even Meister's great hero Hamlet, Fenwick consistently seeks, obeys, and exalts father figures. Rather than deferring, defying, or ignoring his filial duty, he repeatedly seeks new stand-ins for whom to perform it after the death of his birth father, a man whose debts he

MAGICAL MEISTERS   55

has been only too willing to pay. Accordingly, in the novel's opening chapter, Fenwick explains how he has forged his professional medical authority through two forms of paternal relation: his aristocratic patrimony and his dutiful disbursement of his improvident father's bills:

> I was saved from the suspicion of a medical adventurer by the accidents of birth and fortune. I belonged to an ancient family (a branch of the once powerful border-clan of the Fenwicks) that had for many generations held a fair estate in the neighbourhood of Windermere. As an only son I had succeeded to that estate on attaining my majority, and had sold it to pay off the debts which had been made my father, who had the costly tastes of an antiquary and a collector.[60]

Here, in an almost complete reversal of the filial patterning in *Wilhelm Meister*, the prudent son initiates his *Bildung* by paying for the whimsical excesses of an artistically dilettantish father. When Bulwer moves Fenwick's development from the secular into a spiritual world, this paternal reliance only intensifies, even as its object changes. While traveling in Europe, he meets the pathologist Dr. Julius Faber and successfully treats him for his pneumonia. In gratitude, the "childless bachelor" Faber invites Fenwick to share his practice in L__, and ultimately leaves it to him entirely when he retires some years later, finding in the young physician the son he never had.[61]

The death or departure of a parental figure is a common trope of the *Bildungsroman*, typically serving to provide the necessary space for young *Bildungshelden* to come of age and forge their own settlement with the social world. But in *A Strange Story*, neither fathers nor the authority they represent are ever absent for long. Thus, Fenwick's real father is soon replaced by Faber, his name a proximate homophone for father. Although leaving England upon his retirement, Faber as father later returns when his protégé most needs him—just after the young man has been falsely accused and exculpated for the murder of his other older male mentor, Sir Philip Derval. The death of a father in *A Strange Story* always precipitates the emergence of a new one. From then on, Faber acts as Fenwick's chief interlocuter and counsel in the novel, lecturing him with a frequency and exhaustive intensity that must have put heavy demands on *All the Year Round*'s audiences. A Christian, if not a magical believer, he initially explains away Margrave's seeming supernatural abilities in proto-Sherlockian manner as the products of psychological suggestion and cognitive error;[62] nonetheless, in a later, pivotal scene

56   OPEN SECRETS

prior to Fenwick's final confrontation with Margrave, Faber affirms the reality of animal magnetism and of certain, uniquely formed individuals to operate on the minds of others from a distance: "there is in some peculiar and rare temperaments a power over forms of animated organization, with which they establish some unaccountable affinity; and even, though much more rarely, a power over inanimate matter."[63] Like a good Socratic pupil, Fenwick then repeats these arguments back to his mentor for clarification and correction, a rhetorical flourish which positions us as readers too in the role of attentive students. Most of all, Faber insists on the existence of God and the immortality of soul, declaring that, although not a spiritualist himself, "I would rather believe all the ghost stories upon record than believe that I am not even a ghost."[64]

By the novel's close, Fenwick, too, has learned to adopt this position, one he gains not, like Goethe's Meister, by being left alone to discover his own errors under the remote supervision of a secret society, but by the near-relentless battery of explanation provided by his omnipresent surrogate father. Still not quite sure what to think about the true nature of Margrave's powers, he puts this question aside as moot so that he may defer to the ultimate father figure of God. "What mattered henceforth to Faith," Fenwick asks:

> whether Reason, in Faber, or Fancy, in me, supplied the more probable guess at a hieroglyph which . . . was but a word of small mark in the mystical language of Nature? . . . Whatever art Man can achieve in his progress through time, Man's reason, in time, can suffice to explain. But the wonders of God? These belong to the Infinite; and these, O Immortal! will but develop new wonder on wonder, though thy sight be a spirit's, and thy leisure to track and solve an eternity.[65]

Key here is Bulwer's juxtaposition of the historical time frame in which humans may grow, change, and progress with the far superior power of the Infinite in which there are no limits or endings, and where everything that is required is always already present. Fenwick's progress is thus signaled through his final understanding that human developmental time, even after the living enter the afterlife and gain spiritual sight, is as of nothing to the infinite span of eternity.

At its heart, then, Bulwer's occult *Bildungsroman* is a novel in which progressive time is permanently out of joint. It presents us with two contrasting versions of stalled male adolescence—Margrave, who, like J. M. Barrie's Peter

Pan, refuses to grow up, age, and die, and Fenwick, who has no desire to step out from the shadow of his manifold fathers. For both, the plot of occult pedagogical development leads ultimately to a stasis beyond the chronologies of developmental and historical time. Villain and hero alike progress into a state of standing still. The problem of, and with, progress in *A Strange Story* is that it seems fundamentally incompatible with the novel's understanding of true spiritual wisdom.

Perhaps as a reflex of the temporal paradox it presents, the novel triggered in its early critical reception an analogous debate about the nature of progress and its relationship to both spiritual and artistic forms of value. Bulwer published *A Strange Story* just as the sixth decade of his life was ending. Reviewers knew that his literary activity was winding to a close[66] and used the occasion to comment on the novel's place within a longer career trajectory that was either rising to its apogee or futilely circling back on itself. A remarkably perceptive response to the novel in the *Christian Remembrancer* identifies Bulwer as himself the subject and proponent of a lifelong literary *Bildung* who had "from youth, to what, at any rate in authorship, is age" been "anxious we should be alive to a plan, to a gradually unfolding system. Plots and groups of characters have not come to him by chance, he tells us in his prefaces, but by a sort of necessary progression."[67] The terminus of this great and carefully plotted project was always, for this reviewer, going to be "magic," to which Bulwer "has arrived . . . as a goal."[68] At the same time, however, the article suggests that the very idea of progress had consistently been challenged within Bulwer's wider literary corpus, whose major works seemed locked in:

> defiance or hand-to-hand encounter with time. The peculiarity of the story which immediately precedes the present one [*What Will He Do With It?* (1859)] is, that time has no influence, no retarding, checking power on anybody . . . We are not then at all surprised that the next step is . . . to naturalize the process by introducing us to the Elixir Vitae.[69]

Bulwer's literary progress is here fascinatingly styled as a version of Louis Grayle's quest to slip free of the strictures of time and age and to find solace in the eternal. A less flattering way to put this might be to say that Bulwer's *oeuvre* was intellectually and artistically stagnant, mired in repetition, and jejune in its preoccupations. Certainly, there was no shortage of competing critics willing to make just such claims. A perhaps predictably caustic 1865

58   OPEN SECRETS

retrospective of the conservative Bulwer's *oeuvre*, published in the liberal *Westminster Review*, remarks: "Looking . . . at these novels . . . there is little room for praise. If they do really record the growth of the author's mind, all that can be said is that his mind must have grown very badly."[70] Another in *The Saturday Review* laments Bulwer's failure to grow permanently up out of a Gothic adolescence into the mature adulthood of literary realism, depicting him instead as circling repetitively between the two genres in a pathetic cycle of stunted growth. "With most minds," the reviewer declares, "the supernatural loses its attractions after a time, and is discarded for what our author would call the Real. But with Sir B. Lytton the natural and the supernatural seem to take it turn and turnabout. To have been successful in his employment of the one appears a sufficient reason for abandoning it in favour of the other."[71] Targeted specifically at *A Strange Story*, these comments speak to the challenge that all serious works of occult fiction—those inspired by an esoteric philosophical program or form of practice, rather than simply a desire to produce fear or wonder—faced at the mid-century. If occultism itself were consigned to the realm of adolescence, its teachings aligned with a long and deservedly distant past, then it could never fully grow up. The *Bildungsroman* format, adopted as a means of aligning heterodox spiritual seekership with modernity and maturation, might only reveal that occultism, in Bulwer's representational hands at least, was incapable of fostering either. Yet this possibility did not deter the writer's more publicly committed and affiliated occult contemporaries from continuing to co-opt and expand the aesthetic and spiritual capacities of the genre. On the contrary, as we will now see, some attempted to levy their heterodox beliefs to collapse the normative temporal and developmental expectations that had made hostile judgments of Bulwer's occult *Bildungsroman* possible in the first place.

2.4 Emma Hardinge Britten, Authorship, and Occult Fiction

For a very simple reason, Victorian readers were unable to contextualize *Ghost Land; or, Researches into the Mysteries of Occultism* within the course of Britten's development as a fiction writer in the same way as they had *A Strange Story* for Bulwer: namely, she never admitted authorship of the book, which she presented instead as a work of non-fiction that she had only translated from the original German and edited. Nonetheless, a wide scholarly consensus now rejects this claim, as indeed did many of her contemporaries within the transatlantic spiritualist milieu in which she became a leading figure.[72] Born in Bethnal Green in 1823, Britten trained and worked as an actress and musician in Europe and the United States before discovering modern spiritualism in the late 1850s and shortly thereafter establishing herself as one of the movement's most active and influential international proponents. Indeed, her status in this respect was unequaled until Arthur Conan Doyle took up a similar role as international spiritualist propagandist in the 1920s. But her interests were never confined to spiritualism alone; she was also an abolitionist, a woman's suffrage activist, a periodical editor, a prolific writer of spiritualist history and fiction alike, and, in ways that were quite reputationally risky for a prominent spiritualist of her time, an occultist whose pioneering synthesis of esoteric, pagan, and perennialist teachings would exert a significant influence on the Theosophical Society of which she was a founding member.[73] Perhaps the best description of Britten comes from the preface to her posthumously published autobiography, in which the working-class London medium J. J. Morse hails her as "embassadress to the unseen world"[74]—a percipient of and communicant with manifold forms of as yet invisible potential, whether spiritualist, political or artistic. And in her fiction, still the least examined vein of her literary output, we find no exception to this ambition.

Britten's debut as a published fiction writer came hot on the heels of her development as a spiritualist medium, which she dates precisely in her *Autobiography* to February 18, 1856.[75] On this day, she received a posthumous communication from her beloved brother Tom, whose death at sea through the sinking of the *HMS Pacific* had not yet been officially announced.[76] Over the next year-and-a-half, she gave herself wholly to the spiritualist cause, sitting "constantly for all who sought my services as a test medium for a great variety of manifestations"[77] at the Manhattan premises of the Society for the Diffusion of Spiritual Knowledge. The latter enterprise was funded by wealthy spiritualist Horace H. Day, founder also of the Society's in-house newspaper *Christian Spiritualist*.[78] Britten claimed to have been the *de facto* editor of this periodical in early 1857, and to have produced for it some of the stories which appeared in her first fictional collection, *The Wildfire Club* (1861). It is not possible to confirm these claims with any certainty. Of the fourteen tales which appear in *The Wildfire Club*, five are introduced with a headnote which states they were "written for" particular spiritualist papers, including *Christian Spiritualist*, *Spiritual Telegraph*, and *Spiritual Age*. But

60   OPEN SECRETS

the post-1856 runs of these papers reveal little sign of their actual publication; only one of the five—"Haunted Houses 1"—seems to have made it into print as claimed, published under Hardinge's pseudonym "Ezra."[79] It could be that Britten was deploying the phrase "written for" with some liberality here, using it to imply publication intention rather than outcome, and thus authorize the collection through its connection to spiritualism's burgeoning print culture. It is also possible that the composition of some of the stories may have pre-dated her development as a medium, or even her immigration to the United States. Marc Demarest identifies a fascinating reference to Britten in an 1854 letter from Charles Dickens to his friend W. H. Wills, in which he asks the latter to return the papers that Britten had sent to him.[80] Could these papers have included some of her early fictional efforts, sent to Britain's then most popular living writer in the hopes of winning his patronage? We will likely never know, but the record of this contact suggests that Britten was as eager to gain a wide audience for her fictional writings as she would soon be for her spiritualist campaigning. Little wonder that she would, then, enlist the two in each other's service.

The Wildfire Club set the tone for the later published fictional works that would appear under Britten's name: sensational, didactic, sentimental, *louche* in places, and pervaded by a genuine flair for the grotesque. Most of the stories are set in the old European settings inextricably linked to the Gothic brand, including crumbling castles, deserted mansions, and the mountainous haunts of Italian *banditti*; for characters, they feature conventional first-wave Gothic archetypes such as aristocratic *roués*, witch women (here inevitably revealed to innocent and misunderstood spirit mediums), spectral brides, and haunted portraits whose long-dead subjects haunt their ancestral property at night. But Britten was keen to imbue the collection with a serious religious purpose, one irreducible to any cynical act of commercial literary exploitation alone. Her title story, "The Wildfire Club," describes the fate of a group of eighteenth-century debauchers whose plan to kidnap and rape a young village girl after a sham wedding ceremony is thwarted by a providential flood that kills all but one of their members; gifted with spiritual sight, the survivor has a premonition of the catastrophe, and stays away from its site. Later, he draws upon this experience to found a new religious society known as the "Merlinites" who profess "adhesion to no existent form of religious opinion, no respect for creed, sect, worship or church."[81] Instead, "their whole system of belief consisted in faith in the immortality of the soul—a stern, exacting, and uncompromising view of future rewards and punishments for *every act, word, and thought* of every human being,—together with implicit belief in the ability of the spirit (under conditions not yet understood by man) to manifest itself after death in the form of the body it had previously inhabited."[82] Thus prurient horror is turned into a form of didactic propaganda that fictionally backdates the institutional structures of the modern spiritualist movement into an imagined eighteenth-century past. The collection's preface accomplishes the same redirection in the way it explains its title. On the one hand, Britten's "wildfire club" is a clear reference to the notorious real-life Hell Fire clubs of the previous century whose all-male members participated in the anti-clericalism and communal acts of sexual predation described in the story.[83] On the other hand, as she explains in her opening "Address to the Wildfires," the "wildfire" was both a metaphor for the spirit of religious and social reform sweeping through the world, and a direct denotation of the higher ministering spirits with whom she claimed to be in regular contact, entities who formed the real-life inspiration for, and intended legacy of, the collected tales. "Ay, when the pages which now record them are turned to dust," she writes there, "the ages then will do my 'Wildfires' justice, know and call them by their proper names—a club of 'teaching spirits,'—luring no more, but lighting on man's way to that untrodden bourn in which they're shining— the warning and the beacon."[84] Her effort here to exploit, synthesize, and progressively rework the pejorative associations of a deliberately sensational title would be duplicated a couple of decades later in H. P. Blavatsky's and Collins's British Theosophical journal *Lucifer* (1887–1897). The fictional stylings and occult synthesis work of the periodical's pioneering editorial team likely owe more to Britten's influence than has hitherto been acknowledged.[85]

Britten would return to this provocative and prurient Gothic mode in the late-life novel *The Mystery of Number 9 Stanhope Street*, serialized in her Manchester-based periodical, *The Unseen Universe*, between April 1892 and March 1893.[86] It follows the fate of the talented but impoverished artist Richard Stanhope after he becomes obsessed with his model Adina, a young shop clerk. Ultimately and devastatingly, he discovers she is not the pure innocent she appears to be when he finds her dressed as a boy and working as a pool shark at a local billiard hall. To save her from this fate, he offers to marry her, but their engagement is brutally terminated when Adina is tried and executed for murdering the first husband whose existence she had kept hidden from Stanhope.

Occulture enters the narrative with a lighter hand here than in *The Wildfire Club*, manifesting briefly in moments of intuition and vision,

62   OPEN SECRETS

and in the Parisian séance scenes where Stanhope consults the "Sybil of the Ages," Adelaide Lenormand, and attends demonstrations by the mesmerist Monsieur D'Eslon.[87] The focus, as in all Britten's fictional works, is ultimately on redemption; in the wake of Adina's exposure and his ensuing mental collapse, Stanhope gradually rebuilds his life through the love of his talented young wife, Ethel—like Britten, a teacher of music—and their adopted children.

Published some thirty years after *The Wildfire Club*, *The Mystery of No. 9 Stanhope Street* was presented to readers as the close to its author's long hiatus from fiction, one during which she had apparently devoted herself exclusively to non-fictional works of spiritualist history, philosophy, and visionary writing. But recent scholars have challenged this narrative, identifying the most important and influential spiritualist book with which she was associated in those interim years, *Ghost Land; or Researches into the History of Occultism*, as a fictional work of her own composition. Her claims to have merely translated and edited the work on behalf of its pseudonymous author, the European aristocrat Chevalier Louis de B__, ring hollow for several reasons. First, the book appeared several months after the publication of *Art Magic*, another work of occult philosophy initially credited to Louis de B__, but now definitively attributed to Britten by leading Britten expert Demarest.[88] If the Louis de B__ of *Art Magic* was Britten, then Occam's razor suggests that the Louis de B__ of *Ghost Land* likely is as well. Second, many of the esoteric principles, beliefs, and phenomena presented in both *Art Magic* and *Ghost Land* are identical to those advocated in Britten's other occult writings and share with these a common idiom and repertoire of stylistic techniques. Furthermore, both the first and second series of *Ghost Land* explicitly recommend Britten and her works to readers in glowing terms, and attribute to their first-person narrator experiences that Britten describes as experiencing herself in her *Autobiography*. "It is clear," concludes Aren Roukema, "that she did much more than simply edit and translate *Ghost Land* as claimed . . . no other contemporaneous figure embodied a personal philosophy so synonymous with that expressed through the fiction of *Ghost Land*. The novel overwhelmingly reflects Britten's longstanding interest in conflating spiritualism with a wide gamut of occult concepts and practices."[89] It was precisely because of the controversial nature of this synthesis, observe Demarest and Roukema,[90] that Britten adopted a pseudonym in presenting *Ghost Land*, lest its depiction of occult entities, such as elementaries, and practices, such as *vaudoo* possession, alienate the Christian spiritualist audiences that Britten had worked so hard to cultivate, and whose heterodoxy often extended no further than the recognition of the communicative powers of the human dead.

2.5 Paternal Possession and the Illusion of Agency in *Ghost Land*

Another means of establishing Britten's authorship of *Ghost Land* lies in the novel's adoption of a particularly Bulwerian model of occult *Bildung*. If her autobiographical claims to have worked as a child scryer for the London-based Orphic Circle—of which Bulwer was a member—are true, then she must have met the older author.[91] It was possibly through their acquaintance that Britten was put in correspondence with Bulwer's friend Dickens in the 1850s. As Joscelyn Godwin points out, the two certainly shared networks, practices, spirituo-social milieux, and stylistic tendencies,[92] so much so that at least one Victorian occultist, Henry Steel Olcott, thought that *Art Magic* "contain[ed] passages worthy of Bulwer-Lytton; in fact, one would say they were written by him."[93] *Ghost Land* clearly adopts motifs and plot devices from Bulwer's occult *oeuvre*, most notably in its final chapter where the death of adept Louis de B__'s pure and falsely imprisoned wife, Lady Blanche Dudley, is surely meant to evoke the similar demise of Viola Pisani in a French jail cell at the end of *Zanoni*. In the latter finale, the magus seems to die so that his infant son may live, thus catalyzing the novel's closing call for the divine protection of orphan sons who have been wrested from paternal nurture: "*The fatherless are the care of god!*"[94] In *Ghost Land*, this trajectory is reversed; while Louis's newborn child dies alongside its mother, he himself lives and is restored to an occult bachelorhood in which he can continue his enduring quest for a magical father figure he might serve as a compliant son. Here the arrested development that accrues at least *some* negative connotations in *A Strange Story* in its association with the depraved Margrave is almost entirely sanitized, even sacralized. An occult *Bildungsroman* that, in Roukema's words, reveals its protagonist's "progression to occult mastery,"[95] *Ghost Land* goes even further than *A Strange Story* in suggesting that the best way to acquire such knowledge, for male seekers at least, might lie in continually submitting to elite patriarchs.

Ghost Land was serialized in Britten's spiritualist periodical *The Western Star* from July to December 1872, where its author is identified only under

64 OPEN SECRETS

the pseudonym "Austria." Four years later, it appeared in single-volume form as the work of "the author of *Art Magic*." This billing also fronts its sequel, *Extracts from Ghostland, Volume II*, which was serialized alongside *The Mystery of Number 9 Stanhope Street* in *The Unseen Universe* from April 1892 to March 1893.[96] The first series introduces us to narrator and protagonist Chevalier Louis de B__, whose life story provides the necessary context for the occult phenomena and philosophy to be expounded, and without whose biography the latter would make no sense. In the opening chapter, bearing the Bulwerian title of "On the Threshold," Louis offers an *apologia* for this autobiographical structure: "I found it impossible to separate the phenomenal portion of the history from the person with whom they were most immediately connected."[97] To evidence the existence of the supernatural world, then, it is necessary to explicate the life of its percipient. And in *Ghost Land*, this life, like that of Bulwer's Fenwick, has been formed in the shadow of paternal loss and exploitation.

At the age of ten, Louis is sent to Germany from his home in India where his aristocratic Hungarian father had been serving in the British military. Here, on the verge of adolescence, he falls under the tutelage of occultist Felix von Marx, who offers him the opportunity to learn "lore of great wisdom, which few children of your age would be worthy to know."[98] Essentially, the Chevalier is trained to operate as a "flying soul" for von Marx's elite occult Berlin Brotherhood. They teach him to leave his body and travel clairvoyantly across the globe, perceive auras, and participate in magic mirror séances during which angelic and elementary beings manifest in reflecting glass. Although magically adept, the group are spiritually compromised by their atheistic rejection of the possibility of human post-life survival. The anti-spiritualist occultism of their milieu inevitably leads to moral atrocities, such as the murder of Louis's first love, Constance, who had been groomed by her dissolute uncle, Professor Müller, to serve his magical and perhaps also, as the text hints, sexual needs—a fate which echoes Margrave's sinister exploitation of Lilian in *A Strange Story*. After the death of his birth father, Louis travels with von Marx to the United Kingdom where the two embark on an occultural grand tour of the country and Western Europe which only ends with von Marx's sudden death and the bizarre process of life transfer it prompts. No longer living in his own body, von Marx then takes up residence in his *protégé*. For months afterward, Louis speaks in the accent, develops the physical characteristics, and manifests the personality of his erstwhile mentor. It is only with difficulty that von Marx is expelled

MAGICAL MEISTERS   65

through the ministrations of modern spiritualists whose afterlife belief the senior occultist had in life rejected. After this debacle, Louis travels to India, gains initiation within the occult Ellora Brotherhood, headed by the adept Chundra ud Deen, and marries Lady Blanche Dudley, the daughter of von Marx's friend and fellow occult practitioner, John Cavendish Dudley. After his wife falls victim to a black magic revenge plot perpetuated by the lovesick Vaudoo practitioner, Hélène Laval, whose sexual advances he has rejected, Louis sets off to continue his seekership in the modern spiritualist enclaves of the United States. His adventures there are recounted in the second series of *Ghost Land* in *The Unseen Universe*, whose first instalment is preceded, fascinatingly, by a quote from Goethe's *The Sorrows of Young Werther* (1774): "The human race is but a monotonous affair. Most of them labour for the greater part of the time for mere subsistence; and the scanty portion of freedom which remains to them so troubles them that they use every exertion to get rid of it. Oh, the destiny of man!"[99]

Such a despairing lament at humanity's propensity to restrict its own freedom might seem like a strange epigraphic choice with which to preface a tale of expanding occult consciousness, but it perfectly encapsulates the developmental *impasse* presented in both the first and second parts of *Ghost Land*. In neither series is Louis able to get out from under the feet of his fathers, a failure that is presented as no bad thing at all from a magical point of view. Indeed, the inescapability of paternal determination is depicted in a decidedly upbeat and beneficent manner. The most domineering of Louis's father figures is, of course, Professor von Marx, whose personality utterly eclipses his own, providing the younger man with an unearned potency. When the two take up their occult study in England, Louis remarks:

> In his presence I felt strong to act . . . yet by some strange fatuity it seemed to me as if my acts, thoughts, and words took their shape from him, and without the least effort on my part to discover or inquire his will, I know that I lived beneath its influence and derived my chief motives for speech and action from the silent flow of his thoughts. When I was absent from him, I became an indescribably lost creature. I was dreamy, uncertain, wandering; not so much a child as a being without a soul.[100]

Remarkably, the attributes typically assigned to female mesmeric subjects, like Bulwer's Lilian, Du Maurier's Trilby, or Stoker's Lucy Westenra, in the *presence* of their controllers are here given to Louis in von Marx's

66   OPEN SECRETS

absence: dreaminess, lack of agency, and a complete inability to forge his own path. While Lilian, Trilby, and Lucy may at least have a personality to lose in their encounter with their wicked mesmeric antagonists, this point seems more debatable for Louis. On the contrary, here at least, his vigor, expression, and, indeed, very manhood all seem to be the product of von Marx's intrusive influence.

Certainly, this process of imposed masculinization appears to be the intended outcome of the later life transfer process initiated by von Marx, one that he explains in distinctly gendered terms within the explanatory pre-death letter he writes to Louis:

> I WILL GIVE MY LIFE TO YOU . . . In this mysterious transfer *my life can become yours*, my being can incorporate itself within yours, and the effects will be seen and felt when I am gone, in the increased power and primes of your noble manhood and the enlarged capacity of your unfolded spiritual nature . . . I will my life to you, whilst yet I can set it forth in living fires to illuminate the temple of your spirit. Perchance that dying flame may yet retain some spark of consciousness, which, added to your own, shall vitalize your frame, give double manhood to your character . . . and raise you above those grovelling elementary spheres in which we have been doomed to wander.[101]

This magically proffered "double manhood," no less than the singular version that preceded it, is a deeply dependent and reliant one, fundamentally incompatible with the *Bildungsroman*'s typical markers of heterosexual male maturity: marriage, fatherhood, and self-government. Instead, Louis's occult *Bildung* leads to his complete subsumption within the personality of his mentor, losing his own identity as he inherits the latter's flaws and quirks, including a misogynist hatred for von Marx's former wife, Ernestine, who, in one of the novel's few comic flourishes, is deployed to help oust her ex-husband from Louis's body.

While it is true that both Louis and von Marx come to regret this act of overdetermined parental control, they never wholly disavow it; indeed, they lament only its intensity, but not the hierarchy it imposes. Consider how Louis's thoughts toward his erstwhile mentor evolve in the aftermath of the exorcism. Recovering in the care of his new father figure and nurse, John Cavendish Dudley, he initially concludes "I . . . had been robbed of my soul's manhood; . . . [von Marx's] spirit had usurped the right of mine; his will had

MAGICAL MEISTERS   67

superseded mine and left my soul a mere nonentity."[102] The horror of this act is, however, quickly salved through its co-option within the *Ghost Land's* melioristic occult *ethos*. By penetrating Louis, we learn that von Marx has indeed furthered the course of spiritual evolution, even if not necessarily or primarily that of his pupil. A disbeliever in human spiritual survival while alive, von Marx is accordingly consigned to a low spiritual sphere after death; in taking control of Louis, he has gained an upward escape route. "My spirit," declares Louis in a moment of revelation, "should be the ladder on which his soul should rise from the elementary spheres through earth again to home in the better land. This was to be my destiny and his."[103] What is envisioned here is a relationship of charitable parasitism. The risk it poses to Louis as host is presented as a fair price to pay for the immense spiritual debts he owes to his tutor. After all, as Louis reflects during his later travels in India, "I could not think but that Felix von Marx had kept his word; that he had indeed died to add his noble manhood to my constitutional weakness, and that I must be indebted to his towering spirit for the capacity to achieve an amount of physical and intellectual labour under which a more vigorous physique would have sunk."[104]

Ultimately, while *Ghost Land* presents von Marx as overzealous in his paternal and pedagogical ambitions, it stops short of depicting him as the villain of the piece in the same way as does *A Strange Story* to the equally parasitical Margrave. This distinction is brilliantly captured in his curious self-comparison to another anti-hero from the British Gothic pantheon: Mary Shelley's Victor Frankenstein. Discussing Louis with his close associate Dudley, von Marx asks "do you remember the story of the German student, Frankenstein? He made a monster, I an angel. He was the story of a myth, mine that of a scientific truth."[105] The first thing to say about this putative association is that it makes no sense at all, and not simply because the progeny of Shelley's and Britten's heterodox experimenters are completely different. The two creators themselves bear no comparison when it comes to filial relations.

Victor Frankenstein's most infamous act of cruelty lies in his abandonment of the monstrous child he consigns to a solitary life of universal scorn and unbearable loneliness. Von Marx is guilty of the opposite; he clings cloyingly too close to his beloved and over-dutiful son, annexing Louis's personality within his own for the purposes of what he claims to be their mutual edification. And the spiritual *value* of this controlling father–son dynamic, if not necessarily always its *mode*, receives repeated confirmation in *Ghost*

68 OPEN SECRETS

Land long after the Professor's spiritual eviction from his young host. In *Ghost Land*'s second half, we see Louis seek and embrace a new panoply of magical male mentors—John Cavendish Dudley, who nurses him to health, introduces him to modern spiritualism, and, briefly, becomes his father-in-law, and the proto-Theosophical Indian masters Chundra ud Deen and Nanak Rai, who, deep within the Ellora cave complex, initiate Louis into a secret occult brotherhood that practices electrically assisted forms of clairvoyance and astral travel.

This pattern of perpetual filial discipleship is only briefly interrupted by a marriage that is itself pitched more as an act of paternal devotion than mature romantic love. Louis first meets Dudley's daughter Blanche during her stay in India; at her father's request, he has agreed to act as chaperone and been offered "*carte blanche* to act as if she were your own child, or, for the matter of that, your grandchild."[106] While registering her pale, ethereal beauty, Louis feels no immediate amorous stirrings nor temptation to abandon the all-male Ellora Brotherhood that provides him with "the happiest hours of my life."[107] Indeed, when he is subsequently offered Blanche's hand by her Viscount uncle, Louis refuses, explaining awkwardly that "I was a man devoted to a special idea, consecrated to aims wholly foreign to the marriage relation, the duties of which I could not undertake consistently with the religious engagements to which I referred."[108] He only relents when reputationally compelled to do so. The scorned enchantress Hélène Laval mesmerizes Blanche and forces her to enter Louis's room late at night in torn, filthy clothes, hoping that the two will be detected there and smeared respectively as ruined woman and rapist. Their hasty marriage is the only way to deflect this stigma, just as it had been for Fenwick and Lilian in *A Strange Story*. One year later, when Blanche and his son die through the further consequences of Laval's black magical malfeasance, Louis is free to throw off the shackles of his new *pater familias* role and return to contented subjection under occult paternal authority. No longer a husband or father himself, he can resume the position of perpetual son. This readopted role is suggested and compounded by the pseudonym he adopts in *Ghost Land*'s second series, in which he travels *incognito* across America's spiritualist heartland: Louis Gray. Describing himself as "a newly resurrected soul under a new name in an old body," the Chevalier's choice of alias immediately evokes Bulwer's Louis Grayle, the scapegrace son whose occult pursuit of endless, frozen youth turned him into the fiendish Margrave. But Britten's Gray, importantly, never achieves the moral debasement of Bulwer's Grayle;

MAGICAL MEISTERS   69

his permanent adolescence remains a sacralized one, perhaps because realized spiritually rather than physically. At the end of *Ghost Land*'s second series, we see Louis still in the position of humble seeker, newly galvanized by his awareness of the spiritually evolutionary purpose of incarnation and equipped, as the last instalment's final line declares, to greet death with the cry, "Master! I am ready! Aye, ready!"[109]

By this point, readers should not be surprised that *Ghost Land* closes with a gleeful confirmation of its subject's submission to mastery. Such is the dominant keynote and necessary trajectory of the male occult *Bildungsromane* that this chapter has traced, and whose finales could not possibly take any other form. The highly paternalistic model of esoteric knowledge transmission they endorse requires their male *Bildungshelden* to remain in a position of permanent youth, progressing forward and backward into arrested development. While their contemporary secular counterparts may have been criticized by the likes of Moretti for their fairy-tale naïveté or preservationist attitude toward the status quo,[110] novels like Dickens's *Great Expectations* at least permit their protagonists to briefly reject paternal expectations and imposed social roles even if only to ultimately return to them. Such brief escapes do not happen at all in the examples I have discussed. This is not, however, to say that the Victorian occult *Bildungsroman* is more conservative than such non-occult examples in any straightforward way. Fenwick and Louis, after all, defer not to birth but to found fathers; their subservience is the result of hard-earned, sometimes perilously obtained, heterodox knowledge rejected by the social world at large. Far from retaining or preserving an Edenic childhood innocence in the face of numinous contact, it is precisely this occult experience that causes them to embrace a sometimes vilified but often ennobled form of self-elected permanent adolescence where, free from the imperatives of marriage or fatherhood, they are always ready to obey paternal command and control. Their enduring occult boyhood, in other words, is the product of much study and labor; their deference, of unconventionality.

A Strange Story and *Ghost Land* show just how important the *Bildungsroman* was for occult revivalists who sought through it to popularize the spiritual movements in which they participated, and who produced some of the genre's most fascinating, if often neglected, variations. Their efforts require greater recognition within both secular histories of the *Bildungsroman* and literary esotericism studies, which has tended to mine such works primarily for evidence of their author's biographical experience—*Ghost Land*'s reception provides

70   OPEN SECRETS

case in point here[111]—rather than for their complex genre innovation work. Such a shift will allow us to recognize these texts as both outliers, by virtue of their anti-realist supernaturalism, and indwellers to the genre, particularly in light of its recent reappraisal by scholars such as Rosenthal and Elisha Cohn. Both Rosenthal and Cohn challenge long-standing critical interpretations of the *Bildungsheld*'s journey to adulthood as progressive and intentional, with Rosenthal proposing that such characters more often confirm in their actions decisions already made than choices newly formed,[112] and Cohn arguing for the importance of "non-reflection, inaction" and "diminished consciousness" to the genre's classic plots.[113] Such fascinating interventions open up the interpretive possibility for us to see the Victorian occult *Bildungsroman*, not as abandoning or reversing the progressive individualism of the secular novel of development, but rather as radically exaggerating and newly exposing the figurations of stasis, paternal determination, subjective evacuation, and arrested development that it always already contains.

Similarly, my analysis of the male occult *Bildungsroman* also offers us an opportunity to expand and recalibrate our understandings of the gendered paradigms of esoteric practice and magical identity in nineteenth-century Britain. Ever since the publication of Alex Owen's hugely influential *The Darkened Room* in 1989, historians of spiritualism and gender have pointed out the manifold ways in which occult participation posed a simultaneous outlet for, and threat to, women's agency, empowering them as mediums by confirming traditional patriarchal beliefs in their innate feminine passivity.[114] While valuable and well-warranted, this prevailing focus on women's plight has tended to leave intact the notion that the forms of masculine identity available to male seekers within this milieu were somehow less compromised, more authoritative, will-driven, and agential than those offered to female participants. Indeed, this conviction drives Robert Thompson's claim that Britten adopted the male authorial persona of Louis in *Ghost Land* to "escape the stigma of being a passive vessel."[115] As we now know, however, masculinity offers no such antidote to passivity in *Ghost Land* or indeed in *A Strange Story*, nor is it associated with any uncomplicated form of self-directed growth or ideal of normative maturation. On the contrary, Bulwer's and Britten's male seeker figures, whether dangerous spiritual vampires or possessed stepsons, remain forever boys.

In the next chapter, we will turn to another potent encounter between gender and genre in the Victorian occult fictional corpus: the woman's reincarnation romance. As Eastern beliefs in metempsychosis and karmic retribution infiltrated British popular culture at the *fin de siècle*, occultural women writers forged this sensational sub-genre to sacralize, not filial obedience, perennial adolescence, or possessed passivity, but an explosive and forceful strategy of self-assertion in the face of gender and sexual violence. In this emphasis, as we will see, the sub-genre achieves what the occult *Bildungsromane* we have just examined can or will not: namely, a stalwart defiance of, rather than compliance with, patriarchal authority.

3

Self, Sex, and Liberation in the Female Reincarnation Romance

"[D]o you observe," remarks the learned Professor Massilton in A. P. Sinnett's 1885 reincarnation novel *Karma*, "what a large part of Karma is evidently played out in all our cases . . . by our relations with women. What a determining force it seems to be."[1] Written at the vanguard of the new Theosophical movement then sweeping Britain, Sinnett's now forgotten romance here affirms what was rapidly becoming a, if not *the*, keynote of the reincarnationist discourse that had entered Britain's popular cultural mainstream only a few years earlier.[2] Rebirth was a distinctly gendered business, one always already implicated in, and enacted through, the heterosexual relations between men and women. No erotic encounter, however transient or spontaneous, escapes the relentless spiritual accountancy of karma, a fact that Sinnett's own plot bears out in its forensic examination of the metaphysical consequences of the romantic dalliances of an ancient Roman neophyte named Flaccus for a nineteenth-century group of European occult seekers. Bogged down by a heavily didactic prose style, cumbersome plot, and old-fashioned two-volume publication format, the novel sunk like a stone in the contemporary fiction market into which it was launched. Two years later, however, a similar formula would achieve both mass commercial success and critical plaudits in the more capable hands of young author H. Rider Haggard, whose bestselling romance, *She: A History of Adventure* (1887), recounts the efforts of British adventurers Horace Holly and Leo Vincey to avenge the victims of an ancient and extravagant *crime passionnel*. From then onward, sex and reincarnation would form a ready, and heady, fit in the era's occult philosophy and popular fiction alike.

Still the best-known and frequently reprinted work of Victorian reincarnation fiction, Haggard's novel, like Sinnett's, reads the sexual politics of reincarnation through a distinctly masculine lens, centering and evoking reader identification with the men forced to re-encounter the women

Open Secrets. Christine Ferguson, Oxford University Press. © Oxford University Press 2025.
DOI: 10.1093/oso/9780197651599.003.0003

SELF, SEX, AND LIBERATION 73

they abandoned or scorned many lifetimes ago. As such, these novels seed a heavily patriarchal, and sometimes directly misogynistic, tradition of non-fictional reincarnation discourse then emergent, if never dominant, within the Theosophical fold, one through which, as Joy Dixon writes, "women's oppression was rationalized as a karmic debt they themselves had generated."[3] Yet if we are to understand how this naturalization of gender inequity became available to leading popular fictional lions like Haggard—and indeed, how reincarnation itself became distinctly *engendered* in Victorian culture—it is to a different cast of authors and occultists, all women, we must turn. Their role in both feminizing reincarnation and appropriating it for a counter-discourse of esoteric feminism has long been sidelined, obscured by the historiographical tendency to under-reckon the fictional output of the revival discussed in Chapter 1. This neglect has been replicated within the contemporary scholarship on *fin de siècle* popular fiction, where the extent and potency of women's contributions to the often primarily male-identified romance revival remains under-reckoned. Taking aim at these twin lacunae, this chapter examines how late Victorian women deployed reincarnation, both as a claimed experience and a fictional trope, to politicize and sacralize their resistance to a lamentably common form of female experience: namely, women's subjection to gender-based violence.

3.1 Reincarnation Belief in Britain: The Birth of Rebirth

At the most basic level, reincarnation refers simply to "the belief that human beings do not . . . live only once, but on the contrary, live many, perhaps an infinite number of lives, acquiring a new body in each incarnation."[4] It is often linked, but not identical, to the loosely analogs concept of metempsychosis, which holds that individual souls may move into different bodies without necessarily relying on death as a mechanism. Although, as Olav Hammer and Julie Chajes have posited, the belief was largely absent from mainstream British social and spiritual life until the final decades of the nineteenth century, it had some presence, if only as a vague speculative proposition, in earlier literary works such as William Wordsworth's "Ode: Intimations of Immortality" (1807).[5] As it circulates in the West today, reincarnationism has few requisite tenets beyond the belief that individuals may have more than one life; it may or may not be accompanied by a belief in God, or in a system of spiritual adjudication that mandates a causal

74 OPEN SECRETS

relationship between the actions taken in one incarnation and the rewards or penalties doled out in the next.[6] Although most commonly associated with Eastern religious traditions, it also circulates in a number of Western esoteric and philosophical currents, such as Neo-Platonism, Kabbalah, and the writings of Immanuel Kant and Gottfried Ephraim Lessing.[7] In its route into mass cultural dissemination within best-selling late Victorian fiction, reincarnationism was filtered through the heady crucibles of Victorian Egyptomania and Theosophy,[8] the latter ignited with particular force by women. Three, in particular, set the terms through which reincarnation entered the British occult milieu from the 1870s onward: the spiritualist and Theosophist Marie Sinclair, whose esoteric works appeared under her aristocratic title of the Countess of Caithness; the pioneering feminist, physician, and Christian hermeticist Anna Kingsford; and H. P. Blavatsky, the Russian émigré who cofounded the Theosophical Society in Manhattan in 1875, and who subsequently became its foundational theologian—if such a role can be assigned to a movement which has repeatedly refused to identify itself as a discrete and unitary religion—with the publication of her two landmark occult treatises, *Isis Unveiled* (1877) and *The Secret Doctrine* (1888).[9] All equally convinced of the reality and moral necessity of rebirth, these women nonetheless promoted differing modes of reincarnationism that competed for supremacy in this fertile period of occultural innovation. Sinclair and Kingsford were friends and fellow occultists, with the former, according to Olav Hammer, the likely source of the latter's introduction to reincarnation theory; together they endorsed a Westernized brand of rebirth modeled on the Kardecian *spiritisme* from which Blavatsky repeatedly, and somewhat unconvincingly, sought to distance herself.[10] By contrast, Blavatsky's universalist and karmically calibrated strain of reincarnationism drew more from the Eastern religious beliefs she encountered directly and started teaching after her 1879 sojourn in India with the Theosophical Society's then-President, Henry Steel Olcott. Articulated at greatest length in her abstruse magnum opus, *The Secret Doctrine*, Blavatsky's version of reincarnation soon gained ascendancy within the Society, thanks in no small part to the more accessible, user-friendly guides to karmic justice and past-life experience issued by her Theosophical contemporaries Sinnett, E. D. Walker, and Annie Besant.[11] From there, karmically calibrated reincarnationism burst into the *fin de siècle* popular fiction market, featuring in a steady stream of romances produced by new and established big-hitters, such as Haggard and Marie Corelli, and in the more niche works of genre fiction produced for

SELF, SEX, AND LIBERATION   75

proselytization purposes, or via allegedly magical means, by Theosophists such as Rosa Campbell Praed, Mabel Collins, and even Blavatsky herself.[12]

In retrospect, the source of reincarnation's appeal to late Victorian readers might seem obvious, catering as it did to the popular taste for supernaturalism, exotic otherworldly milieux, and a somewhat Manichean moral system in which good and evil were clearly identifiable and directly opposed; it also offered a novel device on which to base subsequent sequels, allowing writers to bring back beloved protagonists or notoriously villainous antagonists from the dead in new bodies, ready to fight again—after the success of *She*, for example, Haggard revivified Ayesha for three subsequent novels: *Ayesha: The Return of She* (1905), *She and Allan* (1921), and *Wisdom's Daughter* (1923). Yet it is worth noting that reincarnationism's affordance for popular fiction was by no means automatic, nor was it necessarily welcomed by the Theosophical believers who had worked so hard to put rebirth on the nation's spiritual radar. In both *The Secret Doctrine* and *Esoteric Buddhism*, Blavatsky and Sinnett had advanced a depersonalized, *longue durée* theory of multiple incarnation, one in which the individualized personalities, local color, dynamic plotting, and suspenseful action necessary to the popular adventure novel played virtually no part. All life, they insisted, inexorably and slowly cycled upward toward reunification with the Divine, and while individuals could by their actions delay or expedite this process, they could not permanently arrest it. Furthermore, the roughly fifteen-hundred-year rest period that, according to Sinnett, necessarily separated incarnations certainly slowed down any sense of rapid momentum or dramatic continuity between lifetimes.[13] Some Theosophists insisted that only the most advanced of spiritual seekers could or should remember their past lives;[14] indeed, with no small degree of irony, Sinnett had his character Baron Von Mondstern denounce such acts of mnemonic self-surgery as vainglorious in *Karma*, declaring, "I am not sure if knowledge about one's previous incarnations could have any other effect than that of fueling personal vanity, and so doing one the worst possible service."[15]

The fact that both Blavatsky and Sinnett would ditch this reticence in their fictional explorations of reincarnation is proof of their willingness to let the requirements of suspenseful literary plotting take precedence over their spiritual precepts. Even less equivocation was required for those women writers working within the more emotive, personalized, intuitive, and mnemonically accessible vein of reincarnationism promoted by Sinclair and Kingsford. The two staked their belief in the reality of rebirth, not on their mastery

76 OPEN SECRETS

of Eastern philosophy and ancient texts, but on direct lived experience. Throughout the 1870s and 1880s, both lectured on, and laid claim to, multiple, closely consecutive past lives—these included Mary, Queen of Scots, for Sinclair, and, for Kingsford, the Old Testament Queen Esther, Faustina the Younger, Mary Magdalen and Joan of Arc. As the latter list demonstrates, no fifteen-hundred-year cooling off period was required between putative incarnations. Another intriguing feature of their reincarnationism was that new identities never wholly replaced, effaced, or subsumed prior selves; as such, both Sinclair and Kingsford would claim to have met and conversed with their previous incarnations in the present, speaking to them as if in conversation with another person.[16] Thus of an alleged midnight meeting at Edinburgh's Holyrood Palace with her past-self Mary Stuart, Caithness claimed that her avatar had offered her the following bespoke counsel:

> You, my child, have a mind capable of grasping truths that are destined to make all nations free and inspired . . . Marie, my beloved one, the faith you have espoused possesses the richest and rarest casket of jewels the world has ever seen. Add something grand to its now fast-advancing literature, its steady tidal wave of sweetly unfolding inspiration.[17]

At this same meeting, the violently deposed Scottish Queen also appeared to align herself with the contemporary cause for female empowerment by declaring that "Men are asleep over the material triumphs they are crowning their brows with . . . they cannot be still and listen to Deific forces. But Woman, earth's Mothers, must do so."[18] The desire for intimacy, continuity, inspiration, and solidarity evinced in accounts such as Sinclair's anticipate what Hammer has described as the "client-centred" form of reincarnationism now ascendent within contemporary New Age cultures, where "ordinary people" claim distinguished and famous past lives to "cast their personal histories in narrative form" and "trans[form] privileged experience into personal experience."[19]

The bespoke and highly colorful past-life testimonials of Sinclair and Kingsford found their fictional counterparts in the *fin de siècle* female-authored reincarnation romances that shared their prioritization of women's lived, physically embodied experience. Connected more by their overlapping political, spiritual, and proto-feminist agendas than by direct influence, these novels espouse a very different model of gender power than the male occult *Bildungsromane* discussed in Chapter 2; far from sacralizing extreme forms of filial subservience to paternal authority, they mobilize their chosen romance genre to incubate and express the sometimes violent forms of female agency suggested by the reincarnative personas favored by Sinclair and Kingsford: Queens, Biblical heroines, spiritual warriors, and murderesses. In the next section, we will consider how their efforts transformed the way gender and genre alike were typically calibrated within the *fin de siècle* literary movement known as the romance revival.

3.2 Engendering the Romance Revival

The late Victorian romance revival has long been understood as an overtly gendered enterprise, one whose leading lights frequently positioned themselves in direct opposition to the supposedly effeminizing forces of a ubiquitous, banal, and prim domestic realism fit only, as Haggard famously declared in "About Fiction" (1887), for "little girls in the schoolroom."[20] The tales of derring-do and far-flung adventure for which Haggard and fellow male romancers, such as R. L. Stevenson, R. M. Ballantyne, and G. A. Henty, became known worked by contrast to champion a spirit of maverick boyish virility imagined as equally necessary to Britain's imperial project than the less glamorous—and certainly less sensationally narratable—apparatus of technocratic state bureaucracy. The masculinity promoted in such works was often staked in distinctly anthropological terms as an expression of a healthy primitivism, one that would unshackle the allegedly innate, universal male traits of bravery and brutality increasingly under threat by an effete modernity. As the genre in which these primal masculine traits were celebrated, the late-Victorian romance, too, was often linked to a socially beneficial form of atavism. Thus, Haggard opined, that "The love of romance flourishes as strongly in the barbarian as in the cultured breast," and forecast confidently that the genre would endure far beyond the "unreal, namby-pamby nonsense" favored by Britain's fiction-reading matrons.[21] Haggard was by no means unique among the romance revivalists in this gender-polarizing project of genre consolidation. A similarly masculinist—if less explicitly misogynist—formulation of romance features in the literary criticism of Haggard's contemporaries Stevenson and Andrew Lang, with the former vaunting the lively "incident" of the boy's adventure tale over the "clink of tea-spoons and the accent of the curate" found in works of literary realism,[22] and the latter pitching his impatience with the literary realism he depicts

78   OPEN SECRETS

as being written primarily *for* and *about* women in pseudo-religious terms. Realist novels, Lang writes in "Realism and Romance" (1887), display "an almost unholy knowledge of the nature of women;"[23] what the current times required was a form of muscular romance that could re-masculinize and re-racialize England's lily-white, effete reading public by appealing to "the savages under our white skin."[24]

Lurking behind—or sometimes directly on the surface of—this masculinist and racist rhetoric of romance, where non-white ethnicities are celebrated because of their supposed anti-modern obsolescence and lack of intricate psychological depth, is the specter of a newly licensed poetics of misogynistic violence. We detect the latter, for example, in the gleeful retribution enacted against the lascivious African cannibal woman in Haggard's *She*, who pays a bloody price for her sexual overtures toward the old English manservant Job and, following her rejection, her roasting of the flesh of the party's Muslim attendant Mahomed. Holly promptly shoots her in the back after this horrific deed, rejoicing in her death "as it afterwards transpired [that] she had availed herself of the anthropophagous customs of the Amahagger to organize the whole thing in revenge of the slight put upon her by Job."[25] An even more devastating retribution is enacted in the novel's finale against Haggard's eponymous white Queen, another female sexual over-reacher whose immoderate desire for Kallikrates, now reincarnated as Leo Vincey, also drives her to homicidal behavior, slaughtering her love rivals past (Amenartas) and present (Ustane). Eager to stay forever young with Vincey, she steps again—and too soon—back into the magical Flame of Life which, instead of boosting her vitality, causes her abrupt decay into a shriveled, simian form "no bigger ... than ... a two-months' child."[26] Beyond the fates of specific female characters, the gendered violence of the imperial romance is also enacted through the genre's triumphalist descriptions of the penetration and conquest of foreign spaces that, as Anne McClintock writes, are "feminized and spatially spread for male exploration, then reassembled and deployed in the interests of massive imperial power."[27] This process she dubs "an erotics of ravishment," exemplified, among other places, in the famous trek of the male adventurers in Haggard's *King Solomon's Mines* (1885) over the mountain range known as Sheba's Breasts as they quest to discover and extract an ancient, lost treasure from the cavernous womb of Kukuanaland.

As this context makes clear, even if late Victorian reincarnationist discourse was not already entangled in discourses of gender power, it would have quickly become so when incorporated within the popular imperial romance, a genre whose best-selling, male-focused narratives both allegorized and reveled in violence against women and racial others. The reaction of women writers within the Theosophical fold to such tendencies, and indeed, to imperial racism per se, was complex, as were their efforts to recuperate the romance for their own ideological and spiritual priorities. The relationship of early Theosophy to Western imperialism and contemporary discourses of white supremacy was by no means as straightforwardly antithetical as the Society's official First Object—to "form a nucleus of the universal brotherhood of humanity without distinction of race, creed, caste, or colour"— might suggest.[28] As Sumathi Ramaswamy reminds us, British occultists benefited immensely from the orientalist scholarship, trade networks, and archaeological acquisitions that Victorian imperialism produced, even as they bemoaned "the empire's materialist excesses, its scientization of the globe, and its participation in the enchantment of the world."[29] Nor was Theosophical anti-imperialism necessarily free of the Anglocentric and racist sentiments used to justify Britain's colonial land grab in Christian and secular circles. Gauri Viswanathan has shown how Besant, for example, was able to maintain a position of "imperial affirmation" within her support for Indian autonomy, stipulating that "her plea for Indian self-government *within* the empire was not quite the same thing as a call for Indian independence from Britain, which more radical Indian nationalists were seeking."[30] Ramaswamy also observes that, while first-wave Theosophy generally eschewed the scientific racism of its day, the movement's "complex geography of human races in which all the black people of the world are either Lemurians or their degenerate descendants . . . arguably . . . is much more racist and hierarchal than that espoused by many a contemporary disenchanted materialist."[31] Certainly, it is not difficult to find examples of virulent racism within the Society's early history, such as Blavatsky's hostile references to the African American sex magician Paschal Beverly Randolph as "the Nigger," or the letters published in the Theosophical press that present colonial genocide as a kind of spiritualized Social Darwinism working providentially to eliminate races now deemed obsolete.[32] If such sentiments were never officially sanctioned or universally held within the *fin de siècle* Theosophical milieu, neither were they particularly rare. Perhaps it is for this reason that the women's occultural reincarnation romances we will soon discuss are generally more forceful in contesting the gendered hierarchies of the male imperial romance than they are its racial ones.

3.3 Reincarnative Scripts of Male Sexuality in Late Victorian Britain

Few other Eastern religious concepts have had such an immediate impact on Victorian popular fiction as reincarnation. From the 1870s onward, it formed an increasing presence in British fantasy, Gothic, and romance novels, where pathos, terror, and narrative suspense were used to leaven the somewhat austere, abstract perspective of first-wave Theosophical reincarnationism. As fictional transposition enlivened and individualized rebirth, so too did reincarnation as concept expand the conventions and affective registers through which writers could write about death. No longer need it serve as the terminal point of normal embodied existence; the afterlife need not be imagined as a site of perfectionist, purgatorial, or infernal stasis, but as a dynamic preparatory ground for the reintroduction of characters back into the flesh.

The reincarnation romance in Britain did not technically originate with Theosophy, but the latter's influence gave the sub-genre the moral seriousness, religious import, and, perhaps most importantly, structure of karmic debt that would by the end of the century render it such an effective vehicle for the critique of gender violence and sexual inequity. We can better appreciate this difference by briefly considering a pre-Theosophical example of reincarnation fiction, Mortimer Collins's proto-science fiction-cum-silver-fork novel, *Transmigration* (1874). Collins is important for this chapter in more ways than one; in addition to being a writer of reincarnation fantasy, he was also the father of Mabel Collins, the British Theosophist and trance writer who produced some of the Theosophical Society's earliest devotional texts and landmark fictional works, including *The Blossom and the Fruit*. It is quite possible that the elder Collins had an influence on his daughter's esoteric pursuits; beyond reincarnation, he was also interested in the heterodox theories of extreme life-extension, writing about these in his highly eccentric self-help book, *The Secret of Long Life* (1871). Yet while heterodoxy and fiction writing may have run in the blood of the Collins family, father and daughter would enter this terrain through dramatically different gendered perspectives.

Transmigration can only be described as a profoundly silly book, one distinguished by both its spiritual irreverence and mildly pornographic fixation on the sexual opportunities that rebirth offers to its male protagonist. It was published in three volumes, each focusing on a separate incarnation of Edward Ellesmere, a privileged son of the English gentry who serves as a kind of reincarnative *picaro*, traveling through realms both astral and mundane without any destination in mind. The first volume sees him leave his loving family home to study at Eton, join the Guards, and fall into a dissolute lifestyle of gambling and spending. After fleeing to the countryside to escape his debtors, he kills the brother of his fiancée, Lucy Lovelace, in a spurious duel and lives out the remainder of his days in penitential scholarly seclusion. This isolation is only tempered by his increasingly close—and to today's readers at least, perhaps unnervingly romantic—friendship with Mavis Lee, the young daughter of a neighbor thirty-five years his junior. When Ellesmere dies at the volume's conclusion, he leaves her a sizeable bequest from which, unknown to him at the time, his returned future self will benefit.

Although a murderer, Ellesmere starts his subsequent incarnation in Volume 2 with no outstanding karmic debt, nor is there any delay before his delivery into a new body optimized for sensory pleasure in the interplanetary realms. He comes to his senses in the beautiful but immaterial Hall of Spirits; while he could opt to stay amidst its aesthetic splendors, his desire for physical contact and embodied experience drives him back into the flesh. Frustrated by his inability to eat, drink, or make love to the beautiful Irish poetess who, like he, exists only in spiritual form, he readily assents to a new physical incarnation on the planet Mars where he consorts with lascivious Greek goddesses and characters from the Western literary canon while subsisting on the beauty-enhancing and intoxicating Martian substance Pyrogen. Following trysts with the Greek seer Cassandra and the entrancing child-woman Alouette, daughter of the Martian king, he tires of constant satiation and returns to earth again in Volume 3 as Reginald Marchmont, the son of his former child companion, Mavis Lee. In this capacity, he becomes heir to his own former fortune and marries the granddaughter of his erstwhile fiancée, Lucy.

As this racy, whimsical, and often absurd plot trajectory demonstrates, pre-Theosophical fictional reincarnationism did not aspire to religious seriousness in the same way that the movement's later in-house novels would. As taken up here by Collins senior, rebirth serves primarily to create a series of erotic playgrounds for its male protagonist-avatar, ones where unrequited or disappointed desire is always eventually satisfied, often with a younger version of its original object. This function strains against the didactic moralism that Collins unconvincingly attempts to shoehorn into the novel's conclusion, where Ellesmere urges readers toward a research-based conviction in human immortality: "What I have done, others may do . . . I *know* the soul to

82 OPEN SECRETS

be immortal: the unfortunate people who only *hope* that it is immortal may get proof if they go the right way to work."[33] Despite this imprecation, it is difficult to see how readers could have finished *Transmigration* with faith in anything but the material pleasures of eating, drinking, and sex.

Although the provocatively non-serious and decidedly non-causal vein of fictional reincarnationism we see in *Transmigration* never entirely disappeared from Britain's literary landscape, it did become less common as Theosophy's fortunes rose and those of the picaresque novel continued to fall.[34] What did endure, in male-authored reincarnation fiction of the late century at least, was the use of rebirth as an erotic gambit. Some exemplification is required here if we are to understand the force of the female-authored counterparts that would take aim at this convention. Haggard's *She* is again apposite here through the unrelentingly libidinal momentum of its plot, in which the central British adventurers encounter increasingly beautiful and sexually available women the further they travel into heart of Kôr, and in its use of rebirth to punish the jealous originary violence of its titular *femme fatale*. Haggard's sexual morality drama presents a cosmos in which women dangerously weaponize their beauty, sometimes via magical means, to manipulate and destroy female romantic rivals and prospective male love objects alike; destructive, erratic, and emotional as Ayesha may be, she is also inevitably defeated, even if more by her own *hubris* than the successful efforts of her enchanted English beholders.

A similar schema of patriarchal sexual politics circulates in other works of male-authored late Victorian reincarnation fiction, both in ones produced within, and outwith, the Theosophical milieu. Some, following *She*, present women as demonic *femme fatales* driven to excess by the same unconquerable possessive desire that keeps them stubbornly in the flesh; some incorporate women into their plots only as two-dimensional instruments of karmic machinery whose role is to expedite the psychological and spiritual development of their modern, disenchanted, male protagonists. Sinnett follows the latter route in *Karma* by focusing on the reincarnative tutelage and rehabilitation of the ancient Roman womanizer Flaccus in his present-day avatar of George Annerly, a London journalist so sexually unattractive and physically misshapen that he himself considers it a "grievous mistake" that "I was suffered to live at all."[35] Despite these limitations, this "very ugly, *chetif*, badly-made fragment of humanity" had, prior to the onset of the main plot, won the love of the New Woman actress Miriam Seaford, whom he was is only prevented from marrying due to his precarious financial situation.[36]

She breaks their engagement; the two then reunite briefly only for Annerly to be spurned a second time when she elopes with the married Professor Massilton, a fellow member of the secret occult cadre to which Annerly also belongs. The novel wraps up with an extended occult exegesis of these events and their karmic significance for Annerly. Seaford, by contrast, has seemingly no karmic stakes worth explaining in this sordid business; her role has only been to serve as the deliverer of deferred cosmic justice. Mondstern underlines her simply instrumental function as he consoles the heart-broken Annerly, reminding him that he alone is in control of his successive life scripts:

> The author of the Karma now governing your life—you yourself under different conditions—enjoyed life but too well... In general terms... you were endowed with extraordinary personal advantages which hurried you into much temptation... you revelled in the love of several women, whose lives were thus partly wrecked through your fault... the circumstances that have made the love of women a sorrow to you in this incarnation, rather than a delight as formerly, were due to the inevitable reaction of the past.[37]

The novel diagnoses Flaccus's romantic transgressions but make no attempt to redress the sufferings of their victims, or even to allot them equivalent narrative space; on the contrary, it simply endows Annerly with a newly strengthened, spiritually honed, and defiantly ascetic masculinity. Seaford, by contrast, having discharged her function of preparing Annerly and Massilton for their next incarnative stage, simply disappears from narrative view like so much eschatological detritus.

Only a few years after the publication of *Karma*, this form of reincarnative female erasure spilled out from the occultic fringe into the work of the era's best-known British literary proponent of hereditary and sexual fatalism: Thomas Hardy. In his scandalous 1891 masterpiece, *Tess of the d'Urbervilles: A Pure Woman*, the narrator had presented the rape of doomed heroine Tess by her distant relation Alec d'Urberville as a regrettable but foreordained fate best described in the passive voice: "it was to be."[38] "Doubtless," we are told, "some of Tess d'Urberville's mailed ancestors rollicking home from a fray had dealt the same measure even more ruthlessly towards peasant girls of their time."[39] Tess's destruction has been destined since her birth, a debt incurred by her male ancestors for whose historical acts of sexual violence she must pay. In this instance—where fatal

84   OPEN SECRETS

inheritance is presented in allusive, hereditary terms rather than in distinctly karmic ones—the narrator at least expresses moral dissatisfaction with the deterministic forces he describes: "though to visit the sins of the fathers upon the children may be a morality good enough for divinities, it is scorned by average human nature; and it therefore does not mend the matter."[40] No similar sense of regret features in Hardy's later metempsychotic sexual fantasia, *The Well-Beloved: A Sketch of a Temperament*, serialized in the *Illustrated London News* between October and December 1892 before being substantially revised for single-volume publication in 1897. It follows the sculptor Jocelyn Pierston as he attempts to find his feminine ideal by consecutively seducing women from three generations of the same family. Neither written nor received as an occult romance, it nonetheless shares a conceptual basis with the latter as it draws upon the Platonic concept of the soul as an eternal monad capable of transmigrating into different bodies. Pierston pursues the spirit he alternately refers to as "Jill-o-the-wisp," "the New Incarnation," "the Goddess," and, of course, "the Well-Beloved," through the female line of the Caro family, who live the Isle of Slingers that he first came to as a young man to practice his craft.[41] At the age of twenty, he finds her in Avice Caro; as a man of forty, in Avice's daughter Ann, who he renames as Avice; finally, as a sexagenarian, in the original Avice's granddaughter, then a blooming young woman in her early twenties. None of these pairings succeed, a fact largely due less to the women's resistance, but to Pierston's own mysticized, amatory capriciousness. For men of his own "strange, visionary race," he explains to his friend Somers, "[e]ach shape, or embodiment" of the Well-Beloved "has been a temporary residence only, which she has entered, lived in a while, and made her exit from, leaving the substance, so far as I have been concerned, a corpse, worse luck!"[42] Once they have ceased to inspire his attraction, in other words, his former love objects become as if dead to him. Pierston ultimately recovers from the grip of his obsession and settles down, in the novel's conclusion, to a late-life companionate marriage and a retirement dedicated to good works. Having successfully converted the sculptor from womanizing aesthete to local philanthropist, the spirit of the Well-Beloved, like Sinnett's Miriam Seaford, becomes narratively obsolete and disappears.

The loosely spiritualized, less explicitly Theosophical form of female erasure enacted in *The Well-Beloved*—where women, whether pitiable or pitiless, serve as requisite but ultimately dispensable tools of male *Bildung*—drew little comment in the novel's enthused critical reception. Instead, contemporary reviewers hailed the novel as a meditation on the universal and essential

SELF, SEX, AND LIBERATION   85

nature of male heterosexuality, despite Hardy's efforts to frame it as the portrait of a singular personality. The *Athenaeum* observed that the author "has imagined a temperament which we believe to be that of the great majority of male human beings—nay of male beings of every species."[43] Similarly, the *Review of Reviews* concluded that the novel simply confirmed the truth of Somers's advice to Pierston: "You are like other men; only rather worse. Essentially all men are fickle like you; but not with such perceptiveness."[44] Such universalizing responses to a plot that simultaneously essentializes, spiritualizes, and exculpates the objectification of women would come to form a central target of the women's reincarnation romances to which we will now turn. Female occulturalists, as we have seen, had been central to reincarnationism's introduction and popularization within late Victorian Britain; so, too, in their fiction, would they resist its enlistment to support patriarchal myths about male sexuality and female victimhood. In their works, karma delivers justice *to*, and not simply *through*, women whose past and present lives take center stage; in the process, the masculinized paradigms of aggressive conquest, whether geographical or sexual, legitimized within the imperial romance are magically undone.

3.4 Gender Violence and Karmic Justice in the Woman's Reincarnation Romance

Despite the effort of some late Victorian male writers to claim the resurgence of the romance as an exclusively masculine enterprise, aimed at the boys small and large who felt ill at ease within the era's over-cultivated and effeminized literary market, women were crucial to the *fin de siècle* romance revival; so, too, were culturally feminized constructions of affect. Even those popular boy's adventure tales that featured few or no female characters, argues Neil Hultgren, relied on melodramatic techniques long associated with "representations of women and excessive emotion."[45] These features are even more visible in the female-authored late Victorian romances that partnered, and exceeded the sales figures, of their male imperial counterparts, ones that Rita Felski has classified as expressions of the "popular sublime."[46] Like masculine imperial romances, such works were typically quest narratives set in exotic and far-flung locales—sometimes, even other worlds—in which a Manichean struggle between good and evil was taking place; their female protagonists were not only combatants on the

86   OPEN SECRETS

side of a particular national or moral cause, but also aspirants to "the transcendent, exalted, and ineffable."[47] Expressed through the seemingly indecorous outlet of mass fiction and, as pursued by female authors, such lofty ambitions were often dismissed as kitsch, a pejorative positioning intended, writes Felski, following Anne Cvetkovich, to quarantine the popular sublime from its more "culturally prestigious" romantic precedents that deployed a similar "structuring of affect."[48] Critically maligned as such works may have been, they had a seemingly insuperable market appeal in the 1880s and 1890s; indeed, Britain's best-selling writer of this period—and, according to some scholars, of the entire Victorian era—was a leading practitioner of the popular sublime: Marie Corelli (1855–1924). Corelli was, writes Felski, "said to be the most famous and highly paid novelist of her generation," with her Faustian smash hit *The Sorrows of Satan* (1895) selling "more copies on first publication than any previous English novel . . . no previous novelist had ever secured such vast audiences or wielded so much."[49] By 1901, the unprecedented popularity of Corelli's fever-pitched tales of mystical adventure, set in the decadent capitals of Europe, the ancient Near East, and the upper spiritual spheres, led liberal weekly *The Speaker* to declare her "one of most powerful people in the world."[50]

From her unrivaled position on the British—and indeed, global[51]—popular fiction stage, Corelli disseminated her own bespoke version of esoteric, Theosophically inflected Christianity. Although she repeatedly, if never wholly convincingly, insisted that her fictional theology was utterly orthodox and entirely consistent with Anglican doctrine, its influence by contemporary Theosophy and spiritualism is undeniable; indeed, these elements of exotic new spirituality were crucial to her success. On the Corellian page, late Victorian audiences could safely encounter aberrant beliefs and occult concepts without being linked by association to an explicitly or sincerely heterodox author, as would be the case, some decades later, for readers of Arthur Conan Doyle's spiritualist novel *The Land of Mist* (1926). In her 1886 debut, *A Romance of Two Worlds*, she introduced the recurring character Heliobas, an Eastern sage and leader of an ancient Chaldean-Christian brotherhood whose mission was to reform the debased and decadent West. Formed a thousand years before the birth of Christ—whose coming it foretold—the Brotherhood adheres to an "Electric Creed" which teaches that God and his creation are connected by a spiritualized electric current.[52] Properly understood, this force could be used by adepts to fuel astral travel and psychic telecommunications, repel assailants, restore health and beauty,

SELF, SEX, AND LIBERATION   87

and defer death. Karma and reincarnation also feature prominently within the Electric Creed, clearly the products of the Theosophical influence that Corelli routinely denied. Her characters repeatedly explain and endorse the karmic framing of reincarnation intrinsic to Theosophy's new religious brand, albeit repackaging it in a superficially Christian form. This strain of Christianized reincarnationism permeates her entire occult fictional *oeuvre*, featuring most prominently in *Ardath, The Sorrows of Satan, Ziska*, and *The Life Everlasting* (1911). *Ardath* follows the adventures of talented but jaded British writer Theos Aldwyn—a familiar Corellian archetype—as he travels in search of artistic and spiritual renewal, first to the remote monastery run by Heliobas's Brotherhood in the Caucasus, and then to the Field of Ardath, a Near Eastern site named in the apocryphal Book of Esdras and located in the ruins of ancient Babylon. There he reunites with his long-lost, and hitherto forgotten, angelic lover Edris and is transported back in time some five thousand years before the rise of Christianity to the last days of the doomed city of Al-Kyris.[53] Here he falls into the company of the vainglorious poet Sah-Lûma, whom he will ultimately recognize as his own previous incarnation. Chastened by this encounter with his vacuous former self, Aldwyn returns to the present with his literary genius reinvigorated, and ready to greet Edris when she next appears in material form.

Ardath is by no means free of dramatic incident—indeed, there are virgin sacrifices, snake gods, earthquakes, and pillars of fire—but these are rolled out at a relatively glacial pace over the thousand-plus pages of the book's original three-volume first edition, where they function less as catalysts for suspense than as prompts for the highfalutin spiritual explication central to Corelli's distinctive literary style. In tension with the slow, tableaux-vivant progression of *Ardath*'s plotting are the frenetic exclamation marks, dashes, exotic names, and incessant diacritical marks that would infuriate her critics over the course of Corelli's publishing career: "For some inexplicable reason," complained *The Quarterly Review* in 1898, "Miss Corelli lays much stress on grave and circumflex accents, distributing them in unlikely places . . . And so we read of Azùl, Niphrâta, Zabâstes, Râphon, Sah-Lûma, Nirjâlis, and Oruzèl. These all belong, apparently, to some antediluvian dialect, the key of which is kept in the author's exclusive possession."[54] Felski identifies such stylistic flourishes as central tools in Corelli's campaign to "achieve an effect of grandiose sublimity" and "inves[t] the most minor descriptive or narrative detail with profound symbolic significance";[55] through them, she sought to champion an unabashedly feminine religious aesthetic

88   OPEN SECRETS

in which often pilloried forms of linguistic or emotional excess could be reimagined as conduits to divine truth. This commitment to a project of aesthetic and spiritual feminization co-existed with, and to a certain extent complicates, the anti-feminism that Corelli expressed in her well-known public political statements against the women's suffrage movement.[56] Even as she distanced herself from her sisters' demands for political representation, her occult fiction asserted and fused women's artistic and spiritual pre-eminence, attributing to her female characters a moral authority that would undergird the gendered delivery of karmic justice at the heart of her most important foray into reincarnative revenge fantasy: *Ziska*.

Ziska was published in 1897, hitting bookstands in the same year as a number of competing high-profile gothic titles—Florence Marryat's *The Blood of the Vampire*, Bram Stoker's *Dracula*, and Richard Marsh's *The Beetle*—which shared *Ziska's* preoccupation with the threat of contamination by a foreign menace. Unlike these, however, *Ziska* depicts Britain not as the target but rather the *source* of this peril; it is, among other things, a novel about the horrors of the English on holiday. The central narrative opens with a lengthy denunciation of a group of British tourists wintering at the Gezirah Palace Hotel in Cairo, a city whose importance for the Western esoteric milieu would reach new heights seven years later when English ceremonial magician Aleister Crowley received *The Book of the Law* while honeymooning there. One wonders how he would have fared from the perspective of *Ziska's* Juvenalian narrator, who unfavorably contrasts the loose social mores, irreverence, and unhealthy constitutions of the Western tourist class with the innate dignity and grace of the indigenous population. "There is nothing of the heroic," we are told, "in the wandering biped who swings through the streets of Cairo in white flannels, laughing at the staid composure of the Arabs, flicking thumb and finger at the patient noses of the small hireable donkeys and other beasts of burden . . . and behaving as if the whole place were but a reflex of Earl's Court Exhibition."[57] With this comment, Corelli seems to separate her romance of the "popular sublime" from the jingoistic nationalism intrinsic to the male imperial adventure tale, while also foreshadowing, via allusion to animal suffering, the greater act of violence on which the plot's pending resolution will hinge. Her narrator then enumerates the small acts of local retaliation, specifically, aggressive demands for *baksheesh*, with which the Egyptians pay back the hordes of marauding European pleasure-seekers who treat their city as a consequence-free pleasure park:

SELF, SEX, AND LIBERATION   89

the desert-born tribes have justice on their side when they demand as much of it as they can get, rightly or wrongly. They deserve to gain some sort of advantage out of the odd-looking swarms of Western invaders, who amaze them by their clothes and affront them by their manners.[58]

More than just one of the bad-tempered narrative asides for which Corelli was well-known, this passage importantly establishes what will soon emerge as the novel's dominant philosophical keynote: namely, the question of justice and how the oppressed might obtain it through material (money) and spiritual (karma) means.

Like Sinnett's European occultists, the denizens of the Gezirah Palace are soon revealed to be the unwitting agents of an ancient tragedy whose consequences continue to resonate in the present day. During the reign of Amenhotep, we learn, the warrior Araxes "betrayed and murdered the only woman that ever loved him," the harem girl Ziska-Charmazel;[59] now, the dead woman's vengeful spirit, incarnated in the body of the beautiful Princess Ziska, has arrived in Cairo to track down the contemporary avatar of her erstwhile destroyer. She finds him in Armand Gervase, a louche French painter who shares the misogynistic views of his Pharaonic predecessor and waxes lyrical for those "early days of civilization" in which men were able to seduce and then kill as many women as they liked: "I would have mercifully killed my sweet favourite as soon as her beauty began to wane. A lovely woman, dead in her exquisite youth,—how beautiful a subject for the mind to dwell upon!"[60] Ziska flirts with, models for, and then, in a secret chamber of the Great Pyramid, murders Gervase, an act that induces his repentance and liberates them both from the cycle of incarnation. Corelli delivers this moment of salvation with melodramatic aplomb; as Gervase's body lies cooling on the tomb floor, a disembodied voice rings out in the air above him, pronouncing:

> [t]he old gods are best, and the law is made perfect. A life demands a life. Love's debt must be paid by Love! The woman's soul forgives; the man's repents—wherefore they are both lifted from bondage and the memory of sin. Let them go hence, the curse is lifted![61]

No dispensable plaything nor discredited witness, Ziska instead becomes ultimate judge and rehabilitative agent of her male assailant.

90   OPEN SECRETS

The karmic justice delivered in *Ziska*'s finale thus upends the patriarchal tropes and jingoistic ideological orientation of the male reincarnation plot and the imperial romance alike, even if, as Niyati Sharma is surely correct to observe, the novel remains elsewhere mired in a deeply orientalist aesthetic.[62] It empowers women, and the space of the East—and more specifically, Eastern women—to act as the arbiters of sexual, social, and moral truth. In imagining the Eastern reincarnated woman, not as fresh sexual fodder for a jaded white male protagonist, but as a female avenger, it extends the anti-imperial tenor of the opening tourist scenes; in particular, the novel seems to take aim at the hoary justification of colonial incursion as a project of noble chivalric intervention whereby, in Gayatri Spivak's famous formulation, "white men" might "sav[e] brown women from brown men."[63] As Rosa Braidotti has powerfully pointed out, this insincere rhetoric of gendered salvationism has only intensified in the West over the last century and in the wake of 9/11 and the Iraq War, when many white neo-liberal feminists and post-feminists unreflexively embraced the imperialist belief that:

> "our women" (Western, Christian, white or "whitened" and raised in the tradition of secular Enlightenment) are already liberated and do not need any more social incentives or emancipatory policies. "Their women" (non-Western, non-Christian, mostly not white and not whitened, as well as alien to the Enlightenment tradition) however, are still backward and need to be targeted for special emancipatory social actions, or even more belligerent forms of enforced "liberation."[64]

Ziska hamstrings this gendered narrative of white male saviorism first, by dissolving the binary of cultural and racial difference on which it rests—the modern French Gervase and the ancient Egyptian warrior Araxes are, after all, the same man, in different bodies—and second, by enabling an Eastern woman to save herself through an act of spiritually authorized if brutal retribution. Like Hardy's Tess, Ziska murders the man who violated her; unlike Tess, this deed is presented not as the tragic, self-destructive reflex of a pre-determined fate, but as an agential act of spiritual redemption enabled by Ziska's occult prowess. In this sense, *Ziska* cannot, as Felski proposes, be categorized alongside later desert romances, such as Edith Maude Hall's *The Sheik* (1919) in which white women are abducted and raped by erotically "primitive" Arab men with whom they subsequently fall in love.[65] While Hull's distinctly non-supernatural *The Sheik* ends with the English heiress

Diana Mayo declaring her undying attachment to abductor Sheik Ahmed Ben Hassan, *Ziska*'s Gervase has a different fate, namely a knife in the heart. *Ziska* operates as a potent woman's revenge fantasy wrapped up in, and given moral weight through, new occultural theories of reincarnationism, deploying rebirth to assure its readers that men who kill women will inevitably pay a price, not simply an undefined spiritual one to be delivered at a non-specific future date, but a viscerally physical one at the hands of their victim.

3.5 The End(s) of Gender in *The Blossom and the Fruit*

Theosophically influenced, if not directly affiliated, *Ziska*, I have argued, offers a dramatic reversal of an increasingly prevalent and misogynistic discourse of fictional reincarnationism that proliferated at the *fin de siècle*, one in which rebirth worked to underline and spiritually naturalize women's dependence upon, and subordination to, men. In its closing sentence, the novel's Theosophical energies and proto-feminist potencies are, however, arguably dissolved into the sentimental affirmation, "Love pardons all."[66] No similarly traditional nostrum was available to those women who, through their closer participation within and adherence to the Theosophical movement, were obliged to take the full theological implications of the movement's nascent karmic philosophy more seriously. It is to such a figure I will now turn. Daughter of Mortimer Collins, Mabel Collins was a crucial figure in the establishment of Theosophy's first-wave public sphere, producing for the movement a steady stream of catechistic, trance, and fictional works, and, with her one-time collaborator and later bitter enemy, Blavatsky, editing the London-based Theosophical journal *Lucifer* from 1887 to 1889. In this periodical, she serialized her pioneering Theosophical novel *The Blossom and the Fruit: A True Story of a Black Magician* between September 1887 and August 1888, after which it promptly appeared in single-volume book edition.

The significance of *The Blossom and Fruit* for the modern occult revival and its fictional traditions cannot be overestimated, although the novel rarely features in surveys of Victorian supernatural fiction, women's writing, or Theosophical literature. It had a formative influence on subsequent generations of British occultists, most notably Crowley, who praises the novel in *Magick in Theory and Practice* (1929) for making a "deep . . . mark on my

92   OPEN SECRETS

early ideas about Magick," and includes it there on a list of recommended literary works geared to give prospective Thelemites "a general familiarity with the mystical and magical tradition . . . and suggest many helpful lines of thought."[67] The struggle of Collins's heroine Fleta to realize her own path without relying upon other seekers, or pulling them out of their own orbits, certainly seems to anticipate *The Book of the Law*'s valorization of the individual will; so, too, does the that fact that Fleta is a magician whose work space is described as a "laboratory" reflect Thelema's promise to integrate "the method of science" with "the aim of the religion."[68] In terms of its wider occultural influence, the text played a crucial role in feminizing the male initiatory plot popularized by Bulwer and Britten in its placement of a woman in the role of seeker-protagonist. *Zanoni*'s inspiration to Collins is signaled directly in the novel's title, which echoes Mejnour's description of Zanoni's spiritual mentorship of Glyndon: "he leaves in thy heart the seeds that may bear the blossom and the fruit."[69] Finally, the novel acted as trigger for various high-profile debates and controversies within the late Victorian Theosophical publishing world, most notably the one over the nature of its own authorship that would ultimately lead to Collins's break with Blavatsky. The most important novel of the late Victorian occult revival, *The Blossom and the Fruit* exposes the complexities attached to gendered forms of reincarnative justice that that *Ziska* had glossed over.

Collins was no novice to fiction writing when she started the work; she had made a name for herself as a reasonably successful author of women's romances well before she publicly took up the Theosophical mantle, publishing her first triple-decker, *An Innocent Sinner*, in 1877. Ten years later, *The Blossom and the Fruit* appeared on the heels of two earlier occult publications—*The Idyll of the White Lotus* (1884) and *Light on the Path* (1885)—that won her acclaim and attention within her surrounding occultural milieu. As Mark S. Morrisson observes, we might see her as an "esoteric version of the 'New Woman' who could mobilise her skills as a journalist and popular writer to propel herself to occult power."[70] When its first instalment appeared in the inaugural issue of *Lucifer* in September 1877, an accompanying byline identified Collins as the author and listed some of her previous works, such as *The Idyll* and *The Prettiest Woman in Warsaw* (1885); the serial story was there subtitled, "A Tale of Love and Magic."[71] In November, this subtitle was changed to "The True Story of a Magician,"[72] a decision likely intended to bolster the narrative's reality effect and distance it from any association with Collins's purely invented former romances.

These were not the last editorial changes to which the novel would be subject while in serialization. Its final two instalments, published in July and August 1888, listed Collins and an unidentified collaborator, identified only by an em-dash, as co-writers. The split authorial attribution was maintained in the single-volume book version that appeared later that year, bearing yet another new subtitle: "A True Story of a Black Magician."

What are we to make of these changes? It is certainly possible that another writer, possibly Blavatsky herself, had contributed to or taken over the authorship of the serial when Collins was incapacitated by the period of illness formally announced as reason for her absence in the October 1888 issue of *Lucifer*.[73] Yet this possibility does not explain the anonymization of her co-author. That decision was likely taken by Blavatsky to boost the esoteric capital of the novel by distorting and shrouding its authorial provenance in mystery. Indeed, she had done this very thing to *Light on the Path*, which Collins had claimed to have received through trance vision and then personally transcribed. Blavatsky then badgered the younger woman into attributing the text to the dictation of the Theosophical Mahatma Koot Hoomi, presumably as an exercise in brand management. When Collins later, at the encouragement of the American Theosophist Elliot Coues, sought to reclaim the book as her own, the fallout was swift and dramatic.[74] In February 1889, her name was stripped from *Lucifer*'s masthead; Collins subsequently lodged and then withdrew a libel action against Blavatsky that July.

As Collins's biographer, Kim Farnell, points out, the reasons for the suit and its abandonment are likely to remain unknown. Animosity between the two women had been growing for some time, driven both by these internecine struggles for authorial identification and by Blavatsky's suspected circulation of scurrilous rumors about Collins's involvement in a tantric sex *ménage* with fellow Theosophists Bertram and Archibald Keightley.[75] Collins and Blavatsky seem also to have disagreed about how the sometimes-harmful magical acts performed by Fleta in *The Blossom and the Fruit* should be morally calibrated and badged. Farnell explains that, at the time of *The Blossom and the Fruit*'s publication, "stories were going around that the original version . . . contained an ending that endorsed black magic. According to Blavatsky, she had to intervene before it was published and rewrite the final chapter."[76] If true—and Farnell is by no means convinced that it is—such a dispute might explain the choice to introduce a more morally explicit subtitle that flagged in advance how the actions of its female magical protagonist were to be understood, namely, as works of *black* magic, albeit ones that

94   OPEN SECRETS

ultimately led to good. Certainly, a similar anxiety is suggested by the pre-emptive plot synopsis that opens the first book edition:

> This book is called the story of a black magician, because it shows the struggles and mistakes of one who has been an adept in black magic, and who is endeavouring with great force, but very blindly, to reach towards the White Brotherhood and learn good instead of evil. Fleta, who in her earlier incarnation, took power selfishly into her own hands, became by virtue of that power a black magician: one who has knowledge and uses it for selfish ends.[77]

This preface deflates the narrative suspense that had been levied to such great success in surrounding reincarnative thrillers such as *She* and *Ziska*, replacing mystery with a statement of absolute moral and didactic clarity. Through this declaration, the paratext manifests a palpable apprehension that the novel's explosive content might be misread without explicit direction, that readers might confuse the simple *representation* of Fleta's magic with an *endorsement* of its means and ends. If not kept on a tight least, occultural readers might mistake black magic for white, or karmic victim for victimizer.

This dangerous potential, for which the preface serves as attempted prophylactic, is amplified in the primal scene of sexual violence that then opens the novel's reincarnative plot. Readers are shown a lush, primordial forest in which a fatal act has just occurred. A "savage, . . . dark, but beautiful" young girl, clothed only by low-hanging "blue-black hair," stands over the bleeding corpse of a youth, a sharp stone in her hand.[78] Anticipating our question, the narrator explains:

> Why had she in this moment of fierce passion taken that beautiful life? She loved him as well as her untaught heart knew how to love; but he, exulting in his greater strength, tried to snatch her love before it was ripe. It was but a blossom, like the white flowers overhead; he would have taken it with strong hands as though it were fruit ripe and ready. And then in a sudden flame of wondrous new emotion the woman became aware that the man was her enemy, that he desired to be her tyrant.[79]

Her lover, it seems, had attempted to sexually coerce her; she, unready and resistant, killed him in an act of spontaneous self-defense. Everything that happens from henceforth represents an attempt to make sense of this action in light of Theosophical principles. We track this "savage" girl through successive, and increasingly white, incarnations in which she sheds her forest glamour to occupy the pale-skinned body of the aristocratic middle-European Princess Fleta in the present day. She is the sub-titular black magician; her devoted protégé, Hilary Estanol, the avatar of her murdered lover. Together, they have traveled through many lives, "learning the strange lesson of incarnation in the world where sex is the first great teacher."[80]

Spanning eons, but mostly set in a vaguely delineated present, *The Blossom and the Fruit*'s narrative defies easy summary and most conventions of popular narrative plotting. After the opening Edenic homicide, readers are given a brief glimpse of the forest girl's subsequent life as, in attempted penitence for her deed, she "trie[s] to learn the lesson that had come upon her" by mating with "one whom she did not love, and whose passion for her was full of tyranny" that "she dared not ... resist."[81] We then see her in a new incarnation as "Wild Blossom," a beautiful young woman who settles down to a life of maternal domesticity with a fisherman. In this union, she abandons "herself, her life, her very soul. The surrender was now complete."[82] Yet the happiness that Wild Blossom hoped would stem from this renunciation never arrives; instead, "spite of all, her heart was hungry and empty."[83] This life too ends in frustrated unfulfillment. Neither of these acts of self-subordination to male partners have repaid and released her from her primary karmic liability. Her next life as the beautiful, accomplished, and aristocratic magician Fleta takes up the main part of the narrative, which recounts her efforts to enter the elite, all-male Order of the White Star under the mentorship of occult adept Ivan and in the companionship of Hilary. In time, she comes to understand that neither Ivan, Hilary, nor her short-lived husband Prince Otto, who dies in battle just past the novel's midway point, can help her obtain her spiritual goals. She can only enter the Temple of the White Star alone, and free from all forms of desire, whether sexual, intellectual, or social. In the novel's final section, she travels to a Norman castle in North-eastern England where she undergoes a final trial that will allow her to expunge her original act of murder. On its successful completion, she falls to the ground dead, now fully ripened in spirit and ready to enter the ascetic ranks of the Brotherhood, her incarnative journey from fleshed self to disembodied non-self complete.

Collins's ponderous female reincarnation romance lacks, to uninitiated readers at least, the immediate moral clarity of *Ziska*. While the latter puts the blame for Ziska-Charmazel's murder firmly on Gervase's shoulders, here

96   OPEN SECRETS

it is the primal Fleta who is held responsible for her attempt to resist rape by her forest lover. Even while depicted as an undeveloped, innocent, and impulsive child of nature who knew not what she was doing, Fleta's act is depicted as inherently selfish, requiring many lifetimes to correct. It is her karmic debt as self-defender, and not Hilary's as initiating assailant, on which the plot revolves. Indeed, Hilary seems to more quickly achieve a spiritual ascent into asexual desirelessness than she. As Ivan explains to Fleta near the novel's finale:

> You know that sorcery is of the same order as the passion of sex; it is selfish, it desires to acquire, to intensify all that is personal. You know this . . . yet you have madly let yourself follow this passion, in its nobler form, and refused to see that by merely elevating it you did not change its character. Hilary Estanol, from the cruel wound you inflicted on him when you flung him from you, will be able to learn the lesson you have failed to learn. He will not love again; he will no longer desire to have or to hold.[84]

This is a deeply provocative, and from most feminist points of view, dismaying passage, one in which the Thelemic resonances identified earlier in our discussion seem most absent—inspired as he may have been by Collins's novel, Crowley saw sexuality, not as negative force to be suppressed or censured, but rather as the core of Thelema's progressive spiritual discipline. Collins, by contrast, chastises sexual desire as selfish and counterintuitively here attributes it, not to Hilary, original sexual aggressor as he may have been, but rather, eye-wateringly, to Fleta, for her attempted resistance of his attack. Thus, the attempted male rapist ascends more quickly than the female self-defender; Fleta will struggle longer than Hilary to enter the Brotherhood even if, ironically, it is the very violent act for which she is sanctioned that expedited his abandonment of desire. Hilary's more rapid progress may also be a consequence of the novel's initiatory prioritization of masculinity. Fleta, who has remained a woman across all her incarnations, is repeatedly counselled that her gender is a near-fatal impediment to her spiritual goals.[85] As her magical mentor Ivan explains, no woman has ever joined the ranks of the White Brotherhood; to succeed in doing so, she must "suffer as no woman has yet had strength to suffer."[86] In fact, he counsels her as she stands on the threshold of her final trial to "forget you are a woman; more, you have to forget you are a person."[87]

SELF, SEX, AND LIBERATION   97

In its emphasis on the allegedly greater selfishness of women's sexual self-defense than of male sexual violence, and on the near-absolute incompatibility of femininity with initiation, *The Blossom and the Fruit* might seem to function as an anti-feminist occult fable, one that centers a female seeker only to indict her gender as selfish and self-defeating. Such a reading, however, would be premature; against its grain runs the novel's fascinating counter-discourse on the value of a specifically feminine, and flagrantly aggressive, selfhood to the formation of magical will. Self-abandonment only gains spiritual value, suggests *The Blossom and the Fruit*, when the seeker first has a considerable self to lose. If Fleta's previous selves, and indeed, all women in general, have failed to enter the Order of the White Star, it is perhaps because they have never been socially enabled to cultivate an assertive personhood sufficiently worthy of sacrifice. Both the Forest girl and Wild Blossom resigned themselves to lives of quiet subordination, assenting, in so doing, to the culturally inscribed and heavily gendered script that, as feminist scholar Lisa Downing argues, understands "female selfishness . . . very differently from, and as far more reprehensible than, its male counterpart for reasons that are deeply embedded in cultural understandings of the nature and function of women and that work in the interests of the patriarchal status quo."[88] While men, Downing writes, "are supposed to be 'full of self,'" women have more often been required to be "nurturing, to be *for the other*, and literally selfless."[89] Women who resist this injunction enact what Downing terms an "identity category violation," whereby their "political affiliations or personal actions are at odds with the perceived normative characters of the group to which they are ascribed."[90] It is as an expression of such an identity category violation that we can understand Fleta's practice of black magic, and indeed, her primary homicidal act. Although stigmatized, these deeds enable her to build the reincarnative experience and force of ego without which her culminating act of magical self-abandonment would mean nothing.

In *The Blossom and the Fruit*, then, the iniquity of Fleta's self-ish magic is tempered—even sanctioned—by the spiritual goals it is enlisted to serve. In this respect, and although violently self-assertive and trained in black magic, she is a far more morally ambiguous figure than the other *fin de siècle* black magical *femme fatales* who followed in her wake: the shape-shifting Helen Vaughan in Arthur Machen's *The Great God Pan* (1895), for example, or the blood-sucking Lucy Westenra in Stoker's *Dracula* (1897), each creations of a masculine occult science or practice who seek only destruction. By serving herself, however, Fleta necessarily works for a greater spiritual good.

Certainly, she repeatedly acts on her own behalf and willingly risks harm to those around her. We are shown this tendency right from the very start of the novel's main section where, disguised as a wizened gypsy fortune teller, she meets Hilary at a ball and tells him they were born "under the same star."[91] Equipped with a magical awareness of their entangled reincarnative histories, Fleta knows that he will have no choice but to fall in love with her; she knows too that his passion will remain unrequited, and that he will suffer great mental tortures as he travels by her side, watching her give her hand to Prince Otto and her heart to Ivan. This jealousy comes with considerable psychological costs, and drives him to near madness; seeing Fleta prostrate herself before Ivan, Hilary flees the scene "like a blind man," running outside to "yiel[d] to an agony of despair which blotted out sky and trees, and everything from his gaze, like a great cloud covering the earth."[92] "The next time I see your gaze fixed on that man's as I saw it but now," he tells her, "I will kill him"[93]—and murder, as the novel's premise makes clear, comes with crushing karmic costs. Continually in what follows, Hilary tries to break free of his fatal attachment; continually, until his final release, he fails. Fleta permits this torturous situation to continue because she believes—falsely, as we learn in the novel's conclusion—that it is necessary for her own progression. "I cannot go in alone," she explains to Hilary of her attempt to enter the Order of the White Star. "I cannot go in for myself . . . I must take a soul in each hand to the door, ready, purified, prepared for the altar, so that they shall even become members of the Great Brotherhood; while I must be content to turn back and sit on the outer steps."[94] Here again, we encounter one of the novel's many paradoxes on the nature of self, one that reiterates the contrasting instructions for self-formation in Collins's earlier Theosophical catechism *Light on the Path* (1885) where seekers are told to "Kill out ambition" and "Kill out desire of life,"[95] but also to "desire power ardently" and "desire possessions above all . . . but these possessions must belong to the pure soul only, and be possessed therefore by all pure souls equally."[96] Fleta, for much of the narrative, seeks to deprioritize herself to advance, to conscript others within her spiritual quest, no matter how they suffer, so that she can gain spiritual capital.

Fleta's use of and dependence on others becomes more explicitly self-focused, even vampiric, in her dramatic encounter with a belligerent elementary spirit during a carriage ride with Hilary and a young, terrified Duchess who knows nothing of their occult studies. Suddenly, an obscure fourth presence, described as a shadowy male figure, seems to fill the corner

SELF, SEX, AND LIBERATION 99

of the carriage; Hilary fights it while Fleta sits in mute trance. When he succeeds in killing it, it suddenly disappears. What has happened? As Fleta explains on her awakening, she has devoured the entity, incorporating it into her own body to increase her strength and beauty. Hilary has been her unwitting and endangered tool in this act of triumphant spiritual ingestion. "My whole being is stronger for his death," she declares. "I absorbed his vital power the instant you wrenched it from him . . . [it] was one of those half-human, half-animal spirits that haunt men to their ill, and which fools call ghosts or demons. I have done him a service by taking his life into my own."[97] Here Fleta in her appetites approaches Bulwer's occult anti-hero Margrave in her willingness to exultantly feed on the vitality of others.

Yet unlike Margrave, who can barely remember his own past and lives only for the present, Fleta maintains a mitigating self-awareness and sense of spiritual mission that persists through these most ostensibly selfish of acts—and even her act of psychic ingestion, we must note, is posited to be beneficial to its victim. Through the novel's free indirect narration, we are given intimate access to her forensic and excoriating stream of internal self-judgment, in which she obsessively diagnoses and castigates the flaws that have daunted her initiatory efforts thus far. "I have always been too impatient, too eager," she explains to Hilary. "I have always tried to take what I longed for without waiting to earn it."[98] But while her impatient precocity may be castigated, her independence of will never is. On the contrary, the novel increasingly pushes her toward more and more radical forms of autonomy. As she explains to Hilary after a failed initiation attempt:

> I have not learned to stand utterly alone and to know myself as great as any
> other, with the same possibilities, the same divinity in myself. I still lean
> on another, look to another, hunger for the smile of another. O, folly, when
> I know so well that I cannot find any rest while that is in me.[99]

Given the sexually possessive, controlling, and violent nature of the men who have surrounded her since her earliest incarnation, Fleta's commitment to absolute independence here functions less as a rejection of community and emotionally healthy forms of interdependence than a spiritual survival technique. Each thwarted attempt to cross the threshold helps to buttress her cultivation of autonomy; these failures become triumphs for her radical project of self-making. "You know," she tells Hilary, "that a little while ago I essayed the initiation of the White Brotherhood. You know that I failed. I do

100   OPEN SECRETS

not regret having had the courage to try. I should have been a coward indeed to draw back."[100]

Through such efforts, founded upon Collins's paradoxical occult theory of selfhood, *The Blossom and the Fruit* subtly transforms black magic into white, rewriting the meaning of its heroine's primal, and self-originating, act of violence. Readers are invited to view the murder of the forest lover as a spiritually valuable if brutal deed that serves Fleta's development far more than femininized submission to patriarchal marriage. This keynote is established in the characterization of Wild Blossom's life after wedding the fisherman and becoming a mother in the main narrative's prelude. Despite achieving these crowning accomplishments of traditional femininity, she is left with a "heart . . . hungry and empty. What could it mean that though she had all, she had none?"[101] These traps she has learned to avoid by the time of her incarnation as Fleta; while she does marry Prince Otto, the suitor to whom she has been betrothed since birth, their marriage is non-hierarchical and brief. Like so many of the real-life female occultists in her surrounding esoteric milieu,[102] Fleta never becomes a mother. These decisions she explains to Hilary as such:

> Sweetheart, wife, mother, these things I can never be again, for the love of any man. I am alone in the world; I can lean on no man, I can love no man any more throughout the ages that I may wander on this earth. That life has gone away from me once and for all, and I stand alone.[103]

Fleta's salvationist trajectory thus becomes markedly different from those featured in Corelli's contemporary reincarnative romances, where liberation is typically achieved, as it would be again in the occult novels of Dion Fortune, in heterosexual dyads; Ziska with Gervase, Theos Alwyn with the reborn Edris in *Ardath*, the unnamed female narrator of *The Life Everlasting* with Rafel Santoris.[104] Hilary's initiation, by contrast, happens off stage and out of time with Fleta's. It could not be otherwise; only entirely alone can she pass the threshold. Her previous endeavors to do so have failed because she has not yet been sufficiently solipsistic.

If Fleta's prior missteps are the understandable, even necessary, consequences of the pressures she faces in a patriarchal society that equates femininity with self-abnegation, what solutions and initiatory routes does *The Blossom and the Fruit* ultimately offer to female magical seekers? The answer is a deeply paradoxical one that both empowers women to reject normative femininity and calls on them to abandon gender altogether. In loving others and putting their salvation head of her own, Ivan tells Fleta, she has been supremely selfish: "Was not the dream that you must save two other souls [Hilary and Otto], and take them with you . . . only another form of your passion for power? Who was it that gave you that order? Was it not your own imperious soul?"[105] To save herself, not only must she jettison these attachments, but also, and more radically, her very gender identity itself. Like Corelli's Ziska, Fleta's karmic destiny has been shaped by her lived experience in a woman's body, in which she has been subject to sexual and gender-based violence; these experiences have made her what she now is. But it is this very identity as a woman that she must abandon if she is to penetrate the austere, sexless space of the Order's temple. Fleta is granted a tantalizing glimpse of this space, situated on the astral plane, in an early trance vision. She leaves her body and enters a vast illuminated plane seething with seekers "of all ages and nationalities, but more than two-thirds of them . . . men."[106] Like her, they are striving toward a vast, white-columned building in the far distance. She quickly pushes past these others and soon finds herself outside the temple's doors, which she is briefly able to push open. Inside, she sees "figures in silver dresses with a jewel like an eye that saw, clasped at the neck," their faces "strange and unfamiliar," and, notably, gender unmarked.[107] They approach as if to greet her, then violently push her back out after she makes the mistake of asking, "Where is Ivan?"[108] This womanly show of attachment to others has foiled her once again. "You love him," they cry in unison, "Go!"[109] She comes back to her body outside in the forest, where the blossoms remain on the bow. If she wishes to join these figures she later describes as "cold abstractions, men no longer! . . . human no longer!"[110] she will need to ungender herself. This goal she seems to achieve in her final collapse out of the body and the tyrannical cycle of physical incarnation. Like the other female reincarnation romances we have discussed, *The Blossom and the Fruit* focalizes the twin phenomena of gender inequality and sexual violence that marked the lived experience of so many women both in and outwith the late Victorian occult fold. Yet the only solution it seems to offer to these blights is the elimination of gender itself. Even with all the imaginative resources of a new syncretic religion at hand, Collins's novel finds it easier to imagine a genderless spiritual future than a one in which different, multiple genders might co-exist in a non-hierarchical way outside patriarchal expectations.

This conclusion testifies to the complexity of the feminist and gender-political positions articulated in the reincarnation writing authored by

102 OPEN SECRETS

British women during Theosophy's first wave. The spiritual significance of gender, and of womanhood in particular, in this corpus is very different from, and by no means assimilable within, the more explicitly essentialist forms of polarity-based sex magic and Goddess spirituality to come in the early twentieth century.[111] As this chapter has shown, late Victorian reincarnationism was both spearheaded by women and used by them to forge imaginative and spiritual solutions to sexual inequality, some taking the form of embodied, retributory violence against male aggression, some of gender transcendence. The female reincarnation romances considered here boldly challenged the increasingly masculinist positioning of their genre within the heated rhetoric of the romance revival; in their plots, the acts of figurative sexual domination and casual gynocide that litter works such as Haggard's *She* are centered, denaturalized, and critiqued. Such deeds, they insist, cannot be brushed aside with levity or resignation; they carry profound spiritual consequences for aggressor and victim alike. In their simultaneous desire to both escape from, but also vindicate, embodied female experience, novels like *Ziska* and *The Blossom and the Fruit* complexify, even undermine, the putative anti-materialism of the esoteric movements that inspired them. They map the stakes of rebirth for women whose gendered bodies were alternately imagined as prime site of spiritual identity formation and as prison from which they must escape. Most of all, they reveal that the appeal of reincarnation to late Victorian women lay not just—perhaps not even primarily—in its offer of escape into a fanciful alternative reality where they might reimagine themselves as exalted queens or legendary seers; rather, it provided a potent conceptual tool through which they could examine, articulate and envision justice for the all-too-mundane experiences of sexual inequality and gender-based violence that impacted women's everyday lives.

4

Journoccultism

Numinous News and the Mantic Fragment

Thus far, our study has been concerned with long-form novel genres, such as the *Bildungsroman* and the romance, which provided the extended space for philosophical explication and narrative amplification that many occult revivalists felt their ideas warranted. They used the novel's expanse both to develop their alternative spiritual ontologies and, equally importantly, to authorize occult knowledge by associating it with depth, readerly endurance, and a highly attentive form of literacy that could penetrate hidden meanings unavailable to lay audiences. These connotations reinforced the deep bibliocentrism infused within the Victorian occult imagination, manifest in its preoccupation with rare, mysterious, and ancient books said to be the few, or even sole surviving, repositories of esoteric wisdom traditions. For an example of this tradition, we need look no further than the first chapter of H. P. Blavatsky's *Isis Unveiled*, which conjures the image of "an old Book—so very old that our modern antiquarians might ponder over its pages an indefinite time, and still not quite agree as to the nature of the fabric upon which it is written."[1] Yet as new technological innovations massively diversified and expanded the spectrum of print media at the *fin de siècle*, the book—preferably long, dusty, and one of a kind—no longer seemed like the best or natural formal fit for occult exposition. This chapter examines the deployment of the more accessible, ephemeral, and diurnal medium of the periodical press to represent and, fascinatingly, *transact* dealings with the numinous through a mode that I will refer to as *journoccultism*. I here identify two compelling and competing forms of journoccultural practice that took root at end of the nineteenth and start of the twentieth century in Britain. The first, paying homage to the factual, informative, and empirical *ethos* of the newspaper, enlisted the apparatus of the press to send dispatches to and from otherworldly spheres and non-human entities. The second exploited the sensational, fragmentary, attention-grabbing, and often non-serious features of the new journalism to produce experiences of ontological disorientation, wonder, and mystical

Open Secrets. Christine Ferguson, Oxford University Press. © Oxford University Press 2025.
DOI: 10.1093/oso/9780197651599.003.0004

104 OPEN SECRETS

epiphany within readers and reporters alike. We will track the development of and tensions between these two arms of press-based literary esotericism through cases studies of the work of four journalistic professionals-cum-heterodox spiritual seekers: W. T. Stead, Hannen Swaffer, Arthur Machen, and Charles Fort. Of this group, only Stead's press practices have previously been recognized as relevant to his spiritualist belief; in the case of the other three, their work as reporters has been viewed at best as coincident, and at worst, as directly antithetical to their pursuit of numinous experience or paranormal contact. In putting these figures together for the first time, I want to demonstrate the diverse formal, philosophical, and spiritual opportunities that the periodical press, in its new journalistic styling most of all, offered to esoterically inclined writers at the end of the nineteenth and start of the twentieth centuries, ones they cultivated and exploited with remarkable *élan*. My goal is to make visible the importance of the newspaper page, in its production, visual style, and mode of consumption, to the heterodox pursuits of these writers and to the evolution of modern occultural literary practice more broadly.

4.1 Occultism and the Press at the *Fin-de-Siècle*: Rivalry and Collaboration

As represented within the plots of late Victorian occult novels, the relationship between new religious seekers and the mainstream secular press was almost exclusively hostile. Time and time again in novels like A. P. Sinnett's *Karma*, Mabel Collins's *Morial the Mahatma* (1891), and Marie Corelli's *The Soul of Lilith* (1892) and *The Sorrows of Satan* (1895), the newspaper trade is repeatedly lambasted for its pitiable inability to understand spiritual truths, and worse, for its mendacious tendency to misrepresent them. In *The Soul of Lilith*, for example, we see the sardonic Eastern adept and Christian esotericist El Râmi taking time out from his magical manipulation of the beautiful seeress Lilith, whose soul he has trapped in her dead but preternaturally preserved body, to scorn the vacuity of the morning papers. While scanning the book review column, he finds "a loftily-patronizing paragraph on the 'Theosophical Movement,'" whose writer, "a gentleman connected with the Press, who wrote excessively common-place verse . . . is inclined to admit that there are great possibilities on the lines of study."[2] The bemused El Râmi reads this comment as a ridiculous under-estimation from a talentless hack unable to appreciate the gravity of occult truth. "This little poetaster," he sneers, "full of the conceit common to his imitative craft, is 'inclined to admit' that there are great possibilities in the study of the invisible! Excellent condescension!"[3] Other contemporary works of occult fiction condemn, not just the ignorance and arrogance of dilettantish journalists, but the more brutal and direct smear tactics applied by the mainstream press to new religious thought. Thus in *Karma*, Sinnett has the pioneering magical circle of the Baron von Mondstern brought down, not by illicit or dangerous forms of spiritual practice, but by a cynical tabloid campaign that falsely accuses it of promoting "Divorce and Demonology."[4] The press resurfaces as anti-spiritualist pariah in Arthur Conan Doyle's mid-1920s spiritualist *roman à clef*, *The Land of Mist* (1926), in which the particular visual style of the tabloid page, no less than the biased and inaccurate nature of its reportage, is taken to task. After the entrapment and arrest of honest medium Tom Linden by a couple of undercover policewomen, the novel briefly interrupts its established typographical layout with the centered, capitalized headline and italicized pull-quote used to report the case in the *Planet*.

IMPOSTER IN THE POLICE COURT

Dog Mistaken for Man
WHO WAS PEDRO?
Exemplary Sentence.[5]

On reading these lines, Conan Doyle's psychic investigator, Edward Malone, remarks in exasperation: "No wonder these Spiritualists feel bitterly. They have good cause."[6] The very format of such articles, this stylistic interjection implies, defies neutrality or balance by quite literally positioning fraudulence above all other explanations of the reported phenomena, and by reducing the complex case to a series of short, syntactical fragments. The truth of Linden's abilities can only be told through the regular, multi-sentence, and left-aligned paragraph style to which the novel quickly returns. What *The Soul of Lilith*, *Karma*, and *The Land of Mist* seem to make clear is that the secular press is no place for spiritual revelation. Its stylistic features, commercial imperatives, rapidity of production, and, hence, superficiality of investigation, militate against the accurate and respectful transmission of occultural ideas.

106 OPEN SECRETS

Yet despite what such fictional salvos might suggest, the late Victorian newspaper trade undeniably furnished a very hospitable and often lucrative professional environment for occult seekers, if not necessarily for their beliefs. Indeed, almost all of the era's leading revivalists spent at least some time earning their living as men and women of the press—Anna Kingsford, Henry Steel Olcott, Sinnett, Collins, Annie Besant, Blavatsky, and Robert James Lees, to name just a few.[7] Further, as Mark S. Morrisson has shown, many occultists drew upon their experiences of writing for the mainstream press to establish and edit niche spiritualist and occult periodicals of their own where they could combat the prejudice they found endemic in the broader public sphere.[8] The most active, prolific, and influential of all these press converts in Britain was the pathbreaking investigative reporter, editor, and new journalistic pioneer, W. T. Stead (1849–1912), whose work I will use to establish the first strand of journoccultism this chapter will consider: namely, the informational one. Stead would do more than any of his contemporaries to establish the newspaper page as a portal for contact with unseen spiritual intermediaries eager to maintain contact with the living. In its practical intentions and prioritization of information-driven content, his brand of journoccultism would also act as a foil for a second, more epiphanic and mystical form of journoccultural writing that aimed, not to disseminate facts about the afterlife or extraterrestrial civilizations, but to defamiliarize our ways of knowing the world and of distinguishing the real from the fictive, the false, and the imaginary.

4.2 W. T. Stead, Julia's Bureau, and the Informational Vein of Journoccultism

Born into a deeply evangelical family in 1849, Stead had, by the mid-1880s, become a giant of the late Victorian press. British readers knew him for his sensational 1885 investigative exposé of London's child prostitution circuit in the "Maiden Tribute of Modern Babylon" articles he had penned for the *Pall Mall Gazette*, the paper in which, as editor, he had spearheaded and championed the popular press style that would become known as the "New Journalism."[9] Although coined first by Stead himself,[10] this latter sobriquet has become more famously associated with the liberal cultural critic Matthew Arnold, who used it in 1887 to describe an emergent form of journalism that, although devised by "a clever, energetic man" (Stead) and "full of ability, novelty, sensation, sympathy, [and] generous instincts," had the "one great fault" of being "feather-brained."[11] For detractors like Arnold, the problem with the new journalism was precisely those features that its proponents, such as Stead, most valued: namely, its unabashed populism and stridently democratic desire to reach and shape as wide an audience as possible. To pursue this aim, it would jettison the long, fact-crammed, and unsigned columns of the mid-Victorian newspaper in favor of a livelier, brasher, more personal, and succinct style—one that prioritized readability, fostered the "human interest" angle, and elevated the visual appeal of the page with lavish photographic reproductions and illustrations. As has been widely recognized, the new journalism both capitalized upon and catered to the new forms of mobility enabled by the era's technological advancements, printing breaking news transmitted at top speed via the transatlantic cable, and suiting the shortened attention span of the commuter on the go "who took their news on the train or omnibus."[12] Finally, in its quest to entertain as well as inform a wide, sometimes only partially attentive, readership, the new journalism gave particular prominence to the attention-grabbing gimmick, curio, oddity, and minor mystery whose strangeness would only be enhanced by the brevity and non-conclusive nature of its reportage in a truncated, whimsically toned paragraph. For writers like Machen and Fort, operating in the second, more mystical, and cognitively disorienting mode of journoccultism we will track later in the chapter, such fragmentary forms of reportage offered a perfect vehicle for the intrusion of the numinous.

Yet in its early decades, the spiritual stakes of the new journalism, as envisioned by Stead at least, lay in its imagined ability to establish informational consensus among living humans about the supernatural world, rather than its promise as a tool for radically altering human consciousness in a distinctly mystical and or non-rational way. Always a deeply religious man, Stead had from the very beginning of his career envisioned the new journalism as a potent spiritual initiative that might represent—or foster—the "'soul' of the nation."[13] This conviction is reflected in his 1886 article on "The Future of Journalism" for the *Contemporary Review*, in which he hails the salutary potential of the newspaper to stem the tide of atheism by publicizing and campaigning against the wrongs inflicted upon the poor and the downtrodden. He writes:

> When men cease to complain of injustice, it is as if they sullenly confessed that God was dead. When they neglect to lay their wrongs before their

108 OPEN SECRETS

fellows, it is as if they had lost all faith in the reality of that collective con-
science of society which Milton finely calls "God's secretary." For every appeal to the public is a practical confession of faith that shuts out despair.[14]

Writing just one year after his conviction and imprisonment for the abduction he performed in the course of his unorthodox undercover work for the
Modern Babylon series,[15] Stead was clearly anxious to insist upon the fundamentally moral impetus of risky acts of muckraking journalism. But the
quasi-religious sentiments expressed in "The Future of Journalism" were
not simply instrumentalist forms of retrospective self-defense. Rather, they
speak to the consistent vision of the press's sanctifying power that Stead
would maintain for the rest of life, imagining the newspaper page as a holy
space where otherwise disparate members of the national community might
come together and aspire for higher things. In "The Future of Journalism,"
Stead had no other way to express this potential than through the language
of Christian resurrection. "To give utterance to the inarticulate moan of the
voiceless is to let light into a dark place," he surmises. "A newspaper in this
sense is a daily apostle of fraternity, a messenger who bringeth glad tidings
of joy, of a great light that has risen upon those who sit in darkness and the
shadow of death."[16]

Stead's conviction in the sacred function of the press would only intensify after his embrace of modern spiritualism. He had attended his first
séance in 1881, where a medium declared that he was destined to be "the
St Paul of Spiritualism."[17] By the early 1890s, Stead was well on his way to
realizing this prophecy, acting, as Roger Luckhurst has shown, as "the most
important, if unpredictable proselytizer" of the newly forged concept of telepathy,[18] and, in 1893, establishing the quarterly periodical *Borderland*,
dedicated to the investigation of a wide and eclectic array of psychical
and supernatural phenomena—spirit communications, clairvoyance,
Theosophy, automatic writing, psychometry, and divination, to name just a
few.[19] Luckhurst is surely right to recognize that, far from being separate or
even opposed, Stead's work as a leading new journalist and as a pioneering
spiritual seeker were essentially inter-connected.[20] These endeavors drew
upon a shared commitment to democratization, resting on the conviction
that elite or restricted forms of knowledge should be available far and wide
to mass audiences. Additionally, Stead's practices of journalism and spirit
mediumship also drew upon the same formal techniques. This continuity is
nowhere more apparent than in his 1909 establishment of the otherworldly

"Julia's Bureau" to serve as a supernatural wire service linking the dead to the living.

Much has been written about this initiative, and I review its coordinates here primarily to establish the particular *brand* of journoccultism that it represented, rather than to argue for its uniqueness in the *fin de siècle* cultural landscape. Indeed, as we will see, Stead was by no means the only or last British press man to envisage an occultural use for the newspaper, even if he was the most famous proponent of this practice in the twentieth century's first decade. He had first conceived the idea for a "Bureau of Intercommunication between the Two Worlds" shortly after his own development as an automatic writing medium in June 1892. Thereafter, he began receiving messages from, he believed, the newly dead American journalist and activist Julia Ames (1861–1891) whom he had met in the summer of 1890 while she was touring through Europe.[21] Although their relationship was neither longstanding nor particularly intimate, Stead felt that Ames had singled him out for contact due to his unrivaled position at the forefront of the British press, from where he could hopefully command authority and wide audiences for her afterlife dispatches. Stead published these first in *Borderland* and then in the 1898 collection *Letters from Julia; or, Light from the Borderland*, later reissued as *After Death; or Letters from Julia*, a title Stead felt to be both "more challenging" and to "indicat[e] more explicitly the subject of the book."[22] As many commentators have pointed out, the content of the letters was very much the typical spiritualist fare, reiterating long-established truisms about the progressive nature of the afterlife and the continuity of individual personality after death in a rhetorical style that Stead himself recognized as being markedly similar to his own trademark "Steadese."[23] "Julia was nothing if not generic," observes Sarah Crofton. "Her teachings were consistent with the ideas of other occultists whose writing Stead had collected, piecemeal, in the pages of *Borderland*."[24] Clichés abound in Julia's descriptions of the "great calm and peace" she felt on passing, and of her reception by an angelic guide who leads her to formerly departed loved ones who "live and lov[e]" as if "they had still plenty to do," even as death has freed them of the necessity to "work for their daily bread."[25] She learns that personality endures and progress, however slow, is assured in the afterlife; that while the dead have no wish to return, they do most ardently "lon[g] to speak to those from they have been parted," but lack "a hand to enable them to write."[26] More striking than the spiritualist platitudes Julia offered was the method and institutional structure that she proposed for afterlife contact, namely, the construction of a

110   OPEN SECRETS

dedicated "bureau of communication between the two sides" staffed by "one or more trustworthy mediums," including Stead himself, who could provide proof of spiritual survival to all comers and free of charge.[27] While Emma Hardinge Britten had participated in a similar free mediumship venture under the aegis of the Society for the Diffusion of Spiritual Knowledge in the late 1850s,[28] never before had such a scheme been proposed by a prominent *grandee* of the journalistic establishment.

First suggested in an automatically written message in 1892, Julia's Bureau officially opened its doors at Mowbray House on the Kingsway on April 24, 1909.[29] The fact that the Bureau had taken so long to establish after its initial proposal arguably anticipates the reasons for—and inevitability of—its ultimate failure, namely, the stalwart worldliness of Stead's version of spiritualism, and of his wider journoccultural pursuits. In his preface to the 1905 edition of *After Death*, he attributed the delay to his demanding schedule and competing engagements as an editor and man of business:

> It may be asked why . . . I have done nothing to establish the Bureau of which my friend writes so much. I have been willing, but I have not felt the imperious call which impels me to thrust aside all obstacles and say it must be done. I am a public man, immersed in public affairs, and I have felt that call in relation to mundane things, which left me neither means nor leisure to attempt to found the Bureau. If any who read this book feel called to cooperate in such an effort, I shall be very glad to hear from them, if they have any practical suggestions to make or help to offer.[30]

When faced with a choice of where to direct his manifold energies, in other words, the everyday world still won out over the spiritual one. One senses a weariness or reticence here; perhaps Stead had hoped that Julia's messages alone would be enough to inspire widespread belief or at least, interest, in spiritualism—although their highly derivative, homespun content proved predictably unable to do so. Certainly, he seems here to be fishing for volunteers who might take up the task of planning and administering the Bureau on his behalf. By 1909, it must have been clear that such assistance was not on the horizon.

When the Bureau finally launched, the Steadian *ethos* of everyday practicality and organizational rationality prevailed within its operations. As Crofton describes, applicants for sittings were interviewed, vetted for their suitability, and provided with a mandatory reading list to whose study they were required to commit in a signed pledge; the chosen few, almost all grieving survivors rather than agnostic investigators, were then paired with mediums on the Bureau's staff who would seek to contact their absent friends on their behalf.[31] Results were middling to poor. Of the six hundred clients who used the Bureau up until the time of Stead's 1912 death aboard the *RMS Titanic*, "only about a third believed that they had established contact with deceased loved ones."[32] Given that they had been handpicked and prepared for acceptance, this figure seems particularly underwhelming. If, as Stewart J. Brown has contended, the aim of Stead's project was to deploy a bureaucratic communication apparatus to *demystify* spiritual contact, then it seems clear that the Edwardian public had limited interest in this mode—or perhaps *tone*—of spiritual encounter. The Bureau fizzled out a few years after Stead's death, eventually merging into the W. T. Stead Borderland Library, the more conventional spiritualist society established by his daughter Estelle in 1914.

The informational vein of journoccultism pioneered by Stead did not, however, disappear with the closing of the Bureau. It was to have a further efflorescence a decade later in the sensational quest of a London journalist and editor, Swaffer, to find and authenticate the spirit of his recently deceased employer Lord Northcliffe (Alfred Harmsworth), the legendary press baron and founder of the *Daily Mail* who died at the age of fifty-seven in 1922. Swaffer serialized his results first in *The People*, for which he was then editor-in-chief, and subsequently in extended form in the pacy and confessional *Northcliffe's Return*, which appeared with Hutchinson and Co. in 1925. More so than *Letters from Julia*, Swaffer's book serves as a stylistic paean to the new journalistic techniques that its posthumous subject had adapted from Stead and others in order to turn the *Mail* into Britain's highest-ever circulating daily, reaching one million readers a day by 1900.[33] It adopts a gossipy, breezy, and often humorous tone as it relays memories of the man affectionately known as "the Chief" before describing his apparent post-death conversion to the spiritualist beliefs he had viewed with an alternate mix of ambivalence and downright hostility in life.[34] Swaffer engages readers with a suspenseful investigative plot in which he sits in séance with all the leading luminaries of the post-war London spiritualist scene—Gladys Osborne Leonard, Albert Vout Peters, Dennis Bradley, the Reverend J. W. Potter and his son Clifford, and Evan Powell—until receiving what he believed to be conclusive evidence of Northcliffe's continuing survival and, equally importantly, ongoing journalistic endeavors, on the other side. Like Conan Doyle's spiritualist *roman à*

112   OPEN SECRETS

clef, The Land of Mist, whose serialization in the *Strand* appeared in the same year, *Northcliffe's Return,* too, reaches its narrative climax in a big public debate on the truth of spiritualism—in Swaffer's case, one held at the Queens Hall on Langham Place in early 1925—and the triumphant conversion of its reporter-protagonist to a belief in spiritual survival.

Although markedly less solemn in approach than Stead, Swaffer—and the Northcliffe entity he claimed to have contacted—shared his predecessor's vision for a journoccultism that would be above all practical, useful, and information-based, aiming to channel quasi-anthropological details about the afterlife to the living. Indeed, Stead even makes a guest appearance in *Northcliffe's Return,* allegedly joining Northcliffe "on the Other Side" to "wor[k] on the same propaganda to put Spiritualism over."[35] Northcliffe's aptitude for this post-life promotional duty is anticipated in the nickname he bore while still alive and working at the *Mail's* Carmelite House headquarters: the "All-Knowing One."[36] What better figure to relay the details of the next world with shrewd-eyed precision than a highly experienced press man renowned for his seeming omniscience of view? Alive and dead, Swaffer emphasizes, Northcliffe had eyes everywhere. Indeed, when the newsroom first learned of their chief's death, he tells us, employees quipped that the truth of spiritualism must rest on whether they ever heard from him again:

> If it were true that he passed over into a spiritual sphere from which all communication were possible, surely he, of all men who ever lived, would strive to communicate with the earth; for in this life he was the arch-propagandist, the master publisher and the greatest publicist of his age. Never was a being so fitted by his earthly training for carrying on a similarly restless, tireless, ceaseless sort of campaign on the Other Side.[37]

Throughout *Northcliffe's Return,* readers are just as, if not more, frequently invited to admire the spirit Northcliffe for the tenacity of its journalistic instincts as for the philosophical quality of its communication. "My God," marvels Swaffer, setting this tone after an early séance, "to think that, even when the Chief got to heaven, he took the trouble to send the story over."[38] His awe here is first and foremost professional, inspired by the posthumous Northcliffe's energy, labor, and new journalistic *nous* as he communicates tidings from a sphere hitherto considered to be stubbornly ineffable.

Swaffer's frequent redirection of reader attention from the content to the method of the messages was also no doubt tactical. After all, the actual substance of Northcliffe's communiqués, very much like that of Julia's, was very thin indeed, offering a pale comparison to the lively and often scathing wit that Swaffer attributes to the living Northcliffe. Dead, the "All-Knowing One" is altogether more po-faced and truistic in his utterances, declaring, for example, through the mediumship of Osborne Leonard that "Wars bring poverty, hatred, crime, destruction, and suffering."[39] A later message is so banal as to be potentially attributable to any spirit in any séance ever recorded: "There will be troublesome times ahead, but keep calm and do what's right."[40] Swaffer insisted that he had received messages of a much more precise and evidential nature than these, but that he could not share their details in print due their intimate and confidential nature. A consequence of this reticence is that many of the most specific spirit messages printed in *Northcliffe's Return* relate not to the qualities of the afterlife or the Chief's personal life, but to the operations of the newspaper trade, thus fulfilling an early joke by one of the *Mail*'s reporters that if "all this Spiritualistic talk of Conan Doyle . . . were true, Northcliffe would . . . come out of his grave and t[ell] us what he thought of the paper."[41] And so, in Swaffer's account, he does. A message delivered via the mediumship of the seventeen year-old Clifford Potter bewails, "what a terrible curse the opinion of a few journalists may be to a nation" and insists that "Journalism . . . has seen its day."[42] Surprising sentiments these may be from an erstwhile newspaper titan, but they are very much in keeping with the mood of a postwar British spiritualist community that had been continuously ridiculed and attacked by tabloids like the *Mail* and *John Bull*. Skeptical readers might well have questioned just who was ventriloquizing who here. At other times, the spirit Northcliffe seems more hopeful about the future of the mainstream press, but only if it embraces the socialist principles to which Swaffer himself was committed: "the thing I look forward to above everything now is the day when the newspapers will become a public national property; not for the imposing of ideas and policies of private individuals, but for the purpose of conveying new and ideas to the common people."[43] The living Northcliffe, needless to say, would never have been so naïve as to view the capitalistic and informational functions of tabloid journalism as easily separable. In a later séance with a different medium, Vout Peters, the Northcliffe entity resumes its here abandoned capitalist tendencies to offer advice on how *People* might be formatted so as to out-sell its rivals, counselling Swaffer "Interest your

114   OPEN SECRETS

public first . . . Short leaders! Short leaders! Many of them. Not long, prosy things, like used to be in the *Standard*."[44]

For many spiritualists, the very prosaic and practical nature of messages such as these that confirmed their authenticity—how better to establish the persistence of individual personality than to demonstrate that our beloved dead maintained the same interests, bugbears, and speech patterns as they had in life? "Triggering a sense of the familiar," observes Sarah Crofton "is one of the most crucial strategies of spirit-writing. It is at the heart of Spiritualism."[45] Yet, as these examples suggest, the entity summoned across *Northcliffe Returns* was rarely consistent enough to be wholly familiar as "the Chief," and never specific or explicit enough—at least, not after Swaffer's editorial interventions—to convince non-spiritualistically inclined readers. *Northcliffe's Return* ultimately lacked the impact of *Letters from Julia*, despite, or perhaps more accurately, *because* of, sharing the same common-sensical and informational orientation, one that may no longer have felt fresh. In the intervening years between their publication, a new, distinctly weirder strain of journoccultism had sprung up in the writing and professional practice of two men who, together, would exert a massive influence on the transatlantic development of twentieth-century horror and science fiction: Machen and Fort. For these figures, as we will now see, the earlier informational current of journoccultism could never describe or prove the existence of other worlds, not only because the information it provided was insufficient—although it often was—but because information alone was incompatible with the radical ontological shift required to sense and contact the numinous. Common sense, coherence, and the genres of facticity could never produce the experience of awe-struck wonder they saw as the main authenticating criterion of the supernatural. Fascinatingly, this conviction led them, not to reject the new journalism as a vehicle for supernatural, extraterrestrial, or mystical apperception, but rather to emphasize and exploit a different set of its qualities, namely, its associations with "the ephemeral, the fleeting, the insubstantial, the unformulated, the informal, personalized, and colloquial."[46] Both professional journalists and fiction writers, Machen and Fort were linked also by their mutual penchant for library reading rooms, their overlapping publication networks, and their similarly ambivalent relationship to the contemporary occult and spiritualist movements in whose in whose literature they were deeply versed.[47] If never dedicated spiritualists or fully committed initiates of any particular occult school—Machen's tenure in the Hermetic Order of the Golden Dawn was brief and in his own recollection dilettanteish—they maintained a life-long fascination with otherworldly horizons, and with the tantalizing possibility that human life might be shaped or directed by an unseen realm of spiritual or extra-terrestrial intermediaries. And most intriguingly for our purposes, their writing would time and time again detect—if never definitively *confirm*—the presence of these forces in the sensational, comic, or trivial headlines, the marginalia, and the elliptical filler paragraphs of the daily newspaper.

4.3 Machenian Gothic and the Mantic Press

Machen is today remembered primarily as a pioneer of late Victorian Gothic fiction, and, somewhat less frequently as a dilettantish dabbler in the modern occult revival via his brief membership in the Hermetic Order of the Golden Dawn and his lifelong friendship with the magical practitioner and self-described "most initiated man in Europe," A. E. Waite.[48] Rarely is he celebrated for his decades-long career as a professional reporter, even though this activity occupied far more of his working life than the other two endeavors. This omission, encouraged by his own often cynical and contemptuous comments about the newspaper trade, has hitherto prevented readers from recognizing the deep continuity between the modes of spiritual seekership and numinous contact articulated across Machen's Gothic fiction and his journalism. Yet it is only by coming to grips with Machen's experiences, and fictional representations, of the press that we can fully understand the occultural stakes of his wider literary *oeuvre*. After all, Machen's involvement with the newspaper business spanned almost the entirety of his adult life. When he first came to London as a callow Welsh teenager in 1881, it was with the intention of establishing a career in journalism,[49] and while his longest period of full-time employment as a reporter did not start until he was appointed to the *Evening News* (a Northcliffe paper) in 1910, he spent the intervening decades honing his journalistic style by contributing freelance reviews, short stories, and popular interest pieces to periodicals and magazines on a regular basis. Early stories appeared in papers such as the *St James Gazette* and *The Whirlwind*;[50] from 1897 to 1899, he wrote a regular review column for *Literature* and later contributed articles to new journalistic weeklies such as *T.P.'s Weekly* and *Vanity Fair*.[51] By 1910, when his fiction writing career had fallen into a slump from which it would never fully recover, Machen was fully established, in James Machin's words, as "a

116 OPEN SECRETS

Fleet Street regular ... whose name appeared in the by-lines of many national newspapers."[52] His press fame would be further cemented a few years later in his sensational and unintentional creation of the Angel of Mons myth in his short story "The Bowmen," published in the *Evening News* on September 29, 1914.[53] Even after his dismissal from the *Evening News* in 1921, Machen remained a regular media hack.[54] Were his scattered corpus of newspaper and magazine commissions, tightly dead-lined and written off-the-cuff, ever gathered and anthologized, it would dwarf the corpus of 1890s occult gothic tales for which Machen remains best known, and on which most accounts of his literary career's occultural significance remain based.

Perhaps because of its duration and extent, Machen critics have come to view his journalistic career dismissively, often treating it as a grubby derogation of the rare genius that would have flourished had it not been for the writer's relentless penury. Early biographer William Francis Gekle insists that Machen "detested" journalism because it was too akin to the literary realism he famously reviled, and describes him as producing "just as much drivel as the average journalist" was expected to yield in the 1890s.[55] More scathingly, Wesley Sweetser refers to Machen's hack work as a form of spiritual harlotry which required the Welshman to "prostitute his soul for a steady income" to "the ugly and venomous toad of journalism."[56] Admittedly, Machen had adopted similar terminology in *The London Adventure* (1924), the final of his three memoirs, to describe journalism as "a prostitution of the soul, compared with which the prostitution of the body is a little thing."[57] Such sentiments were well known to the author's intimates and family members. In the foreword to an 1988 collection of his father's letters, Hilary Machen recollects "the grim sadness with which my father set out each morning to his highly paid journalism: as in the way with all good families, his sadness affected both my mother and myself, and is not yet forgotten, and has bequeathed to me a valuable asset: an overwhelming hatred and contempt for the popular press."[58] Professional journalism features repeatedly in Machen's letters and memoirs as a source of intellectual, emotional, spiritual, and aesthetic privation, a career "unfit for any decent man of feeling" and "the most illiterate occupation in the world."[59]

Yet too often in their assessment of this aspect of his career, critics have been diverted by the intensity of Machen's horror of waged labor away from the parallel moments of revelatory rapture that simultaneously animate his fictional deployments of, and autobiographical commentary on, the newspaper trade. Indeed, in *The London Adventure*, he admits that his newspaper work had never only been a form of debasement; on the contrary, he declares "that as a newspaper reporter I saw queer things and odd prospects which, otherwise, I should not have seen."[60] In assignments to report on the Hornsey Poltergeist case, the murder trials of Steinie Morrison and Frederick Seddon, or the Battle of Sidney Street,[61] journalism took Machen down some very strange paths indeed, ones in which the peripatetic business of reportage triggered encounters with the numinous. These experiences he referred to as "precious jewels" strewn through the "squalid vestments" of the "newspaper business"; in their wake, he would feel "dazed, bewildered, uncertain; curious as to whether I had not somehow strayed into a world of illusion which was not wholly of our earth."[62]

Incidents of such journoccultural illumination saturate Machen's gothic fiction and autobiographical ruminations alike. In the former, press extracts, abandoned newspapers, and the ominous cries of itinerant news sellers pervade the London cityscape, endowing the ancient or arcane horrors they limn with an uncanny modernity. In "The Lost Club" (1890), one of Machen's earliest tales, his recurring *flâneur* characters Austin and Phillips stumble by chance upon a hidden London club where terrified members are summoned to open a mysterious book at random; if the page they reveal is printed in solid black, the club president announces, they will be "at the disposal of the committee and myself."[63] After witnessing this absurd if, in their estimation, harmless game, the pair leave; a few weeks later, Austin passes a newsstand and learns that the hapless discoverer of the black page, one Mr. St John D'Aubigny, has now mysteriously disappeared. "Since the above date," a paragraph reports, "the unfortunate gentleman who was much liked in London society, has not been heard of... The police are extremely reticent."[64] A clear homage to Robert Louis Stevenson's "The Suicide Club" (1878), Machen's tale departs from this initiating source text in its more deliberate obscuration of the nature of the club's operations and of its members' fates; we never find out if D'Aubigny was murdered, compelled to suicide, forced into exile, or something else. By its very concision and inconclusion, hinting, perhaps, at conspiratorial silence, the newspaper paragraph becomes the perfect vehicle to signal this capacious mystery.

Here and elsewhere in Machen's fiction, pithy press articles are interjected into the narrative not to express or share, but rather to *destabilize* information, to introduce more uncertainty into already enigmatic incidents, and to lead characters into a menacing non-human world. In "The Novel of the Black Seal" (1895), for example, one such *Tit-Bits*-style article lures Professor

118   OPEN SECRETS

Gregg into his ultimately fatal investigations of the ancient, malevolent fairy folk who survive in the Welsh countryside—"many years ago," he explains to Helen Lally, "a chance paragraph in a newspaper caught my attention, and focused in an instant the vagrant thoughts and half-formed fancies of many idle and speculative hours into a certain hypothesis."[65] A similarly arresting tabloid story on the "West End Horrors"—namely a bizarre rash of suicides among wealthy titled men—lures Austin and Villiers toward an ancient pagan horror and its feminine avatar, Helen Vaughan, in *The Great God Pan* (1894). When Villiers discovers a deeply unnerving drawing of the malevolent Helen in an abandoned Soho house, it is no surprise that it wedged within "a pile of newspapers littered on the floor."[66] Machen's early stories train us to expect the numinous in exactly such places, amidst the discarded pages of newspapers whose portentous significance is only partially scrutable to attuned seekers who know that yesterday's news can contain terrifying spiritual auguries.[67]

Machen's most extended fictional exploration of journoccultural mystery comes in his final, and long underappreciated, novel *The Green Round* (1933), a *doppelgänger* story that brings the writer's career-long fascination with the stubborn weirdness of the press to a fevered apex. The novel opens with a prologue in which a seemingly mundane, even perversely boring, exchange in the correspondence column of a London newspaper takes an unnerving turn. An indignant member of the public—here lampooned with the generic name of "Brown of Clapham or Smith of Wimbledon"[68]—writes in to complain about the growing vulgarization of Britain's former beauty spots. On a recent family holiday to the seaside town of Porth in West Wales, he was horrified to find upon the once tranquil promenade:

> a hideous building, of staring red brick and grotesque design . . . On a balcony, a jazz band was emitting ear-splitting cacophonies, swings, roundabouts, and shooting galleries were all in evidence, and seemed fully patronized. The more popular entertainments were surrounded by a surging mass of people; the noise was deafening.[69]

A predictable exchange ensues, with contributors vociferously debating the benefits and demerits of the mass entertainment industry's encroachment on the countryside. Amidst this *fracas*, one important letter gets overlooked. Porth's town clerk writes in, not to take any particular side in this lively dispute, but rather to reject the initial claim that triggered it. For, as he angrily insists, there are simply no places fitting this description in Porth; the dunes remain, as ever, undeveloped and placid. "I can only conclude," he writes bitingly, "that your correspondent, under the influence of some temporary confusion, mistook his right hand for his left, and thus took the wrong turning."[70] Well before the main narrative takes off, Machen thus establishes Porth as a liminal space where things are not what they seem, where two worlds— one bucolic, peaceful, relaxing, and implicitly white, the other ferociously modern, urban, overpopulated, and, as the reference to jazz suggests, possibly racially hybrid—have come to inexplicably overlap. The formal structure of the correspondence column is ideally suited to host this mysterious co-existence, first, because it has no requirement to offer any conclusion to the ephemeral debates it instigates and drops in accordance with the whims of reader interest, and second, because its non-serious nature minimizes the extent to which these contradictory experiences represent an assault on the illusion of a shared consensual reality, one which the newspaper is more typically enlisted to support than to undermine.

It is into this ontologically compromised milieu that Machen's hapless protagonist, the middle-aged literary recluse Laurence Hillyer, is launched. Too much alone in his London lodgings, he has fallen prone to spells of incoherent muttering and depressive thoughts; what he needs, declares his doctor, is a change of air, a new routine, and some restorative company. And a truly terrifying kind of company indeed he finds on the sands of Porth. Shortly after his arrival, a local farmer's wife is abducted and brutally murdered. Hillyer falls under suspicion when his fellow lodging house guests see him out walking with a "horrible-looking. . . deformed" stranger whose face emanates pure malevolence. One or both of this pair of outsiders, they conclude, must be the culprit,[71] and they descend upon the two to make a vigilante-style arrest in the dunes. This effort quickly descends into panicked confusion as this terrifying companion, of whom Hillyer denies all knowledge, seems to disappear into thin air. Hillyer has, he insists, only ever been alone in his walks. Terrified, he flies back to London only to have this malevolent presence follow, instigating mayhem in the form of violent poltergeist activity and uncanny nocturnal illuminations. He is ultimately forced to flee the country altogether, taking only a brown paper parcel and leaving no notice of his whereabouts. It really was, remarks the doctor who first sent Hillyer to Porth, "an odd case."[72]

Far more than simply an opening gambit, the newspaper emerges in Machen's novel as a key participant in the protagonist's ongoing

120 OPEN SECRETS

psychodrama, a source and site of the uncanny forms of sociality later exaggerated in grotesque form through Hillyer's relationship with his unseen foe. Eager to engage with his fellow guests, he scours the pages of new journalistic weeklies for fresh conversational topics that almost always misfire in comic and perverse ways when he gives them air. Sitting in the lounge over coffee one night, for example, he asks Mrs. Sykes about her jeweled pipes. When she balks in confusion, he explains that "he had read only that morning in the woman's page of a popular paper, that fashionable women were all smoking briar pipes heavily jewelled, and that rubies and emeralds were the most popular combination."[73] This particular episode is resolved easily enough when she laughs and replies that "nobody paid any attention to that nonsense," but others are not.[74] More scandalously, he asks the "very pretty dark daughter" of his co-lodger General Clinton, recently returned from years of long service in India, why she has no caste mark on her forehead. The General is enraged, suspecting Hillyer to be insinuating that she is of mixed race—another reflection, perhaps, of the novel's paranoid fascination with hybridity. Of course, the hapless writer intends no such thing; he had merely "seen a paragraph to the effect that with smart women the caste-mark on the forehead had become a craze."[75] Pondering these missteps afterward, he concludes:

> a great part of the daily paper dealt with a world of pure fiction, reporting its news with all the gravity of one who deals with the plain and common facts of life. Women did not smoke jewelled briars, they did not paint Hindoo caste marks on their brows . . . The reason of these strange inventions puzzled Hillyer profoundly . . . If he had ever thought of the mysteries as things hidden away and apart, remote from the general stream of life, he saw now that he was mistaken. The mysteries were part of the very tissue and being of man; they were not to be avoided. The quest for that which was concealed by the gold and jewelled world of the Arabian nights was conducted in the columns of the daily press; behind Persian lattice-work, in a tiled court, deep azure, where the music of falling water rang from the fountain, he saw the appearance of the dark lady with the jewelled pipe, the castemark on her forehead, her feet gleaming golden on the rose-marble floor.[76]

These musings present the newspaper as a textual medium in which the esoteric is made fleetingly exoteric, and divine mystery brought ever so briefly down to earth. The choice of the women's fashion pages as the catalyst for

Hillyer's epiphany here is both telling and somewhat sinister, hinting at a possible alternate explanation for violence that starts to accompany Machen's protagonist. When Hillyer reads the paper, he seems increasingly driven by a desire, not to gain a general knowledge of the world and its major geopolitical events, but to indulge in a series of *Arabian Nights*-tinged fantasies about mysterious, seductive, and exotic women. The most famous woman of all in the *Nights* is, of course, Scheherazade, who spins her wondrous tales as protection against the nightly threat of gynocidal violence. When Hillyer finds himself drawn to the figure of the beautiful "dark lady with the jewelled pipe," is it of she that he is thinking? And if so, does this fantasy cast him in the supporting role of Shahryar, the murderous king for whom Scheherazade's tales of wonder serve as temporary distractions from his urge to kill? These intertextual allusions align Machen's protagonist, if only allusively, with the murderer of the local farmer's wife; perhaps the fiendish and volatile companion who accompanies him is no supernatural agent, but a manifestation of his own unacknowledged misogynistic psychosis, fostered and fueled by his eccentric perusal of the tabloid beauty columns. A great strength of Machen's final novel is its ability to evoke this possibility without fully letting it break through the textual surface—a function which, is after all, key to the newspaper's uncanny force here. Far from consolidating public opinion in its Steadian styling as "the daily apostle of fraternity,"[77] the new journalistic newspaper in *The Green Round* instead acts as both a catalyst and conduit for highly individualistic forms of aberration, both supernatural and psychological, summoned down and across its column lengths.

4.4 Machen as Journoccultist on the Numinous Beat

The fictional examples of Machen's journoccultural imagination we have just discussed are connected, perhaps inevitably, by what Marco Pasi has described as a "negative epistemology" of esotericism, one which frames human interactions with the numinous as uniformly terrifying, and destructive, and is a requisite feature of "horror or supernatural fiction" whose "purpose . . . is to frighten the reader."[78] For Pasi, this negative epistemology lies at the heart of Machen's Gothic corpus and acts as a reflex of the author's deep cultural pessimism and skepticism about modernity.[79] Certainly it is not difficult to find elements of misanthropy and reactionary conservatism scattered across Machen's *oeuvre*; we detect them for example, in the peevish

122   OPEN SECRETS

series of essays he would collect and publish as *Dr Stiggins: His Views and Principles* (1906) and in his pro-fascist contribution to *Authors Take Sides on the Spanish Civil War* (1937), in which, of the 148 authors featured, he was one of only five to write in support of General Franco. Yet Machen's literary engagement with the numinous, and with the numinous newspaper most of all, cannot be reduced to reactionary anti-modernism and repulsive dread alone. In the trilogy of memoirs he produced in the early 1920s—*Far Off Things* (1922), *Things Near and Far* (1923), and *The London Adventure* (1924)—he would adulate the new and positive forms of numinous contact made available by one of modernity's most distinctive textual forms: the newspaper. Collectively, these volumes represent a fascinating multi-part spiritual autobiography whose stages are transacted via its autobiographical subject's mystical interactions with the periodical press, first as a child reader of the London weeklies at home in Caerleon, and then as a reporter for the London press, where his assignments would repeatedly lead him down otherworldly byways.

Although most concentrated within *The London Adventure*, which covers his time on the *Evening News*, journoccultural elements run through all three of Machen's autobiographies, surfacing most vividly in their praise for the imaginative and spiritual effects of the periodical press's disorienting eclecticism and occult content. In *Far Off Things*, he recalls his childhood delight in reading the bound volumes of London weeklies, such as *Chambers's Journal*, *All the Year Round*, *Welcome Guest*, and *Household Words*, which populated his father's library. He credits his life-long interest in alchemy to a series of "singularly well-informed and enlightened" articles published in the latter in 1855.[80] "I see myself sitting on a stool by the rectory hearth," he recalls:

> propping up "Household Words" against the fender, quite ravished by the story of Nicholas Flamel, who found by chance, "The Book of Abraham the Jew," who journeyed all over Europe in search of one who could interpret figures for him, and who succeeded at last in the Operation of the Great Work, and was discovered by the King's. Chamberlain living in great simplicity, eating cabbage with Perenelle his wife.[81]

Unlikely reading material for an eight- or nine-year old this may be, but Machen was after all no ordinary child, and the alchemical quest serves in his recollection the same function as the imperial adventure tale might have held for other boys, opening for him an arena of wonder and awe. His early contact with occultism, transacted through the pages of a popular family weekly, was clearly premised on a distinctly positive epistemology, one that underlined the considerable spiritual gains attainable through alchemical study and made manifest in Flamel's noble humility and preference for homespun domesticity over vulgar wealth.

This youthful enchantment with the occult potencies of the press is tempered somewhat in *Things Near and Far*, the volume that covers the late-century period in which Machen first came to London, attempted to launch a career in the "sorry trade" of journalism, and briefly joined the Hermetic Order of the Golden Dawn, which he here mocks as offering only "impotent and imbecile Abracadabras. It knew nothing whatever about anything and concealed the fact under an impressive ritual and a sonorous phraseology."[82] The most pessimistic of his memoirs, it nonetheless manages to find some spiritual value in the entangled dross of press work and occult practice. Downplaying his first forays into column writing as "harmless and agreeable" rather than profoundly wise, he nonetheless credits them "in a small way" with setting him on the path of "his true subject: the country of my childhood and my youth."[83] Similarly, despite his cynical assessment of the order's grandiose spiritual claims, he nonetheless recognizes that the practices of the Golden Dawn:

> did me a great deal of good—for the time. To stand waiting at a closed door in a breathless expectation, to see it open suddenly, and disclose two figures clothed in a habit that I never thought to see worn by the living, to catch for a moment the vision of a cloud of incense smoke and certain dim lights glimmering in it before the bandage was put over the eyes and the arm felt a firm grasp upon it that led the hesitating footsteps into an unknown darkness; all that was strange and admirable indeed; and strange it was to think that within a foot or two of those closely curtained windows the common life of London moved on the common pavement.[84]

Machen is most likely describing here his participation in an early neophyte ritual in the Order's Isis-Urania Temple; his brief membership period did not permit him to advance to the higher grades. Hierarchical ascension within the order does not seem to have ever interested Machen, who here instead focuses on the sensory and phenomenological dimensions of the ritual practice rather than its initiatory outcome. Through touch, scent, and sight, he is lifted beyond the everyday world; or rather, it is the discordant juxtaposition

124 OPEN SECRETS

of that mundane world with the uncommon sensory and aesthetic effects of the ritual that allows him to experience a sense of transport.

This focus on praxis and sensory affect forms the dominant keynote of the journoccultural recollections in *The London Adventure*, the most press-focused of all his three memoirs. It is no small irony that Machen's most positive depictions of journoccultural experience appear within this most extended account of the profession he loathed and which he repeatedly accused of inducing in him a kind of spiritual bankruptcy. Authentic as these sentiments may be, *The London Adventure* nonetheless shows that reportage also offered a means to replenish the spiritual stocks it simultaneously depleted by leading Machen, like the less fortunate Hillyer, toward portents and unseen intermediaries. After a lengthy opening digression about the author's procrastination in starting the book, *The London Adventure* curates and partially explicates the strangest incidents of its author's eleven-year employment with the *Evening News*. Two key episodes demand our attention in this respect: Machen's investigation of the Hornsey Poltergeist case and of the Campo Tosto inheritance suit. Fascinatingly, they both represent incidences of journalistic failure in the sense that the experiences his investigations produce are inexpressible within the stylistic conventions of the popular interest articles they are intended to produce. In contrast to the previously discussed fictional examples, here Machen focuses on how the practice of investigative reportage—rather than the readerly reception of its published end products—evokes numinous encounter and occult intimations.

The Hornsey poltergeist case caused a media sensation in 1921. Papers reported on a series of strange happenings taking place in the North London home of the Frost family—lumps of coal jumping out of the fire by their own apparent volition, and pieces of crockery levitating and smashing in mid-air.[85] Eager to capitalize on the sensation, the *Evening News* duly dispatched Machen to investigate. The nature of the events, whether paranormal or fraudulent, that took place in the Frost home are not Machen's key concern in *The London Adventure*. Instead, he here lingers on an episode that occurred along his way to the North London suburbs, when he paused en route to interview a brass founder—possibly a colleague of Mr. Frost's—in Clerkenwell. Machen never explains this man's connection to the case, but instead speculates on the esoteric significance of the seemingly trivial and random small talk in which they engage. In response to a question about the methods of his trade, the brass founder reveals that he is a Freemason and asks if Machen is also "on the square."[86] The reporter is not, but nonetheless finds himself sent into a reverie by the odd suggestive confluence of brass work, freemasonry, the ancient mystery religions of Egypt, and the prosaic poltergeist phenomena of floating China on which he has been assigned to write:

> We resumed our enquiry into a particular instance of that other ancient and insoluble mystery, the Poltergeist, which had been manifesting in a northern suburb. Now here was an intelligent and fervent Mason, but how little he realised that his Father in the Craft was much more than a Brassfounder, much more than a Master Builder, that he belonged to a race removed from man, and that his true name was, very possibly Sabazius; that he was perhaps of the house of Osiris? I think this good Son of the Widow knew little of all this; and so, as I say, with the vast majority of his brethren. Yet the ancient rite is duly performed, and so other ancient rites are performed in the rawest, reddest suburbs.[87]

Eschewing the framing of ancient esoteric traditions as rejected or forbidden, this passage invites us to recognize their survival in everyday practices kept alive by common workers with no understanding of their original spiritual import. The "rite" to which he refers—perhaps a Freemasonic one, or perhaps simply the performance of foundry work—has value not because it is spiritually intentional, instrumental, or authentic, but because it is performed only half-consciously in the starkly unspiritual site of the city's margins. This story of serendipitous encounter and esoteric survival is not, needless to say, the one that he has been sent write, and it never makes it into the *Evening News*. But in Machen's autobiographical reflection, it is this moment of contact—between the reporter and the skilled tradesman, the ancient and the modern, the solemn ancient mystery rite and the absurd suburban psychical efflorescence—that forms the epiphanic center of the case.

An even stranger irruption of this correspondential strain of journoccultism occurs during Machen's investigation of a light local color story about the peculiar will of one Mr. Campo Tosto, late of a London hamlet that he identifies as Burnt Green.[88] Much to the consternation of his surviving family, Tosto—an eccentric art collector known to shoot arrows at trespassers—has bequeathed his extremely valuable mediaeval art collection to his servants Mr. and Mrs. Turk. When Machen arrives to interview the lucky legatees, the publicity-shy Mr. Turk says he will not say or show him anything—except, that is, his ability to read a newspaper upside down.

126 OPEN SECRETS

Promptly taking up Machen's copy of the *Daily News*, he proceeds to give him a demonstration. At its conclusion, he declares contentedly to the baffled reporter: "You see... I was a farm labourer for years, but lately I've a lot to do with fuller's-earth."[89] None of this, of course, makes any sense whatsoever, and again Machen comes away with no story fit for print. Yet what he has acquired is a genuine experience of psychological disorientation and spiritual awe induced by the irreducible oddness, uncanny correspondences, and eclecticism of this bizarre episode of quasi-sacred non-sense. He recalls:

> I drove back to Reigate in a "dwam," as the Scots say; really not knowing whether I stood on my head or heels, feeling rather like an actor who has been "rushed on" for a small part in a mad drama which he has had no time to study. For consider; here was a man called Campo Tosto living in a place called Burnt Green, which is, practically a translation of Campo Tosto. Here was a man whose property consisted chiefly of Madonnas and mediaeval candlesticks... Here was his heir, with the good old English country name of Turk. And here was Turk, who could read print upside down, because he had been a farm labourer and a worker in fuller's-earth... I went home in that "dwam" and wondered what on earth I was to do, and at last wrote the whole, true story, just as it happened, and ended by wondering whether it were, somehow, a parable, written for our example, though, as I said, I could not conceive what the moral of the story might be. But my news editors would not print.[90]

This editorial decision is hardly surprising; after all, Machen's reported experience has neither the contemporaneity nor the communicability of a pithy news article. Rather it captures the ineffability of the mystical experience or the dream; the percipient feels himself in the presence of a great mystery whose sacred nature he perceives without being able to articulate or rationalize it. Although catalyzed by particular press practices—the pursuit of a special interest interview, the reading of newsprint upside down—its oddness cannot be represented within that instigating medium. Machen registers the incident not as terrifying but rather as edifying, although the spiritual lesson it is intended to convey remains resistantly unclear. A communiqué, however inscrutable, has been attempted; the mysterious grandeur of the numinous realm is only intensified through its choice to manifest itself through such commonplace and absurd details, inassimilable to any known interpretive system or occult tradition.

4.5 Charles Fort and the Damned Data of the Press

Mr. Turk's provocative act of reading the newspaper upside down—quite literally in the wrong direction and against the grain—provides a fitting segue into the final, and most experimental form of journoccultural practice this chapter will consider, one that wholly reverses and subverts the informational impulses of Stead's spiritualist bureau to vaunt instead the mystery of inconclusive data and unreliable reportage. Fort (1874–1932) is one of the most important if misunderstood figures in the early twentieth-century transatlantic occult milieu, a reporter, editor, and fiction writer from upstate New York who, after an inheritance freed him from burden of full-time employment, spent the rest of his life in reading rooms in Manhattan and London collecting and collating instances of unexplained phenomena reported in scientific journals and newspapers. He then compiled these in four remarkable compendia of the bizarre, all written in his characteristically accretive, puckish, and gnomic verbal style: *The Book of the Damned* (1919), *New Lands* (1923), *Lo!* (1931), and *Wild Talents* (1932). Fort is remembered today less for these works than for his influence on both the subsequent generations of science fiction writers inspired by his speculations on extraterrestrial activity and on the *Fortean Times*, a monthly magazine which continues his investigation of "strange phenomena and experiences, curiosities, prodigies, and portents."[91] The formal radicality of his literary expression, and its incubation in his press experience, has been almost entirely side-lined within Fort's reception history; indeed, as Damon Knight points out, "Fort has so often been described as a hermit that people forget he was a newspaper reporter."[92] Yet the distinctive character and unsettling power of the Fortean paranormal comes directly from its duplication of press parataxis. To recognize this quality is to claim Fort for literary esotericism studies by positioning him as one of most radical and innovative practitioners of twentieth-century journoccultism, a figure whose juxtapositional and compositional play with the newspaper approaches the anarchistic *découpage* of his Dadaist contemporaries in Europe.

Fort's deliberate rejection of any established system or tradition for interpreting the unexplained has made him difficult to situate within esotericism and religious studies, and only a few scholars have attempted to do so.[93] An important exception is Jeffrey J. Kripal, whose 2010 study *Authors of the Impossible: The Paranormal and the Sacred* establishes Fort as a key figure in the twentieth-century history of religion due to his popularization

128   OPEN SECRETS

of a paranormal paradigm that aligns with Rudolf Otto's concept of the sacred as the *mysterium tremendum et fascinans*—or, as Kripal memorably paraphrases it, "the mystical (*mysterium*) as both fucking scary (*tremendum*) and utterly fascinating (*fascinans*)."[94] In making this case, however, Kripal, like Fort's many of Fort's biographers, is compelled to project a greater coherence onto the Fortean project than it warrants—and that its accretive press-based methodology deliberately defies. He detects a single "Super-Story woven into the heart of his four books," one that belongs to the emergent genre of "science mysticism" and attests "that the earth was being visited by ships from outer space."[95] Certainly, one can find such claims scattered throughout Fort's books—but do they constitute a coherent single story, or, indeed, a story at all? The topical and formal eclecticism of the works complicates such a reading, as do what Kripal himself recognizes as the "constant qualifications, . . . distancing humour, and . . . explicit rejection of the entire epistemology of belief" that form the hallmarks of the Fortean style.[96] Such textual qualities are not easily assimilable within the sincere and focused purpose (that is, arguing for the reality of extra-terrestrial contact) that Kripal attributes to Fort. Yet he is far from alone in taking what we might call an overly systematic or earnest lens to Fort's paranormal compendia. Knight, too, presents the corpus as evidencing, if indirectly, a broad scientific hypothesis than can be empirically confirmed when its supporting "data"—the word Fort uses to describe the reports of anomalous phenomena he draws from the press—is subject to statistical analysis. This Knight does, producing graphs and charts that prove, in his estimation, that anomalous occurrences sweep the globe in waves and are likely attributable to a single, over-arching catalyst: namely, extra-terrestrial interference. Surveying his results, he declares that "[t]he conclusion is inescapable that . . . [t]he cause of the cycles, the controlling force that keeps them in synchrony, must lie outside the earth."[97]

For such extrapolations from Fort's books to be true, both readers, and indeed, the author himself, would need to have faith in the objective validity of their reported data, none of which Fort collected at first hand. The accounts of mysterious disappearances, rains of blood, frogs, and gelatine, strange geoglyphic marks, spontaneous fires, and poltergeist activity come from mediated reports whose reliability we would do well to scrutinize, and whose specific genre provenance and production conditions are often downplayed or simply misrepresented by the champions of Fortean coherence. Consider, for example, Knight's response to an anticipated objection that "the frequency of reports does not correlate to frequency of occurrence, but to some other factor—interest of newspaper editors in mysterious happenings, say."[98] He claims first that editors are not so fickle as to notice anomalies in one year and not the next, and then that scientific journals were the main source of Fort's data. Such professional periodicals, he insists, can be trusted fully, being more objective, reliable in their judgment, and empirically robust than the more dubious format of the newspaper. "[T]he words 'newspaper editors,' above, are a red herring," he claims, "Fort drew most of his data from scientific publications, not newspapers."[99] Yet Knight is wrong here on both counts. The history of retraction, debate, and supersession within scientific periodicals shows that their contents are nowhere near as incontrovertible or final as Knight would like to make them, even if their findings are more rigorously reviewed than those reported in the daily press. And it is simply untrue that Fort consistently favored the scientific over the mainstream press, a fact nowhere more evident than in in his final book, *Wild Talents*, a compendium of strange deaths, disappearances, and superhuman abilities whose contents are drawn entirely from the newspapers. To understand the formal impact and innovation of Fort's writing, we need to put the newspaper at the center of its interpretative frame, and to consider more cautiously the authority and ontological status which he attributes to the press.

We can approach this task by first examining Fort's attitudes to the journalistic profession in which he spent most of his salaried working life, and from whose outputs, in *Wild Talents* at least, he drew his data. His career as a pioneering armchair paranormal researcher came at the end of a long apprenticeship in the press. As a young man, he was employed as a reporter for the Albany *Democrat* and the Brooklyn *World*, and then as editor of the short-lived Queens-based weekly, the *Independent*.[100] These experiences forged his livelihood and fueled his creative imagination alike, forming the subject of many of the comic short stories he produced in the first decade of the twentieth century when he was trying to launch his career as a fiction writer. These repeatedly draw humorous effect from the fundamentally untrustworthy and often fabricated contents of the daily newspaper. In stories like "I Meddled," "In a Newspaper Office," "Glencliff's Mysterious Burglar," "With the Assistance of Fryhuysen," and "Fryhuysen's Colony,"[101] all published between 1905 and 1906, we repeatedly encounter Barnumesque reporters who conceal, skew, and err, and who invent the details of events they are too lazy to attend in person. Thus, en route to an assignment at a political meeting, the seasoned reporter-narrator of "In a Newspaper Office"

130   OPEN SECRETS

reflects that no "reporting was necessary. Just describe any meeting you've seen, and the description will do. As to the speech—it was in typewriting, and there was not copies enough to go around. Bungway of the *Standard* got a copy, and I went with him to his room to take it down, both of us agreeing at what points to interpolate 'Applause!' 'Laughter!' 'Great Applause!'"[102] More than just a sendup of lax journalistic ethics, this passage is also a tribute to the keen creativity of a profession whose members, however work-shy, have an unerring ability to understand the public mind, and to know what readers will expect and accept to have happened, regardless of whether it did or not.

Indeed, in Fort's short stories, this ability to scry the public mind is sometimes so strong as to equip reporters with quasi-magical abilities, rendering them able to conjure into reality the fictions they invent so as to spare themselves the labor of reportage. Consider the eponymous layabout reporter in "Fryhuysen's Colony" who writes up for his Sunday column an improbable story about a bizarre urban squatters' colony peopled with "a cave dweller," an "old woman with . . . seventeen goats," and a "one-legged sailor."[103] Back in the office, he brags to his peers about this latest feat of his superlative imagination: "Why, I never wrote a story more than a fifth true in all my life. Anybody could just sit down and describe what he sees. Where's the art in that?"[104] This pride turns to panic when the editor, sensing his bluff, requests that Fryhuysen and the paper's in-house artist escort him to the colony so he can see it for himself. All three are astonished when, arriving at the named location, they find the colony in place and exactly as described, complete with monopedal maritimer, the troglodyte, and seventeen goats. Intriguingly, Fryhuysen reacts not with relief but shame. "Humiliated," we are told, he "hung his head. He had boasted of his imagination, but this time, perhaps for the novelty of it, had written up things that only existed."[105] Fort's deliberately ambiguous phrasing here allows for a range of interpretation. Perhaps Fryhuysen had known all along that the colony was real, and simply wanted to pass off this oddity as a creation of his own remarkable invention. But the sentence does not absolutely confirm this pre-knowledge; it simply states that the things of which he had written "merely existed," whether he knew of them or not. Certainly, Fryhuysen's anxiety about the expedition allows for the possibility that he might have expected a very different outcome. However we read this coy conclusive statement, this story establishes, like so many of Fort's newspaper-focused tales, that in the world of the press the distinction between the real and the invented is by no means stable, and that the latter may in any case prove superior to the former.

It would be naïve to believe that Fort simply abandoned such reservations about the factuality of the press, ones experientially derived from his own work as reporter and editor, when he took up the mantle of paranormal researcher. Indeed, Fort's "damned" data is not presented as having any definite ontological character at all; his stories have been chosen less for their specific content or relationship to the truth, than for what he presents as the injustice of their rejection by what he calls "Dogmatic Science."[106] Any clear binaristic distinction between truth and falsehood would, in any case, betray the "intermediatism" that forms the centerpiece of Fort's thought. Described in Jack Hunter's words as a "kind of ontological indeterminacy,"[107] Fortean intermediatism sees all existence as "a flow, or a current, or an attempt, from negativeness to positiveness, and is intermediate to both."[108] This sense of flow between poles is also captured by the verbs Fort repeatedly used to describe the anomalous phenomena he termed "damned"—they do not stand or sit; they march and process. Thus, *The Book of the Damned* opens by hailing "A procession of the damned" made up "of data that Science has excluded. Battalions of the accursed, captained by pallid data that I have exhumed, will march . . . they'll go by like Euclid arm in arm with the spirit of anarchy."[109] And this incessant mobility is best captured—or indeed produced—by the non-cumulative serial periodical print forms from which the data is culled. Fort suggests as much when he explains, in the latter work, his decision not to consult book sources:

> it is from periodicals that we must get our data. To the writers of books upon meteorites, it would be as wicked—by which we mean departure from the characters of an established species—quasi-established, of course— as would be, to something in a barnyard, a temptation that it climb a tree and catch a bird. Domestic things in a barnyard: and how wild things from forests outside seem to them. Or the homeopathist—but we shall shovel data of coal.[110]

One of the most stylistically fascinating passages in Fort's corpus, the words here break down syntactically into the very indeterminacy that the writer lauds in his chosen periodical dataset. Books, he suggests, are fixed species with set rules that confine their contents within accepted parameters. Periodicals, by contrast, are more open to ontological subversion, able to straddle both the domestic and the wild because their audiences do not expect them to deliver orthodoxy. Lacking any requirement to connect all their parts, to exhaust their topics, or indeed, to endure, periodicals become the ideal staging ground for the procession of damned data.

The qualities that *The Book of the Damned* attributes to periodicals are only more pronounced in the newspaper medium that provides the entirety of his source base for *Wild Talents*. Like all of Fort's works, its content is diffuse and eclectic; if the work is definable at all, it as a collection of events that superficially seem like crimes—fires, disappearances, sudden deaths, vandalism, mass infection outbreaks—but which are implied to be the result of extraordinary and paranormal human abilities, the "wild talents" of its title. These data are drawn from a wide array of regional, national, and specialist newspapers that were published in Britain and the United States largely between 1876 and the 1920s: the *Derby Mercury*, the *News of the World*, *Lloyd's Sunday News*, the *Philadelphia Public Ledger*, the *St. Louis Globe-Democrat*, the *Brooklyn Eagle*, the *Medium and Daybreak*, and *The Spiritualist*, to name just a few. The inclusion of the latter two long-established spiritualist titles does not reflect any investment or endorsement on Fort's part of the wider claims of the movement they represent; on the contrary, the spiritualist hypothesis becomes in *Wild Talents* just one among many explanatory systems that fails to adequately explain or understand the anomalies recorded in the press. Thus, in a discussion of acheiropoietic images, Fort opines that "almost all spirit photographs have been frauds, but . . . a few may not have been—. . . no spirits were present, but . . . occasionally, or very rarely, a quite spookless medium has, in a profound belief in spirits, engendered, out of visualizations, something wraith-like that has been recorded by a camera."[111] Similarly, when reflecting on "poltergeist girls"—young women in whose presence telekinetic phenomena, or, to use a spiritualist lexicon, feats of physical mediumship, had taken place—he suggests that they are not "mediums, controlled by spirits, but that effects in their presence are phenomena of their own powers, or talents, or whatever."[112] Ever a maverick, Fort did not wish to associate himself with any existing theory of the supernatural, however much it might have shared his suspicion of mainstream science—although a closer familiarity with spiritualist literature might have shown him that thought transference was by no means an uncommon explanation within it.[113] Such a recognition would have required the kind of depth-based research and interpretive synthesis that he here and elsewhere deliberately and defiantly eschews. The purpose of *Wild Talents* is not to test or synthesize its sources into a coherent theory, but, via their unruly juxtaposition, to train Fort's readers in the kind of

JOURNOCCULTISM 133

dissociative, conspiratorial reading practices that will short-circuit rational thought and allow the *affective* qualities of the numinous—wonder, awe, terror, ecstasy, mystical connection—to creep in.

In many respects, then, Fort was seeking through his accretive press methodology to reproduce an experience of journoccultural transport akin to the "dwam" state Machen describes in *The London Adventure*. The anomalous, portentous, absurd, and invented coincidences of the Campo Tosto episode are replicated in *Wild Talents*' reflection on a 1911 *New York Herald* human interest story on the seventeenth-century murder of English magistrate Sir Edmund Berry Godfrey. Three men were sentenced and hung for the crime "on Greenberry Hill, London. The names of the murderers were Green, Berry, and Hill. It does seem that this was only a matter of chance. Still, it may have been no coincidence, but a savage pun mixed with murder."[114] Important to note here is that either Fort, or the *New York Herald*, has simply got things wrong.[115] Green, Berry, and Hill were indeed executed—but on London's Primrose Hill, which only afterward came to be named by locals as Greenberry Hill in memory of the execution. Whether the error is Fort's or the newspaper's is moot and of minimal importance; accuracy, after all, was never high on the author's literary priorities. Where nominative determinism does not exist, it can be retrospectively invented to produce the thrill of an unknown that will never resolve into certainty. Indeed, almost immediately after this interlude, Fort cuts off speculation on its import to move onto a new topic, claiming that "near the beginning of a book, I don't like to come out so definitely."[116] Definitiveness is anathema to the mobility of the Fortean project, and the best way to ward it off was through a journalistic source base whose concision, rapidity of composition, and sloppiness of fact checking defies authoritative closure.

Ultimately, Fortean journoccultism does not prize information exchange or knowledge production, but rather something much more visceral and immediate: feeling—the feeling of languorous, vertiginous wonder experienced when reading, in no particular order, and without any urge to fact-check, old newspaper reports of odd occurrences that range from the tragic to the terrifying to the absurd. *Wild Talents* thus operates through an epistemic of affect rather than of objectivity.[117] "Sometimes I am a collector of data," Fort tells us here:

> other times I have joys, when unexpectedly coming upon an outrageous story that may not altogether be a lie . . . but always there is present a

134 OPEN SECRETS

feeling of unexplained relations of events that I note; and it is this far-away haunting, or taunting, awareness, or suspicion, that keeps me piling on.[118]

Among other things, this passage makes clear that attempts to validate and resolve Fort's data into empirical conclusions completely miss the point. Such conclusivity would beggar the joy only possible through the ontological destabilization that his often-unreliable newspaper sources are particularly well equipped to produce. "I can't be somewhat happy, as a writer," he admits, "unless I'm also mauling something."[119] Fort's interest in the affective and sensory aspects of paranormal press reportage is also conveyed in what is perhaps the least acknowledged quality of his work: its rich aesthetic beauty. As a writer he extracts images and incomplete phrases from the newspaper to produce lush prose poems that pay tribute to the mysterious and the ephemeral, reproducing in his syntax the fragmentary form of the clippings from which he compiles his books. Consider the stunning imagistic quality of this passage inspired by a discussion of anomalous rain falls in *The Book of the Damned:*

Black rain—red rains—the fall of a thousand tons of butter.
Jet-black snow—pink snow—blue hailstones—hailstones flavoured like
oranges.
Punk and silk and charcoal.[120]

The sensory, pleasure-driven, and affective quality of Fort's writing is entirely lost if we attempt to reduce it to just one particular "super-story" about a particular hypothesis—about extra-terrestrial visitation, esoteric correspondences, or human psychical abilities—derived from factual sources. A mistake of much twentieth-century Forteana has been to try to validate the books by annexing them within the domain of the social or even natural sciences, to view Fort himself as a rigorous if untrained anthropologist, a collector of neglected but nonetheless true facts that would yield rich results if subject to scientific testing. It is far more accurate to position him as a poet of the paranormal press, a journoccultist whose response to the earlier, informational project of press mediumship is to explode its primary ontological and epistemological tenets. Stead's Julia and Swaffer's Northcliffe would be completely ill at ease and out of place in the resulting Fortean milieu, where inconclusive newspaper paragraphs, phrases, and images accrete endlessly in defiance of organizing principle, narrative, or headline.

The subversive force is Fort's journoccultural technique is only strengthened by what might seem like his counterintuitive decision to present his findings in the very print book form he repeatedly rejected within his source base. Although, since the 1973 launch of *Fortean Times*, Forteanism is now firmly associated with the magazine format, it was in Fort's lifetime a book brand. In making this choice, the author seemed to align his findings with the established print hierarchies of the occult milieu on whose fringes he would circulate. As discussed earlier in the chapter, the book—preferably rare, ancient, singular, and cryptic—had become by the late nineteenth central a central imaginative and ideological totem for many occult revivalists, representing the cultural prestige, tradition, intellectual extension, and knowledge capital that they so ardently wanted to associate with their movements. The periodical, by contrast, favored the eclectic, the non-linear, and the ephemeral, epitomizing in its serial form not ancient, fixed truths but the constant march of all print into desuetude. "Read today and rubbish tomorrow," writes Margaret Beetham, "each number of a periodical becomes obsolete as soon as the next comes out."[121] Furthermore, she continues, the individual issue:

> does not demand to be read from front to back in order. It is an unusual reader of any periodical who reads every word "from cover to cover," let alone in the order in which they are printed. Most readers will construct their own order ... The average reader will also select and read only a fraction of the whole. The periodical, therefore, is a form which openly offers readers the chance to construct their own texts.[122]

What works like *Wild Talents* achieve is to deploy an anarchically eclectic and non-conclusive structure that encourages—even compels—audiences to read the book *as if* it were a continuing periodical, and hence without the requirement of commitment, the intention of exhaustivity, or the expectation of linear development and conclusion. Neither the latter's narrative, nor the newspaper excerpts which comprise its evidence, are presented in any kind of structured chronological order. The book opens with a report of a mysterious fire in Derby in 1905 and closes with the case of a supposed perpetual motion engine whose inventor, John Worrell Keely, died in 1898. The connection between these two events is never spelled out; they are as much, or as little, linked as any of the phenomena in the Fortean universe, which is to say both entirely and not at all.

136   OPEN SECRETS

Wild Talent's final sentence—a fragment, of course—offers a last and gleeful riposte to the hegemony of the book, and to its conventions of narrative closure. It comes in the form of a detached subordinate clause that speculates on Keely's personal beliefs about the engine. "Justifying himself," Fort writes, "in the midst of promises that came to nothing, because he could say to himself something that Galileo should have said, but did not say— 'Nevertheless it does move!'"[123] From the vantage of readers with bookish and, indeed, grammatical, expectations, this line feels clumsy and incomplete. Yet its composition in the form of a subclause whose grammatical subject is yet to come acts a tribute to the continuity on which serial publications rely. The book may have ended, this phrasing suggests, but its occultural enterprise, and the incessant flood of print on which it relies, moves endlessly forward. It marches.

This chapter has traced the evolution of a distinctive journoccultural literary mode spawned by and developed in tandem with the late Victorian advent of the new journalism, a popular reportage style in whose rhetorical features and attention-grabbing techniques it would seek to detect the numinous. At the heart of this mode sits a rejection of the book and of depth reading as the privileged means through which to transact textual encounters with spiritual or paranormal beings; instead, it finds in the newspaper column a superior spiritual tool. Yet, as we have seen, not all forms of journoccultism approached this task with the same motives, nor achieved the same outcomes. The rationalistic, information-focused work of early Spiritualist journalists like Stead and Swaffer sought to bring the other world distinctly down to earth on the newspaper page, to mine it for practical detail about post-life existence and to interview its denizens as a means of confirming their identities and retrieving important professional advice. For them, the journalistic framing and presentation of spiritualist communication extended the movement's wider commitment to *familiarizing* the supernatural, to making the doings of the dead, and the activities of the spirit world no more remarkable than the contents of the daily newspaper. For Machen and Fort, however, it was the very strangeness of the press—its erratic, unreliable, content, and the sometimes ludicrous and serendipitous coincidences thrown up by journalistic work—that equipped it to probe an ultimately much more ludic, inscrutable, disorienting, and sinister occult world than modern spiritualism was typically willing to entertain. Far from simply providing new concrete facts about the other world, their vein of journoccultism launches a full-scale attack on the idea of information as a straightforward process of knowledge transfer from A and to B, and between people with shared ontological presumptions. Instead, the newspaper becomes an agent of profound disorientation, sending its reporters into epiphanic dwams and breaking the ability of its readers to tell fact from fiction, beginning from end, and one thing from another. The differences between these two forms of journoccultism no doubt reflect and extend wider social responses to the new journalism itself, one in whose reception history they play a notable if often overlooked role. What, they ask, should the press page do—consolidate a new consensual reality linking the public and otherworldly spheres, or rather revel in the fragmentation of such a prospect? However they answered this question, journoccultists knew it could only be approached by looking squarely *at* rather than *through* the formal features of the newspaper, by centering the role of the latter in shaping and intensifying the meaning of the esoteric subjects they addressed. These literary innovators moved beyond the book to find and foster the numinous in the ultra-modern headlines and paratactic paragraphs of the daily newspaper, a form ideally suited, in their estimation, to reveal the incessant flux, rather than enduring permanence, of the unseen world.

5

Occult Detection in the Aeon of Horus

Crime and its detection are ubiquitous within occult fiction, offering compelling pretexts through which to expound and model the moral, philosophical, and simply practical benefits of an esoteric worldview. Nearly all of the texts we have encountered in our study thus far are punctuated by at least one murder, whether it be of Haroun of Aleppo and Sir Philip Derval in *A Strange Story*; of the German woman, Frau Ebenstein, in Emma Hardinge-Britten's *Ghost Land*, whose assailant is tracked clairvoyantly by the proto-occult detective Zwingler; or, in Corelli's *Ziska*, of the titular ancient Egyptian temple dancer who waits through the ages to deliver bloody justice to the lover who killed her in the reign of Amenhotep. In their fascination with the occult dimensions of murder and its investigation, Bulwer, Britten, and Corelli extended a religiously inflected tradition of crime writing that, argues Maurizio Ascari, has its origins in the Book of Genesis and in mediaeval morality plays where "the primal detective and judge is God himself."[1] The ostensibly rationalist mode of literary detection associated with Sherlock Holmes—himself, ironically, the creation of a spiritualist author—may remain one of detective fiction's best-known global brands, but it is not the genre's oldest or exclusive form, nor, as we will explore in greater detail in this chapter's first half, was it itself ever wholly devoid of theological resonance. The intimacy between detective fiction and heterodox spirituality became closer than ever in the early decades of the twentieth century, as the genre consolidated its enduringly central position within Britain's popular literary market and the occult revival reached its peak. In this period, esoteric students, seekers, and practitioners of all stripes increasingly turned to the detective plot to stage and solve the problems of a deeply unjust world desperately in need of the spiritual, moral, and legal reform that they believed their movements were uniquely equipped to provide. The genre's appeal for such writers lay not just in its potential to reach wide audiences disinclined to pick up arcane magical treatises, nor in the empirical, evidence-based techniques of its protagonists that evoked the patina of scientific authority increasingly important to modern occultism; it was encapsulated also in the detective narrative's

---

Open Secrets. Christine Ferguson, Oxford University Press. © Oxford University Press 2025.
DOI: 10.1093/oso/9780197651599.003.0005

provision of a textual-philosophical space through which to stage questions of spiritual ethics, legality, and justice. In its pages, readers could consider which secular and spiritual laws required adherence, and which it was their duty or destiny to transgress; so, too, might they imaginatively assess the spiritual fitness of the classic juridical responses—"retribution, deterrence, incapacitation, rehabilitation" or "restoration"[2]—meted out to those who fail to make the right distinction.

This chapter examines how these questions are taken up within the remarkable occult detective stories written by Britain's most influential—and indeed, notorious—twentieth-century magical practitioner: Aleister Crowley (1875–1947). Starting in 1916, Crowley penned twenty-three stories featuring the Thelemic investigator Simon Iff, one of the most philosophically invested and morally anarchic occult detectives ever to appear on page. Of these, only the first six appeared in print during Crowley's lifetime, serialized as "The Scrutinies of Simon Iff" in *The International* between September 1917 and February 1918; it is on these that we will focus. In what follows, I will situate Iff within the contemporary forms of rationalist and occult literary detection that inspired his creation, and from whose canons and critical histories he has for too long been absent. The sometimes socially conservative tenor of these surrounding genre expressions, particularly as manifested within Golden Age detection, throws the revolutionary character of Crowley's detective into sharper relief; so, too, however, does the comparison allow us to recognize the deeply reactionary, retrograde, and elitist currents into which Iff's spirituo-legal philosophy often flowed. "The Scrutinies of Simon Iff" offered Crowley a fertile ground through which to apply the controversial and cryptic tenets of *The Book of the Law* (1904), the received text on which his new religious system of Thelema was founded, to fictionalized transgressions of secular and spiritual law. In their investigative solutions, the stories also render the hard limits of Crowley's radical, anti-bourgeois philosophy dramatically apparent.

Before turning to Crowley's fiction, we will first trace two lines of development within modern British detective fiction that made the genre particularly ripe for Thelemic intervention and subversion: first, its increasing embourgeoisification, and, second, its growing accommodation of an enchanted worldview, one signified both through its accommodation of fatalistic or eschatological notions of justice and through its incubation of an occult sub-genre, one to which the *Iff* stories, grounded in esoteric philosophy but empty of supernatural content, stand as outliers. In the figure of

140 OPEN SECRETS

Simon Iff, the Aeon of Horus and the Golden Age come together in an explosive combination that allows us rethink established histories of the occult detective genre and of Crowley's social politics alike.

5.1 Forming Murder in the Golden Age

When Crowley composed his first *Iff* stories in December 1916, he was entering the lists of a well-established and hugely popular fictional genre then blossoming into what would become known retrospectively as its "Golden Age." Dated loosely between the First and Second World Wars,[3] the golden age of British detective fiction was long viewed as the most conservative and formulaic—indeed, conservative *because* formulaic—era in the genre's history. While this broad characterization of the golden age's political orientation and formal logic has been persuasively nuanced in recent years,[4] it was commonplace in the early decades of the twentieth century and deserves our attention for its likely influence on Crowley's own more deliberately defiant approach. Perhaps the most important innovation, and widely recognized convention, of the golden age plot is its standardization of the "plot-puzzle formula,"[5] one that minimizes the morally disturbing and emotionally traumatizing aspects of murder—its bloodiness and visceral devastation, or the tragically sacrificed potential of its victims—to focus instead on the mechanics of its detection. Heather Walton summarizes its features as such:

> A crime occurs—usually a murder—the circumstances of which are mysterious. A detective appears or is appointed, and an investigation is launched. Evidence and alibis are required, and false solutions are considered and discarded. Finally, a solution is proposed. Arrest or another form of "containment"—suicide, perhaps, or the death of the murderer at the hands of a member of the cast—is the next step. A marriage between former suspects—in Christie, frequently of the young and attractive kind—often completes the mood or resolution.[6]

We can see this formula in action in Agatha Christie's landmark first novel. *The Mysterious Affair at Styles*, written in 1916 and published in 1920, in which the controlling family matriarch, Mrs. Emily Inglethorp, is poisoned by her much younger new husband, Alfred, and his second cousin, Evie Howard. The murderous duo successfully deflect suspicion onto competing members of household until the superior "little grey cells" of master detective Hercule Poiret see through their ruse.[7] The novel then closes with the union of two young couples: the estranged married couple John and Mary Cavendish and the long unrequited lovers Cynthia Murdoch and Lawrence Cavendish. Their relationships are now free to flourish because they have been purged of mutual suspicion by the arrest of the true culprits.

Critics have attributed the appeal of this formula to its delivery of soothing familiarity to an early-twentieth-century audience reeling from the combined traumas of the First World War and the 1918–1920 flu pandemic. In the place of uncertainty and chaos, it offered a number of seeming guarantees: first, that its instigating murder, although sensational, would not be so upsetting as to detract attention from the game of detection; then, that its plot would move at a bracing but not exhausting or unbalanced pace toward a definite solution; and finally, that its solution would neither be too obvious, nor impossible, to guess, and hence a sense of "fair play" would be preserved in the reader–author contract.[8] In fulfilling these expectations, golden age detection came to acquire what Lee Horsely dubs a "cozy" quality, one in which "a comfortably recognizable pattern . . . is acted out in a familiar domestic setting, with the restoration of reassuring orderliness guaranteed."[9] Yet while formulaic repetition and a reassuring restoration of order—whether emotional, moral, social, or political—are common within golden age detection, these qualities are not ubiquitous nor mutually inclusive. Indeed, as we will see, "The Scrutinies of Simon Iff" reproduces some of the era's most familiar detective tropes to lead its readers into a distinctly unsettling moral and philosophical terrain.

Beyond its formulaic plotting, perceptions of golden age detection's conventionality have been deepened also by its dominant geographical settings, class milieu, gender and racial coordinates, and indeed, generalized ontology. Murders cluster in the country houses and genteel, lily white villages of England's shrinking post-First World War rural arcadia; even when shifting to urban locations, Horsely notes, golden era writing remains based largely "within the restricted milieu of fashionable society . . . in an *exclusive* setting,"[10] one into which only certain kinds of characters are permitted to enter. Literary detectives were being increasingly retooled for respectability and normality at the time of Crowley's writing, continuing an upward social trajectory underway since the nineteenth-century origins of modern crime fiction in the Newgate novel.[11] More and more, eccentric geniuses like Arthur Conan Doyle's Holmes were being crowded out by respectable

142   OPEN SECRETS

plain men sleuths like G. K. Chesterton's Father Brown and Christie's Miss Marple, who needed no elaborate disguise to pass as bourgeois within the polite social and domestic environments in which their investigations regularly took place. Their prevailing investigative focus on the home and village encouraged yet another perceived transformation within the genre's identity, namely, its dissociation from "the typical heroic quest of the masculine knight errant" in favor of a much more distinctly "feminized" mode that prioritized sleuthing techniques based on "connection, empathy or ethical feeling" and psychological rapport.[12] This emphasis on the investigative superiority of intuition and empathy to cold, empirical deduction is also embedded within the *Iff* stories, but, again, accompanied by very different moral valences than it would be in non-Thelemic detection.

5.2 Divine Justice and Mumbo Jumbo: Enter the Occult Detective

In the early decades of the twentieth century, as one vein of British detective fiction veered toward formal familiarity, femininity, middle-class mundanity, and respectability, another advanced the genre in an entirely different direction—into the territory of a terrifying, unpredictable, and untamable occult world best navigable by the eccentric male investigators that this particular sub-genre privileged. With roots in earlier Gothic and sensation fiction modes, the occult detective story rose to prominence at the *fin de siècle* in response to both the success of Sherlock Holmes and the ambition of the Society for Psychical Research, a Cambridge-based organization formed in 1882 to subject alleged psychic phenomena to rigorous scientific testing. The occult detective was typically either (or sometimes both) an occult adept or a natural psychic who tackled supernatural mysteries: cases of possession, murder by telepathic suggestion, attack by nature spirits, spiritual vivisection, abduction by fairies, or, most commonly, the inconvenient haunting of stately family houses.[13] During its *fin de siècle* efflorescence—although the sub-genre's popularity, as Nick Rennison and Paul Green remind us, never really went away[14]—it produced landmark fictional investigators such as Kate and Hesketh Prichard's Flaxman Low, dubbed "the Sherlock Holmes of the Ghost World"; Algernon Blackwood's John Silence; W. H. Hodgson's Carnacki the Ghost-Finder; and Sax Rohmer's Moris Klaw, the Dream Detective. These characters advertised their direct debts to the contemporary occult revival by embracing its terminology, peppering their deductive explanations with references to Theosophical shells and elementaries, spirit controls, the akashic library, telepathy, and the astral plane. In this way, they ensured that the occultism they deployed was understood as thoroughly modern and up to date, and not a nostalgic holdover from an eclipsed age suitable only for folk tale and legend. Although some of the sub-genre's best-known practitioners were directly connected with the revival through membership in its societies—both Blackwood and, as we have seen, Arthur Machen spent some time in the Hermetic Order of the Golden Dawn—such affiliation was by no means a requirement of authorship or indeed, success. Far more important than the sincerity, coherence, and accuracy of the eso-teric beliefs and practices represented in this *oeuvre* was its ability to gen-erate a thrilling, pithy plot within the relatively limited space of the short story format that the sub-genre favored. It was only when Crowley and, later, the ceremonial magician Dion Fortune entered its ranks—by far the most eminent and invested occult practitioners to do so—that this balance would shift:[15] an exciting story remained key, but their narratives devote more space than any of their literary peers to the explanation of the guiding eso-teric principles that shape crime in this world and the next.

The relationship between these two divergent strands of British inter-war detective fiction—respectable and familiar, eccentric and occult—is com-plex; certainly, it was never as oppositional or mutually exclusive as some contemporary literary practitioners, both earnestly, or with tongue firmly in cheek, suggested.[16] True, a number of prominent secular golden age writers insisted that the supernatural had no place in what should, they argued, be a thoroughly disenchanted genre. Consider, for example, the stipulation of American author S. S. Van Dine in his 1928 article, "Twenty Rules for Writing Detective Stories" that:

> the problem of crime must be solved by strictly naturalistic means. Such methods for learning the truth as slate-writing, Ouija-boards, mind-reading, spiritualist séances, crystal gazing, and the like, are taboo. A reader has a chance when matching his wits with a rationalistic detective, but if he must compete with the world of spirits and go chasing through the fourth dimension of metaphysics, he is defeated *ab initio*.[17]

Out of respect for readerly fair play alone, Van Dine felt occultism had to be ruled ontologically out of bounds, as no uninitiated lay reader could be

144 OPEN SECRETS

expected to anticipate or reach independently the esoteric rationale for a given crime. One year later, in his own "Ten Rules for a Good Detective Story," the Catholic priest and crime novelist Ronald Knox would repeat this prohibition, asserting that "All supernatural or preternatural agencies are ruled out as a matter of course."[18] Perhaps the most proscriptive version of this principle appears in the playful oath that aspirants to membership within the Detection Club, a literary social club formed by golden age luminaries Knox, Chesterton, Dorothy L. Sayers, and others, were required to pledge: "Do you promise," they were asked, "that your detectives shall well and truly detect the crimes presented to them using those wits which it may please you to bestow upon them and not placing reliance on nor making use of Divine Revelation, Feminine Intuition, Mumbo Jumbo, Jiggery-Pokery, Coincidence or Act of God?"[19]

Despite such prohibitions, the occult detective continued to flourish during the high-water era of the genre's secular golden age and remains a staple popular cultural archetype to this day, having successfully migrated from page to small screen in several landmark paranormal series, such as *The X-Files* (1993–2018), *Supernatural* (2005–2020), and *Medium* (2005–2011). The trope's persistence, even in an earlier twentieth-century period when some writers were campaigning for its eradication, is attributable to many factors, not least the fact that the secular Anglo American detective fiction tradition, as a growing scholarly consensus now recognizes, had always already been infused with the spiritual from its nineteenth-century origins in the work of Edgar Allan Poe, Charles Dickens, Mary Elizabeth Braddon, Wilkie Collins, and Conan Doyle.[20] The work of such early genre pioneers has been widely hailed for its ostensibly scientific *ethos*, evident in its prioritization of empirical observation and evidence, incorporation of new forensic and visual technologies, engagement with emergent medical and psychological theories of human behavior, and routine metaphoric borrowings from the biological, geological, anthropological, and philological sciences.[21] Yet, as Andrea Goulet reminds us, Victorian detective fiction took shape at a time when the "boundaries between science and pseudo-science, reason and mystery" remained "blurred";[22] hence, in its pages, we find references to and deployments of heterodox investigative practices such as mesmerism and bertillonage alongside more orthodox techniques of chemical analysis or footprint comparison.[23] Furthermore, even as it oriented itself toward science, both orthodox and otherwise, the genre's genealogical underpinnings in the Gothic remained in place and continued to generate at least the semblance of supernatural threat in works such as Conan Doyle's *The Hound of the Baskervilles* (1902).[24] Even if ultimately debunked via logical explanation, supernatural mumbo-jumbo and divine intervention were never absent from the main stage of British detective fiction.

Perhaps the best example of this entanglement can be found in the legendary consulting detective renowned above all others for his cold, almost mechanistic rationalism and his sometimes-unnerving dedication to scientific inquiry: Sherlock Holmes. In his 1887 fictional debut, *A Study in Scarlet* (1887), Holmes is described to Watson by his associate Stamford as being "a little too scientific for my tastes—it approaches to cold-bloodedness. I could imagine his giving a friend a little pinch of the latest vegetable alkaloid, not out of malevolence, you understand, but simply out of a spirit of inquiry in order to have an accurate idea of the effects."[25] Yet the phenomenally popular stories subsequently serialized in *The Strand* as *The Adventures of Sherlock Holmes* between July 1891 and June 1892 would see the super-sleuth indulge time and time again in providential forms of magical thinking. Thus in "The Boscombe Valley Mystery," Holmes tells the terminally ill murderer John Turner, whose daughter he wishes to protect from scandal, that he will not turn him into the police because "you will soon have to answer for your deed at a higher court than the Assizes."[26] Similarly, in "The Blue Carbuncle," he explains, after dismissing the penitent jewel thief John Ryder without securing his arrest:

> I suppose I am commuting a felony, but it is just possible that I am saving a soul. This fellow will not go wrong again . . . Chance has put in our way a most singular and whimsical problem, and its solution is its own reward.[27]

The power of providence is not only anticipated but borne out in other of the *Adventures*, including "The Five Orange Pips," where a group of murderous Ku Klux Klan conspirators are drowned aboard the *Lone Star* before they can be apprehended, and "The Speckled Band," in which the poisonous snake that the degenerate Anglo-Indian medic Dr. Grimesby Roylott has trained to murder his stepdaughters turns its venom back on him. Holmes describes this outcome as if it were inevitable: "Violence does, in truth, recoil upon the violent, and the schemer falls into the pit which he digs for another."[28] If that were true, however, then surely there would be no need for the investigative intrusions of a detective; justice would simply deliver itself without need of an intentional human agent. Such sentiments represent a magical

146 OPEN SECRETS

form of wish fulfilment, albeit one accommodable within, rather than antagonistic to, the scientific *ethos* that Holmes elsewhere champions. This gentle project of accommodation anticipates the far more extreme form of magico-scientific synthesis that Crowley would seek to forge in his *Iff* stories and, indeed, in his wider magical career.

Far from being wholly disenchanted, then, the Holmes stories incorporate a subtle supernaturalism that is tacit, allusive, optimistic, and providential, assuring readers that justice will inevitably prevail whether within or outside the court system.[29] In the occult detective tradition, by contrast, encounters with the numinous are simultaneously much more explicit and often far more pessimistic, emphasizing the unbridgeable division between the maverick occult investigator and the secular audiences who follow this exploits. Because occult detection relies on knowledge of arcane occult principles and supernormal psychological abilities, so, too, as Dine had charged, does it lack the sense of readerly fair play so important to disenchanted traditions of literary detection. Where readers are guaranteed in the Holmes stories a full, accessible, and empowering deductive explanation that grants them imagined parity with the sleuth—"when I hear you give your reasons," remarks Watson in "A Scandal in Bohemia," "the thing always appears to me to be so ridiculously simple that I could easily do it myself"[30]—they are, in the occult detective tale, more often pawned off with mystifications. "I am sorry that I cannot give you all the links in my chain of reasoning," apologizes Flaxman Low to his baffled client Colonel Daimley at the close of the Prichards's "The Story of the Moor Road" (1898) but "much is still obscure."[31] In this fictional example, as so often in real life, the occultist insider recognizes that his claims can never satisfy the normative evidentiary standards held by nonbelievers; he simply urges his hearer to take it on trust. Similarly, the narrator of Blackwood's 1908 occult detective story, "A Psychical Invasion" (1908), deems the attempt to forge a shared evidentiary consensus with readers so pointless as to refuse to attempt it altogether; after describing the experiences of "physician extraordinary" John Silence in a haunted house, he asserts: "It is impossible here, nor would it be intelligible to the reader unversed in the knowledge of the region known to a scientifically trained psychic like Dr Silence, to detail these observations. But to him, it was clear, up to a certain point."[32]

Just as occult detection's solutions were less commonly predictable—because more esoteric—than those of the secular detective plot, so, too, were they implicitly less reassuring; indeed, they are often stubbornly futile. This is not to say that the sub-genre's plots never conclude with happy endings or

OCCULT DETECTION IN THE AEON OF HORUS   147

successful exorcisms, but rather that such outcomes are never guaranteed, nor is the delivery of the instigating criminal, often dead for centuries or non-human, to law. Indeed, the fact that such spectral transgressors have been able to haunt the living at all suggests that the providential post-life courts alluded to in the Holmes stories might be ineffective or non-existent. The occult detective story can, at best, provide *knowledge* of otherworldly criminality, but satisfying triumph over its supernatural agents is far more elusive. We can see this tendency in two of the earliest British examples of the sub-genre: Samuel Warren's *Passages from the Diary of a Late Physician* (1830–1837) and Sheridan Le Fanu's *In a Glass Darkly* (1872). In these are presented the case histories of Warren's eponymous physician and of Le Fanu's Swedenborgian doctor, Martin Hesselius, respectively; while the former only occasionally ventures into occult territory, the latter always does. In Warren's "The Spectral Dog," a respectable Church of England clergyman seeks relief from a persistent canine apparition which follows him wherever he goes; moreover, he wants assurance that it is the product of a somatic disruption or an optical illusion, and not, as he fears, an actual manifestation of a chaotic supernatural world in which he desperately does not want to believe. Himself perplexed by the case, Warren's physician can offer no such consolatory explanation, and, while the specter ultimately disappears, the narrative offers no guarantee that it will not return as suddenly and unexpectedly as it arrived. Even less fortunate than Warren's clergyman is the hapless patient Mr. M. in "The Spectre-Smitten," a young London lawyer with a penchant for "*diablerie* and mysticism"[33] who comes home one night to find the phantom of his newly dead neighbor sitting in his armchair. This malevolent presence proceeds to haunt his every waking moment and ultimately drives him to madness by plaguing him with horrific visions of the hell to which he believes himself now bound. Attempting and failing to find a medical basis for these symptoms, the late physician reluctantly finds himself pulled toward a supernatural hypothesis when, in full mania, Mr. M. describes with total accuracy the events in a nearby room which he could have had no earthly means of witnessing. After a long asylum stay, Mr. M. seems to recover most of his wits only to spontaneously relapse several years later and commit suicide during a family holiday to Brussels.

Le Fanu's Hesselius stories bring us even closer to the sub-genre's mature *fin de siècle* expression by replacing the agnosticism of Warren's physician, who occasionally entertains but never commits to a wholly supernatural explanation of mental illness, with absolute belief in the spirit world. In

148 OPEN SECRETS

"Green Tea," the opening story in *In a Glass Darkly*, Hesselius immediately recognizes the otherworldly provenance of the fiendish monkey who stalks his beleaguered patient, the Reverend Mr. Jennings, with "unfathomable malignity."[34] Hard at work on a book about "the religious metaphysics of the ancients,"[35] Jennings has, as Hesselius explains, unintentionally opened his spiritual inner eye by drinking large quantities of green tea; in consequence, he is now able to see, and worse yet, be seen by, hostile elementary spirits who "hate man with a deadly hatred."[36] Before Hesselius can properly treat his symptoms, the despairing Jennings take a razor to his own throat. Despite his patient's suicide, the doctor insists on framing the case as success: "I have not," he declares, "the slightest doubt that I should have first dimmed and ultimately sealed that inner eye which Mr Jennings had inadvertently opened . . . I have never yet failed."[37] Yet with victories such as these, one wonders, who needs failures? Similarly pyrrhic victories pervade occult detection's early twentieth-century corpus, evident in works such as the Prichards's "The Story of the Moor Road," Claude and Alice Askew's "The Fear" (1914), and Katherine Mary Dalton Renoir's "The Case of the Fortunate Youth" (1927) in which the victims of psychic attack are forced to flee or destroy their homes in order to ensure their own survival. In such forced concessions to an aggressively expansionist—and simply aggressive *tout court*—supernatural milieu, it is very difficult to identify the fulfilled fantasy of Edenic restoration that W. H. Auden famously hailed as definitive feature of golden age detection, asserting that "[t]he phantasy . . . which the detective story addict indulges is the phantasy of being restored to the Garden of Eden, to a state of innocence, where he may know love as love and not as the law."[38] In its loosening of the implied connections between detection, justice, and redemption, the occult detective narrative furnished the conditions in which the radically amoral, extra-legal, and often deeply noninterventionist meanderings of Crowley's Simon Iff could thrive. It is to this character, and its radically reactionary incubation of the most pessimistic, fatalistic, and misanthropic aspects of its host sub-genre, that I will now turn.

5.3 The Birth of Simon Iff

Conceived during what Crowley would later describe as "an ecstasy of creative energy," the Thelemic detective Simon Iff was as much a child of need as of inspiration.[39] His forty-one-year-old creator was near destitute and mired in the controversies—personal, moral, political, and religious—that would form a dominant keynote of his subsequent reputation.[40] The first six *Iff* stories, written between late December 1916 and mid-January 1917,[41] were intended to alleviate Crowley's penury by packaging Thelemic philosophy in an accessible, lively, and commercially proven popular fictional format, aimed at a much larger audience than his more abstruse non-fictional writings that were then available only in extremely limited edition. They were published in *The International* between September 1917 and February 1918 under the series heading *The Scrutinies of Simon Iff* and signed by "Edward Kelly," the pseudonym that Crowley borrowed from the magical partner of Renaissance magus Dr. John Dee. Never one to hide his light under a bushel, Crowley, then also editor of *The International*, billed the Thelemic sleuth as "the greatest sensation since Sherlock Holmes. Simon Iff is an entirely original character, and his method of detection is the most fascinating in all literature."[42] Although Iff never achieved the public recognition anticipated here, he clearly captivated his creator. Crowley would return to Iff again and again in the following years, featuring him as presiding millenarian magus in the war thriller-cum-occult *roman à clef*, *The Butterfly Net*, written in 1917 and first published as *Moonchild* in 1929, and then as protagonist in three new short story sequences, *Simon Iff in America*, *Simon Iff Abroad*, and *Simon Iff, Psychoanalyst*, none of which saw print during their author's lifetime. Indeed, there would be no republication of the *Iff* stories at all until 1987, when Martin P. Starr edited a single volume version of *The Scrutinies* for Teitan Press. All four *Iff* collections would only be published together— the latter three for the very first time—in William Breeze's 2012 edition of *The Simon Iff Stories and Other Works*, which appears in Wordsworth's Tales of Mystery and the Supernatural series. Among other consequences, this protracted publication history meant that Iff was largely unavailable to readers during Crowley's revival as a counter-cultural icon in the 1960s and plays little part in his *mythos* or new religious legacy. As a result, contemporary Crowley scholars have had very little to say about the *Scrutinies* beyond identifying their thinly veiled basis in the incidents and associations of Crowley's interwar biography. I seek, by contrast, to position *The Scrutinies*, and the affordance of their framing genre, at the very heart of Crowley's creative and magical program in this period, recognizing Iff as a dynamic creative vehicle through the magus sought to test, apply, and shape the reception of the most controversial implications of the still nascent Thelemic philosophical system he had received over a decade earlier.

150   OPEN SECRETS

To take *The Scrutinies* seriously in this way requires us first to reject the trivialization, implicit elitism, and biographical reductionism in which the very few existing critical accounts of the stories have been mired, even those produced by some of Crowley's most important scholarly defenders. In his introduction to the 1987 Teitan Press edition of *The Scrutinies*, for example, Starr contends, "They were intended to be entertainment, not serious literature."[43] This idea that high cultural literary seriousness might be neatly separated from the mere diversion offered by commercially focused genre fiction—that the two forms of expression were classes apart, and hard opposites—is one that was already unsustainable at the time of Crowley's writing. In the early twentieth century, as Andreas Huyssen observes in his influential *After the Great Divide* (1986), "modernism's insistence on the autonomy of the art work, its obsessive hostility to mass culture, its radical separation from the culture of everyday life, and its programmatic distance from political, economic, and social concerns was always challenged as soon as it arose."[44] Indeed the *Iff* stories furnish an excellent example of this very challenge, adopting a popular fictional form to explore the radical new ideas about human subjectivity and personality fostered by the ascension of psychoanalytic theory and the traumatic resonances of First World War.[45] Furthermore, it makes little sense to impute such an iron-cast view of the distinction between high and low culture—between amusement and elevation—to a magical iconoclast who, from his provocative 1909 publication of rites of the Hermetic Order of the Golden Dawn in *The Equinox*, had dedicated his career to the project of occult expansion and popularization. Crowley himself refused to quarantine these different dimensions of his literary *oeuvre*; thus, even while commenting negatively on the later unpublished *Iff* stories (of which he thought less highly than *The Scrutinies*), he concedes: "I find it hard to consider this sort of thing as serious literature, and yet so ineradicable is the artistic instinct in me that the Old Adam peeps out sufficiently often to remove these stories from the category of *jeux d'esprit*."[46]

Despite the author's own insistences on their aesthetic significance, thus far the main—even only—role allotted to the stories within Crowley scholarship has been as containers of useful biographical information. In his foreword to the Wordsworth edition of Crowley's *The Drug and Other Stories*, David Tibet deems the contents of the collection to be "manifestations of a continual autobiography" which "resonate on several levels," including "that of pure entertainment . . . self-promotion and occult instruction," but not, it seems from the subsequent discussion, of literary innovation.[47]

Now, it certainly is possible to read the *Iff* canon as an index to its author's life, with the detective, as has been widely acknowledged, functioning as a highly romanticized prospective self-portrait of how Crowley would have liked to be seen in old age—witty, sage, calm, universally respected, and living a life of comfort and ease. *The Scrutinies* also contain barely veiled allusions to Crowley's real-life lovers, magical, partners, and enemies, such as Rose Kelly, Jeanne Merton, Jeanne Robert Foster, Robert Murray Leslie, Ananda Kentish Coomaraswamy, and Ratan Devi.[48] Yet to read the stories only as gossipy clues to Crowley's personal relationships is to significantly impoverish our understanding of their aesthetic complexity and ambition. The ease with which *The Scrutinies*, and indeed, the wider *Iff* oeuvre, lend themselves to biographical interpretation must not shut down other, more formally cognizant and genre-focused approaches to their interpretation, especially when their primary genre was of such demonstrable significance to their writer.

As his one-time secretary and fellow occult practitioner, Israel Regardie observed that Crowley was "an inveterate reader and connoisseur of detective stories,"[49] his passion for the genre triggering some of his earliest acts of insubordination against the rigid constraints of his repressive Plymouth Brethren upbringing. In *The Confessions*, Crowley recounts how virtually all works of secular popular fiction were barred to him in his youth, lest they lead him into moral turpitude and hedonism: "I was absolutely cut off from literature. One or two books of Scott and Dickens were permitted. Ballantyne was approved, G. A. Henty winked at rather than openly tolerated."[50] Nonetheless, he defiantly smuggled illicit titles into the house to read furtively in the family water-closet; fascinatingly, the text *The Confessions* names as object of this practice is Fergus Hulme's *The Mystery of a Hansom Cab* (1886), the phenomenally popular Australian detective novel that outperformed Conan Doyle's *A Study in Scarlet* when it was published in Britain in 1887. "My mother considered the hansom cab as an engine devised by the devil," Crowley here remarks, "and any reference to one was considered obscene."[51] There is something undeniably apposite in this image of a youthful Crowley squatting over a toilet while voraciously consuming a ripping bestseller whose genre and ultra-modern subject had been deemed obscene within his strenuously evangelical household; it pleasingly augurs and aggregates his future interests in fiction, filth, and pleasurable rebellion. Detective fiction, as this episode suggests, appealed to Crowley's iconoclastic imagination as a subject of prohibition, and hence as a powerful vehicle, like

152 OPEN SECRETS

the cab itself, for moral transgression; it is little wonder then, that references to the genre's classic works and major authors pervade the *Confessions* and indeed, his wider literary *oeuvre*.[52] The Beast's lifelong intimacy with literary detection and fascination with its potentially subversive cultural capital rendered it an staging ground for his interwar reckoning with the volatile tension between—and within—the secular legal systems whose principles detective fiction had traditionally served, and the Thelemic Law of absolute self-liberation that his new philosophical system mandated.

5.4 Books of the Law

It is difficult to conceive of a more fitting choice than the detective story for the fictional experimentation of an occult practitioner whose entire magickal career can be understood as an attempt to interrogate and overturn extant social, moral, and religious understandings of legality.[53] The roots of this project lie in the remarkable revealed text, *The Book of the Law*, that Crowley received while on honeymoon with his first wife, Rose Kelly, in Cairo in 1904. Delivered by the otherworldly messenger Aiwass, a "discarnate . . . intelligence, both alien and superior to myself, yet acquainted with my inmost secrets,"[54] the book is composed of three parts attributed to the ancient Egyptian deities Nuit, Hadit, and Ra-Hoor-Khuit, respectively. It announces the coming of a new era that would jettison what Crowley saw as the tyranny, repression, and slavish groupthink of western Christianity in favor of a new era of pleasure, individual liberation, and strength: the Aeon of Horus. The *ethos* of this dawning age would be served and cultivated by Thelema, the new religious movement based upon *The Book of the Law* and named after the Greek word for will. Thelema's central spiritual philosophy is encapsulated in *The Book of the Law*'s three well-known axioms: "Do What Thou Wilt Shall be the Whole of the Law"; "Love is the law, love under will"; and "There is no law beyond Do what thou Wilt."[55] As Crowley would explain, these directives were in no way to be interpreted as endorsements of an erratic, impulsive, and undisciplined hedonism that licensed individuals to do whatever they wanted, regardless of consequence; on the contrary, they demand that seekers take seriously the attempt to study, reveal, and fulfil the dictates of their true will; that is, their wholly unique, authentic inner nature, the "purpose to which [they] must devote [themselves] . . . to the exclusion of all else."[56] Far from being simply personal or even solipsistic, this disciplined

OCCULT DETECTION IN THE AEON OF HORUS 153

investigation and embrace of the will would have, Crowley insisted, profoundly positive social and political consequences of great benefit to humanity at large; namely, it would eliminate strife, suffering, and the sources of all human conflict, leading to a truly Utopian state of bliss. "To Crowley," writes Henrik Bogdan, "the Law of Thelema was the answer to all the political, religious, social, ethical, and psychological problems facing mankind: . . . all forms of conflict are rooted in the fact at least one of the parties involved in the conflict is not aware of his or her True Will."[57] Thelemic individualism would usher in the conflict-free, crimeless state that parliamentary democracy had thus far failed to deliver.

From the first, *The Book of the Law*'s radically individualistic understanding of what it meant to serve the law proved controversial, not least of all with Crowley himself. Would there really be no more misery and discord if everyone followed their true will? If our wills are all utterly unique, is it not possible that somewhere in this endless variety, the will of certain individuals might comprise the commission of violent or harmful acts against noncompliant others? If Thelema did indeed offer a route into a conflict-free world devoid of suffering, as Crowley often suggested, why were so many of *The Book of the Law*'s pronouncements exuberantly bellicose, so seemingly eager to luxuriate in the anguish of those it deems feeble and infirm? The section attributed to Hadit, for example, counsels:

> We have nothing with the outcast and unfit; let them die in their misery. For they feel not. Compassion is the vice of kings: stamp down the wretched and the weak; this is the law of strong; this is our law, and the joy of the world.[58]

Such sentiments intensify in the closing book of Ra-Hoor-Khuit, the self-described "god of war and vengeance," who calls for an end to the alleged compassion of the Christian era and an obliteration of the weak.[59] "Mercy be let off," he exhorts, "damn them who pity! Kill and torture; spare none; be upon them!"[60] How were seekers to understand such explicit panegyrics to cruelty, mercilessness, and violence in light of the imperative to develop their will?[61] Crowley claimed to have been repelled by such directives on their first receipt, so much so that he ignored *The Book of the Law*'s revelation for several years before finally accepting its truth and adopting his role as Thelema's prophet in 1909.[62] "The fact of the matter was that I resented *The Book of the Law* with my whole soul," he recollects in the *Confessions*:

154   OPEN SECRETS

> I was bitterly opposed to the principles of the Book on almost every part
> of morality. The third chapter seemed to me gratuitously atrocious. My
> soul, infinitely sad at the universal story, was passionately eager to raise
> humanity. And lo! The Magical Formula denounced pity as damnable,
> acclaimed war as admirable, and in almost every other way was utterly re-
> pugnant to my ideas.[63]

Nonetheless, accept the *Book*'s truth he would, and while he would later insist, particularly in his own encounters with the secular legal system, that
selfishness, criminality, and violence were expressions of a black magic
wholly incompatible with Thelema, it is surely not difficult to see why a
neutral reader might perceive a celebration of these qualities in *The Book of
the Law*.[64]

Sympathetic interpreters have suggested that *The Book of the Law*'s calls
for an end to compassion, and, indeed, to those suffering human subjects
who might benefit from it, should be understood as rhetorical adornments
of its anti-Christian polemic rather than direct calls to brutal action; alternately, they identify such statements as too metaphorically complex to be
interpreted literally. Richard Kaczynski, for example, argues that "so much
of the *Book of the Law*'s meaning lies not in its literal interpretation but
in the highly codified meaning of its words that one is tempted to call it
a stylistic forebear of James Joyce's *Finnegan's Wake*."[65] This comparison,
however, is strained. *Finnegan's Wake* is a vast, linguistically experimental
modernist novel written in a recondite prose style that defies familiar interpretation of any kind; it is not, like *The Book of the Law*, a pithy treatise composed of imperative statements that appear to command certain
actions in a direct and accessible language, such as "Be strong, o man! Lust,
enjoy all things of sense and rapture: fear not that any God shall deny thee
for this."[66] Furthermore, Joyce never produced for *Finnegan's Wake* any
supporting commentaries that insisted on the literal meaning of its leg-
ible pronouncements, as Crowley repeatedly did for *The Book of the Law*.
Although recognizing the moral unpalatability of Ra-Hoor-Khuit's message to most readers, Bogdan writes, "Crowley stressed the importance of
interpreting it literally, although he would continue the search for more
subtle esoteric meanings."[67] Thus in *The Law is for All*, the extended exegesis of *The Book* which compiles several of the commentaries he produced
between 1919 and 1922, Crowley affirmed that "the thesis concerning
compassion is of the most palmary importance in the ethics of Thelema.

It is necessary that we stop, once for all, this ignorant meddling with other people's business. Each individual must be free to follow his own path!"[68] Here the attempt to alleviate suffering and seek social justice is dismissed as a form of meddling, and poverty, pain, and disenfranchisement are imagined as freely chosen paths in which true initiates should not intervene. This view is underlined again in *The Confessions* when Crowley pronounces, "We should not protect the weak and the vicious from the results of their inferiority."[69]

Crowley's advocacy of non-interference in the face of suffering or violence takes a darker turn again in *The Law for All* when, in a move that has curiously escaped comment from Crowley's feminist interpreters, he seems to offer a Thelemic justification of rape and murder. While every man and woman is a star, and thus must be "absolutely free to interpret and communicate self by means of any sexual practices,"[70] he writes:

> Physical constraint, up to a certain point, is not so seriously wrong . . . Some of the most passionate and permanent attachments have begun with rape. Rome was actually founded thereon. Similarly, murder of a faithless partner is ethically excusable, in a certain sense; for there may be some stars whose nature is extreme violence.[71]

Although conceding that this startling sentiment represents "merely my personal view," he then defensively affirms, "Yet nature's unspeakable variety, though it admits cruelty and selfishness, offers us no examples of the puritan and the prig!"[72] The passages implies that acts of sexual violence or homicide at least have the virtue of being "natural," while puritans and prigs— presumably, people who disapprove of such actions—do not; furthermore, these deeds should be recognized in some cases as authentic manifestations of true will and hence necessary to express. The magus further defends the potential spiritual value of rape later in *The Law for All* when he qualifies the claim that "it may . . . be considered improper, as a general rule, for your sexual gratification to destroy, deform, or displease any other star" with the stipulation: "It must, of course, be understood that such consent is not always explicit. There are cases where seduction or rape may be emancipation or initiation to another. Such acts are to be judged by the results."[73] By the results of such acts on who, one wonders? Crowley's decision to float the possibility that rape might be experienced as liberating, not just by its perpetrators, but also by its victims, is not only ethically execrable, but also in contradiction

156 OPEN SECRETS

with the liberationist, individualist, and harm-free *ethos* he would vaunt for Thelema elsewhere.

5.5 Thelemic Ethics at Play in *The Scrutinies of Simon Iff*

In these tensions around the meaning and permissibility of violence within *The Book of the Law* and its commentaries, we detect a, perhaps even *the*, chief dilemma of Crowley's early articulation of Thelemic ethics. How are liberated individuals to situate themselves in relation to preventable human suffering, willful aggression, and crime? Should they ignore or celebrate these phenomena? Or should they, like the detective, intervene, if only through the pursuit of interpretation and revelation? And how might acts defined as criminal by the secular legal system—theft, rape, and murder— be interpreted from a Thelemic point of view? Were they, as perhaps a best-case application of Thelemic principles would indicate, simply the la- mentable results of a suppressed or stunted will, and hence destined for ex- tinction once all have realized their true selves? Or, as Crowley would often publicly deny, but as some of his writings certainly allow, did Thelema imply that criminality simply *was* the true will of some individuals and thus its ex- pression was spiritually necessary? Crowley had to publicly downplay the latter possibility at different points in his career, particularly when he was being smeared by right-wing British tabloid *John Bull* as leading a sexually depraved, financially exploitive, and possibly pederastic human sacrifice cult at the Abbey of Thelema in Cefalù following the 1923 death of his fol- lower, Raoul Loveday, there.[74] In the court room and in the public sphere, it was very important to Crowley that Thelema not be seen as inciting crime. Detective fiction, however, provided him with a much safer space in which to play with and probe the disjunctions between the Law as pronounced through Aiwass and the law of the state. In *The Scrutinies*, he deploys genre conventions to push to the limit contrasting understandings of the will as both antithesis to, and spiritual sanction for, violent crime without risking any real-world reputational or legal harm.

Crowley establishes the terms of his radical occult engagement with detective fiction in the first *Iff* story, "The Big Game," published in *The International* in September 1917. As an example of the genre, it is a very odd production indeed, one in which Crowley's Thelemic sleuth Iff—his name surely a homonymic pun on the Masonic Hiram Abiff, keeper of the Temple's

OCCULT DETECTION IN THE AEON OF HORUS   157

secrets—only makes a very belated appearance long after the story's criminal perpetrators have been identified. Readers might easily have failed to realize they were reading a detective tale at all until the final few pages, when Iff appears in the Hemlock,[75] the ultra-elite London gentleman's club that forms a running setting throughout the series. His late arrival is in part a necessary reflex of the activity that Crowley here associates with detection and flags in the series title: unlike Sherlock Holmes, Simon Iff does not himself *adventure*, rather he *scrutinizes*. His type of investigation need not necessarily intervene, solve, or save; all it must do is observe and examine—activities that could take place at any point before, during, or after the commission of crime. Iff's absent sense of investigative urgency, influenced possibly by Crowley's engagement with Daoism in this period,[76] alone separates from many of his fictional contemporaries, both occult and secular. Of these, the one he most closely approaches is Chesterton's clerical sleuth Father Brown, a fellow interpreter of crime through a spiritual lens, albeit a very different one than Iff.

When Iff finally does pronounce on the murders committed in "The Big Game," it is in a manner shockingly at odds with the moral coordinates typical of golden age detection and in a spirit clearly intended to *épater la bourgeoisie*. In the tale's opening scene, two successful urban professionals, the criminal lawyer Dick Ffoulkes—his name reflecting Crowley's penchant for pornographic pun—and leading journalist Jack Flynn celebrate the success of their combined efforts to acquit Ezra Robinson on the charges of having murdered his employer, Richard Marsden, in an elaborate locked-room stratagem. Ffoulkes had punched holes in the circumstantial evidence and convinced jurors that Marsden had accidentally stabbed himself while knife-juggling in the bath during a power cut; Flynn had assisted his colleague and, as the narrative implies, possible former lover, by penning "long articles on miscarriages of justice; others on the weakness of circumstantial evidence where no strong motive was evident; others again on strange accidental deaths."[77] But their victory represents no triumph for the secular law. As Ffoulkes casually admits to Flynn, Robinson was indeed guilty; he had spontaneously plotted and carried out the murder with his lover Maud Duval, a fellow cocaine addict and former member of "some kind of devil-worshipping club."[78]

Delighted with their successful evasion of the law, the two men plan further illicit amusements, specifically, the "big game" hunt of the title; they each resolve to commit a motiveless murder within the next twelve months, one

158   OPEN SECRETS

of a "purely adventurous nature, not . . . inspired by greed or animosity," but rather pursued for "the joy of baffling the stupid police, fooling the detectives with false clues, triumphantly proving yourself innocent when you know you are guilty!"[79] Ffoulkes selects for his victim the elderly sister of the murdered Marsden, who married Robinson on his release; he bludgeons her to death on the first anniversary of her brother's death, knowing that this odd coincidence will provoke "the clever-clever novelist-detectives" to "fabricate a mystery of revenge in connection with the date."[80] This meta-fictional allusion to the operations of the genre impishly takes aim at both writers and readers of detection fiction whose shared predilection for pattern-seeking will do them no good here. Flynn, meanwhile, goes to Paris on this same date, where Robinson and Maud are meeting covertly to celebrate their crime. There, in the guise of a rouged-up, homosexual cocaine peddler, he lures the drug-addled pair back to his rooms, in which they are later found dead by hanging. So it is that Ffoulkes and Flynn effortlessly fulfil their bet.

At this point, readers who had been promised "the greatest sensation since Sherlock Holmes" might well have thrown their hands up in despair. Where is the promised detective, and where is the judgment and ensuing punishment for criminal transgression that Holmes always pronounced, even if he sometimes delegated its delivery to providence? Moreover, where were the magical tools and manifestations so central to the occult detection genre and certainly co-extensive with the author's reputation? In fact, nothing at all supernatural happens in "The Big Game," or, indeed, in most of *The Scrutinies*. Instead, and almost too late to fulfil the requirements of the genre, Iff haphazardly enters the scene, running into Ffoulkes at the Hemlock Club and playing with him a few games of chess. Described as a "little old man, who was known as a mathematician of great eminence, with a touch of the crank,"[81] he effortlessly wins each contest not, he explains, on the basis of his superior skill, but rather of his deeper psychological understanding: "I can gauge your intellect . . . it is limited in certain directions."[82] Indeed, Iff surmises to his opponent, it is exactly such a mind—too narcissistic to sense its own blind spots—that could have committed the recent murder of old Mrs. Marsden without realizing the vulnerabilities it would incur; the murderer has put himself in checkmate to another criminal player. "There may be someone hunting him who is as superior intellectually to him as he is to the police," Iff casually remarks, careful not to directly accuse Ffoulkes of murder. "[H]e would have no experience in his own person that such monsters as himself were at large; therefore, I ask you, how does he know, every night, that someone will not kill him in his sleep?"[83] This magical suggestion works like poison, and within a month Ffoulkes has descended into a full-blown paranoid mania that requires his incarceration within a mental institution from which he is unlikely to ever be discharged.

Had "The Big Game" ended here, it might be seen as offering only a more lurid version of golden age detection's morally satisfying and conventional narrative arc in which criminal actions are shown to inevitably cause their own retribution. And Iff does in fact espouse this causal view in the story's conclusion, somberly declaring that "we are all punished ... exactly where we have offended, and in the measure thereof."[84] But the subject of this homily is not who we might expect. He is here speaking to Flynn, whose own act of double murder, and whose complicity in the false exoneration of Marsden's killer, Iff absolves instantly and almost without comment after the journalist's unforced confession. "You have perhaps erred in some ways," judges Iff, "—ways which I find excusable—but you need never lose a night's sleep over the business."[85] Instead, as the following stories make clear, Flynn not only escapes punishment, but is in fact rewarded for his homicidal actions by becoming a *de facto* initiate of the secret esoteric brotherhood that Iff heads, and appearing in stories such as "The Conduct of John Briggs" and "Not Good Enough" as a kind of Watson to his occult master. What are we to make of the drastically different fates of the two murderous co-conspirators in "The Big Game"? Why does Iff find Flynn's actions more "excusable" than Ffoulkes's? If punishment is calibrated in relation to the nature of the offense, then does not the fact that Flynn seems to benefit from his crime, retaining his position at the top of his profession and gaining access to hidden wisdom, suggest that he has not offended at all? These contrasting outcomes exemplify the highly individualistic soteriology for which Thelema would become known,[86] while also troubling the universalized ethical and social claims that Crowley often made for his philosophy. If crime was truly inimical to Thelema, a spiritual system whose global adoption would allegedly end all human conflicts, why do its principles here seem to reward murder? Alternately, if the Thelemic system allowed the possibility that crime might form a necessary, even permissible, form of will expression for some individuals, why is the libidinally named Dick Ffoulkes driven to madness for his transgression, while his associate Flynn, a more prolific murderer, is left free to pursue a course of personal spiritual development in the top tiers of London club land? These questions are evoked but left unanswered in story's laconic finale, offering a

160   OPEN SECRETS

philosophical challenge which the ensuing *Scrutinies* will address with only limited success.

The most humanitarian application of Thelemic criminology within *The Scrutinies*—in the sense that it presents Thelema as conducive to the reduction and elimination, rather than the acceptance or celebration, of homicidal violence—comes in the sequence's gruesome second story, "The Artistic Temperament." Inspired by J. G. Frazer's *The Golden Bough* (1890),[87] it tells the story of the professionally successful but talentless Royal Academician Lord Cudlipp who kills and drains the blood of his own son on a remote Scottish island, hoping, following his recent reading of Frazer's comparative religious opus, that this act will magically imbue his canvases with the visionary power they have always lacked. As in "The Big Game," Iff takes up the case by chance after meeting and feeling compassion for the young sea painter, André de Bry, who was falsely accused and then acquitted of the murder under the notorious Scottish verdict of "Not Proven"—"the Verdict of the Sitter on the Fence," as it is here described.[88] Iff decides to investigate, or rather, *scrutinize*, the case, to free de Bry from the stigma that now clings to his name, and more importantly, to illustrate the tragic consequences of rejecting the Thelemic imperative, "Do what thou wilt shall be all of the Law."[89] "Failure to observe this precept is the root of all human error," he explains to his associates in one of the story's moments of direct Thelemic tutelage: "It is our right and duty—the two are one, as Éliphas Lévi very nearly saw—to expand upon our own true centre, to pursue the exact orbit of our destiny. To quit our orbit is to invite collisions."[90] Such an act of orbital straying, the narrative wants us to see, has led to the junior Cudlipp's murder. His father, a rich manufacturer's son with grandiose artistic aspirations, used his ample fortune to buy himself an artistic career for which he was eminently unsuited, and whose frustrations and failures would eventually force him to a gruesome act of pagan filicide. All of this could have been avoided, Iff insists, if he had simply followed his authentic, albeit unglamorous, inner will to be a biscuit maker. "Suppose," says Iff, "I think it my will to steal my neighbour's watch. I am caught; police-court, prison, and general disaster. Merely the result of my ignorance in regard to my true destiny. Failure in life and especially criminal failure: collision."[91] A separate orbit for all, and each in their orbit; if humans could but adhere to this principle, the sage here suggests, criminal collisions would surely cease to occur.

Yet even as it advances this form of what we might call Thelemic criminological idealism, so, too, does "The Artistic Temperament" simultaneously

OCCULT DETECTION IN THE AEON OF HORUS 161

derail it for the purposes of venting antisemitic and anti-democratic spleen. Certainly, Iff insists, some forms of violence, like Cudlipp's, are the preventable products of stifled will; yet others, like the French Revolutionary executions, or what Iff cavalierly describes as the Jewish ritual murder of infants—blood libel presented here as if it were uncontroversial fact—are intimated to be the result of an innate atavism wholly incompatible with the agential individualism on which Thelemic philosophy depends. It is only possible to do one's will, after all, if one is capable of choice, and not simply a slave to incorrigible racial instincts and urges. By casting French revolutionary leaders, however "humanitarian," as subject to "primitive tribal passions," and presenting "the sacrifice of the first-born" as a Jewish religious ritual still alive in contemporary Russia, Iff conjures subjects whom Thelema presumably could not reach;[92] indeed, he even concedes that Cudlipp himself might belong to this biodeterministic category. Speculating that his savage act of filicide could have been catalyzed, not just by the strains of his artificially imposed artistic temperament, but also by racial memory, Iff remarks "Cudlipp's family was originally Armenian, . . . the offshoot of some old Babylonian tribe . . . The recent impressions combined with some far strain of atavism, and he resolved to the murder."[93]

This conviction—that certain human types are biologically predisposed to criminal vice or legal conformity alike and are hence incapable of self-chosen spiritual development—is further developed in the final two instalments of the *Scrutinies*, "Not Good Enough" and "Ineligible." These stories are the most provocative and reactionary of the collection, far more so than the surrounding golden age detective stories whose admittedly conservative suspicion of outsiders never extended to their quite literal dehumanization, as it does here. In the former, Iff exculpates the despicable but nonetheless falsely accused Eurasian academic Ananda Haramzada Swamy from the charge of murdering his rich older lover, Lady Brooke-Hunter on the basis that he, as a biracial man, is, as the title anticipates, constitutionally "not good enough" to have performed a gynocidal deed styled here as noble and praiseworthy; its true perpetrator, the victim's outraged blue-blooded husband, Sir Reginald, is ritually absolved for his action and in the story's finale offered the Presidency of the Board of Education.[94] With his name drawn from the Hindi word for "bastard," Haramzada, as Crowley scholars have recognized, is a thinly veiled and ferocious portrait of the art historian Coomaraswamy, whose wife, Ratan Devi, had recently and painfully ended an affair with Crowley.[95] The spitefulness of this characterization utterly collapses here the

162   OPEN SECRETS

air of ironic Wildean insouciance that Crowley seeks to cultivate elsewhere in the series, and indeed, as Bogdan suggests, throughout his wider magickal corpus as evidence of his class distinction;[96] instead, Crowley writes here like a man enragedly attempting to salve the wounds of romantic rejection with a series of manic racialized slurs and corrosive eugenic fantasies.

"Ineligible," the only historical story of the *Scrutinies*, relates the shocking back story of Joshua Glass, a nearly successful candidate for membership within the Hemlock Club whose admission, had it not been thwarted by Iff, would have led the club "and therefore the universe (which revolves around it)" into "irreparable disaster."[97] In an earlier Iff story, "Outside the Bank's Routine," Crowley had established that the Hemlock only admitted men who had "done something 'notorious and heretical,'"[98] a criterion that Glass, author of a controversial religious tract entitled *A Jealous God*, about the perverse misanthropy of the Christian God, seems amply to fulfil. Far from being heretical, however, Iff argues that Glass's polemic represents a thoroughly orthodox extrapolation from John 111:16 (a scriptural book which does not exist and must be cited here as joke or in error),[99] one fully compatible with the theology of the Exclusive Plymouth Brethren sect in which Glass, like Crowley himself, was raised. Worse yet, after "insist[ing] upon a physical examination," Iff discovers that Glass has a "a malformation so curious and monstrous that, despite his human parentage, it was impossible to admit him any title to membership of our race."[100] The magus does not specify what this defect might be, but given that it is only detectable via intimate physical exam, it seems to relate to the sexual organs. In any case, Glass is quite literally an anatomical monster for whom the magico-heretical tutelage of the Hemlock Club can do no good, and who must accordingly be kept outside its precincts; he is at once too offensively normal and horrifically different to be let in.

The eruptions of biological fatalism and racial essentialism we see in "Not Good Enough" and "Ineligible" undermine both the liberationist reach of Thelemic philosophy and, accordingly, the straightforward didactic function that both Crowley and subsequent critics have attributed to the *Scrutinies*. In *The Confessions*, Crowley had claimed that the tales, while being "perfectly good detective stories," were intended "to show a master of the law as competent to solve the subtlest problems by considerations based upon the Law," illustrating "the way in which crime and unhappiness of all sorts may be traced to a breach of the Law. . . The way to keep out of trouble is to understand and therefore to love every impression of which one becomes conscious."[101] Starr affirms this pedagogical function in his introduction to the 1987 Teitan Press edition, where he writes that Crowley "managed to incorporate subtly the principles of the Law of Thelema to an astonishing degree, demonstrating that they are the basis of rational human conduct, and how neglect of them leads in turn to crime and unhappiness."[102] There are, I suggest, two reasons to question such summations. First, there is surely nothing subtle about the exposition of Thelemic philosophy, nor indeed the *grand guignolesque* crimes it is deployed to investigate, within the tales. Thelemic axioms such as "Do what thou wilt" are shoehorned into the stories with a blatancy that even non-occultural readers would struggle to miss, and their fast-moving, intricate, and bizarre criminal plots are repeatedly interrupted by sustained lectures on Thelemic principles. The frequency and directness of these interjections offers but a poor cover, however, for their inconsistency with, even inapplicability to, the baroque fever-dream narratives on offer. And herein lies a second objection to exclusively didactic interpretations of the *Scrutinies*: they lack—and, indeed, flaunt their lack of—the philosophical or moral coherence on which purportedly homiletic literature relies. If crime is indeed the result of neglecting Thelemic principles, then why are the murders committed by Flynn and Brooke-Hunter granted spiritual sanction, and allowed to serve as basis for initiation? How is the maxim that we can avoid trouble by loving our conscious impressions applicable to the very different fates of the murderous conspirators Ffoulkes and Flynn? And most importantly, what is the point of venturing a campaign of fictional didacticism within a worldview that identifies certain individuals as constitutionally ineducable, incapable of resisting hereditary thrall, or even, quite literally, inhuman? If such views are reconcilable with Thelemic philosophy, then it is surely not in any immediate, obvious, or universal way; the version of Thelemic philosophy on display in *Scrutinies* is incompatible with the conviction that if we all simply realize and follow our true will then crime will cease to exist. Instead, the stories reveal the same irreconcilable tensions within Crowley's fictionalized representation of Thelemic criminology that Marco Pasi has identified within the author's political thinking more broadly and render them deserving of the same caveat: "the attempt to interpret Crowley's thought as a coherent whole," writes Pasi, "is a risky operation, most likely doomed to failure from the outset."[103]

To recognize these oppositions, however, is not to deny that there are any recurrent ideological throughlines across the *Scrutinies*—there certainly are, albeit not ones of a particularly liberatory or individualistic nature.

164   OPEN SECRETS

On the contrary, what connects these stories more tightly than any *ethos* of occultural liberation is their shared investment in the exclusion of impure and non-elite outsiders from the magickal precincts of the Hemlock Club. Indeed, it is toward this end that the over-arching narrative logic of the series moves, opening with a tale of inclusion—the Thelemic redemption of murderous urban professional Flynn in "The Big Game"—and closing with a firm renunciation of those who are ineligible for both club and human species membership. In the early stories, this process of gate-keeping is handled with a relative lightness of touch; by the final instalment of *The Scrutinies*, it is pursued with a xenophobic and anti-democratic vehemence unparalleled in the works of even the most conservative of the era's secular genre practitioners, fellow detective fiction writers like Christie and Sayers whose suspicion of foreign interlopers never quite extends to a denial of their human identity, or a call for their mass culling. The series' second story, "Outside the Bank's Routine," lays the seeds of this exclusionist trajectory in its gentle parody of the Scottish bank manager Ian Macpherson, a grasping, bourgeois social climber who consults Iff about the seeming embezzlement of funds by his loyal employee, Mr. Fraser. After agreeing to take on the case, Iff invites the aspirational lowlander to join him at the Hemlock, where Macpherson unwittingly falls afoul of an arcane rule designed to showcase the membership's elite eccentricity; anyone who quotes Shakespeare must forfeit a sum of £5. Dazzled by the distinguished premises and eager to show off his learning, Macpherson constantly spouts the bard until he is presented with a bill of £95, which Iff generously agrees to pay. "Don't think of it, I beg you!" says Iff as the startled Macpherson catches sight of the exorbitant bill. "I am a rich man and an old one: I shall never miss it. Besides the fine goes to a most worthy object: the Society for Destroying Parliamentary Institutions."[104]

Played for laughs, this episode underlines that fact that vulgar outsiders will pay a price for attempting to infiltrate the inner sanctum with their cheaply purchased and vulgarly displayed cultural capital—true rebellion, such as the effort to destroy parliamentary institutions, is only for an elite inner cadre, not upstarts like Macpherson. A far graver penalty awaits the story's second "ambitious, money-loving Scotsman,"[105] the doctor who has facilitated the conspiracy behind the bank theft. Simon's scrutinies reveal that the money was in fact stolen by Macpherson's other employee Mr. Fisher, who cooked up the plan with Fraser's sadistic, sexually hysteric, and drug-addicted fiancée, Clara Clavering—a fictionalized Scarlet

Woman who Iff compares in passing to three other such women he knew in real life, one of whom was his wife.[106] Together, he reveals, Clara and Fisher stole the money, abducted Fraser, tortured him into making mysterious phone calls about its whereabouts, and, after Fraser's accidental death of a heart attack during these trials, planted his corpse, along with another mutilated one stolen from a morgue, across the country as decoys. Heinous acts these may be, but they receive little philosophic or practical censure from Iff: Clara he assigns to a mental hospital, en route to which she escapes by seducing her escort. Fisher, like Flynn before him, is taken under the magus's wing as a pupil-initiate and placed "in conditions most favourable to his proper development."[107] As Clara and Fisher enjoy their freedom, the full punitive debt for their crime is paid by their co-conspirator Dr. Leslie, who aided the plot by supplying the extraneous corpse and who had earlier introduced Clara to drugs. Unlike the plot's lovers, Leslie is "a common type," one of many predatory Scotsmen in the imperial center who use their good looks and charm to "become woman's doctors . . . seduce their patients . . . make them drug fiends . . . perform abortions; and to the extortionate charges for their crimes they add a tenfold profit by blackmail," thus becoming "the curse of London."[108] Leslie, Iff declares, "I mean to hang."[109]

Crowley's anti-Caledonian ire here—as distinct from and opposed to the romantic Jacobitism he embraced elsewhere—seems a product of his equation of lowland Scottish identity with the dour, deterministic Calvinism that formed a central target of Thelema's pleasure-focused philosophy. Yet the Thelemic insights offered in *The Scrutinies* rarely offer a more liberating alternative to this predestinarian theological foil, least of all to the racialized outsiders who Iff presents as socially, morally, and spiritually irredeemable. In "Not Good Enough," Iff "purse[s] his lips" when told about Haramzada Swamy's Eurasian identity as the son of "a black, a Tamil" and an white English mother;[110] he makes "another gesture of disgust"[111] after learning about the Swamy's habit of making his wife clean the pornography-strewn suite he uses for his extra-marital sexual liaisons. This might seem like a strangely prudish reaction from the proponent of an overtly sexually liberationist and non-monogamous credo, but as the story proceeds, it becomes clear that Iff's distaste is more racially than morally based. As the mixed-race son of a white mother, Swamy is deemed constitutionally and irredeemably corrupt, doomed to carry the defects of his necessarily degenerate mother— "all white women who marry coloured men," Flynn opines, "must be classed

166　OPEN SECRETS

as such."[112] To this anti-miscegenationist contention, Crowley's sage replies simply, "I agree."[113]

Iff's assent to this deeply racist and misogynistic premise leads him, however, to a very different conclusion than his protégé. For Flynn, Swamy's miscegenate nature suggests that he is innately criminal, and hence the true murderer of Sybil Brooke-Hunter. For Iff, however, it means something that he presents to Flynn, and accordingly, readers, as even worse: namely, that the Swamy is *not good enough* to commit what the text depicts as a justifiable crime, namely, the murder of a promiscuous, unattractive woman. Instead, Iff explains, the Swamy's racial degeneracy plays out in more pathetic criminal acts such as theft, blackmail, and the authorship of a woefully ill-conceived book that misreads Buddha as a hedonist.[114] Such a colossal act of misjudgment, opines Iff, reveals the wrongly accused to be akin to "a fly, whose time-sense is extremely rapid compared to ours" and "cannot perceive movement in a body which travels more slowly than about a yard a minute."[115] The Swamy's "nature," Iff concludes in the story's finale:

> is not his own fault, any more than a toad's. But this I want you to understand, that as sex is the most sacred thing in life, so the sins of the fathers are visited on the children most of all in violations of eugenics. Whether it's tubercule, or alcoholism, or marriage between kin too close, or sub-race too distant, the penalty is fulminating and disastrous. Generation becomes degeneration.[116]

Such a gloomy prognosis segues into a curt discussion of how Thelemic philosophy might proactively prevent the perpetuation of such types. When Flynn asks, "What's the remedy?,"[117] Iff advances what would be defined as a positive eugenic solution, in that it encourages the right kind of reproduction instead of prohibiting undesirable couplings—namely, he calls for a restoration of "the worship of Dionysus and Priapus and Mithras" and polygamy, so that the elite might freely couple without social stigmatization.[118] But this is not the only solution that Iff advocates. Earlier, on hearing that, among his many sordid infamies, Swamy had forced his wife to abort her lover's child,[119] Iff advocates a negative eugenic interpretation of such deeds: "To let the degenerates drop out is the true kindness—certainly to the race, perhaps even to them."[120] In addition to being morally reprehensible, this startling sentiment also completely sells out Thelemic individualism to the imagined good of the racial collective. After all, the duty of realizing one's true will is hardly compatible with forced subjection to euthanasia.

Some scholars have attempted to distance these sentiments, virulent as they may be, from any real or deeply held racism on Crowley's part; Keith A. Cantú, for example, writes that "Crowley's unfortunate use of insulting epithets in personal contexts is not exemplary of any kind of broader racism against Asians or any people of mixed ancestry for that matter. Instead, in Crowley's writings we usually find quite the opposite: admiration."[121] Yet as postcolonial critics, such as Edward Said, have powerfully argued, and as the history of imperialism demonstrates, racism has never precluded the countervailing tendency to venerate or admire certain aspects of the racial other; just as, observes Tomoko Masuzawa, the "highly laudatory, unrealistically exalted" representations of non-Western societies produced by European Orientalists in the eighteenth and nineteenth centuries "proved no detriment to their self-esteem or to their universalist ideals."[122] Furthermore, it is very clear that the hostility toward mixed-race subjects in "Not Good Enough" is not simply the product of an unfortunate choice of words—although why even were this the case they should be exempt from critique remains, I admit, unclear to me—but rather of a quasi-biological theory that is developed and articulated at length. Less exonerative is Starr, who acknowledges in his notes to "Not Good Enough" that "Crowley disliked Eurasians" on the basis of his belief that the stigma they faced from European and Asian communities alike caused them to internalize shame and thus behave in a base manner. In the story in question, however, as Starr rightly recognizes, the Swamy's turpitude is not attributed to adverse social conditioning but rather to the alleged biological inferiority commonly assigned to racial others within the mainstream of white supremacist thought in early twentieth-century Britain. "Crowley," he concludes, "uses the same elements of contemporary race prejudice to build the case for the Swamy's vileness."[123] Echoing this positioning, Crowley biographer Lawrence Sutin observes that the Beast "embodied many of the worst John Bull racial and social prejudices of his upper-class contemporaries" and, like many of the writers in his surrounding intellectual milieu, combined "deeply held racist viewpoints" with "a fascination with people of colour."[124] While the ultimate question of Crowley's personal racial beliefs is likely to remain moot, and certainly lies beyond the scope of this chapter, there can be no denying that the sentiments expressed in "Not Good Enough" are absolutely compatible with the logic of a deeply misogynistic and eugenicist white supremacy that pathologizes the white women

168   OPEN SECRETS

who sleep with non-white men, and the offspring such unions produce, as dangerous racial degenerates.

What is most remarkable in *The Scrutinies* is not its reproduction of depressingly familiar and contemporarily prevalent racist platitudes, but rather its baffling representation of these views as the products of a secret or taboo form of knowledge available only to an elite, heretical inner circle of magickal initiates. Heretical to whom, one wonders? The far-right *John Bull* magazine whose hostility toward racial others Sutin aligns with Crowley's own was, after all, Britain's top-selling weekly during the years of the First World War;[125] the fact that this paper regularly crusaded against Crowley and branded him a "traitorous degenerate" for his affiliation with George Sylvester Viereck's pro-German papers does not mean that the two did not sometimes endorse the same sentiments.[126] During the war, Bottomley's tabloid regularly attacked non-white migrants to Britain, condemned pacifism with a truly Ra-Hoor-Khuitian vehemence, and suggested that there were certain kinds of individuals—British-based Germans, homosexuals, and left-wing politicians such as Ramsay MacDonald—whose murder would not only be acceptable but also desirable.[127] As the conclusion to "Ineligible" fascinatingly demonstrates, Crowley was very much aware of the possibility that certain forms of apparent unorthodoxy—the misanthropic theology of the demi-human zealot Joshua Glass—might actually represent the orthodox views of an existing status quo wrapped up in unfamiliar dress. This insight, however, he seems in *The Scrutinies* incapable of applying to the fictionalized philosophy of its own elite occult detective, or to the prestigious club environs whose social purity Iff polices and protects from contamination. Instead, Crowley's prophet-sleuth not only fails to reject the xenophobia of the same right-wing populist public sphere that often took Thelema as target, but effectively uses his magickal scrutiny to authorize it.

The golden age detective story was in many ways a perfect vehicle through which to express these tensions between a modernist *ethos* of individualistic liberation and a countervailing impulse to reactionary containment, functioning as it did to both restore order to, and expel interlopers from, an increasingly middle-class English social milieu while also calling attention to the failures of conventional policing, legal, and ethical systems. In this way, we can recognize *The Scrutinies of Simon Iff*, not simply as a genre outlier by virtue of its often-scandalous new religious content, but also as deeply paradigmatic of the transformations underway within the classic and occult detective fiction traditions from which Crowley took inspiration. The stories develop what we have seen to be crime fiction's longstanding entanglement with questions of spiritual justice and magical ontology into a new direction, one where what might elsewhere read as a failure to fulfil the genre contract—criminals may be detected here, but are as likely to be celebrated as judged—is recoded as a triumph of Thelemic perspective. They warrant our attention, not because they seamlessly evangelize the necessity to realize and do what one wilt, but rather for their exposure, even if unintentional, of how fraught and difficult the process of will realization might be, and how indeterminate its ethical consequences. Some individuals might be capable of developing their will, they suggest, while others may be bound instead by fixed hereditary instinct and racial conditioning that leaves them no freer than a prisoner in a cage. It is no easy thing to distinguish between, and serve justice toward, these two very different kinds of subjects, if indeed wholly separable they may be. Within its fictional exposition in *The Scrutinies*, Thelemic criminology equivocates between announcing an end to crime through self-realization, and installing it as a spiritual necessity whose suppression, more than its performance, would violate the dictates of the Law. Through the format of the popular detective tale, Crowley was able to linger and imaginatively experiment with, rather than gloss over, these philosophical and ethical tensions, to represent their complexity through the different fictional fates of his characters and the elaborate plots pursued within the individual stories and across the wider narrative arc of the series. As such, *The Scrutinies* offer an ideal closing point for our study, one that has sought to establish the fiction of Britain's occult revival, not simply as a didactic vehicle or transparent biographical index to the lives of its authors, but as a site of political challenge, aesthetic innovation, and sophisticated genre mobilization.

6

Conclusion

Forming Occult Fiction in the Secular Age

Nearly a century after the publication of Edward Bulwer Lytton's *Zanoni*, a radically reimagined version of *Zanoni*'s inaugurating central London bookshop would appear on Britain's occult fictional landscape. Situated only a few streets and a short walk away from Mr. D__'s Covent Garden premises, the beckoning shopfront of T. Jelkes, the antiquarian bookseller in ceremonial magician Dion Fortune's initiatory romance, *The Goat Foot God* (1936), offered readers and seekers a very different entrance into the unseen world; in its greater ease of approach, it demonstrates just how far the revival's genre fiction had expanded and diversified in the intervening years. Likely inspired by one, or both, of two real-life London-based establishments—Watkins Books (established in 1897) and the Atlantis Bookshop (established 1922)—Jelkes's shop catches the eye of Fortune's grief-stricken and emasculated protagonist, Hugh Paston, as he takes a desultory early evening stroll through Bloomsbury after the funeral of his wife, Frida, who has died alongside her lover (and Paston's best friend), Trevor Wilmott, in a car crash. Its wares, displayed haphazardly in pavement discount bins rather than hawkishly guarded on dusty interior shelves, will, as the narrative unfolds, come to save his life. For it is there, amidst a grimy, mislabeled, and eclectic assortment of ex-library stock, "fly-blown" and "fruity" after long years of public circulation,[1] that he will first be inspired toward the seeker's path. Searching for a "good detective novel . . . sufficiently exciting to catch the attention,"[2] he picks up a battered copy of *The Prisoner in the Opal* (1928), a black magic thriller by best-selling, jack-of-all-genres author A. E. W. Mason, and finds himself captivated by its salacious description of a black mass. Venturing inside to pay, he discovers richer literary wares that will transform his initially prurient intrigue into a higher quest for sexuo-spiritual rejuvenation; no less importantly, he will find in the proprietor an experienced occult mentor to guide his initiation and introduce him to a requisite female magical partner, the artist Mona Wilton. Together,

Open Secrets. Christine Ferguson, Oxford University Press. © Oxford University Press 2025.
DOI: 10.1093/oso/9780197651599.003.0006

CONCLUSION   171

they ultimately achieve communion with Pan, the goat-foot god of the title, in the pagan, rural space of Monk's Farm. Paston consummates their erotic invocation of the deity—and concludes the novel—by uttering the Golden Dawn ritual formula "Hekas, Hekas, este bibleloi! Be ye far from us, O ye profane."[3] In the context of Fortune's bibliophilic, magical plot, this declaration serves not simply to banish the impure, but also to redefine things hitherto registered as profane—whether they be sexual acts or sordid pulp novels—as vessels of the sacred.

That *The Goat-Foot God*, the fourth of Fortune's six long-form works of occult fiction,[4] should end with this resolution is hardly surprising; after all, the form of magical sexual polarity deployed by Paston and Wilton at the novel's close lay at the heart of the Golden Dawn-inspired Inner Light magical system that the author taught from 1924 until her death in 1946. "The sex-forces," Fortune had maintained in her non-fictional occult writing, were "in their higher aspects . . . powerful regenerative agents"[5] able to remedy the psychological and spiritual alienation from which so many moderns were suffering. Fiction allowed her to extrapolate theory into practice, and indeed all her occult novels, as John Algeo, Gareth Knight, and others have pointed out,[6] revolve around a common heterosexual initiatory plot in which a hero and heroine are restored through culminating magical acts that, in Claire Fanger's words, "evoke sex without actually describing sex."[7] The constancy with which Fortune's novels emplot salvation through sexual polarity evidences a key dimension, not just of her magical, but of her *fictional* practice as well. In her literary criticism, Fortune made it repeatedly clear that she viewed popular fiction as much more than a form of entertainment or commercial enterprise; rather, it was an immersive, didactic mode that could lead correctly attuned readers, whether they were actively seeking esoteric wisdom or not, toward initiation and regenerative contact with the inner planes. When based on the real occult experiences of their writers—as had been, she claimed, *The Secrets of Dr Taverner*[8]—initiatory fictions might be so formulated as to produce pre-determined magical effects on their readers, constituting a form of alternative spiritual bibliotherapy whose operations Fortune often described in a top-down, programmatic way that left little room for reader agency. In her preface to *The Sea Priestess* (1935), for example, she invited her audiences, not to scrutinize, but, in an immersive way, to "identify themselves with one or the other of the characters according to taste," so as to "be led to a curious psychological experience—the therapeutic use of phantasy, an unappreciated aspect of psychotherapy."[9] This

172 OPEN SECRETS

advice has a curiously de-aestheticizing quality, encouraging the public to approach the novel as if it were a cookbook or a self-help manual valuable more for the pre-determined skills or benefits it would help them to acquire than for the quality and pleasures of its prose. It seems impossible to imagine the authors of contemporaneous works such as *Finnegan's Wake* (1939) or *The Years* (1936) offering similar advice to their readers, as if the aesthetic intensities of their fiction were to be subordinated to a single didactic *ethos* enacted upon a highly suggestible readership. Yet this seems to be exactly the position Fortune adopts in the self-reflective essay "The Novels of Dion Fortune," which she published in *The Inner Light* in 1936:

> There is a surprisingly large number of people in the world today who, though they have never seen the inside of a lodge, are of an advanced grade of enlightenment; and owing to the deservedly ill repute into which occultism has fallen ... will have nothing to do with it. To these, and especially to those in whom the realization is subconscious rather than conscious ... a book such as my "Winged Bull" can have all the effects of an initiation because it speaks directly to the subconscious by the method of imagery, which is the only language the subconscious understands.[10]

By reproducing her trademark trope of sexual initiation across the novels, then, Fortune seems in this essay to imagine herself as implanting gnosis directly into the mind of a supine reader whose subconscious is preconditioned to receive a universal esoteric symbolism.

The merits and, indeed, credibility of this highly instrumentalist conception of reading popular fiction, whether occult or otherwise, are perhaps best debated elsewhere; I will simply observe that, while subconscious initiation was certainly *one* of the "affordances"—that is, following Caroline Levine, "the range of uses" to which a literary form can be put[11]—of the occult revival's genre fiction, it was never the only one. As our preceding chapters have shown, this rich occultural corpus was neither conceived, structured, or received in just one way, nor destined for only a singular community of (literary or religious) practice. Moreover, its rich genre awareness militates against its reduction to nothing more than a covert spiritual information delivery system. I wish to linger instead on the ways in which the interlude in Jelkes's shop actually undoes the very mode of earnest, top-down textual initiation that *The Goat-Foot God* seems to have been designed to produce. For in the eclectic, sporadic, distracted, and dreamy nature of Paston's reading

CONCLUSION 173

amidst the stacks, all occult fictional roads must eventually lead to Rome, regardless of the initiatory status or aims of its writers, the sincerity or focus of its readers, or the verisimilitude of the phenomena and experiences it describes. The novel that Paston first picks up, *The Prisoner in the Opal*, is a sexploitationist potboiler whose Satanism is ultimately revealed by Mason's proto-Poirotian French detective, Hanaud, and his Watsonian sidekick, Julius Ricardo, to be wholly ersatz. Together, this investigative duo have been investigating the abduction of American socialite Joyce Whipple and the murder of financier's daughter Evelyn Devenish, both women ultimately revealed to be victims of a Satanic cabal operating out of the Chateau Suvlac in Bordeaux. Far from representing a sincere attempt to raise the devil (who notably never appears here), Mason's plot establishes Evelyn's stabbing atop the group's altar as a purely pragmatic means for her bored lover, the defrocked Catholic priest Robin Webster, to dispense with her and pursue a new affair.

Any spiritual seeker mining *The Prisoner in the Opal* for emic knowledge of esoteric philosophy or practice will find themselves sharply disappointed. Its vision of occultism, here synonymized with Satanism, is wholly cynical and disenchanted, representing it as a means through which men might control and exploit women. And yet, Paston finds himself drawn through it further into the esoteric fold. Recognizing that Mason's Satanism is a sham, he is nonetheless allured by the novel's central organizing metaphor of the opal as an obfuscating medium in which all humans are trapped, and whose hallmark opacity prevents us from seeing the numinous world face to face. Explaining this image at the novel's start, Ricardo reflects:

> The affair gave me quite a new vision of the world . . . I saw it as a vast opal inside which I stood. An opal luminously opaque, so that I was dimly aware of another world outside mine, terrible and alarming to the prisoner in the opal. It was what I called a fire opal, for every now and then a streak of crimson, bright as the flash of a rifle on a dark night, shot through the twilight which enclosed me. And all the while I felt that the ground underneath my feet was dangerously brittle just as an opal is brittle.[12]

Offered retrospectively, these remarks reveal that Ricardo's awareness of and interest in the occult world has not been deflated by Webster's fraudulence, just as Fortune's Paston, reading about Ricardo's fictional exploits in *The Prisoner in the Opal*, is not put off by Mason's sensationalized diablery. On the contrary, the thriller's very omissions and failures serve to goad him

174 OPEN SECRETS

further into what he will come to call the "Search for the Absolute,"[13] a quest sparked by "the idea of following up the clue that the author of 'The Prisoner in the Opal' had dangled for an instant before the ideas of his readers, and then snatched away again."[14]

The subsequent books that Paston will read, incompletely and with wavering levels of focus, in his ensuing trips to Jelkes's shop can be understood as so many flashes of light through the confining opal of mundane perception. That these occultural texts neither thoroughly convince, mutually cohere, or command complete attention only deepens their impact on Paston, inspiring in him something like the "dwam" effect whose description by Arthur Machen we discussed in Chapter 4. First, he turns to J. K. Huysmans's *The Damned* (1890), a classic work of Satanic decadence that follows the attempts of jaded Parisian writer Durtal to both complete his biography of the notorious fifteenth-century child murderer and occultist Giles de Rais and to observe a modern performance of the Black Mass led by the infamous Canon Docre, former lover of his own current paramour Hyacinthe. In Huysmans's rendering, both pursuits are driven less by an epistemophilic desire for spiritual knowledge than a need to escape *fin-de-siècle* ennui. Durtal is an atheist who yearns for genuine supernatural experience as a means to salve his feelings of emptiness; "he did not believe," we are told, "and yet he admitted the supernatural; he admitted it because how was it possible to deny, right here on earth, that we are surrounded by mystery on all sides, in our hearts, on the streets, everywhere when you came to think about it?"[15] Nonetheless, when Durtal does finally gain access to the mass, it fills him not with inspiration but disgust, and the novel closes with his assent to the gloomy observation of his friend Des Hermies: "this century does not give a fig for the coming glory of Christ; it adulterates the supernatural and vomits over the over-worldly."[16] In *The Great God Pan*, Paston's response to these fictional occurrences is far less somber and invested; "skipping skilfully" through the Rais sections of the novel that leave him cold, he pays attention only to the Docre plot.[17] And far from identifying himself "with one or the other of the characters according to taste," as counselled in Fortune's bibliotherapeutic introduction to *The Sea Priestess*, he forges an entirely independent response to the Black Mass not shared by any of Huysmans' fictional cast: "he couldn't see anything horrific about it. It appeared to him simply funny."[18]

This light-hearted bemusement is a world away from the bitter disgust that sends Huysmans's horrified Durtal fleeing into the streets; moreover,

CONCLUSION 175

it does not signify, as it does in *The Damned*, an end to the spiritual quest. Paston keeps reading—again selectively, lightly, nonchalantly, and sometimes notably negligently, as we see in what follows. His next two titles are historical novels recommended by Jelkes: first, Naomi Mitchison's *The Corn King and the Spring Queen* (1931), a sweeping Frazerian epic of contact between an ancient Black Sea-based Scythian magical community, the proto-socialist Sparta of Kleomenes III, and the Alexandrian court of libertine Pharaoh Ptolemy IV; and, second, *The Devil's Mistress* (1915) by Scottish Golden Dawn occultist J. W. Brodie-Innes, which fictionalizes the experiences and motives of the real-life Scottish woman Isobel Goudie, who confessed to practicing witchcraft in 1662. Paston is perplexed, if intrigued, by these works, having "heard that Naomi Mitchison was the daughter of a Professor of Greek, or some such classical subject, so probably her facts were correct,"[19] but refusing to let this awareness drive him into a reductively literalist reading of the text, one for which, in any case, he seems patently ill-equipped. After all, he manages to completely miss the pervasive and explicitly queer erotic content of *The Corn King*'s Spartan and Alexandrian plots, which describe in detail the love affair between Kleomenes and Panteus, and Nikomedes's attempted seduction of Ptolemy.[20] How else could he possibly conclude that "Naomi Mitchison was discreet; she left something to the imagination, which was more than Huysmans did; it was possible that a maiden lady might have read her books without noticing anything"?[21] Whether Paston's seeming ignorance of the novel's erotic homosexual content is due to his inattentive reading—he admits to finding the Spartan scenes less interesting than the Scythian ones[22]—or to Fortune's own well-documented and magically framed homophobia remains unclear.[23]

Paston adopts a similarly independent, even insubordinate, approach to Brodie-Innes's high-toned efforts to reclaim the Goudie case both for contemporary psychical research and as basis for a Christian conversion narrative. In his author's note to *The Devil's Mistress*, Brodie-Innes had justified his historical retelling on the basis that "the incidents in the tale, and their subsequent confirmation by documents, and much concerning the writing the book itself, would form exceedingly interesting matter for the Society for Psychical Research";[24] in the novel itself, he transports Goudie's experiences from the psychical to the theological realm by presenting her voluntary confession as the product of a rediscovered Christian faith that compels her to repent and offer, in publicizing her story, "somewhat of a warning to others."[25] "She was called of God,"[26] remarks her confessor Father Blackhall

176   OPEN SECRETS

in the novel, positioning her death, like that of Bulwer's Zanoni, as an act of noble and spiritually motivated self-sacrifice. Paston takes no notice of these emphases whatsoever; instead, he revels in the apparent ribaldry of *The Devil's Mistress*, "chuck[ling] to himself at the idea of some respectable burgher playing the part of the Devil, complete with the cow's horns, two on his head, and one in his hand. What a vogue, he thought, a well-run coven would have in Mayfair!"[27] The value of these occultural works by Mason, Huysmans, Mitchison, and Brodie-Innes to Paston lies not in the authenticity of their esoteric content, in the conscious intentions—didactic, initiatory, subversive, parodic, commercial—of their authors, nor indeed, in the sum of their parts. Rather, it lies in his feeling that, as he explains to Jelkes, "in a very odd way . . . they're alive. These things are alive. They have a kick in them."[28]

As formulated through Paston's sojourn in Jelkes's bookshop, the "liveliness" of occult fiction comes, not through its authorial intentionality, historical verisimilitude, or theological consistency, but rather in the readerly pleasure and impulsive momentum of the suspenseful action that it delivers through its diverse popular genre identifications. In this sense, his initial response to *The Prisoner in the Opal* sets the pattern for all his subsequent interactions with literary occulture: "There was a curious fascination in the rhythm of the prose, and he read on, hoping for more."[29] On and on and on he reads; in a Fortean sense, and with equal eschewal of definite closure, he marches. In so doing, he provides not only a potent rebuttal of the narrowly determinative sense of textual transmission and initiatory reception that Fortune would espouse in her non-fiction, but also a fruitful model for the newly expansive, and more formally sensitive, approach that *Open Secrets* has sought to bring to the popular fiction of Britain's occult revival. While the works examined in this study were selected on the basis of their writers' direct involvement in, or close proximity to, the long occult revival, it should be clear by now that such identifications do not consolidate any exclusively biographical understanding of their import or use. On the contrary, the existence of such historical affiliations and authorial positions only throws the discordant "liveliness" of our focal texts into sharper relief, rendering their reduction to the exclusive affordance of initiation all the more unfeasible. This is not to say that the criterion of authorial "belief," however elusive this quality might be to define and substantiate, is of no value to the interpretation of occult fiction. It matters very much that the highly ambivalent and often philosophically inconsistent

CONCLUSION   177

fictional depictions of spiritualist self-development or Thelemic ethics we have examined were produced by writers within these movements, rather than by, say, orthodox Christians. But the relationship between the two was never wholly seamless, with the "real" belief pre-determining the fictional inscription, and the fiction passively echoing back the alternative spiritual convictions and experiences that inspired it. On the contrary, the revival fictions we have examined pluralize and expand the range of interactions between popular genre, occult tradition, authorial inscription, and reader use, showing how spiritual practice and literary form are mutually transformed through contact.

What unites the writers considered in the preceding chapters—Bulwer, Emma Hardinge Britten, Marie Corelli, Mabel Collins, Arthur Machen, Charles Fort, and Aleister Crowley—is not a singular vision of literature's magical effects, but rather a shared commitment to popular genre fiction that implicitly rejects the rhetoric of biblio-elitism and exclusivity manifest in other arenas of revival discourse, most notably in the trope of the ancient, arcane book accessible only to initiated readers. Whether high-profile esoteric practitioners, life-long alternative spiritual seekers, or intermittent participants in occult networks, they recognized the value of the popular literary forms that people read every day—the *bildungsroman*, the romance, new journalistic tit-bit, and the detective story—in giving shape to, sharing, and testing the heterodox religious ideas newly articulable within the secular landscape of nineteenth- and twentieth-century Britain; moreover, they recognized the potential of alternative spiritual philosophies, experiences, and identities to introduce innovation within established genres and their familiar conventions. In their embrace of popular fiction *tout court*, they also refused their assent to what Pierre Bourdieu has identified as a central logic of bourgeois cultural production and its categories of artistic taste, namely the "supreme affirmation of . . . [one's] spiritual point of honour in the negation of popular materialism."[30] Rather, they insist that the immaterial realm of spirit and the commercial imperatives of popular fiction are inextricably connected and, potentially, reciprocally beneficial. This is not to say that they all realized this connection in a commercially (or artistically) successful manner; in their lifetimes, only Bulwer and Corelli gained significant fortune and reputation through their occultural fiction, while others obtained largely niche audiences for their efforts and remained in enduringly straitened circumstances. More important than the immediate reach or sales figures of the authors examined in *Open Secrets* to the history of British literary

178   OPEN SECRETS

occulture is their mutual conviction that occult ontology could and should be *popular* in the most basic sense; that is, of and for the people.

Collectively, the target public formed across these works is not a supine, homogenous, or passive one, waiting, sometimes with no conscious awareness, to receive top-down instruction drawn from real-life experiences wrapped in fiction or covert initiation within a single master-tradition or super-story. Rather, it is an unruly, co-participatory body invited to enter a fictional testing ground where thorny questions are posed, not only to a consensual material reality that seems to mitigate against the supernatural, but also to esoteric traditions, beliefs, and practices. The dilemmas evoked, but never firmly resolved, in the occult fiction we have encountered target the very heart of the revival's philosophical and moral enterprise: is occult study best understood as a means for self-development or self-obliteration? Might the extended periods of human existence offered through the revival's new religious movements—via theosophical reincarnation, for example, or personal spiritual survival—ensure the eventual delivery of justice to the oppressed, or simply create space to rationalize their suffering and eliminate its material bases? Were spiritual realms and paranormal worlds exploitable sources of information beneficial to earth-bound mortals, or rather did they stand outside of all established forms of human knowledge formation, their workings signifiable only through absurd juxtaposition and linguistic fragmentation? Were the laws of the mundane and magical realms fundamentally opposed or covertly committed to maintaining a similar status quo? In the ability, and even eagerness, of the texts we have encountered to probe such questions, we see the foolishness of relegating occult fiction to the status of confirmatory handmaiden to philosophies more definitively expressed elsewhere, such as in revealed writing or magical practice.

As we gain a greater understanding of the complexity of revival fiction, so, too, can we better grasp the latitude of its ideological spectrum. Our chapters have shown that the willingness of our focal authors to engage wide readerships with the numinous via popular genres was no indicator of their commitment to liberal democracy, or indeed, to any other singular political position. Their fiction thus offers us the means to inflect monolithic accounts of the ideological work of the specific occultural currents they alternately championed or courted, and indeed, of their own personal positions. Certainly, some of the texts examined in *Open Secrets*—*Zanoni*, *A Strange Story*, *Ghost Land*, and *The Scrutinies of Simon Iff*—evince a reactionary emphasis on the priority of social elites and the supremacy of patriarchal modes

CONCLUSION   179

of knowledge transmission. Many reflect the largely white, and sometimes explicitly white supremacist, orientation of nineteenth- and early-twentieth-century British occulture, evident in the ways they consign non-Western occultists to subordinate roles within the magical *Bildung* of European main characters and deploy occult philosophy to denigrate racial others as biological defectives incapable of spiritual evolution. Yet others, like Corelli's *Ziska* and Collins's *The Blossom and the Fruit*, emplot the ways in which esoteric world systems might provide—sometimes quite literally—weapons for historically disempowered groups, most notably women, as they seek violent retribution against their oppressors. Such contrasting ideological stances are evident not simply across, but sometimes also *within*, the works discussed, perhaps nowhere more vividly than in that Ur-text of modern British occulture, *Zanoni*, a novel that manages to condemn what it pitches as the destructive egalitarianism of revolutionary France while with the same breath appealing for the democratization of occult knowledge. In the popular fiction of Britain's occult revival, calls for the reinforcement of existing power structures routinely circulated alongside and comingled with demands for the rejection and complete remaking of the world.

Through their literary efforts, writers such as Bulwer, Britten, Corelli, Collins, Machen, Fort, Crowley, and Fortune helped to make modern occultism fully at home within popular genre fiction, where, as even a brief glance at contemporary young adult, horror, crime, fantasy, and science fiction lists reveal, it retains a significant presence to this day. The popularity of supernatural themes and magical motifs in widely adapted works by best-selling authors such as Terri Pratchett, J. K. Rowling, and Stephen King means that more English-language readers will encounter occultism first as a fictional trope than as a historical tradition or living spiritual practice. This is not to say that the occult revival's major currents survive only or primarily in popular culture; modern spiritualism, Theosophy, Thelema, Fortean Ufology, and Fortune's Society of the Inner Light all remain active, even if the exact number of their adherents—or indeed, the question of what constitutes adherence—may be difficult to ascertain, and is in some cases no doubt relatively small. In the twentieth and twenty-first centuries, these collectives have been joined by newer magical communities and alternative spiritual movements that take their inspiration, or even instigating source, directly from the pages of modern popular fiction: Lovecraftian chaos magic, for example, or the Grey School of Wizardry.[31] The increasingly symbiotic relationship between popular genre fiction and new religious expression has

180   OPEN SECRETS

much to tell us about what it means to seek spiritual experience in the secular age.

Indeed, it is precisely through the conditions of the secular that the occult revival's popular fiction was able to achieve the rich formal, philosophical, and spiritual innovation that I have been arguing for it in *Open Secrets*. In situating these works in this way, I join the powerful challenges of Talal Asad, Charles Taylor, and Callum Brown to a once-ascendent "secularization theory" that equated modern secularity with an uncomplicated and unidirectional decline of religious belief in the decades of my study, one manifested through "people turning away from God, and no longer going to Church."[32] Famously described by Taylor as a "subtraction story" that imagines moderns as "having lost, or sloughed off, or liberated themselves" from belief,[33] this narrative has been replaced by an understanding of how the context of modernity has instead multiplied the ways in which religion might be understood, practiced, and contested beyond the dominance of state authority. From a time when "it was virtually impossible not to believe in God," Taylor writes, we now inhabit an age where "faith, even for the staunchest believer, is one human possibility among others ... Belief is God is no longer axiomatic. There are alternatives."[34] Secularity's expansion of spiritual possibility beyond a single hegemonic model has been linked to its simultaneous privatization and interiorization of religion, a process that, as Tomoko Masuzawa has argued, operated through a new, ostensibly universal, but deeply Eurocentric, understanding of world religions as equivalent expressions of interiorized belief, of an "individual personal conviction" separable from the public sphere.[35]

Such challenges to the secularization-as-subtraction narrative have, as yet, had an uneven reception with the English literary scholarship of the long nineteenth-century period that *Open Secrets* surveys. As Deidre Lynch, Charles LaPorte, Sebastian Lecourt, and others have pointed out,[36] the now tenuous story of religion's decline played a foundational role in the disciplinary identity and canon formation of modern English literary studies. For a long time, the identity attributed to great literary works—that is, ones deemed worthy of inclusion on university syllabi or of scholarly attention—within this field was a distinctly disenchanted one which, as Jerilyn Sambrooke observes, saw "the rise of the novel ... narrated in relation to the fall of religious forms like the saint's life, the epic, or the spiritual autobiography."[37] This context functioned, not so much to exclude religious literary works—no such claim can be made of Victorian studies, whose traditional

CONCLUSION 181

canon is suffused with writing by and about ardent spiritual believers—as to emphasize, if I may borrow the famous words of T. S. Eliot on Lord Alfred Tennyson's *In Memoriam, A.H.H.*, "the quality of [their] doubt,"[38] and sometimes to quarantine their religiosity from their formal accomplishments and innovations. As Justin Neuman remarks, "no critic would deny the existence of religious novels, but according to the dominant line of reasoning, works of religious fiction achieve their religiosity despite the form, structure, and history of the genre."[39]

What Mark Knight and LaPorte have dubbed a millennial "religious turn" in eighteenth- and nineteenth-century literary studies has started to change this landscape by eroding a once-prevalent critical queasiness about the persistence of belief in post-Enlightenment literature.[40] But the latter's legacy lives on in the textual application and purview of this turn, indeed, in its designation as a "turn" at all. As we saw in our introduction, occult beliefs, magical practices, and esoteric traditions have been on the radar of literary critics for far longer than contemporary esotericism scholars have been willing to recognize. The fact that many literary scholars themselves have not recognized this critical heritage as a threat to disenchanted or anti-religious framings of their disciplinary history—ones that identify the reclamation of the spiritual as a twenty-first century phenomenon[41]—suggests that they, too, may not recognize occult fiction as worthy of inclusion within serious scholarly conversations about "real" religion in literature. Certainly, this exceptionalism is understandable; as we have seen, the literary sub-discipline that has historically been most welcoming to the recovery and study of occult fiction—namely, Gothic studies—has also long consigned supernaturalism to the category of psychological symptom or anxiogenic cultural metaphor, although there are welcome signs that this tide is beginning to change. As the religious turn within modern literary studies continues to gain momentum, it is crucial that the fiction of the occult revival not be left behind, dismissed as either too weird to fit an often-tacit definition of religion, or too clearly affiliated with high-profile new religious proponents or popularizers to be anything but crude, sub-literary propaganda.

Ultimately, the power of the literary works examined in *Open Secrets* lies in their refusal to hierarchize the relationship between the spiritual and the aesthetic, to subordinate one into the service of the other. Literary genre and spiritual seekership, they show, are inextricably connected in a relationship of mutual innovation. In this way, they offer invaluable tools for thinking through the messiness of what religion might mean, and how its literary

182   OPEN SECRETS

presence might manifest, in the secular age. Some were written by committed practitioners of specific new religious movements, some by disaffiliated seekers, and some by disillusioned former initiates; all were produced from perspectives that entertained the reality of a numinous world that orthodox religious traditions alone could not fully express. The modes of spiritual experience they emplot both follow and deviate from the pattern assigned to secular expressions of religiosity, being at once private and inward— consider the journoccultural epiphanies of Machen on the beat, ultimately incommunicable on the tabloid page, if not in personal memoir—and defiantly public and outward-facing, as in Simon Iff's manipulation of the British government under the aegis of the Hemlock Club in *The Scrutinies of Simon Iff*. Indeed, their very adoption of popular fictional form itself demonstrates an enduring commitment to publicizing and communalizing spiritual seekership, to staking claims for the numinous firmly within the public sphere and the domain of mass entertainment, and to synthesizing forms of fictional and religious practice. In these ways, the popular fiction of Britain's occult revival offers us new ways to understand the emergence of modern literature beyond paradigms of dis- or re-enchantment, and beyond a binaristic juxtaposition of private belief to public practice. It leads us to a threshold that is open and unguarded.

Notes

Chapter 1

1. As example of such dire consequences, *Zanoni*'s introduction mentions the case of the Abbé de Villars, the seventeenth-century French author of the Rosicrucian novel *Le comte de Gabalis* (1670) who was brutally murdered in 1673. The simultaneously erotic and sacred nature of the books in Mr. D__'s shop is manifest in their description as "idols" in their "niches" and as "favourite sultanas of his wizard harem." Edward Bulwer Lytton, *Zanoni* (London: Routledge, Warne, and Routledge, 1864), ix.
2. Following the usage guidelines set out in the *Oxford Dictionary of National Biography*, I will henceforth refer to the author simply as "Bulwer," the last name by which he was known for most of his writing life. Andrew Brown, "Lytton, Edward George Earle Lytton Bulwer [*formerly* Edward George Earle Lytton Bulwer], first Baron Lytton," *Oxford Dictionary of National Biography*, https://www-oxforddnb-com.
3. Joscelyn Godwin, *The Theosophical Enlightenment* (Albany: State University of New York Press, 1994), 28. For more on the occult influence and reception of *Zanoni*, see J. Jeffrey Franklin, *Spirit Matters: Occult Beliefs, Alternative Religions, and the Crisis of Faith in Victorian Britain* (Ithaca: Cornell University Press, 2018), 27–44; David Huckvale, *A Dark and Stormy Oeuvre: Crime, Magic and Power in the Novels of Edward Bulwer Lytton* (Jefferson, NC: McFarland and Co., 2015), 28.
4. Bulwer, *Zanoni*, 173.
5. On Bulwer's declining reputation and readership, see Marie Mulvey-Roberts, "Edward Bulwer-Lytton and Poisoned Prose," in *The Palgrave Book of Steam Age Gothic*, ed. Clive Bloom (Cham: Palgrave Macmillan, 2021), 91–112.
6. This figure is discussed, for example, in Rudolf Steiner's *An Outline of Occult Science*, trans. Max Gysi (London: Theosophical Publishing Society, 1914) and in *The Guardian of the Threshold* (1912), one of Steiner's *Four Mystery Dramas* (Hudson: Steiner Books, 2007); see also Dion Fortune's *The Mystical Qabalah* (London: Williams and Norgate, 1935). The Dweller forms the subject and title of a track on Van Morrison's 1982 album, *Beautiful Vision*.
7. Robert Gilbert, "The Great Chain of Unreason: The Publication and Distribution of the Literature of Rejected Knowledge in England During the Victorian Era" (PhD diss., University of London, 2009), 24.
8. Robert Gilbert, "The Great Chain of Unreason," 24.
9. Bulwer, *Zanoni*, ix.
10. Bulwer, *Zanoni*, ix.
11. Bulwer, *Zanoni*, x.
12. Bulwer, *Zanoni*, xv.
13. Bulwer, *Zanoni*, xvi.
14. For example, in the novel's closing prison scenes, as the adept Zanoni prepares to sacrifice his life for his beloved Viola, the narrator observes that here "the reverence that comes from great emotions restored Nature's first and imperishable, and most noble Law—THE INEQUALITY BETWEEN MAN AND MAN!" Bulwer, *Zanoni*, 291.
15. Bulwer, *Zanoni*, xvi. This is a clear reference to *Zicci*, a textual precedent for *Zanoni* published in the *Monthly Chronicle* in 1838.
16. Hugh Urban, *Secrecy: Silence, Power, and Religion* (Chicago: University of Chicago Press, 2022), 6–7.
17. Urban, *Secrecy*, 17.
18. On these developments, see Richard Noakes, *Physics and Psychics: The Occult and the Sciences in Modern Britain* (Oxford: Oxford University Press, 2019); Nick Freeman, "The Black Magic Bogeyman: 1908-1935," in *The Occult Imagination in Britain, 1875–1947*, ed. Andrew Radford and Christine Ferguson (London: Routledge, 2018), 94–109.

184 NOTES

19. The Centre for the History of Hermetic Philosophy and Related Currents was established at the University of Amsterdam in 1999, followed by the launch of the Exeter Centre for the Study of Esotericism at the University of Exeter (now the Centre for Magic and Esotericism Studies) in 2005; these scholarly initiatives built on the momentum of Antoine Faivre's appointment as Chair in the History of Esoteric and Mystical Currents at the Sorbonne's *École Practique des Hautes Études* in 1979. The field is today served by a major disciplinary society, the European Society for the Study of Western Esotericism (founded in 2005), several dedicated academic journals—*Aries: Journal for the Study of Western Esotericism* (relaunched in 2001) and *Correspondences* (inaugurated 2013)—and various book series, including the one in which this volume appears.

20. Michael Bergunder, "What is Esotericism? Cultural Studies Approaches and the Problems of Definition in Religious Studies," *Method and Theory in the Study of Religion* 22, no.1 (2010): 12.

21. Wouter Hanegraaff, *Esotericism and the Academy: Rejected Knowledge in Western Culture* (Oxford: Oxford University Press, 2012), 152.

22. Kocku Von Stuckrad, "Western Esotericism: Towards an Integrative Model of Interpretation," *Religion* 35, no. 2 (2005): 88.

23. For an insightful recent discussion of the exclusions produced during the institutional formation of esotericism studies, see Egil Asprem and Julian Strube's edited collection, *New Approaches to the Study of Esotericism* (Leiden: Brill, 2021).

24. Hanegraaff, *Esotericism and the Academy*, 369, 7.

25. Christine Ferguson, "Beyond Belief: Literature, Esotericism Studies, and the Challenges of Biographical Reading in Arthur Conan Doyle's *The Land of Mist*," *Aries: Journal for the Study of Western Esotericism* 22 (2021): 205–230.

26. Wouter J. Hanegraaff, *Western Esotericism: A Guide for the Perplexed* (London: Bloomsbury, 2013), 152. For similar claims of the absence or neglect of occulture in literary studies scholarship, see also Tessel Bauduin and Henrik Johnsson, "Conceptualizing Occult Modernism," in *The Occult in Modernist Art, Literature, and Cinema*, ed. Tessel Bauduin and Henrik Johnsson (Cham: Palgrave Macmillan, 2018), 3.

27. Miriam Wallraven, *Women Writers and the Occult in Literature and Culture: Female Lucifers, Priestesses, and Witches* (London: Routledge, 2015), 2.

28. Egil Asprem and Julian Strube, "Esotericism's Expanding Horizon: Why This Book Came to Be," in *New Approaches to the Study of Esotericism*, ed. Egil Asprem and Julian Strube (Leiden: Brill, 2021), 1.

29. Pierre Georges Castex, *Le conte fantastique en France: de Nodier à Maupassant* (Paris: Librairie José Corti, 1951), 13. Castex defines this "Renaissance de l'Irrational" as a particularly modern wave of scientifically aligned mysticism whose practices included mesmerism, spiritism, and Swedenborgianism.

30. Nicholas Goodrick-Clarke, *The Western Esoteric Traditions: A Historical Introduction* (Oxford: Oxford University Press, 2008), 11.

31. Per Faxneld, *Satanic Feminism: Lucifer as the Liberator of Women in Nineteenth-Century Culture* (Oxford: Oxford University Press, 2017), 19.

32. Faxneld, *Satanic Feminism*, 185.

33. Faxneld, *Satanic Feminism*, 22.

34. Chris Baldick and Robert Mighall, for example, damningly accuse much modern Gothic criticism of having "abandoned any credible historical grasp upon its object, which it has tended to reinvent in the image of its own projected intellectual goals of psychological 'depth' and political 'subversion'" and of "mistakenly presenting Gothic literature as a kind of 'revolt' against bourgeois rationality, modernity, or Enlightenment." Chris Baldick and Robert Mighall, "Gothic Criticism," in *A New Companion to the Gothic*, ed. David Punter (Oxford: Blackwell, 2012), 268.

35. Terry Eagleton, *Ideology: An Introduction* (London: Verso, 1990), 2.

36. Adam Drazin, "The Object Biography," in *Lineages and Advancements in Material Culture Studies: Perspectives from UCL Anthropology*, (London: Routledge, 2020), 64.

37. Julian Strube, "Towards the Study of Esotericism without the 'Western': Esotericism from the Perspective of a Global Religious History," in *New Approaches to the Study of Esotericism*, ed. Egil Asprem and Julian Strube (Leiden: Brill, 2021), 45.

38. Victoria Nelson's *The Secret Lives of Puppets* (Cambridge: Harvard University Press, 2001) traces this process of religious sublimation in art from antiquity to the twentieth century; *Gothicka* picks it up in the Gothic and cultural production on the twenty-first century, where she bases her analysis "on the foundational argument laid down in *The Secret Life of Puppets*." Victoria Nelson,

NOTES 185

Gothicka: Vampire Heroes, Human Gods, and the New Supernatural (Cambridge: Harvard University Press, 2012), xii.

39. Nelson asserts this bold act of dating by stating, "After the year 1700, Western artists and writers would continue to express, though often in an unconscious manner, hidden and increasingly taboo notions of immortality, divinity, and the incorruptible body." Nelson, *The Secret Lives of Puppets*, 43.

40. Nelson, *The Secret Lives of Puppets*, 18.

41. Nelson, *Gothicka*, xii.

42. As Owen Davies—one of many scholars to make this point—observes: "despite the so-called Enlightenment, the practice of magic never disappeared in Europe, manifesting itself in the activities of treasure seekers and cunning-folk, and in the rarefied esoteric religious and Freemasonry movements of the eighteenth century. During the early nineteenth century new pseudo-sciences such as mesmerism renewed intellectual interest in universal hidden forces." Owen Davies, *Grimoires: A History of Magic Books* (Oxford: Oxford University Press, 2009), 175. Other recent challenges to the assumed extent and scope of secular disenchantment in the West can be found in Egil Asprem, *The Problem of Disenchantment: Scientific Naturalism and Esoteric Discourse, 1900–1939* (Leiden: Brill, 2014); Jason Josephson Storm, *The Myth of Disenchantment: Magic, Modernity, and the Birth of the Human Sciences* (Chicago: University of Chicago Press, 2017); Noakes, *Physics and Psychics*.

43. So, too, does Nelson refrain from "survey[ing] the present state of Gothick scholarship and position[ing] [her] own thinking within it," as doing so, she writes, would have deprived her of the "room either mentally or on the page, for the explorations presented here." Nelson, *Gothicka*, xii, xiii.

44. She quickly adds that this warning "is perhaps not so threatening as secular humanists ... might fear." Nelson, *Gothicka*, xii.

45. Arthur Versluis, *Restoring Paradise: Western Esotericism, Literature, Art, and Consciousness* (Albany: State University of New York Press, 2004), 3.

46. Versluis, *Restoring Paradise*, 12.

47. Jeffrey J. Kripal, *Authors of the Impossible: The Paranormal and the Sacred* (Chicago: University of Chicago Press, 2010), 25.

48. Versluis, *Restoring Paradise*, 5.

49. Across these two different perspectives, it seems that literary scholars cannot win, either always already too ideological and fanciful, or too dogmatic and empirical, in their approach to occult fiction. Faxneld's study at least has the virtue of evidencing and explaining the critical tendencies he finds problematic. Versluis's *Restoring Paradise*, by contrast, shows far fewer signs of sustained contact with the state of contemporary literary studies, and nowhere presents examples of the kind of quantitative data-collection methods he argues to be ascendent within a field which is in fact home to an ever-growing methodological variety, including (but by no means limited to) formalism, affect theory, eco-theory, digital humanities, post-colonialism, gender studies and queer theory, cultural materialism, creative criticism, new historicism, book and publishing studies, reception history, fan studies, medical humanities, and adaptation studies.

50. For a compelling account of the disciplinary and literary-critical formation of Gothic Studies, see Tim Jones, *The Gothic and the Carnivalesque in American Culture* (Cardiff: University of Wales Press, 2015), 15–20 and Scott Brewster, "Gothic Criticism in the Twentieth Century: Who is this Who is Coming?" in *Twentieth-Century Gothic: An Edinburgh Companion*, ed. Sorcha Ni Fhlainn and Bernice Murphy (Edinburgh: Edinburgh University Press, 2022), 64–80.

51. Talia Schaffer, "Canon," *Victorian Literature and Culture* 46, no. 3/4 (2018): 595.

52. These include the International Gothic Association (launched in 1991); the University of Stirling's International Centre for Gothic Studies (founded in 1998) and accompanying MLitt in the Gothic Imagination programme, which ran until 2020; the Manchester Centre for Gothic Studies; the Centre for the History of the Gothic at the University of Sheffield; and the MA in Victorian Gothic at the University of Portsmouth. Key Gothic studies journals and presses include *Gothic Studies* (founded in 1991) *Studies in Gothic Fiction, Irish Gothic Studies, Horror Studies,* the University of Wales's *Gothic Literary Studies* series and *Anthem Studies in Gothic Literature.*

53. Jarlath Killeen, *Gothic Literature, 1825–1914* (Cardiff: University of Wales Press, 2009), 124.

54. Christopher Partridge, "Occulture is Ordinary," in *Contemporary Esotericism*, ed. Egil Asprem & Kennet Granholm (Sheffield: Equinox Press, 2013), 113.

186 NOTES

55. The same cannot be said of the field's engagement with the role of orthodox religious traditions and theology in Gothic writing, which has seen a considerable upsurge in recent years; see Sam Hirst's *Theology in the Early British and Irish Gothic, 1764–1834* (London: Anthem Press, 2023); Madeline Potter's *Theological Monsters: Religion and the Irish Gothic* (Cardiff: University of Wales Press, 2025); and the Gothic Bible Project at the University of Sheffield. At the time of writing, the impact of new and heterodox religions on the genre has yet to receive the same depth of treatment.

56. For a discussion of this kind of de-occulting critical practice in the reception history of Bram Stoker's *Dracula* (1897), see Christine Ferguson, "Dracula and the Occult" in *The Cambridge Companion to Dracula*, ed. Roger Luckhurst (Cambridge: Cambridge University Press, 2017), 57–65.

57. Hirst, Theology in the Early British and Irish Gothic, 105.

58. Patrick Brantlinger, *The Reading Lesson: The Threat of Mass Literacy in Nineteenth-Century British Fiction* (Bloomington: Indiana University Press, 1998), 35.

59. Nicola Bown, Carolyn Burdett, and Pamela Thurschwell, "Introduction," in *The Victorian Supernatural*, ed. Nicola Bown, Carolyn Burdett, and Pamela Thurschwell (Cambridge: Cambridge University Press, 2004), 12, 9.

60. Alexandra Warwick, "Feeling Gothicky," *Gothic Studies* 9, no. 1 (May 2007): 5–15, 8.

61. Catherine Spooner, *Post-Millennial Gothic: Comedy, Romance, and the Rise of Happy Gothic* (London: Bloomsbury, 2017), 2.

62. Jones, *The Gothic and the Carnivalesque in American Culture*, 60.

63. Baldick and Mighall, "Gothic Criticism," 273.

64. Baldick and Mighall, "Gothic Criticism," 271.

65. Baldick and Mighall, "Gothic Criticism," 271.

66. Norman Paige, "Permanent Re-Enchantments: On Some Literary Uses of the Supernatural from Early Empiricism to Modern Aesthetics," in *The Re-Enchantment of the World: Secular Magic in a Rational Age*, ed. Joshua Landy and Michael Saler (Stanford: Stanford University Press, 2009), 160–161.

67. Paige, "Permanent Re-Enchantments," 172.

68. Fred Botting, *Gothic* (Abingdon: Routledge, 2014), 1.

69. Botting, *Gothic*, 2.

70. Marco Pasi, "Arthur Machen's Panic Fears: Western Esotericism and the Irruption of Negative Epistemology," *Aries* 7 (2007): 74.

71. Of the mysteriously curative and life-lengthening powers of the Chaldean-Rosicrucian collective to which he belongs, occult adept Mejnour claims, "All we profess to do is but this—to find out the secrets of the human frame, to know why the parts ossify and the blood stagnates, and to apply continual preventatives to the effects of Time. This is not Magic; it is the Art of Medicine rightly understood." Bulwer, *Zanoni*, 154.

72. Botting, *Gothic*, 9.

73. Roberts, *Gothic Immortals*, 157.

74. Godwin, *The Theosophical Enlightenment*, 218. For a further challenge to claims of Bulwer's Rosicrucian adepthood, and that French magus Éliphas Lévi visited him at Knebworth House, see David Huckvale, *A Dark and Stormy Oeuvre: Crime, Magic and Power in the Novels of Edward Bulwer Lytton* (Jefferson, NC: McFarland and Co., 2015), 128.

75. Killeen, *Gothic Literature 1825–1914*, 128.

76. In his opening presidential address to the society in 1882, Cambridge intellectual Henry Sidgwick stated, "[W]e are all agreed that the present state of things is a scandal to the enlightened age in which we live . . . I say it is a scandal that the dispute as to the reality of these phenomena should still be going on, that so many competent witnesses should have declared their belief in them, that so many others should be profoundly interested in having the question determined, yet that the educated world, as a body, should still be simply in the attitude of incredulity." Henry Sidgwick, "Address of the President at the First General Meeting," in *The Fin de Siécle: A Reader in Cultural History, c. 1880–1914*, ed. Sally Ledger and Roger Luckhurst (Oxford: Oxford University Press, 2000), 273.

77. A discussion of the range of intellectual, religious, and philosophical positions accommodated within the SPR can be found in Janet Oppenheim, *The Other World: Spiritualism and Psychical Research in England, 1850–1914* (Cambridge: Cambridge University Press, 1985) and Noakes, *Physics and Psychics*.

78. In Doyle's angry letter of resignation from the society in January 1930, he deems the Society "unscientific and biased" and complains that it had "confined its energies to the misrepresentation and hindrance of those who have really worked at the most important problem ever presented to mankind." "Sir Arthur Conan Doyle's Resignation," *Journal for the Society of Psychical Research* (March 1930): 45–46, 46.

79. Killeen, *Gothic Literature 1825–1914*, 142.

80. Bulwer and Marie Corelli were among the best-selling authors of the nineteenth century; Arthur Machen, although he never obtained wealth or even consistent financial stability from his authorship, gained international acclaim as a weird fiction pioneer.

81. Ken Gelder, *Popular Fiction: The Logics and Practices of a Literary Field* (London: Routledge, 2004), 22.

82. David M. Earle, *Re-Covering Modernism: Pulps, Paperbacks, and the Prejudice of Form* (Burlington: Ashgate, 2009), 8.

83. For more on Bulwer's relationship with Lévi, see Leslie Mitchell, *Bulwer Lytton: The Rise and Fall of a Victorian Man of Letters* (London: Hambledon, 2003).

84. Charles Maturin, *Melmoth the Wanderer: A Tale* (Edinburgh: Constable and Company, 1820), 4:441.

85. Bulwer, *Zanoni*, 285.

86. Mark Turner, "Seriality, Miscellaneity, and Compression in Nineteenth-Century Print," *Victorian Studies* 62, no. 2 (2020): 283–294, 283.

87. A fuller discussion of cultural anxieties around mass literacy in this period, and their representation in the novel, can be found in Brantlinger's *The Reading Lesson* (1998).

88. The dependence of Modern Spiritualism on emergent mass entertainment and media industries is treated at greater length in Simone Natale's excellent *Supernatural Entertainments: Victorian Spiritualism and the Rise of Modern Media Culture* (University Park: Pennsylvania State University Press, 2016).

89. In her classic study of the decade's realist fiction, Kathleen Tillotson observes "One reason why the novel is particularly interesting in the eighteen-forties is that it was in the process of becoming the dominant form. In the eighteen-forties critics began to say what they continued to say more forcibly for the next forty years or so, that the novel was the form of expression most suited to the age ... that it had become what the epic and the drama had been in previous ages"; at this point, "the demand for novels was larger than ever before". See Kathleen Tillotson, *Novels of the Eighteen-Forties* (Oxford: Clarendon Press, 1954), 13, 15. Writing nearly half a century later, Patrick Brantlinger confirms Tillotson's account of the novel's authorization in this decade: "by the 1840s novels and novel-reading were growing respectable. With Jane Austen and Sir Walter Scott, and through the emergence of new publishing and circulating-library practices and institutions such as Mudie's, the novel gained widespread cultural acceptance." Brantlinger, *The Reading Lesson*, 2.

90. For more on Bulwer's association with these genres and his popularity in this period, see Mitchell, *Bulwer Lytton* and Lawrence Poston, "1832," in *A New Companion to Victorian Literature and Culture*, ed. Herbert Tucker (Oxford: John Wiley & Sons, 2014), 12–13.

91. Mitchell, *Bulwer Lytton*, 111.

92. Brantlinger, *The Reading Lesson*, 18–19.

93. On Bulwer's transformation from a youthful radical to a late-life Tory, see Mitchell, *Bulwer Lytton*.

94. Recent accounts of the historical emergence, thematics, and style of the early Victorian penny blood, see Jarlath Killeen, "Victorian Gothic Pulp Fiction," in *The Victorian Gothic: An Edinburgh Companion*, ed. Andrew Smith and William Hughes (Edinburgh: Edinburgh University Pres, 2012): 43–46; Anna Gasperini, *Nineteenth-Century Popular Fiction, Medicine and Anatomy: The Victorian Penny Blood and the 1832 Anatomy Act* (Cham: Palgrave Macmillan, 2019).

95. In an early letter to his friend Frederick Moncton, Falkland describes a disastrous early love affair which causes him to "[pass] ... like Melmoth, from youth to age"; later, he gives his own volume of Maturin's novel to the Lady Emily, so that their shared reading of it may cement their budding love. She writes in her journal, "He left a book here; it is a volume of 'Melmoth.' I have read every word of it, and whenever I have come to a pencil-mark by him, I have paused to dream over that varying and eloquent countenance, the low soft tone of that tender voice, till the book has fallen from my hands, and I have started to find the utterness of my desolation!" Edward Bulwer Lytton, *Falkland* in *The Greatest Gothic Novels of Edward Bulwer-Lytton* (Chicago: Musaicum Books, 2021), 1297, 1336.

188 NOTES

96. For more on Bulwer's short-lived and largely unsuccessful editorial tenure at the *New Monthly Magazine*, see Mitchell, *Bulwer Lytton*, 117.
97. One cause of this confusion lies in the story's later separate publication within the Bulwer Lytton's collection of stories and essays, *The Student* (1835), where readers could encounter it independently of *Asmodeus at Large*.
98. Godwin, *The Theosophical Enlightenment*, 125; Roberts, *Gothic Immortals*, 167.
99. Edward Bulwer Lytton, *Asmodeus at Large* (n.p.: OK Books, 2021), 56. The supernatural being in question is described in suggestively pagan terms as a "gigantic, motionless, and aged Man, or rather a man-like Shape. His vast countenance was unutterably and dreadly calm; his brows, like the Olympian Jove's, overhung his majestic features; but the orbs beneath were dull and lifeless, there was no ray in them." Bulwer, *Asmodeus at Large*, 56.
100. Bulwer, *Asmodeus at Large*, 68.
101. Bulwer, *Asmodeus at Large*, 4.
102. Peter France characterizes Le Sage's novel as offering "a combination of modern rationalism, lightness of tone, and playful use of the supernatural." Peter France, "*Le Diable Boiteux*," in *The New Oxford Companion to Literature in French*, ed. Peter France (Oxford: Oxford University Press, 1995), 240.
103. Peter Brooks, *Realist Vision* (New Haven: Yale University Press, 2005), 3.
104. Bulwer, *Asmodeus at Large*, 14.
105. Edward Bulwer Lytton, "Asmodeus at Large—No. X," *The New Monthly Magazine and Literary Journal* 37, no. 146 (February 1833): 155–168, 168.
106. Bulwer, "Asmodeus at Large—No. X," 168.
107. Mitchell, *Bulwer Lytton*, 259.
108. In *Gothic Immortals*, for example, Marie Roberts identifies *Zicci* as the text alluded to in the introduction to *Zanoni*, the "shorter version of a hieroglyphic manuscript passed on to the narrator by a suspected Rosicrucian." Roberts, *Gothic Immortals*, 168.
109. *Zicci* closes with Glyndon following "an impulse that he could not resist . . . to seek the mystic. He would demand, that hour, his initiation into the worlds beyond our world; he was prepared to breathe a diviner air. He entered the castle, and strode through the shadowy and star-lit gallery which led to Mejnour's apartment." Edward Bulwer Lytton, "*Zicci* (1838)," in *The Greatest Gothic Novels of Edward Bulwer-Lytton* (n.p.: OK Books, 2021) 1397–1512, 1511–1512. This exact paragraph is duplicated at the end of Book 4, Chapter 2 of *Zanoni*.
110. Bulwer, *Zicci*, 1417–1418.
111. Bulwer, *Zicci*, 1420.
112. Bulwer, *Zicci*, 1449.
113. See the Kindle edition of *Zicci*, published by OK Books, which subtitles it as a "prequel to *Zanoni*." Edward Bulwer Lytton, *Zicci*, 1397.
114. Bulwer, *Zanoni*, 112.
115. Bulwer, *Zanoni*, 93.
116. Bulwer, *Zanoni*, 93.
117. Bulwer, *Zanoni*, 284.
118. Bulwer, *Zanoni*, 154–155.
119. Bulwer, *Zanoni*, 155.
120. Bulwer, *Zanoni*, 181.
121. Bulwer, *Zanoni*, xi.
122. Book Seven, titled "The Reign of Terror," footnotes in its first chapter the *Papiers inédits chez Robespierre* as source for the following words that Robespierre speaks: "Adieu! This day itself, I go forth to riot on thy fears!" Another of Bulwer's notes, earlier in the chapter, states: "Not to fatigue the reader with annotations, I may here observe that nearly every sentiment ascribed in text to Robespierre, is to be found expressed in various discourses." Bulwer, *Zanoni*, 236.
123. These are launched chiefly through the demonization of Jean Nicot, a lecherous and hideously ugly painter committed to the artistic realism and political revolution that Bulwer presents as dead ends here. Warning Glyndon to stay away from him, Zanoni declaims "See you not that The Grander Art, whether or poet or painter, ever seeking for the TRUE, abhors the REAL." Bulwer, *Zanoni*, 63.
124. Bulwer, *Zanoni*, 143–151; 196–198.
125. Anna Maria Jones, "Inductive Science, Literary Theory, and the Occult in Edward Bulwer-Lytton's 'Suggestive' System," in *Strange Science: Investigating the Limits of Knowledge in the*

Victorian Age, ed. Lara Karpenko and Shalyn Claggett (Ann Arbour: University of Michigan Press, 2017), 229.

126. Bulwer, *Zanoni*, 302.
127. Huckvale, *A Dark and Stormy Oeuvre*, 143.
128. Jones, "Inductive Science," 216.
129. Harriet Martineau, "Zanoni Explained," in Edward Bulwer Lytton, *Zanoni* (London: Routledge, Warne, and Routledge, 1864), 302.
130. Jones, "Inductive Science," 230.
131. Martineau, "Zanoni Explained," 393.
132. For example, Blavatsky here refers to "the vicious beings which move in the astral waves like fish in the water; being who surround us, and whom Bulwer-Lytton calls in *Zanoni* 'the dwellers in the threshold.'" H. P. Blavatsky, *Isis Unveiled: A Master Key to the Mysteries of Ancient and Modern Science and Theology* (New York: J. W. Bouton, 1877), 1:158.
133. "Zanoni," *Sheffield Independent*, January 2, 1847, 2; for a similar response, see also "Zanoni: by the Author of 'Night and Morning,' 'Rienzi,' etc.," *The Metropolitan Magazine* 33, no. 132 (April 1842): 354–364.
134. "The book is less designed to amuse than to set its readers thinking—to what amount of good purpose, must depend on the readers themselves . . . we may add that, whether its whole drift is or is not perceived, it has qualities which cannot fail of instant appreciation. It is an eloquent and thoughtful book beyond question." "Zanoni," *The Literary Gazette*, February 26, 1842, 4. See also "Literature," *Caledonian Mercury*, April 4, 1842, 4.
135. "Literature," *Morning Post*, June 16, 1843, 6.
136. "Esoteric Bosh," *Saturday Review of Politics, Literature, Science, and Art* 58, no.1499 (July 19, 1884): 70.
137. Bulwer, *Zanoni*, vi.

Chapter 2

1. Goethe's *Ur-Bildungsroman* was first introduced to Anglophone readers as *Wilhelm Meister's Apprenticeship* in Thomas Carlyle's 1824 translation.
2. *Bildungsromane* by these writers include Paschal Beverly Randolph, *The Wonderful Story of Ravalette* (New York: Sinclair Tousey, 1863); Mabel Collins, *The Blossom and the Fruit: The True Story of a Black Magician* (London: Published by the Authors, 1888) and *The Idyll of the White Lotus* (London: Reeves and Turner, 1884); David Duguid, *Hafed, Prince of Persia: His Experiences in Earth-Life and Spirit-Life* (London: J. Burns, 1876); Marie Corelli, *A Romance of Two Worlds* (London: Richard Bentley & Son, 1886); Edward Bulwer Lytton, *Zanoni* (London: Saunders & Otley, 1842) and *A Strange Story*, 2 Vol. (London: Sampson Low, Son, and Co., 1862); *Ghost Land, or Researches into the Mysteries of Occultism, Illustrated by a Series of Autobiographical Sketches*, ed. and trans. Emma Hardinge Britten (Boston: Published for the Author, 1876). Although Emma Hardinge Britten was initially identified only as the translator and editor of the latter, she is now widely agreed to be its author. I will present the arguments for her authorship, and the text's fictional status, later in the chapter.
3. Sara Lyons, "Recent Works in Victorian Studies and the *Bildungsroman*," *Literature Compass* 15, no. 4 (April 2018): 1.
4. Richard Salmon, "The English *Bildungsroman*," in *The Oxford History of the Novel in English: Volume Three: The Nineteenth-Century Novel, 1820–1880*, ed. John Kucich and Jenny Bourne-Taylor (Oxford: Oxford University Press, 2012), 90.
5. Suzanne Howe, *Wilhelm Meister and his English Kinsmen: Apprentices to Life* (New York: Columbia University, 1930), 4.
6. For more on the gendered stakes of the *Bildungsroman*, see Lorna Ellis, *Appearing to Diminish: Female Development and the British Bildungsroman, 1750–1850* (Lewisburg: Bucknell University Press, 1999); Susan Fraiman, *Unbecoming Women: British Women Writers and the Novel of Development* (New York: Columbia University Press, 1993).
7. Lyons, "Recent Work in Victorian Studies and the Bildungsroman," 2.
8. Franco Moretti, *The Way of the World: The Bildungsroman in European Culture* (London: Verso, 1987), 10.
9. M. M. Bakhtin, "The *Bildungsroman* and Its Significance in the History of Realism (Toward a Historical Typology of the Novel)," in *Speech Genres and Other Late Essays*, ed. Caryl Emerson and Michael Holquist, trans. Vern McGhee (Austin: University of Texas Press, 1987), 23.

190 NOTES

10. Julia Brown Prewitt, "The Moral Scope of the English *Bildungsroman*," in *The Oxford Handbook of the Victorian Novel*, ed. Lisa Rodensky (Oxford: Oxford University Press, 2013), 663.

11. Sarah Vandergrift Eldrige and C. Allen Speight, "Introduction," in *Goethe's Wilhelm Meister's Apprenticeship and Philosophy*, ed. Sarah Vandergrift Eldrige and E. Allen Speight (Oxford: Oxford University Press, 2020), 3.

12. Jesse Rosenthal, for example, argues that genre develops its notion of *Bildung* from Lord Shaftesbury's *Characteristicks of Men, Manners, Opinions, Times*, which was published in 1711; see Jesse Rosenthal, *Good Form: The Ethical Experience of the Victorian Novel* (Princeton: Princeton University Press, 2016), 131. For a further discussion of the debates around the genre's origin point, see also John Frow, Melissa Hardie and Vanessa Smith, "The Bildungsroman: Form and Transformation," *Textual Practice* 34, no. 12 (December 2020): 1906.

13. Scholars have pointed out that Carlyle's translation and introduction of *Meister* worked to reinforce his own philosophical agenda rather than to reveal Goethe's. In the first major study of the novel's reception in England, Suzanne Howe observes that "[t]hrough Carlyle the sane and corrective power of action was the moral lesson Wilhelm Meister taught its English readers and imitators" and "Carlyle used the mildly pantheistic sage of Weimer to bolster up a shaky Presbyterian Christianity" (Howe, *Wilhelm Meister and his English Kinsmen*, 10, 89).

14. This usage was perhaps borrowed from the earlier Boston-based spiritualist newspaper *The Spiritual Age*, which ran between 1858 and 1860, and also bore the epigraph "Light! More Light" on its masthead, although without attribution to Goethe.

15. "5 Ephesians 13," in *The Bible: Authorized King James Version and Apocrypha*, ed. Robert Carroll and Stephen Prickett (Oxford: Oxford University Press, 1997), 243.

16. William Howitt, "Spiritualist Idiosyncrasies in the Goethe Family," *The Spiritual Magazine* (September 1866): 416–426.

17. Steiner's commentaries are collected in *Nature's Open Secret: Introductions to Goethe's Scientific Writings*, trans. John Barnes and Mado Spiegler (New York: Anthroposophic Press, 2000).

18. Edward Lingan, *The Theatre of the Occult Revival: Alternative Spiritual Performance from 1875 to the Present* (New York: Palgrave Macmillan, 2014), 63.

19. Johann Wolfgang von Goethe, *Wilhelm Meister's Apprenticeship*, 3 vols., trans. Thomas Carlyle (Edinburgh: Oliver & Boyd, 1894), 1:30.

20. Rosenthal, *Good Form: The Ethical Experience of the Victorian Novel*, 132. Similarly skeptical of the novel's putative realism, Thomas Jeffers remarks that "it is ... freighted ... with fairy tale motifs, forced coincidences, sudden deaths, paranormal sexuality, outbursts of poetry, seminar-style philosophical disquisitions, and self-reflexive meditations on Hamlet and aesthetics generally." Thomas Jeffers, *Apprenticeships: The Bildungsroman from Goethe to Santayana* (New York: Palgrave Macmillan, 2005), 15.

21. Goethe, *Wilhelm Meister's Apprenticeship*, 1:134.

22. Goethe, *Wilhelm Meister's Apprenticeship*, 1:340.

23. Goethe, *Wilhelm Meister's Apprenticeship*, 1:321.

24. Goethe, *Wilhelm Meister's Apprenticeship*, 2:180.

25. Carolyn Abbate and Roger Parker, *A History of Opera: The Last Four Hundred Years* (London: Penguin, 2015), 177.

26. Theodore Ziolkowski, *The Lure of the Arcane: The Literature of Cult and Conspiracy* (Baltimore: Johns Hopkins University Press, 2013), 95.

27. Jeffers, *Apprenticeships*, 27.

28. Goethe, *Wilhelm Meister's Apprenticeship*, 3:310.

29. Goethe, *Wilhelm Meister's Apprenticeship*, 3:126.

30. Goethe, *Wilhelm Meister's Apprenticeship*, 3:217.

31. Michael Bell, *Open Secrets: Literature, Education, and Authority from J.J. Rousseau to J.M. Coetzee* (Oxford: Oxford University Press, 2007), 97.

32. Goethe would continue Wilhelm's story in *Wilhelm Meisters Wanderjahre, oder Die Entsagenden*, a sequel published in 1821 and then substantially revised in 1829.

33. Goethe, *Wilhelm Meister's Apprenticeship*, 3:304.

34. Moretti, *The Way of the World*, 213.

35. Although he was still regularly attending séances and consulting mesmeric healers in the early 1860s, Bulwer made sure to distance himself from spiritualist adherence in his writing. Thus, in an unpublished chapter of *A Strange Story* now held at the Hertfordshire Country Record Office, he had one character remark that "I have had the curiosity to read much of the 'spirit-manifestation' literature, and I cannot find in the whole of it a single new idea—a single idea

NOTES 191

for which an express revelation seems in the least degree called for." Bulwer, quoted in Andrew Brown, "The 'Supplementary Chapter' to Bulwer Lytton's *A Strange Story*," *Victorian Literature and Culture* 26, no. 1 (1988): 169. The ambiguous nature of Bulwer's relationship to the Society of Rosicrucians is discussed in Chapter 1 of this book.

36. Brown, "The 'Supplementary Chapter,'" 157.
37. Howe, *Wilhelm Meister and his English Kinsmen*, 126.
38. Richard Salmon, "The Genealogy of the Literary *Bildungsroman*: Edward Bulwer-Lytton and W.M. Thackeray," *Studies in the Novel* 36, no. 1 (Spring 2004): 42.
39. Bulwer, *Asmodeus at Large*, 61.
40. Bulwer, *Asmodeus at Large*, 61.
41. Bulwer, *Asmodeus at Large*, 73.
42. When, in *A Strange Story*'s final section, Fenwick immigrates to Australia with his new bride, he finds gold on his land that is then used in an alchemical ritual to extend Margrave's life and save Lilian's. In *Great Expectations*, Pip finds himself the beneficiary of a mysterious fortune that he believes to have come from Miss Havisham but is in truth the product of the transported convict Magwitch's labour in New South Wales.
43. Brown, "The 'Supplementary Chapter,'" 60.
44. Although unidentified in the narrative, a contemporary review of *A Strange Story* identifies the likely location of Fenwick's practice to be Lincoln, where Bulwer had sat for MP. "Art V.—*A Strange Story*. By the Author of 'My Novel,'" *The Christian Remembrancer*, April 1882, 453.
45. Bulwer, *A Strange Story*, 1:10.
46. Bulwer, *A Strange Story*, 1:159.
47. Describing his impressions of Hyde to his companion Mr. Utterson, Enfield states, "He is not easy to describe . . . I never saw a man I so disliked, and yet I scarce know why. He must be deformed somewhere; he gives a strong feeling of deformity, although I couldn't really specify the point. He's an extraordinary looking man, and yet I really can name nothing out of the way." Robert Louis Stevenson, *The Strange Case of Dr Jekyll and Mr Hyde*, ed. Martin Danahay (Peterborough: Broadview, 2005), 35–36.
48. Bulwer, *A Strange Story*, 1:194.
49. Bulwer, *A Strange Story*, 1:150.
50. Bulwer, *A Strange Story*, 1:314.
51. Bulwer, *A Strange Story*, 1:167.
52. Bulwer, *A Strange Story*, 1:184.
53. Bulwer, *A Strange Story*, 1:186.
54. Bulwer, *A Strange Story*, 1:217.
55. Bulwer, *A Strange Story*, 1:218.
56. Bulwer, *A Strange Story*, 1:218.
57. Bulwer, *A Strange Story*, 2:309.
58. Bulwer, *A Strange Story*, 2:308.
59. Bulwer, *A Strange Story*, 2:309.
60. Bulwer, *A Strange Story*, 1:4.
61. Bulwer, *A Strange Story*, 1:2.
62. In Chapter XLV, after hearing Fenwick's account of the Scin-Laeca apparition, Faber explains it as a result of the younger man's suggestibility and pre-disposition to the fantastic, declaring "I mock the sorcerer and disdain the spectre." Bulwer, *A Strange Story*, 2:58.
63. Bulwer, *A Strange Story*, 2:213.
64. Bulwer, *A Strange Story*, 2:233.
65. Bulwer, *A Strange Story*, 2:382.
66. Indeed, Bulwer would pen only four novels in the remaining eleven years of his life, the last of which remained unfinished: *The Coming Race* (1871), *Kenelm Chillingly* (1873), *The Parisians* (1873), and *Pausanias, The Spartan* (1873).
67. "Art V.—*A Strange Story*. By the Author of 'My Novel,'" 448.
68. "Art V.—*A Strange Story*. By the Author of 'My Novel,'" 448.
69. "Art V.—*A Strange Story*. By the Author of 'My Novel,'" 449.
70. "Art IV. Modern Novelists: Sir Edward Bulwer-Lytton," *Westminster Review*, April 1865, 495.
71. "A Strange Story," *The Saturday Review*, March 8, 1862, 273–275, 273.
72. Marc Demarest identifies the spiritualist contemporaries who believed *Ghost Land*'s Chevalier Louis de B__ to be none other than Britten herself in his preface to her earlier, and also pseudonymously published, *Art Magic*; see Marc Demarest, "Introduction to the Annotated Edition,"

192 NOTES

in *Art Magic; or Mundane, Sub-Mundane, and Super-Mundane Spiritism*, ed. Marc Demarest (Forest Grove: Typhon Press, 2011), xxxix.

73. For more on these aspects of her career, see Bridget Bennett, "Crossing Over: Spiritualism and the Atlantic Divide," in *Special Relationships: Anglo-American Affinities and Antagonisms*, ed. Janet Beer and Bridget Bennett (Manchester: Manchester University Press, 2002), 89–109; Robert Mathiesen, "Britten, Emma [Floyd] Hardinge," in *Dictionary of Gnosis and Western Esotericism*, ed. Wouter Hanegraaff (Leiden: Brill, 2006), 202–206; Robert Mathieson, *The Unseen Worlds of Emma Hardinge Britten: Some Chapters in the History of Western Occultism* (New York: Theosophical History, 2001); Robert Thompson, "The Chevalier's Secret: Emma Hardinge Britten and the Dawn of American Occultism," *Literature and Theology* 33, no. 4 (December 2019): 451–475; Wallraven, *Women Writers and the Occult in Literature and Culture*; Molly Youngkin, "A 'Duty' to 'Tabulate and Record': Emma Hardinge Britten as Periodical Editor and Spiritualist Historian," *Victorian Periodicals Review* 49, no. 1 (Spring 2016): 49–75. Marc Demarest's *Emma Hardinge Britten* website (ehbritten.org) and *Chasing Down Emma* blog (ehbritten.blogspot.com) remain the fullest and most comprehensive web resources on Britten.

74. J. J. Morse, "Preface," in Emma Hardinge Britten, *Autobiography of Emma Hardinge Britten*, ed. Mrs Margaret Wilkinson (Manchester: John Heywood, 1900), v–ix.

75. As various scholars have pointed out, Britten's involvement with the occultic milieu likely long pre-dated this publicly declared advent of her mediumistic development. In her autobiography, she refers to working briefly as a clairvoyant seer for a London-based occult collective known as the Orphic Circle in the 1830s; key members are known to have included the astrologer 'Zadkiel' (Richard James Morrison, 1795–1874), the fourth (Philip Henry) Earl Stanhope (1781–1855), and, strikingly, Edward Bulwer Lytton. See Emma Hardinge Britten, *Autobiography*, 4. For more on Britten's involvement with this group, see Joscelyn Godwin, *Theosophical Enlightenment*, 205–212.

76. Britten, *Autobiography*, 31.

77. Britten, *Autobiography*, 34.

78. Britten, *Autobiography*, 39. This claim of Britten's unacknowledged role in the editorship of *The Christian Spiritualist* was reiterated in the second series of *Ghost Land*, published in her later periodical *The Unseen Universe*. Here the Chevalier de B__, newly arrived in New York, visits the journal's headquarters and declares that "the chief portion" of its contents as being "written and edited by Mrs Hardinge." Emma Hardinge Britten, "Extracts from 'Ghost Land,' Volume II; Or Researches into the Realm of Spiritual Existence. By the Author of 'Art Magic,'" *The Unseen Universe* 1, no. 3 (June 1892): 116.

79. Ezra, "Haunted Houses 1: The Picture Spectres," *Spiritual Telegraph* VI, no. 30 (November 21, 1857): 233–234.

80. Charles Dickens, "Letter to W.H. Wills, 25 January 1854," in *The Letters of Charles Dickens: Volume 7, 1853–55*, ed. Graham Storey, Kathleen Tillotson, and Angus Easson (Oxford: Clarendon Press, 1993), 258. Demarest speculates on the potential content of the papers and nature of their correspondence in "Emma (Harding) and Charles (Dickens)," *Chasing Down Emma*, January 27, 2009, http://ehbritten.blogspot.com/2009/01/emma-harding-and-charles-dickens.html.

81. Emma Hardinge Britten, "The Wildfire Club," in *The Wildfire Club* (Boston: Berry, Colby, and Company, 1861), 340.

82. Britten, "The Wildfire Club," 340–341.

83. As Evelyn Lord writes, in sex-focused Hell Fire club collectives such as the Medmenham Friars, "Priapus became king, and Bacchus god; hell-fire took a classical turn that had to be reached by crossing the River Styx. Public and respected men became satyrs, and decency fled, to the delight of the hack writer and gutter press, which like today sold itself on sensational exaggerated stories." Evelyn Lord, *The Hell-Fire Clubs: Sex, Satanism, and Secret Societies* (New Haven: Yale University Press, 2010), xxvii–xxviii.

84. Britten, "The Wildfire Club," 7.

85. For more on *Lucifer* and its fictional publications, see Christine Ferguson, "The Luciferian Public Sphere: Theosophy and Editorial Seekership in the 1880s," *Victorian Periodicals Review* 53, no. 1 (Spring 2020): 76–101.

86. Britten's title here may be an allusion to Orphic Circle member Philip Henry Stanhope.

NOTES 193

87. Emma Hardinge Britten, "The Mystery of No. 9 Stanhope Street: A Romance of Real Life," *The Unseen Universe: A Monthly Magazine Devoted to Spiritualism, Occultism, Ancient Magic, Modern Mediumship, and Every Subject that pertains to the Whence, What, and Whitherword of Humanity* 1, no. 7 (October 1892): 351; Emma Hardinge Britten, "The Mystery of No. 9 Stanhope Street," *The Unseen Universe* 1, no. 8 (November 1892): 408.
88. Demarest, "Introduction to the Annotated Edition," iii–lvi.
89. Aren Roukema, "Naturalists in Ghost Land: Victorian Occultism and Science Fiction," in *The Occult Imagination in Britain, 1875–1947,* ed. Christine Ferguson and Andrew Radford (London: Routledge, 2018), 186.
90. "Having laboriously built up the persona of the author of *Art Magic,*" writes Demarest, "Britten found herself with ready and exclusive access to a male occult adept cut-out, into whose mouth Britten could put controversial material." "Introduction to the Annotated Edition," xlvi.
91. Britten, *Autobiography,* 3–4.
92. Godwin, *The Theosophical Enlightenment,* 204.
93. Henry Steel Olcott, *Old Diary Leaves: The True Story of the Theosophical Society* (London: G. P. Putnam's Sons, 1895), 189.
94. Bulwer, *Zanoni,* 299.
95. Roukema, "Naturalists in Ghost Land," 184.
96. My analysis of *Ghost Land*'s first series takes the first book edition as base text.
97. Britten, *Ghost Land,* 17.
98. Britten, *Ghost Land,* 21.
99. This epigraph appears on page 27 of the first issue of *The Unseen Universe,* positioned directly before the opening of the opening instalment of *Ghost Land*'s second series. See *The Unseen Universe* 1, no. 1 (April 1892): 27.
100. Britten, *Ghost Land,* 78.
101. Britten, *Ghost Land,* 182–183.
102. Britten, *Ghost Land,* 214.
103. Britten, *Ghost Land,* 214.
104. Britten, *Ghost Land,* 323.
105. Britten, *Ghost Land,* 240.
106. Britten, *Ghost Land,* 407.
107. Britten, *Ghost Land,* 368.
108. Britten, *Ghost Land,* 424.
109. Emma Hardinge Britten, "Extracts from Ghostland, Volume II; Or Researches into the Realm of Spiritual Existence. By the Author of 'Art Magic.'" *The Unseen Universe* 1, no. 12 (March 1893): 619.
110. Moretti, *The Way of the World,* 185, 182.
111. Until very recently, scholarly debate on *Ghost Land* focused largely on identifying its pseudonymous author so as to align their recorded biographical experience with the work's textual representation. See Godwin, *The Theosophical Enlightenment,* 206–212; Mathiesen, *The Unseen Worlds of Emma Hardinge Britten.* Only with the publication of Roukema's "Naturalists in *Ghost Land*" has this focus started to shift toward questions of genre.
112. Rosenthal, *Good Form,* 133.
113. Elisha Cohn, *Still Life: Suspended Development in the Victorian Novel* (Oxford: Oxford University Press, 2015), 2.
114. Alex Owen, *The Darkened Room: Women, Power, and Spiritualism in Late Victorian England* (Chicago: University of Chicago Press, 1989), 6.
115. Thompson, "The Chevalier's Secret," 459.

Chapter 3

1. A. P. Sinnett, *Karma* (London: Chapman and Hall, 1886), 223.
2. The emergence and circulation of reincarnation belief in Victorian Britain is treated in Olav Hammer, *Claiming Knowledge: Strategies of Epistemology from Theosophy to the New Age* (Leiden: Brill, 2004) and Julie Chajes, *Recycled Lives: A History of Reincarnation in Blavatsky's Theosophy* (Oxford: Oxford University Press, 2019).
3. Joy Dixon, *Divine Feminine: Theosophy and Feminism in England* (Baltimore: Johns Hopkins University Press, 2001), 160.
4. Paul Edwards, *Reincarnation* (Amherst: Prometheus Books, 2002), 11.

194 NOTES

5. William Wordsworth, "Ode: Intimations of Immortality from Recollections of Early Childhood," *Poems, in Two Volumes, Vol. 2* (London: Longman, Hurst, Rees, and Orme, 1807).
6. Edwards, *Reincarnation*, 12.
7. The presence of reincarnationism in these bodies of thought is examined at greater length in Chajes, *Recycled Lives*, and Hammer, *Claiming Knowledge*.
8. Late Victorian Britain's fascination with ancient Egypt and its religious culture was intensified via the simultaneous developments of Egyptology as an academic discipline and by British imperial conquest in the near East. See Roger Luckhurst, *The Mummy's Curse: The True History of a Dark Fantasy* (Oxford: Oxford University Press, 2012); David Gange, *Dialogues with the Dead: Egyptology in British Culture and Religion, 1822–1922* (Oxford: Oxford University Press, 2013); Maria Fleischhack, *Narrating Ancient Egypt: The Representation of Ancient Egypt in Nineteenth-Century and Early Twentieth-Century Fiction* (Frankfurt: Peter Lang, 2015); Eleanor Dobson, *Writing the Sphinx: Literature, Culture, and Egyptology* (Edinburgh: Edinburgh University Press, 2020); *Victorian Alchemy: Science, Magic, and Ancient Egypt* (London: UCL Press, 2022); Maria Fleischhack, ed., *Victorian Literary Culture and Ancient Egypt* (Manchester: Manchester University Press, 2020).
9. James Santucci, "Theosophy," in *The Cambridge Companion to New Religious Movements*, ed. Mikael Rothstein and Olav Hammer (Cambridge: Cambridge University Press, 2012), 231. This list of female reincarnationists operating with late Victorian Britain is far from exhaustive; others include the American spiritualist and medium Cora Scott Tappan (1840–1923), who delivered trance speeches on rebirth during her 1875 London lecture tour, and the socialist, feminist, and Theosophist Annie Besant (1847–1933).
10. Hammer, *Claiming Knowledge*, 465. Despite Blavatsky's protestations, Kardec's influence on her thinking, as both Joscelyn Godwin and Julie Chajes have documented, remains clear. See Godwin, *The Theosophical Enlightenment*, 303; Chajes, *Recycled Lives*, 88.
11. A. P. Sinnett, *Esoteric Buddhism* (London: Trübner & Co., 1888); E. D. Walker, *Reincarnation: A Study of Forgotten Truths* (New York: John W. Lovell, 1888); Annie Besant, *Reincarnation* (London: Theosophical Publishing Society, 1898).
12. See Rosa Campbell Praed, *Nyria* (London: T. Fisher Unwin, 1904); Mabel Collins, *The Idyll of the White Lotus* (London: Reeves & Turner, 1884); Mabel Collins, with —, *The Blossom and the Fruit: A True Story of a Black Magician* (London: Published by the Authors, 1888); H. P. Blavatsky, *Nightmare Tales* (London: Theosophical Publishing Society, 1892).
13. As Sinnett explains in *Esoteric Buddhism*, this rest period of one-and-a-half millennia was to be spent in the *devachan*, a "condition of . . . subjective enjoyment," or, as Sinnett lyrically describes it, "rosy sleep" in which individuals recovered before returning to reap the penalties or rewards accrued during their last life. Sinnett, *Esoteric Buddhism*, 83, 85.
14. Annie Besant attributed this amnesia to the fundamental lack of fixed personal essence in humans. What survived from incarnation to incarnation, she suggested, was not a continuous personality, but a depersonalized spirit with no unique or exclusive connection to any of its previous historical avatars. As she explains in *Reincarnation*, "Sashital Dev does not reincarnate as Caius Giabrio, and then as Johanna Wirther, blossoming out as William James in nineteenth-century England, but it is the one eternal son of Mind that dwells in each of these in turns . . . William Johnson in the nineteenth century cannot look back on, or remember, *his* rebirths, for *he* has never been born before, nor have *his* eyes seen the light of an earlier day" (18). Nonetheless, she was able to accommodate the position that *certain* people might, with appropriate training and spiritual qualities, be able to clairvoyantly excavate their own former lives and those of others. For an example of this Theosophical mnemonic practice, see Annie Besant and C. W. Leadbeater, *The Lives of Alcyone* (Adyar: Theosophical Society, 1924).
15. Sinnett, *Karma*, 184.
16. Such encounters between past incarnation and present self are described in Countess of Caithness, *A Midnight Visit to Holyrood* (London: C. L. H. Wallace, 1887), and in Edward Maitland, *Anna Kingsford: Her Life, Letters, Diary, and Work* (London: George Redway, 1896).
17. Caithness, *A Midnight Visit to Holyrood*, 39–40.
18. Caithness, *A Midnight Visit to Holyrood*, 38.
19. Hammer, *Claiming Knowledge*, 479.
20. H. Rider Haggard, "About Fiction," *Contemporary Review* 51 (February 1887): 177.
21. Haggard, "About Fiction," 172, 177.
22. R. L. Stevenson, "A Gossip on Romance," *Longman's Magazine* 1, no. 1 (November 1882): 73.
23. Andrew Lang, "Realism and Romance," *Contemporary Review* 52 (November 1888): 688.

NOTES   195

24. Lang, "Realism and Romance," 689.
25. Haggard, *She*, 100.
26. Haggard, *She*, 294.
27. Anne McClintock, *Imperial Leather: Race, Gender, and Sexuality in the Colonial Contest* (London: Routledge, 1995), 23.
28. P. Pavri, *Theosophy Explained in Questions and Answers* (Adyar: Theosophical Publishing House, 1930), 7.
29. Sumathi Ramaswamy, *The Lost Land of Lemuria: Fabulous Geographies, Catastrophic Geographies* (Berkeley: University of California Press, 2004), 54.
30. Gauri Viswanathan, *Outside the Fold: Conversion, Modernity, and Belief* (Princeton: Princeton University Press, 1998), 204.
31. Ramaswamy, *The Lost Land of Lemuria*, 68. For a discussion of early Theosophy's relationship to surrounding concepts of race and racist ideologies, see James Santucci, "The Notion of Race in Theosophy," *Nova Religio: The Journal of Alternative and Emergent Religions* 11, no. 3 (February 2008): 37–63.
32. Blavatsky's use of this racial slur is documented in John Patrick Deveney, *Paschal Beverly Randolph: A Nineteenth-Century Black American Spiritualist, Rosicrucian, and Sex Magician* (Albany: State University of New York Press, 1997), 254. For an example of Theosophical apologetics for colonial genocide, see A. Banon, "Racial Development," *The Theosophist* 9, no. 97 (October 1885): 76–77. Here Banon, a Fellow of the Theosophical Society, declares that "the white men, the last sub-race of the fifth race, have a mission to perform in crowding out and so causing to die out the remnants of the third and fourth races, as the natives of America have already nearly all passed from view. The year 2000 will see the Aryan race sole possessors of the world, the older races having died out from want of stamina" (77).
33. Mortimer Collins, *Transmigration* (London: Hurst and Blackett, 1873), 3:290–291.
34. We can sense the latter part of this shift in the complaint of one of *Transmigration's* reviewers that "There is no sequence in Mr Collins's idea of transmigration; neither duty or agency is involved in it. It is a mere fancy dependent on the fates, not upon ourselves." "Transmigration," *British Quarterly Review* 118 (April 1874): 574.
35. Sinnett, *Karma*, 15.
36. Sinnett, *Karma*, 15.
37. Sinnett, *Karma*, 265–266.
38. Thomas Hardy, *Tess of the d'Urbervilles* (London: W. W. Norton, 1991), 58.
39. Hardy, *Tess of the d'Urbervilles*, 57.
40. Hardy, *Tess of the d'Urbervilles*, 57.
41. Thomas Hardy, *The Well-Beloved and Alicia's Diary* (Paris: Zulma Classics, 2005), 64, 68, 67.
42. Thomas Hardy, *The Well-Beloved and Alicia's Diary*, 50–51.
43. "The Well-Beloved," *The Athenaeum* 3624 (April 10, 1897): 471.
44. *The Well-Beloved*, quoted in "The Quest of the Well-Beloved," *The Review of Reviews* (April 1897): 394.
45. Neil Hultgren, *Melodramatic Imperial Writing: From the Sepoy Rebellion to Cecil Rhodes* (Athens: Ohio University Press, 2014), 54.
46. Rita Felski, *The Gender of Modernity* (London: Harvard University, 1995), 115.
47. Felski, *The Gender of Modernity*, 119.
48. Felski, *The Gender of Modernity*, 120.
49. Felski, *The Gender of Modernity*, 115.
50. E. C., "Problems of Popularity," *The Speaker* 5, no. 106 (October 12, 1901): 50–51, 51.
51. Corelli's fiction—like Bulwer's—was also popular in Britain's colonies, most notably in India and in West Africa. Her reception in these sites is discussed in Prodosh Bhattacharya, "The Reception of Marie Corelli in India," in *New Readings in the Literature of British India, c. 1780–1947*, ed. Shafquat Towheed (Hanover: Ibidem-Verlag, 2014), 219–244; Priti Joshi, *In Another Country: Colonialism, Culture, and the English Novel in India* (New York: Columbia University Press, 2002); Stephanie Newell, *Literary Culture in Colonial Ghana* (Manchester: Manchester University Press, 2002).
52. Marie Corelli, *A Romance of Two Worlds* (London: Methuen, 1922), 229.
53. Here as elsewhere, Corelli plays fast and loose with archaeological evidence. The First Babylonian Empire was in ascendancy between the nineteenth to the sixteenth century BCE— three full millennia after the dating that *Ardath's* mystic Zuriel offers for Al-Kyris when he

196 NOTES

describes Christianity as "a Creed that shall not be declared to men for full five thousand years!" Marie Corelli, *Ardath: The Story of a Dead Self* (London: Richard Bentley & Co., 1889), 2:143.

54. "A Romance of Two Worlds," *Quarterly Review*, October 1898, 119.

55. Felski, *The Gender of Modernity*, 125.

56. For a fuller discussion of the vehemence and complexity of Corelli's opposition to female suffrage, see Annette Federico, *Idol of Suburbia: Marie Corelli and Late Victorian Literary Culture* (Charlottesville: University of Virginia Press, 2000).

57. Marie Corelli, *Ziska: The Problem of a Wicked Soul* (New York: Frederick A. Stokes Company, 1897), 12. Corelli had launched a similar attack on the invasive nature of the Western tourist industry in *Ardath*, whose narrator laments that "soon there will not be an inch of ground left on the narrow extent of our poor planet that has not been trodden by the hasty, scrambling, irreverent footsteps of some one or other of the ever-prolific, all-spreading, English-speaking race." Corelli, *Ardath*, 1:129–130.

58. Corelli, *Ziska*, 16.

59. Corelli, *Ziska*, 190.

60. Corelli, *Ziska*, 133.

61. Corelli, *Ziska*, 300.

62. Niyati Sharma, "Race and the Entranced Mind in Late Victorian Popular Fiction" (D.Phil, University of Oxford, 2018), ch. 4.

63. Gayatri Chakravorty Spivak, "Can the Subaltern Speak?" in *Marxism and the Interpretation of Culture*, ed. Cary Nelson and Lawrence Grossberg (Basingstoke: Macmillan, 1988), 296.

64. Rosa Braidotti, "In Spite of the Times: The Postsecular Turn in Feminism," *Theory, Culture, and Society: Explorations in Critical Social Science* 25, no. 6 (2008): 6.

65. Felski, *The Gender of Modernity*, 139.

66. Corelli, *Ziska*, 315.

67. Aleister Crowley, *Magick in Theory and Practice* (London: Published for Subscribers Only, 1929), 289.

68. "Editorial," *The Equinox: The Official Organ of the A∴A∴, The Review of Scientific Illuminism* 1, no. 1 (1909): 2.

69. Bulwer, *Zanoni*, 138.

70. Mark S. Morrisson, "Women, Periodicals, Esotericism in Modernist-Era Print Culture," in *Women, Periodicals and Print Culture in Britain, 1890s–1920s* (Edinburgh: Edinburgh University Press, 2019), 379.

71. Mabel Collins, "The Blossom and the Fruit: A Tale of Love and Magic," *Lucifer* 1, no. 1 (September 15, 1887), 23.

72. Mabel Collins, "The Blossom and the Fruit: The True Story of a Magician," *Lucifer* 1, no. 3 (November 15, 1887), 193.

73. "H. P. Blavatsky begs leave to announce that owing to the continued severe illness of her co-editor Mabel Collins, she accepts, until further notice, the sole editorial responsibility for the magazine." "Editorial Notice," *Lucifer* 3, no. 14 (October 1888): 138.

74. This episode, known as the Collins–Coues affair, is covered in detail in Kim Farnell, *Mystical Vampire: The Life and Works of Mabel Collins* (Oxford: Mandrake, 2005), 92–100.

75. Farnell, *Mystical Vampire*, 82–84.

76. Farnell, *Mystical Vampire*, 82.

77. Collins and —, The Blossom and the Fruit, 4.

78. Collins and —, *The Blossom and the Fruit*, 5.

79. Collins and —, *The Blossom and the Fruit*, 6.

80. Collins and —, *The Blossom and the Fruit*, 15.

81. Collins and —, *The Blossom and the Fruit*, 8.

82. Collins and —, *The Blossom and the Fruit*, 13.

83. Collins and —, *The Blossom and the Fruit*, 13.

84. Collins and —, *The Blossom and the Fruit*, 325–326.

85. In the consistency of Fleta's gender identity across many incarnations, Collins seems to break ranks with other first-wave Theosophical contemporaries such as Annie Besant and Charles Leadbeater who posited that individual monads could change sex across their many lives. For an account of such Theosophical theories of gender mutability, see Dixon, *Divine Feminine*, 112–116.

86. Collins and —, *The Blossom and the Fruit*, 110.

87. Collins and —, *The Blossom and the Fruit*, 328.

NOTES 197

88. Lisa Downing, *Selfish Women* (London: Routledge, 2019), 1.
89. Downing, *Selfish Women*, 1.
90. Downing, *Selfish Women*, 1–2.
91. Collins and —, *The Blossom and the Fruit*, 22.
92. Collins and —, *The Blossom and the Fruit*, 85.
93. Collins and —, *The Blossom and the Fruit*, 87.
94. Collins and —, *The Blossom and the Fruit*, 162.
95. Mabel Collins, *Light on the Path: With Notes and Comments* (London: Kegan, Paul, Trench, Trübner, & Co., 1895), 1.
96. Collins, *Light on the Path*, 8.
97. Collins and —, *The Blossom and the Fruit*, 149.
98. Collins and —, *The Blossom and the Fruit*, 80.
99. Collins and —, *The Blossom and the Fruit*, 134.
100. Collins and —, *The Blossom and the Fruit*, 158.
101. Collins and —, *The Blossom and the Fruit*, 13.
102. There is no record of either Blavatsky, Fortune, or Collins herself giving birth to or raising children; while Anna Kingsford did bear a daughter prior to her uptake of occultism, she lived apart from her for much of her life.
103. Collins and —, *The Blossom and the Fruit*, 159.
104. An important exception to these examples of heterosexual co-initiation lies in *A Romance of Two Worlds*, where it is in erotic partnership with the beautiful sculptress Zara that Corelli's heroine forges her initiation. See Christine Ferguson, "Zanoni's Daughters: Fin de Siècle Fictions of Female Initiation," in *The Cosmic Movement: Sources, Contexts, Impacts*, ed. Boaz Huss and Julie Chajes (Beersheba: Ben Gurion University Press, 2021), 91–126.
105. Collins and —, *The Blossom and the Fruit*, 328.
106. Collins and —, *The Blossom and the Fruit*, 100.
107. Collins and —, *The Blossom and the Fruit*, 101.
108. Collins and —, *The Blossom and the Fruit*, 101.
109. Collins and —, *The Blossom and the Fruit*, 102.
110. Collins and —, *The Blossom and the Fruit*, 234.
111. For more on the presence of gender essentialism in twentieth-century British paganism, see Shai Feraro, *Woman and Gender Issues in British Paganism, 1945–1990* (London: Palgrave Macmillan, 2020); for an example of its presence in the magical theory of Dion Fortune, see Dion Fortune, *The Esoteric Philosophy of Love and Marriage* (York Beach: Weiser, 2000).

Chapter 4

1. Blavatsky, *Isis Unveiled*, 1:1.
2. Marie Corelli, *The Soul of Lilith* (London: Richard Bentley and Son, 1892), 240.
3. Corelli, *The Soul of Lilith*, 240.
4. Sinnett, *Karma*, 235.
5. Arthur Conan Doyle, *The Land of Mist* (London: Hutchinson & Co., 1926), 129.
6. Conan Doyle, *The Land of Mist*, 130.
7. Outwith their occult activities, these figures owned, edited, or contributed to secular papers such as the *Lady's Own Paper* (Kingsford), the *New York Tribune* (Olcott), *The Pioneer* (Sinnett), *The World* (Collins), *Our Corner* (Besant), *Moskovskiya Vedomosti* and *Russkiy Vestnik* (Blavatsky), and the Manchester *Guardian* and *Tit-Bits* (Lees).
8. See Mark Morrisson, "The Periodical Culture of the Occult Revival: Esoteric Wisdom, Modernity and Counter-Public Spheres," *Journal of Modern Literature* 31, no. 2 (2008): 1–22; "Women, Periodicals, and Esotericism in Modernist-Era Print Culture," in *Women, Periodicals, and Print Culture in Britain, 1880s–1920s: The Modernist Era*, ed. Faith Binckes and Carey Snyder (Edinburgh: Edinburgh University Press, 2019): 374–388.
9. Matthew Rubery, "Journalism," in *The Cambridge Companion to Victorian Culture*, ed. Francis O'Gorman (Cambridge: Cambridge University Press, 2010), 191; Nelson O'Ceallaigh Ritschel, *Bernard Shaw, W.T. Stead, and the New Journalism: Whitechapel, Parnell, Titanic, and the Great War* (Cham: Springer International, 2017), 2.
10. W. T. Stead, "The Future of Journalism," *Contemporary Review* 50 (1886): 677, 678. For more on the common misidentification of Arnold rather than Stead as the term's originator, see Owen Mulpetre, "W.T. Stead and the New Journalism." M.Phil, University of Teesside, 2010.
11. Matthew Arnold, "Up to Easter," *The Nineteenth Century* CXXIII (May 1887): 638.

198 NOTES

12. Rubery, "Journalism," 191.
13. Laurel Brake, "Revolutions in Journalism: W.T. Stead, Indexing, and 'Searching,'" in *Nineteenth-Century Radical Traditions*, ed. Joseph Bristow and Josephine McDonagh (London: Palgrave Macmillan, 2016), 162.
14. Stead, "The Future of Journalism," 669–670.
15. Stead received this sentence for posing as a client to procure the thirteen-year-old virgin Eliza Armstrong and thus expose the rampancy of the urban underage sex trade.
16. Stead, "The Future of Journalism," 670.
17. Stewart J. Brown, *W.T. Stead: Nonconformist and Newspaper Prophet* (Oxford: Oxford University Press, 2019), 139.
18. Roger Luckhurst, "W.T. Stead's Occult Economies," in *Culture and Science in the Nineteenth-Century Media*, ed. Louise Henson, Geoffrey Cantor, Gowan Dawson, Richard Noakes, Sally Shuttleworth, and Jonathan R. Topham (Aldershot: Ashgate, 2004), 125.
19. For a summary of the periodical's purview and outlook, see "How We Intend to Study the Borderland" (3–6) and "The Study of Psychical Phenomena" (24–26) in *Borderland* 1, no. 1 (July 1893).
20. Luckhurst, "W.T. Stead's Occult Economies," 125. For other accounts of the continuity between Stead's journalism and spiritualism, see Sarah Crofton, "'Julia Says': The Spirit-Writing and Editorial Mediumship of W.T. Stead," *19: Interdisciplinary Studies in the Long Nineteenth Century* 16 (2013), https://19.bbk.ac.uk/article/id/1547; Barbara D. Ferguson, "'My Spook Writes Steadese': Voice, Mediation, and the New Journalism in W.T. Stead's *Borderland*," *Victorian Review* 47, no. 1 (Spring 2021): 135–152.
21. Brown, *W.T. Stead: Nonconformist and Newspaper Prophet*, 141.
22. W. T. Stead, *After Death; or, Letters from Julia* (Chicago: Progressive Thinker Publishing House, 1910), 5.
23. W. T. Stead, "My Experience in Automatic Writing," *Borderland* 1, no. 1 (July 1893): 40.
24. Crofton, "'Julia Says.'"
25. Stead, *After Death*, 16, 17.
26. Stead, *After Death*, 23.
27. Stead, *After Death*, 24.
28. Britten, *Autobiography*, 36.
29. Stead, "My Experience in Automatic Writing," 39. As Stewart J. Brown explains, the Mowbray House premises operated until May 1910, after which the Bureau moved to Stead's home at Cambridge House in Wimbledon. See Brown, *W.T. Stead: Nonconformist and Newspaper Prophet*, 159.
30. Stead, *After Death*, 9.
31. Crofton, "'Julia Says.'"
32. Brown, *W.T. Stead: Nonconformist and Newspaper Prophet*, 159.
33. Ritschel, *Bernard Shaw, W.T. Stead, and the New Journalism*, 157.
34. Northcliffe's position vis-à-vis spiritualism and the occult was complex. Under his editorship, the *Daily Mail* took a strong anti-spiritualist line, and in 1904 led a scandalous sting operation against the London-based palmist Keiro and his wife (Charles and Martha Stephenson) which resulted in their arrest and trial for attempted fraud. As Owen Davis has shown, although the Stephensons were ultimately convicted, they were able to use the trial to expose the hypocrisy of Northcliffe's position by showing that several of his own papers ran advertisements for fortune-telling services. Fifteen years later, Northcliffe wrote a prefatory "Appreciation" for leading spiritualist Reverend George Vale Owen's collection of spirit messages *The Life Beyond the Veil* (1921). Here his position on such practices seems to have softened, although he remained guarded. "I have not had an opportunity of reading the whole of *The Life Beyond the Veil*," he admits, "but among the passages I have perused are many of great beauty. It seems to me that the personality of the Reverend G. Vale Owen is a matter of deep importance and to be considered in connexion with these very remarkable documents. During the brief interview I had with him I felt that I was in the presence of a man of sincerity and great conviction." Lord Northcliffe, "An Appreciation by Lord Northcliffe," in Rev. George Vale Owen, *The Life Beyond the Veil: Book 1* (New York: George H. Doran Company, 1921), n.p. See also "The West-End Palmistry Case," *Civil and Military Gazette* (October 27, 1904): 7; Owen Davies, "Newspapers and the Popular Belief in Witchcraft and Magic in the Modern Period," *Journal of British Studies* 37, no. 2 (April 1998): 139–165.
35. Hannen Swaffer, *Northcliffe's Return* (London: Psychic Press, 1939), 159.

NOTES   199

36. Swaffer, *Northcliffe's Return*, 20.
37. Swaffer, *Northcliffe's Return*, 110.
38. Swaffer, *Northcliffe's Return*, 59.
39. Swaffer, *Northcliffe's Return*, 48.
40. Swaffer, *Northcliffe's Return*, 48.
41. Swaffer, *Northcliffe's Return*, 41.
42. Swaffer, *Northcliffe's Return*, 84.
43. Swaffer, *Northcliffe's Return*, 85.
44. Swaffer, *Northcliffe's Return*, 144.
45. Crofton, "'Julia Says.'"
46. Kate Jackson, *George Newnes and the New Journalism in Britain, 1880–1910: Culture and Profit* (Aldershot: Ashgate, 2001), 66.
47. For example, Machen wrote a regular column for *T.P.'s Weekly* between 1908–1909 whose contents were later collected and published as *Notes and Queries* (London: Spurr and Swift, 1926); Fort, as Jeffrey Kripal points out, published several letters on unexplained phenomena in this journal. See Kripal, *Authors of the Impossible,* 123.
48. R. A. Gilbert, *A.E. Waite: Magician of Many Parts* (Wellingborough: Crucible, 1987), 123.
49. Aaron Worth, "Introduction," in Arthur Machen, *The Great God Pan and Other Horror Stories* (Oxford: Oxford University Press, 2018), xii.
50. For example, "A Double Return" was published in the *St James Gazette*, September 11, 1890, and "The Lost Club," *The Whirlwind*, December 20, 1890.
51. For Machen's involvement with these papers, see Aidan Reynolds and William Charlton, *Arthur Machen* (Oxford: Caermaen Books, 1987), 63–66, 106–107, 157.
52. James Machin, *Weird Fiction in Britain, 1880–1939* (Cham: Palgrave Macmillan, 2018), 127.
53. A full account of story's reception within British popular culture and folklore can be found in Richard J. Bleiler, *The Strange Case of "The Angel of Mons": Arthur Machen's World War I Story, the Insistent Believers, and his Refutations* (Jefferson, NC: McFarland & Co., 2015).
54. For example, he authored a Forteanesque column called "Queer Things" for *The Observer* from 1926–1927 and corresponded with the US-based *Dalton Citizen* between the mid-1920s and early 1930s.
55. William Francis Gekle, *Arthur Machen: Weaver of Fantasy* (Millbrook, NY: Round Table Press, 1949), 145, 43.
56. Wesley Sweetser, *Arthur Machen: Weaver of Fantasy* (Millbrook, NY: Round Table Press, 1960), 10.
57. Arthur Machen, *The London Adventure* (Newport, South Wales: Three Impostors, 2014), 11.
58. Hilary Machen, "Foreword," in *Arthur Machen: Selected Letters*, ed. Roger Dobson, Godfrey Brangham, and R. A. Gilbert (Wellingborough: Aquarian Press, 1988), 13.
59. Arthur Machen to Oliver Stonor, January 17, 1927, File 7.1, Arthur Machen Collection, Harry Ransom Center; Arthur Machen to Oliver Stonor, January 19, 1927, File 7.1, Arthur Machen Collection, Harry Ranson Center.
60. Machen, *The London Adventure*, 73.
61. Machen reminisces about his investigation of these cases in "The Ready Reporter," in *The Book of Fleet Street*, ed. T. Michael Pope (London: Cassell & Company, 1930), 143–153.
62. Machen, *The London Adventure*, 79.
63. Arthur Machen, "The Lost Club," in *The Great God Pan and Other Horror Stories*, ed. Aaron Worth (Oxford: Oxford University Press, 2018), 6.
64. Machen, "The Lost Club," 7.
65. Arthur Machen, "The Three Impostors" in *The Great God Pan and Other Horror Stories*, ed. Aaron Worth (Oxford: Oxford University Press, 2018), 119.
66. Arthur Machen, *The Great God Pan* in *The Great God Pan and Other Horror Stories*, ed. Aaron Worth (Oxford: Oxford University Press, 2018), 29.
67. For similar example of such gothic deployments of the newspaper paragraph, see Machen's "The Inmost Light" (1894) and "Ritual" (1937).
68. Arthur Machen, "The Green Round," in *Delphi Complete Works of Arthur Machen* (Hastings: Delphi Classics, 2013), 587.
69. Machen, *The Green Round*, 587.
70. Machen, *The Green Round*, 591.
71. Machen, *The Green Round*, 616.
72. Machen, *The Green Round*, 696.

200 NOTES

73. Machen, *The Green Round*, 604.
74. Machen, *The Green Round*, 604.
75. Machen, *The Green Round*, 604.
76. Machen, *The Green Round*, 605.
77. Stead, "The Future of Journalism," 670.
78. Marco Pasi, "Arthur Machen's Panic Fears," 77.
79. Pasi, "Arthur Machen's Panic Fears," 81.
80. Arthur Machen, *Far Off Things* (London: Martin Secker, 1922), 37. The articles he is no doubt referring to here are "Specimens of the Alchemists," *Household Words* 11, no. 273 (June 16, 1855): 457–465 and "More Alchemy," *Household Words* 11, no. 276 (July 7, 1855): 540–543.
81. Machen, *Far Off Things*, 39.
82. Arthur Machen, *Things Near and Far* (London: Martin Secker, 1923), 66, 152.
83. Machen, *Things Near and Far*, 97.
84. Machen, *Things Near and Far*, 151.
85. "Hornsey Spirit Mystery," *Daily News*, April 11, 1921, 5; "That Mischievous Spirit," *Nottingham Evening Post*, February 23, 1921, 5.
86. Machen, *The London Adventure*, 33.
87. Machen, *The London Adventure*, 33.
88. There is no London hamlet of this name. Given its putative proximity to the Surrey town of Reigate, it is possible that the actual location was Beare Green, and that Machen has misremembered or, for imaginative effect, deliberately recast its name.
89. Machen, *The London Adventure*, 81.
90. Machen, *The London Adventure*, 82. For accuracy's sake, it is worth pointing out that the Italian name "Campo Tosto" is not, in fact, practically the same thing as "Burnt Green" in translation. The phrase it comes closest to in rough translation would be "tough field."
91. *Fortean Times: The World's Weirdest News*, https://subscribe.forteantimes.com.
92. Damon Knight, *Charles Fort: Prophet of the Unexplained* (Golden, CO: Reanimus Press, 2021), 43.
93. At the time of writing, there exist only two major English-language academic studies of Fort's relationship to esotericism and religious studies: Kripal, *Authors of the Impossible*; Jack Hunter, ed., *Damned Facts: Fortean Essays on Religion, Folklore, and the Paranormal* (Paphos: Aporeitic Press, 2016).
94. Kripal, *Authors of the Impossible*, 9.
95. Kripal, *Authors of the Impossible*, 122, 123.
96. Kripal, *Authors of the Impossible*, 122.
97. Knight, *Charles Fort: Prophet of the Unexplained*, 103.
98. Knight, *Charles Fort: Prophet of the Unexplained*, 102.
99. Knight, *Charles Fort: Prophet of the Unexplained*, 102.
100. Knight, *Charles Fort: Prophet of the Unexplained*, 29.
101. The following publication details for each of these stories can be found on *The Fortean Website of Mr X*, http://www.resologist.net/ryook001.htm; "I Meddled," *Popular Magazine*, December 1905; "In a Newspaper Office," *Smith's*, July 1906; "Glencliff's Mysterious Burglar," *Smith's*, May 1906; "With the Assistance of Fryhuysen," *Popular Magazine*, June 1905; "Fryhuysen's Colony," *Smith's*, May 1906.
102. Charles Fort, "In a Newspaper Office," *The Fortean Website of Mr X*, http://www.resologist.net/story02.htm.
103. Charles Fort, "Fryhuysen's Colony," *The Fortean Website of Mr X*, http://www.resologist.net/story05.htm.
104. Fort, "Fryhuysen's Colony."
105. Fort, "Fryhuysen's Colony."
106. Charles Fort, *The Book of the Damned* in *The Complete Books of Charles Fort*, ed. Damon Knight (New York: Dover, 1974), 3–310, 3.
107. Jack Hunter, "Intermediatism and the Study of Religion," *Paranthropology: Journal of Anthropological Approaches to the Paranormal* 7, no. 1 (July 2016): 51.
108. Fort, *The Book of the Damned*, 7.
109. Fort, *The Book of the Damned*, 3.
110. Fort, *The Book of the Damned*, 75.
111. Charles Fort, "Wild Talents," in *The Complete Books of Charles Fort*, ed. Damon Knight (New York: Dover, 1974), 961.

NOTES 201

112. Fort, *Wild Talents*, 989.
113. For example, both psychical researcher Charles Richet and spiritualist Arthur Conan Doyle argued that some spiritualist phenomena, such as spirit photography or telekinesis, might be the result of extraordinary human mental powers rather than the intervention of the dead. See Charles Richet, *Thirty Years of Psychical Research, Being a Treatise on Metapsychics*, trans. Stanley de Brath (London: Macmillan & Co., 1923); Arthur Conan Doyle, *The History of Spiritualism* (London: Cassell & Co., 1926).
114. Fort, *Wild Talents*, 848.
115. This error is not an isolated incident. Elsewhere, for example, he misnames a colliery-adjacent town in central Scotland as "Coalbridge;" it is clearly Coatbridge that he is referring to. Fort, *Wild Talents*, 856.
116. Fort, *Wild Talents*, 848.
117. By "epistemic objectivity" here, I follow Howard Sankey's definition of this term as referring to "the adoption of norms which promote truth about the objective world." Howard Sankey, "Realism and the Epistemic Objectivity of Science," *Kriterion* 35, no. 1 (2021): 5.
118. Fort, *Wild Talents*, 861–862.
119. Fort, *Wild Talents*, 905.
120. Fort, *The Book of the Damned*, 19.
121. Margaret Beetham, "Towards a Theory of the Periodical as a Publishing Genre," in *Investigating Victorian Journalism*, ed. Laurel Brake, Aled Jones, and Lionel Madden (London: Palgrave Macmillan, 1990), 19.
122. Beetham, "Towards a Theory of the Periodical as a Publishing Genre," 26.
123. Fort, *Wild Talents*, 1062.

Chapter 5

1. Maurizio Ascari, *A Counter-History of Crime Fiction: Supernatural, Gothic, Sensational* (London: Palgrave, 2007), 17.
2. Susanna Lee, "Crime Fiction and Theories of Justice," in *The Routledge Companion to Crime Fiction*, ed. Janice Allan, Jesper Guiddal, Stewart King, and Andrew Pepper (Milton Keynes: Routledge, 2020), 284.
3. In this approximate dating, I follow Stephen Knight, who writes, "The golden age of crime fiction is usually taken as the period between the two world wars, though some start it earlier, with the publication of E. C. Bentley's *Trent's Last Case* in 1913, and the first critic to use the term dated it from 1918 to 1930." Stephen Knight, "The Golden Age," in *The Cambridge Companion to Crime Fiction*, ed. Martin Priestman (Cambridge: Cambridge University Press, 2006), 77.
4. As Knight observes, "The term 'golden age' has been criticized as being unduly homogeneous and seen as 'replete with romantic associations;' in fact the types of crime fiction produced in this period were far from uniform—the psychothriller and the procedural began, there was a wide range of practice in the mystery and the stories do regularly represent types of social and personal unease that would contradict a notion of an idyllic 'golden' period." Knight, "The Golden Age," 77. For other challenges to the alleged formal and political conformity of golden age detection, and indeed, of modern crime writing in general, see Clare Clarke, *Late Victorian Crime Fiction in the Shadows of Sherlock* (Basingstoke: Palgrave Macmillan, 2014); Samantha Walton, *Guilty but Insane: Mind and Law in Golden Age Detective Fiction* (New York: Oxford University Press, 2015); Janice Allan, Jesper Guiddal, Stewart King, and Andrew Pepper, "Introduction: New Directions in Crime Fiction Scholarship," in *The Routledge Companion to Crime Fiction*, ed. Janice Allan, Jesper Guiddal, Stewart King, and Andrew Pepper (Milton Keynes: Routledge, 2020), 1–9; Stefano Serafini, "The Gothic Side of Golden Age Detective Fiction," *Gothic Metamorphoses Across the Century: Contexts, Legacies, Media*, ed. Maurizio Ascari, Serena Baiesi, and David Levente Palatinus (Bern: Peter Lang, 2020), 117–130; Chene Heady, "Father Brown, Labour Priest: G. K. Chesterton and the Class Politics of Golden Age Detective Fiction," *Journal of Popular Culture* 53, no. 4 (Autumn 2020): 865–885.
5. Richard Bradford, *Crime Fiction: A Very Short Introduction* (Oxford: Oxford University Press, 2013), 19.
6. Walton, *Guilty but Insane: Mind and Law in Golden Age Detective Fiction*, 51.
7. Agatha Christie, *The Mysterious Affair at Styles* (London: Pan Books, 1954), 145.
8. Unlike in its Victorian precedent, writes Knight, in golden age detection "the reader is challenged to match the detective's process of identifying the murderer and there should be 'fair play': the reader must be informed of each clue that the detective sees." Knight, "The Golden Age," 79.

202 NOTES

9. Lee Horsely, *Twentieth-Century Crime Fiction* (Oxford: Oxford University Press, 2005), 38.
10. Horsely, *Twentieth-Century Crime Fiction*, 37.
11. Horsely, *Twentieth-Century Crime Fiction*, 22. See also Christopher Pittard, *Purity and Contamination in Late Victorian Detective Fiction* (London: Routledge, 2016) for an account of this process of genre sanitization and social upgrading in the late nineteenth century.
12. Susan Rowland, "The 'Classical' Model of the Golden Age," in *A Companion to Crime Fiction*, ed. Charles J. Rezpka and Lee Horsely (Oxford: Blackwell Wiley, 2010), 122, 123. For more on the twentieth-century feminization of detective fiction, see Megan Hoffman, *Gender and Representation in British "Golden Age" Crime Fiction: Women Writing Women* (London: Palgrave Macmillan, 2016).
13. These scenarios form the basis of, respectively, Blackwood's "A Psychical Invasion" (1908), Fortune's "The Scented Poppies" (1922), the Prichards' "The Story of the Moor Road" (1898), Machen's "The Inmost Light" (1894), Machen's "The Shining Pyramid" (1923), and Hodgson's "The Gateway of the Monster" (1910).
14. See Nick Rennison, "Introduction," in *Supernatural Sherlocks: Stories from the Golden Age of the Occult Detective* (Harpenden: No Exit Press, 2017), 7–13; Paul Green, *Encyclopaedia of Weird Detectives: Supernatural and Paranormal Elements in Novels, Pulps, Comics, Film, Television, Games, and Other Media* (Jefferson, NC: McFarland & Company, 2019).
15. Fortune launched her occult detective character Dr. Taverner in a series of six stories serialized in *The Royal Magazine* between May and October 1922, later combining these with six new stories to form the collection *The Secrets of Doctor Taverner* (1926). Fortune took her inspiration for Taverner from her real-life former teacher, the Irish occultist and psychotherapist Dr. Theodore Moriarty at whose private treatment center in Bishop Stortford she studied in the early years of the First World War. She was there introduced, as Alison Butler describes, to "alternative therapies for mental affliction . . . including understanding past incarnations as the source for current emotional disorder." Alison Butler, "Dion Fortune and the Society of the Inner Light," in *The Occult World*, ed. Christopher Partridge (Abingdon: Routledge, 2014), 316.
16. See Ascari, *A Counter-History of Crime Fiction: Supernatural, Gothic, Sensational*; Serafini, "The Gothic Side of Golden Age Detective Fiction."
17. S. S. Van Dine, "Twenty Rules for Writing Detective Stories," *The American Magazine*, September 1928, 130.
18. Ronald Knox, "Ten Rules for a Good Detective Story," *The Publisher's Weekly*, October 5, 1929, 1729.
19. Quoted in Walton, *Guilty but Insane*, 58.
20. For accounts of the gothic, supernatural, and religious dimensions of the early Anglo American detective canon, see Ascari, *A Counter-History of Crime Fiction: Supernatural, Gothic, Sensational*; Srdjan Smajić, *Ghost-Seers, Detectives, and Spiritualists: Theories of Vision in Victorian Literature and Science* (Cambridge: Cambridge University Press, 2010); James Carney, "Supernatural Intuition and Classic Detective Fiction: A Cognitivist Appraisal," *Style* 48, no. 2 (2014): 203–218.
21. See Andrea Goulet, "Crime Fiction and Modern Science," in *The Routledge Companion to Crime Fiction*, ed. Janice Allan, Jesper Guiddal, Stewart King, and Andrew Pepper (Milton: Taylor and Francis, 2020), 291–300; Ronald R. Thomas, *Detective Fiction and the Rise of the Forensic Science* (Cambridge: Cambridge University Press, 1999); Lawrence Frank, *Victorian Detective Fiction and the Nature of Evidence: The Scientific Investigations of Poe, Dickens, and Doyle* (London: Palgrave Macmillan, 2003).
22. Goulet, "Crime Fiction and Modern Science," 294.
23. For an example of mesmerism in classic detective fiction, see Wilkie Collins, *The Moonstone: A Romance* (London: Tinsley Brothers, 1868); of Bertillonage, see Arthur Conan Doyle, *The Hound of the Baskervilles* (London: George Newnes, 1902).
24. The presence of the gothic within nineteenth-century detective fiction is discussed in Ascari, *A Counter-History of Crime Fiction*; Catherine Spooner, "Crime and the Gothic," in *A Companion to Crime Fiction*, ed. Charles J. Rzepka and Lee Horsely (Oxford: Blackwell Wiley, 2010), 245–257; Smajić, *Ghost-Seers, Detectives, and Spiritualists*; Michael Cook, *Detective Fiction and the Ghost Story* (Cham: Palgrave Macmillan, 2014).
25. Arthur Conan Doyle, "A Study in Scarlet," in *Sherlock Holmes: The Complete Novels and Stories* (New York: Bantam Dell, 1986), 16.

NOTES   203

26. Arthur Conan Doyle, "The Boscombe Valley Mystery," in *The Adventures of Sherlock Holmes*, ed. Richard Lancelyn Green (Oxford: Oxford University Press, 1993), 100.
27. Arthur Conan Doyle, "The Blue Carbuncle," in *The Adventures of Sherlock Holmes*, ed. Richard Lancelyn Green (Oxford: Oxford University Press, 1993), 170.
28. Arthur Conan Doyle, "The Speckled Band," in *The Adventures of Sherlock Holmes*, ed. Richard Lancelyn Green (Oxford: Oxford University Press, 1993), 96.
29. Revisionary accounts of Holmes as an anti-rationalist, spiritualist, or "enchanted" figure, as opposed to a beacon of logical ratiocination, have flourished over the last two decades; see Michael Saler, *As If: Modern Enchantment and the Literary Prehistory of Virtual Reality* (Oxford: Oxford. University Press, 2012); Smajić, *Ghost-Seers, Detectives, and Spiritualists*; Brian McCuskey, *How Sherlock Pulled the Trick: Spiritualism and the Pseudoscientific Method* (University Park: Pennsylvania State University Press, 2021).
30. Arthur Conan Doyle, "A Scandal in Bohemia," in *The Adventures of Sherlock Holmes*, ed. Richard Lancelyn Green (Oxford: Oxford University Press, 1993), 7.
31. Kate Prichard and Hesketh Prichard, "The Story of the Moor Road (1898)," in *The Ghost Slayers: Thrilling Tales of Occult Detection*, ed. Mike Ashley (London: British Library, 2022), 28.
32. Algernon Blackwood, "A Psychical Invasion (1908)," in *The Ghost Slayers: Thrilling Tales of Occult Detection*, ed. Mike Ashley (London: British Library, 2022), 78.
33. Samuel Warren, "The Spectre-Smitten," in *Passages from the Diary of a Late Physician* (London: Routledge, 1832), 149.
34. Sheridan Le Fanu, "Green Tea," in *In A Glass Darkly* (Oxford: Oxford World's Classics, 1993), 26.
35. Le Fanu, "Green Tea," 21.
36. Le Fanu, "Green Tea," 14.
37. Le Fanu, "Green Tea," 39.
38. Le Fanu, "Green Tea," 412.
39. Aleister Crowley, *The Confessions of Aleister Crowley*, ed. John Symonds and Kenneth Grant (London: Routledge & Kegan Paul, 1979), 777.
40. As Hugh Urban notes, Crowley moved to the United States in 1914 and, within one year, had exhausted most of his fortune; see Hugh Urban, *Magia Sexualis: Sex, Magic, and Liberation in Modern Western Esotericism* (Berkeley: University of California Press, 2006), 118. He then started contributing to two pro-German papers run by Viereck, *The Fatherland* and *The International*. These activities would lead to accusations that he was spying against his own country during the war, ones that Crowley always vehemently denied but was never able to completely dispel. For more on Crowley's relationship with Viereck, see Patrick J. Quinn, *Aleister Crowley, Sylvester Viereck, Literature, Lust, and the Great War* (Newcastle-Upon-Tyne: Cambridge Scholars Publishing, 2021).
41. William Breeze, "Introduction," in Aleister Crowley, *The Simon Iff Stories and Other Works*, ed. William Breeze (Ware: Wordsworth Editions, 2012), 11.
42. William Breeze, "Introduction," 12.
43. Martin P. Starr, "Introduction," in *The Scrutinies of Simon Iff* (Chicago: Teitan Press, 1987), ix–xviii, xvi.
44. Andreas Huyssen, *After the Great Divide: Modernism, Mass Culture, Postmodernism* (Bloomington: Indiana University Press, 1986), vii.
45. Alex Owen has identified this proto-modernist programme as central to Crowley's Edwardian magickal practice, writing that his desert workings with Victor Neuberg in 1909 "taught Crowley that the apparent coherence of human selfhood is illusory." Alex Owen, *The Place of Enchantment: British Occultism and the Culture of the Modern* (Chicago: University of Chicago Press, 2004), 209.
46. Crowley, *The Confessions of Aleister Crowley* (1979), 830.
47. David Tibet, "Foreword," in Aleister Crowley, *The Drug and Other Stories*, ed. William Breeze (Ware: Wordsworth Editions, 2010), viii.
48. Breeze discusses the function of Iff as self-portrait in "Introduction," in *The Simon Iff Stories and Other Works*, 7; See also Richard Kaczynski, *Perdurabo: The Life of Aleister Crowley* (Berkeley: North Atlantic Books, 2010), 310. Starr identifies the real-life inspirations for some of the characters in *The Scrutinies* in his notes to the Teitan Press edition. See Aleister Crowley, *The Scrutinies of Simon Iff*, ed. Martin P. Starr (Chicago: Teitan Press, 1987), n176.
49. Quoted in Marco Pasi, *Aleister Crowley and the Temptation of Politics* (Durham: Acumen, 2014), n195.
50. Aleister Crowley, *The Confessions of Aleister Crowley* (London: Mandrake Press, 1929), 78.

204 NOTES

51. Crowley, *The Confessions of Aleister Crowley* (1929), 80.
52. See Crowley, *The Confessions of Aleister Crowley* (1979), 411, 567. Crowley was still immersed in detective fiction in 1920, the year he established the Cefalù colony; after falling ill in Tunis that June, he writes "A most unpleasant day of severe illness. I think I may have been poisoned by reading Conan Doyle" (quoted in Kaczynski, *Perdurabo*, 264). Several stories in *The Scrutinies* pay homage to the plots of classic works of detective fiction. In "The Artistic Temperament," Eleanor Cudlipp's refusal to indict the culprit she has witnessed in the criminal act reminds us of Rachel Verrinder's silence after observing Franklin Blake's theft of the diamond in *The Moonstone* (1868), while the threat of using white-hot pokers to torture a confession out of Fisher in "Outside the Bank's Routine" conjures up Rudyard Kipling's "The Mark of the Beast" (1891).
53. As has been widely documented, Crowley adopted the "k" to distinguish the modern scientific, results-based identity he sought for his practice from mere conjuring or spiritualist delusion. For his own account of this rationale, see Aleister Crowley, *Magick in Theory and Practice* (1929), ed. John Symonds and Kenneth Grant (London: Routledge and Kegan Paul, 1973), 130.
54. Crowley, *Confessions of Aleister Crowley* (1979), 397.
55. Aleister Crowley, *The Book of the Law* (London: O.T.O. BCM/ANKH, 1938), 9.
56. Kaczynski, *Perdurabo*, 127.
57. Henrik Bogdan, "Aleister Crowley: A Prophet for the Modern Age," in *The Occult World*, ed. Christopher Partridge (London: Routledge, 2015), 296.
58. Crowley, *The Book of the Law*, 31.
59. Crowley, *The Book of the Law*, 39.
60. Crowley, *The Book of the Law*, 41.
61. Crowley, *The Book of the Law*, 29.
62. Pasi, *Aleister Crowley and the Temptation of Politics*, 14.
63. Crowley, *The Confessions of Aleister Crowley* (1979), 403.
64. In 1934, Crowley sued Constable and Co. for libel for their publication of what he considered to be a defamatory account of Thelema in Nina Hamnett's *Laughing Torso* (1932). On the stand, Crowley condemned black magic as being "not only foul and abominable, but, for the most part criminal. To begin with, the basis of all black magic is that utter stupidity of selfishness which cares nothing for the rights of other people." Kaczynski, *Perdurabo*, 473. It is very difficult, well-nigh impossible, to reconcile this sentiment with the words of Ra-Hoor-Khuit.
65. Kaczynski, *Perdurabo*, 562.
66. Crowley, *The Book of the Law*, 31.
67. Henrik Bogdan, "Envisioning the Birth of a New Aeon: Dispensationalism and Millenarianism in the Thelemic Tradition," in *Aleister Crowley and Western Esotericism: An Anthology of Critical Studies*, ed. Henrik Bogdan and Martin P. Starr (Oxford: Oxford University Press, 2012), 96.
68. Aleister Crowley, *The Law is For All: An Extended Commentary on The Book of the Law*, ed. Israel Regardie (St. Paul: Llewellyn Publications, 1975), 90.
69. Crowley, *The Confessions of Aleister Crowley* (1979), 401.
70. Crowley, *The Confessions of Aleister Crowley* (1979), 114.
71. Crowley, *The Confessions of Aleister Crowley* (1979), 99.
72. Crowley, *The Confessions of Aleister Crowley* (1979), 99.
73. Crowley, *The Confessions of Aleister Crowley* (1979), 126.
74. See "A Wizard of Wickedness," *John Bull*, March 17, 1923, 9; "The King of Depravity," *John Bull*, March 10, 1923, 10; "King of Depravity Arrives," *John Bull*, March 14, 1923, 9.
75. A clear allusion to the Diogenes Club in the Holmes universe.
76. As Johann Nilsson discusses, Crowley started work on a commentary on the *Daodejing* in the summer of 1918, just a few months after the final instalment of the *Scrutinies* appeared in *The International*. In his interpretation, writes Nilsson, Daoism was positioned as a philosophy based on "laissez-faire individualism" and "non-action." Johann Nilsson, "Defending Paper Gods: Aleister Crowley and the Reception of Daoism in Early Twentieth-Century Esotericism," *Correspondences* 1, no. 1 (2013): 103–127.
77. Aleister Crowley, "The Big Game," in *The Simon Iff Stories & Other Works*, ed. William Breeze (Ware: Wordsworth Editions, 2012), 25.
78. Crowley, "The Big Game," 26.
79. Crowley, "The Big Game," 29, 28.
80. Crowley, "The Big Game," 33.
81. Crowley, "The Big Game," 37.

NOTES 205

82. Crowley, "The Big Game," 37.
83. Crowley, "The Big Game," 40.
84. Crowley, "The Big Game," 43.
85. Crowley, "The Big Game," 43.
86. As Richard Kaczynski writes in *Perdurabo*, "the epigram 'Do what though wilt shall be the whole of the Law' is a statement of moral relativism. Depending on one's True Will, what's right for one person may not be right for another" (560). As such, it promoted no universal prohibition of particular acts in the same way as does the Mosaic code.
87. *The Golden Bough* was much on Crowley's mind in this period. Alongside the *Scrutinies*, he was simultaneously publishing a series of short stories inspired by Frazer's opus in *The International* under the pseudonym "Mark Wells"; these were posthumously collected and published as *Golden Twigs* (Chicago: Teitan Press, 1988). For an account of Frazer's influence on Crowley's magickal thinking, see Jason Ananda Josephson-Storm, *The Myth of Disenchantment: Magic, Modernity, and the Birth of the Human Sciences* (Chicago: University of Chicago Press, 2017).
88. Aleister Crowley, "The Artistic Temperament," in *The Simon Iff Stories & Other Works*, ed. William Breeze (Ware: Wordsworth Editions, 2012), 49.
89. Crowley, "The Artistic Temperament," 52.
90. Crowley, "The Artistic Temperament," 52. Crowley, "The Artistic Temperament," 52.
91. Crowley, "The Artistic Temperament," 52.
92. Crowley, "The Artistic Temperament," 54, 56. Crowley's antisemitic evocation of blood libel here draws upon a real-life contemporary case whose details he, writing at speed, seems only to have partially remembered. Iff suggests that Cudlipp might have been motivated by his reading of, not only *The Golden Bough*, but also recent newspaper reports of a Russian Hassid tried for the murder of a Christian child. The case in question is surely that of Menahem Mendel Beilis, subject of one of the most notorious antisemitic witch hunts in early twentieth-century Russia. A respectable local factory worker, Beilis was arrested in Kiev in 1911 for the murder of the thirteen-year-old Andriy Yuschinskyi on the sole testimony, later retracted, of a lamplighter who claimed he had seen a Jew take the boy away. The prosecution relied heavily on a blood libel hypothesis exposed as nonsense at the trial. After his acquittal in 1913, Beilis became an international symbol of Jewish fortitude in the face of antisemitic conspiracy. Crowley, however, ignores, or forgets, the fact of Beilis's innocence, and has Iff say that the concept of "the sacrifice of the first-born" is one "which the Jews only adopted at third or fourth hand from older and autochthonous races," and notes that before Cudlipp's act, "the newspapers were filled with long arguments about the Hasidim and ritual murder, the trial of that man somewhere in Russia—can't think of his name, begins with a B—was on at this time" ("The Artistic Temperament," 56–57). This antisemitic interjection operates on two levels: first, it casually presents child murder as a Jewish cultural tradition, and second, as not even an original one at that, but rather as a practice stolen from other, more ancient groups, thus invoking stereotypes of Jews as grasping and avaricious.
93. Crowley, "The Artistic Temperament," 56.
94. Aleister Crowley, "Not Good Enough," in *The Simon Iff Stories & Other* Works, ed. William Breeze (Ware: Wordsworth Editions, 2012), 115.
95. For more on this relationship and its impact on and aftermath in Crowley's magickal writing, see Keith A. Cantú, "A Triangle of Art: The Relationship Between Aleister Crowley, Ananda Coomaraswamy, and Ratan Devi," *Religion and the Arts* 28 (2024): 89–106.
96. Bogdan observes that Crowley "used irony and humour as a means of distancing himself from other actors on the occult market" and to "distanc[e] himself from the 'common' or 'dull' occult believer." Henrik Bogdan, "Aleister Crowley as an Advertiser of the Occult," *Religion and the Arts* 28 (2024): 15, 58.
97. Aleister Crowley, "Ineligible," in *The Simon Iff Stories & Other* Works, ed. William Breeze (Ware: Wordsworth Editions, 2012), 117.
98. Aleister Crowley, "Outside the Bank's Routine," in *The Simon Iff Stories & Other* Works, ed. William Breeze (Ware: Wordsworth Editions, 2012), 63.
99. Crowley, "Ineligible," 130. The Book of John only has twenty-one chapters. It is possible that Crowley intended to refer to John 11:1–16, which concerns the resurrection of Lazarus. Here, Jesus tells Mary and Martha that the sickness of their ailing brother Lazarus is "for the glory of God, that the Son of God might be glorified thereby" (John 11:4), and thus delays his trip to heal him. When he does finally arrive in Judaea, Lazarus is already dead. "I am glad for your sakes that I was not there," Jesus tells his disciples, "to the intent ye may believe" (John 11:15).

206 NOTES

To a reader such as Crowley, this episode may have suggested that Jesus allowed Lazarus to suffer and die for his own aggrandizement.

100. Crowley, "Ineligible," 130.
101. Crowley, *The Confessions of Aleister Crowley* (1979), 828.
102. Starr, "Introduction," *The Scrutinies of Simon Iff*, xiv.
103. Pasi, *Aleister Crowley and the Temptation of Politics*, 24.
104. Crowley, "Outside the Bank's Routine," 67.
105. Crowley, "Outside the Bank's Routine," 81.
106. Crowley, "Outside the Bank's Routine," 82. As Starr notes, the three women alluded to here are clearly Crowley's first wife Rose Kelly and his subsequent lovers and magickal partners, Jeanne Merton and Jeanne Robert Foster. Starr, *The Scrutinies of Simon Iff*, n. 176–177.
107. Crowley, "Outside the Bank's Routine," 82.
108. Crowley, "Outside the Bank's Routine," 81.
109. Crowley, "Outside the Bank's Routine," 81.
110. Crowley, "Not Good Enough," 101.
111. Crowley, "Not Good Enough," 102.
112. Crowley, "Not Good Enough," 106.
113. Crowley, "Not Good Enough," 106.
114. Crowley, "Not Good Enough," 105.
115. Crowley, "Not Good Enough," 106.
116. Crowley, "Not Good Enough," 116.
117. Crowley, "Not Good Enough," 116.
118. Crowley, "Not Good Enough," 116.
119. In this incident, we see Crowley again trying to settle personal scores. In 1916, Alice Coomaraswamy, wife of Swamy's real-life prototype Ananda Coomaraswamy, had become pregnant as a result of her affair with Crowley. She later miscarried, a loss that is here fictionalized as the deliberate result her husband's interference.
120. Crowley, "Not Good Enough," 109.
121. Cantú, "A Triangle of Art," 101.
122. Tomoko Masuzawa, *The Invention of World Religions; or, How European Universalism was Preserved in the Language of Pluralism* (Chicago: University of Chicago Press, 2005), 311.
123. Starr, *The Scrutinies of Simon Iff*, n. 178.
124. Lawrence Sutin, *Do What Thou Wilt: A Life of Aleister Crowley* (New York: St. Martin's Press, 2014), 2, 366.
125. David Renton, *Horatio Bottomley and the Far Right Before Fascism* (London Routledge, 2022), 134.
126. "Another Traitor Trounced," *John Bull*, January 10, 1920, 8.
127. Renton, *Horatio Bottomley and the Far Right Before Fascism*, 133–134.

Chapter 6

1. Dion Fortune, *The Goat-Foot God* (York Beach: Weiser Books, 1999), 5.
2. Fortune, *The Goat-Foot God*, 5–6.
3. Fortune, *The Goat-Foot God*, 382. In Israel Regardie's four-volume compilation of the teachings, ceremonies, and rites of the Hermetic Order of the Golden Dawn, this phrase is attached to several rituals, including those related to the consecration of magical objects, neophyte initiation, spiritual development, and the invocation of the higher genius. See Israel Regardie, *The Golden Dawn: A Complete Course in Ceremonial Magic* (Woodbury: Llewellyn Publications, 1989), 118, 131, 214, 303, 318, 442.
4. Fortune's first extended work of occult fiction was *The Secrets of Dr Taverner*, a collection of occult detective stories (some of which had been previously serialized in *The Royal Magazine*) published by Noel Douglas in 1926. It was followed by five novels: *The Demon Lover* (1927), *The Winged Bull* (1935), *The Goat-Foot God* (1936), *The Sea Priestess* (1935), and the posthumously published *Moon Magic* (1957).
5. Dion Fortune, *The Esoteric Philosophy of Love and Marriage* (York Beach: Weiser, 2000), 2.
6. For more on the role of sexual polarity in Fortune's occult philosophy, practice, and fiction, see John Algeo, "The Integrated Alien: Ritual Magic in the Fiction of Dion Fortune," in *The Shape of the Fantastic*, ed. Olena Saciuk (New York: Greenwood Publishing, 1990), 211–218; Gareth

NOTES   207

Knight, *Dion Fortune and the Inner Light* (Loughborough: Thoth, 2000); Susan Johnston Graf, *Talking to the Gods*; Anne Parker-Perkola, "Dion Fortune and the Temples of the Numinous," in *Essays on Women in Western Esotericism*, ed. Amy Hale (Cham: Springer International, 2022), 357–373.

7. Claire Fanger, "Mirror, Mask, and Anti-Self: Forces of Literary Creation in Dion Fortune and W. B. Yeats," in *Esotericism, Art, and Imagination*, ed. Arthur Versluis, Lee Irwin, John D. Richards, and Melinda Weinstein (East Lansing: Michigan State University Press, 2008), 178.

8. Thus, Fortune claimed that the stories in *The Secrets of Dr Taverner* were drawn from her time practicing occult psychotherapeutics with Dr. Theodore Moriarty in Bishop Stortford in the early years of the First World War. In this collection, she remarks in *Psychic Self-Defence* (1930), "there were presented under the guise of fiction, a number of cases illustrative of the hypotheses of occult sciences. Some of these stories were built up to show the operation of the invisible forces; others were drawn from actual cases; and some of these were written down rather than written up in order to render them readable by the general public." Dion Fortune, *Psychic Self-Defence* (London: Global Grey, 2018), 20.

9. Dion Fortune, *The Sea Priestess* (York Beach: Weiser Books, 2003), xvii.

10. The house journal of Fortune's Society of the Inner Light, the *Inner Light* is an extremely rare periodical that is not indexed on WorldCat or available in any of the major UK copyright libraries or the International Association for the Preservation of Spiritualist and Occult Periodicals (IAPSOP) database. I rely here on the transcription of this article that appears in Gareth Knight, *Dion Fortune and the Inner Light*, 223.

11. Caroline Levine, *Forms: Whole, Rhythm, Hierarchy, Network* (Princeton: Princeton University Press, 2015), 10.

12. A. E. W. Mason, *The Prisoner in the Opal* (Kelly Bray, Cornwall: House of Stratus Books, 2009), 3.

13. Fortune, *The Goat-Foot God*, 49.

14. Fortune, *The Goat-Foot God*, 11.

15. J. K. Huysmans, *The Damned*, trans. Terry Hale (London: Penguin, 2001), 12.

16. Huysmans, *The Damned*, 264–265.

17. Fortune, *The Goat-Foot God*, 24.

18. Fortune, *The Goat-Foot God*, 24.

19. Fortune, *The Goat-Foot God*, 29.

20. Naomi Mitchison, *The Corn King and the Spring Queen* (Edinburgh: Canongate, 1930), 327–330, 535–539.

21. Fortune, *The Goat-Foot God*, 30.

22. Fortune, *The Goat-Foot God*, 30.

23. As an advocate of "polarized"—read, heterosexual and gender binarized—sex magic, Fortune repeatedly pathologized homosexuality and transgender identity as unnatural phenomena that thwarted esoteric progress; the former, as practiced between men, she presented as synonymous with pederasty. In *The Esoteric Phenomena of Love and Marriage* (1924), for example, she had argued that "we are equipped with physical bodies in which the configuration of the generative organs determines the part we shall play in the polarity of life; we are born male or female and have to abide by the decision of our conception, the phenomena of the hermaphrodite and the homosexual being regarded as pathological by the esoteric as well as the exoteric scientist" (37). In *Sane Occultism* (1929), she called male homosexuality "a very cruel form of vice" whose "victims are usually boys and on the threshold of life. It is also very infectious, spreading in an ever-widening circle as those who have become habituated to it in their turn proselytize for victims." Dion Fortune, *Sane Occultism and Practical Occultism in Daily Life* (Wellingborough: Aquarian Press, 1987), 83.

24. J. W. Brodie-Innes, *The Devil's Mistress* (London: William Rider and Son, 1915), xii.

25. Brodie-Innes, *The Devil's Mistress*, 329.

26. Brodie-Innes, *The Devil's Mistress*, 357.

27. Fortune, *The Goat-Foot God*, 31.

28. Fortune, *The Goat-Foot God*, 36.

29. Fortune, *The Goat-Foot God*, 5.

30. Pierre Bourdieu, *Distinction: A Social Critique of the Judgment of Taste*, trans. Richard Nice (Cambridge: Harvard University Press, 1984), 316.

31. A rich and growing body of scholarship has started to address the modern proliferation of fiction-based religions: see, for example, Markus Altena Davidsen, "Fiction-Based

208 NOTES

Religion: Conceptualizing a New Category against History-Based Religion and Fandom," *Culture and Religion* 14, no. 4 (2013): 378–395; Kateryna Zorya, "If One Knows Where to Look, Fiction is Magic: Reading Fictional Texts as Manuals of Magic in Post-Soviet Ukraine, Russia, and Belarus," in *Fictional Practice: Magic, Narration, and the Power of Imagination*, ed. Bernd-Christian Otto and Dirk Johannsen (Leiden: Brill, 2021), 261–288; Justin Woodman, "'Cthulhu Gnosis': Monstrosity, Selfhood, and Secular Re-Enchantment in Lovecraftian Occultural Practice," in *Fictional Practice: Magic, Narration, and the Power of Imagination*, ed. Bernd-Christian Otto and Dirk Johannsen (Leiden: Brill, 2021), 289–313; Carole Cusack, "A Magickal School in the Twenty-First Century: The Grey School of Wizardry and its Prehistory," *Fictional Practice: Magic, Narration, and the Power of Imagination*, ed. Bernd-Christian Otto and Dirk Johannsen (Leiden: Brill, 2021), 314–333.

32. Charles Taylor, *A Secular Age* (Cambridge: Harvard University Press, 2018), 2. See also Talal Asad, *Formations of the Secular: Christianity, Islam, Modernity* (Stanford: Stanford University Press, 2003); Callum Brown, *The Death of Christian Britain: Understanding Secularization, 1800–2000* (London: Routledge, 2001).

33. Taylor, *A Secular Age*, 26.

34. Taylor, *A Secular Age*, 3.

35. Tomoko Masuzawa, *The Invention of World Religions, Or, How European Universalism Was Preserved in the Language of Pluralism* (Chicago: University of Chicago Press, 2005), 322.

36. See Charles LaPorte and Sebastian Lecourt, "Nineteenth-Century Literature, New Religious Movements, and Secularization," *Nineteenth-Century Literature* 73, no. 2 (2018): 147–160; Deidre Lynch, "Keeping Faith with Literature," *Modern Language Quarterly* 83, no. 2 (2022): 539–547.

37. Jerilyn Sambrooke, "Secularism, Religion, and the 20th/21st-Century Novel," *Literature Compass* 15, no. 1 (2018): 3.

38. T. S. Eliot, "In Memoriam," in Lord Alfred Tennyson, *In Memoriam, A.H.H.*, ed. Erik Gray (London: W. W. Norton & Co., 2004), 138.

39. Justin Neuman, *Fiction Beyond Secularism* (Evanston, IL: Northwestern University Press, 2014), 183.

40. Mark Knight and Charles LaPorte, "Talking about Religion in Eighteenth- and Nineteenth-Century Literature," *Modern Language Quarterly* 83, no. 4 (2022): 368.

41. For an example of this dating of the "religious turn" in modern literary studies, see Charles LaPorte's claim that "The question of Victorian secularization is more complicated in the twenty-first century than it was in the twentieth. A few decades ago, a scholar of English literature might take for granted that modernity militates against religious ways of thinking and that post-Enlightenment history evidences as much." Charles LaPorte, "Victorian Literature, Religion, and Secularization," *Literature Compass* 10, no. 3 (March 2013): 277. Similar positionings can be found in Sara Lyon, "Secularism and Secularization at the *Fin de Siècle*," in *The Edinburgh Companion to the Fin de Siècle: Literature, Culture, and Arts*, ed. Josephine Guy (Edinburgh: Edinburgh University Press, 2018), 124–145; Mark Knight, "The Limits of Orthodoxy in a Secular Age: The Strange Case of Marie Corelli," *Nineteenth-Century Literature* 73, no. 3 (2018), 379–398.

Bibliography

Online Sources

Auden, W. H. "The Guilty Vicarage." *Harper's Magazine*. May 1948. https://harpers.org/archive/1948/05/the-guilty-vicarage/.

Brown, Andrew. "Lytton, Edward George Earle Lytton Bulwer (*formerly* Edward George Earle Lytton Bulwer), first Baron Lytton." *Oxford Dictionary of National Biography*.

September 2004. https://www-oxforddnb-com.ezproxys1.stir.ac.uk/display/10.1093/ref:odnb/9780198614128.001.0001/odnb-9780198614128-e-17314?rskey=fBu1Vr&result=2.

Crofton, Sarah. "'Julia Says': The Spirit-Writing and Editorial Mediumship of W.T. Stead." *19: Interdisciplinary Studies in the Long Nineteenth Century* 16 (2013). https://19.bbk.ac.uk/article/id/1547/.

Fort, Charles. "Fryhuysen's Colony." *Smith's Magazine*. May 1906. *The Fortean Website of Mr X*. http://www.resologist.net/story05.htm.

Fort, Charles. "Glencliff's Mysterious Burglar." *Smith's Magazine*. March 1906. *The Fortean Website of Mr X*. http://www.resologist.net/story03.htm.

Fort, Charles. "I Meddled." *The Popular Magazine*. December 1905. *The Fortean Website of Mr X*. http://www.resologist.net/story03.htm.

Fort, Charles. "In a Newspaper Office." *Smith's Magazine*. July 1906. *The Fortean Website of Mr X*. http://www.resologist.net/story02.htm.

Fort, Charles. "With the Assistance of Fryhuysen." *The Popular Magazine*. June 1905. *The Fortean Website of Mr X*. http://www.resologist.net/story04.htm.

France, Peter. "Le Diable boiteux." In *The New Oxford Companion to Literature in French*, edited by Peter France. Oxford: Oxford University Press, 1995. Online Resource.

Nilsson, Johann. "Defending Paper Gods: Aleister Crowley and the Reception of Daoism in Early Twentieth-Century Esotericism." *Correspondences* 1, no. 1 (2013): 103–127. https://correspondencesjournal.com/ojs/ojs/index.php/home/article/view/6/6.

Reilly, John R. "Violence." In *The Oxford Companion to Crime and Mystery Writing*, edited by Rosemary Herbert. Oxford: Oxford University Press, 2005. Digital Resource.

Unpublished Works

Machen, Arthur. Letter to Oliver Stonor, January 17, 1927, File 7.1, Arthur Machen Collection, Harry Ransom Center.

Machen, Arthur. Letter to Oliver Stonor, January 19, 1927, File 7.1, Arthur Machen Collection, Harry Ranson Center.

Published Works

Abbate, Carolyn, and Roger Parker. *A History of Opera: The Last Four Hundred Years*. London: Penguin, 2015.

Ainsworth, Harrison. *Auriol; or, the Elixir of Life* (1844). London: George Routledge and Son, 1898.

Aiyar, C. P. Ramaswami. *Annie Besant*. New Delhi: Publications Division, Ministry of Information and Broadcasting, 1963.

210 BIBLIOGRAPHY

Algeo, John. "The Integrated Alien: Ritual Magic in the Fiction of Dion Fortune." In *The Shape of the Fantastic*, edited by Olena Saciuk, 211–218. New York: Greenwood Publishing, 1990.

Allan, Janice, Jesper Guiddal, Stewart King, and Andrew Pepper. "Introduction: New Directions in Crime Fiction Scholarship." In *The Routledge Companion to Crime Fiction*, edited by Janice Allan, Jesper Guiddal, Stewart King, and Andrew Pepper, 1–9. Milton Keynes: Routledge, 2020.

"Another Traitor Trounced." *John Bull*. January 10, 1920. British Newspaper Archive.

Aponte, Sally Ortiz. *La esoteria en la narrative hispanoamericana*. San Juan: Editorial Universitaria, Universidad de Puerto Rico, 1977.

Arnold, Matthew. "Up to Easter." *The Nineteenth Century* 123 (May 1887): 629–643.

"Art IV. Modern Novelists: Sir Edward Bulwer-Lytton." *Westminster Review* 27, no. 2 (April 1865): 468–503.

"Art V. A Strange Story. By the Author of 'My Novel.'" *Christian Remembrancer* 43, no. 116 (April 1862): 448–466.

Asad, Talal. *Formations of the Secular: Christianity, Islam, Modernity*. Stanford: Stanford University Press, 2003.

Ascari, Maurizio. *A Counter-History of Crime Fiction: Supernatural, Gothic, Sensational*. London: Palgrave, 2007.

Asprem, Egil. *The Problem of Disenchantment: Scientific Naturalism and Esoteric Discourse, 1900–1939*. Leiden: Brill, 2014.

Asprem, Egil, and Julian Strube, eds. *New Approaches to the Study of Esotericism*. Leiden: Brill, 2021.

Austen, Jane. *Northanger Abbey*. London: John Murray, 1817.

"Authors Take Side on the Spanish Civil War." *Left Review*. 1937.

Bakhtin, M. M. "The *Bildungsroman* and its Significance in the History of Realism (Toward a Historical Typology of the Novel)." In *Speech Genres and Other Late Essays*, by Mikhail Bakhtin, edited by Caryl Emerson and Michael Holquist, and translated by Vern McGhee, 10–59. Austin: University of Texas Press, 1987.

Banon, A. "Racial Development." *The Theosophist* 9, no. 97 (October 1885): 77.

Banta, Martha. *Henry James and the Occult: The Great Extension*. Bloomington: Indiana University Press, 1972.

Basham, Diana. *The Trial of Women: Feminism and the Occult Sciences in Victorian Literature and Society*. Basingstoke: Palgrave Macmillan, 1992.

Bauduin, Tessel, and Henrik Johnsson. "Conceptualizing Occult Modernism." In *The Occult in Modernist Art, Literature, and Cinema*, edited by Tessel Bauduin and Henrik Johnsson, 1–30. Cham: Palgrave Macmillan, 2018.

Beetham, Margaret. "Towards a Theory of the Periodical as a Publishing Genre." In *Investigating Victorian Journalism*, edited by Laurel Brake, Aled Jones, and Lionel Madden, 19–32. London: Palgrave Macmillan, 1990.

Bell, Michael. *Open Secrets: Literature, Education, and Authority from J.J. Rousseau to J.M. Coetzee*. Oxford: Oxford University Press, 2007.

Bennett, Bridget. "Crossing Over: Spiritualism and the Atlantic Divide." In *Special Relationships: Anglo-American Affinities and Antagonisms*, edited by Janet Beer and Bridget Bennett, 89–109. Manchester: Manchester University Press, 2002.

Bergunder, Michael. "What is Esotericism? Cultural Studies Approaches and the Problems of Definition in Religious Studies." *Method and Theory in the Study of Religions* 22, no. 1 (2010): 9–36.

Besant, Annie. *Reincarnation*. London: Theosophical Publishing House, 1898.

Besant, Annie, and C. W. Leadbeater. *The Lives of Alcyone*. Adyar: Theosophical Publishing House, 1924.

Bhattacharya, Prodosh. "The Reception of Marie Corelli in India." In *New Readings in the Literature of British India, c. 1780–1947*, edited by Shafquat Towheed, 219–244. Hannover: Ibiden-Verlag, 2014.

BIBLIOGRAPHY 211

The Bible: Authorized King James Version and Apocrypha. Edited by Robert Carroll and Stephen Prickett. Oxford: Oxford University Press, 1997.

Blackwood, Algernon. "A Psychical Invasion (1908)." In *The Ghost Slayers: Thrilling Tales of Occult Detection,* edited by Mike Ashley, 31–96. London: British Library, 2022.

Blavatsky, H. P. *Isis Unveiled: A Master-Key to the Mysteries of Ancient and Modern Science and Theology.* New York: J. W. Bouton and Co., 1877.

Blavatsky, H. P. *Nightmare Tales.* London: Theosophical Publishing House, 1892.

Blavatsky, H. P. *The Secret Doctrine: The Synthesis of Science, Religion and Philosophy.* London: Theosophical Publishing Society, 1888.

Bleiler, Richard J. *The Strange Case of the "Angel of Mons": Arthur Machen's World War I Story, the Insistent Believers, and his Refutations.* Jefferson, NC: McFarland & Co., 2015.

Bogdan, Henrik. "Aleister Crowley: A Prophet for the Modern Age." In *The Occult World,* edited by Christopher Partridge, 293–302. London: Routledge, 2015.

Bogdan, Henrik. "Aleister Crowley as an Advertiser of the Occult." *Religion and the Arts* 28 (2024): 13–65.

Bogdan, Henrik. "Envisioning the Birth of a New Aeon: Dispensationalism and Millenarianism in the Thelemic Tradition." In *Aleister Crowley and Western Esotericism: An Anthology of Critical Studies,* edited by Henrik Bogdan and Martin P. Starr, 89–106. Oxford: Oxford University Press, 2012.

Borges, Jorge Luis. "The House of Asterion." In *The Aleph,* translated by Andrew Hurley, 51–53. London: Penguin Books, 2000.

Botting, Fred. *Gothic.* Abingdon: Routledge, 2014.

Bourdieu, Pierre. *Distinction: A Social Critique of the Judgement of Taste.* Translated by Richard Nice. Cambridge: Harvard University Press, 1984.

Bown, Nicola, Carolyn Burdett, and Pamela Thurschwell. "Introduction." In *The Victorian Supernatural,* edited by Nicola Bown, Carolyn Burdett, and Pamela Thurschwell, 1–17. Cambridge: Cambridge University Press, 2004.

Braddon, Mary Elizabeth. *The Trail of the Serpent.* London: Ward, Lock, 1861.

Bradford, Richard. *Crime Fiction: A Very Short Introduction.* Oxford: Oxford University Press, 2013.

Braidotti, Rosa. "In Spite of the Times: The Postsecular Turn in Feminism." *Theory, Culture and Society: Explorations in Critical Social Science* 25, no. 6 (2008): 1–24.

Brake, Laurel. "Revolutions in Journalism: W.T. Stead, Indexing, and 'Searching.'" In *Nineteenth-Century Radical Traditions,* edited by Joseph Bristow and Josephine McDonagh, 157–187. London: Palgrave Macmillan, 2016.

Brantlinger, Patrick. *The Reading Lesson: The Threat of Mass Literacy in Nineteenth-Century British Literature.* Bloomington: Indiana University Press, 1998.

Breeze, William. "Introduction." In *The Simon Iff Stories and Other Works,* by Aleister Crowley, edited by William Breeze, 7–18. Ware: Wordsworth Editions, 2012.

Brewster, Scott. "Gothic Criticism in the Twentieth Century: Who is This Who is Coming?" In *Twentieth-Century Gothic: An Edinburgh Companion,* edited by Bernice Murphy and Sorcha Ni Fhlainn, 64–80. Edinburgh: Edinburgh University Press, 2022.

Britten, Emma Hardinge. *Autobiography of Emma Hardinge Britten.* Edited by Mrs. Margaret Wilkinson. Manchester: John Heywood, 1900.

Britten, Emma Hardinge. "Extracts from 'Ghostland,' Volume II; Or Researches into the Realm of Spiritual Existence. By the Author of 'Art Magic.'" *The Unseen Universe* 1, no. 3 (June 1892): 114–123.

Britten, Emma Hardinge. "Extracts from 'Ghostland,' Volume II; Or Researches into the Realm of Spiritual Existence. By the Author of 'Art Magic.'" *The Unseen Universe* 1, no. 12 (March 1893): 613–619.

Britten, Emma Hardinge. *Ghost Land; or Researches into the Mysteries of Occultism.* Translated and edited by Emma Hardinge Britten. Boston: Published for the Author, 1876.

212 BIBLIOGRAPHY

Britten, Emma Hardinge. "The Mystery of No. 9 Stanhope Street: A Romance of Real Life." *The Unseen Universe* 1, no. 7 (October 1892): 405–412.

Britten, Emma Hardinge. "The Mystery of No. 9 Stanhope Street: A Romance of Real Life." *The Unseen Universe* 1, no. 8 (November 1892): 349–359.

Britten, Emma Hardinge. "The Wildfire Club." In *The Wildfire Club*, 340–366. Boston: Berry, Colby, and Rich, 1861.

Brodie-Innes, J. W. *The Devil's Mistress*. London: William Rider and Son, 1915.

Brooks, Peter. *Realist Vision*. New Haven: Yale University Press, 2005.

Brown, Andrew. "The 'Supplementary Chapter' to Bulwer Lytton's *A Strange Story*." *Victorian Literature and Culture* 26, no. 1 (1998): 157–182.

Brown, Callum. *The Death of Christian Britain: Understanding Secularization, 1800–2000*. London: Routledge, 2001.

Brown, Julia Prewitt. "The Moral Scope of the English *Bildungsroman*." In *The Oxford Handbook of the Victorian Novel*, edited by Lisa Rodensky, 663–678. Oxford: Oxford University Press, 2013.

Brown, Stewart J. *W.T. Stead: Nonconformist and Newspaper Prophet*. Oxford: Oxford University Press, 2019.

Bulwer Lytton, Edward. *Alice; or, the Mysteries*. London: Saunders & Otley, 1838.

Bulwer Lytton, Edward. *Asmodeus at Large* (1832–1833). Chicago, IL: OK Books, 2021. Kindle Edition.

Bulwer Lytton, Edward. "Asmodeus at Large—No. X." *The New Monthly Magazine and Literary Journal* 37, no. 146 (February 1833): 155–168.

Bulwer Lytton, Edward. *The Coming Race*. Edinburgh: William Blackwood and Sons, 1871.

Bulwer Lytton, Edward. *The Disowned*. London: J & J Harper, 1829.

Bulwer Lytton, Edward. *Ernest Maltravers*. London: Saunders & Otley, 1837.

Bulwer Lytton, Edward. "*Falkland* (1827)." In *The Greatest Gothic Novels of Edward Bulwer-Lytton*, 1288–1396. Chicago, IL: OK Books, 2021. Kindle Edition.

Bulwer Lytton, Edward. *Godolphin*. London: Bentley, 1833.

Bulwer Lytton, Edward. *Kenelm Chillingly*. Edinburgh: William Blackwood and Sons, 1873.

Bulwer Lytton, Edward. *The Parisians*. London: George Routledge and Sons, 1873.

Bulwer Lytton, Edward. *Pausanias, the Spartan*. London: George Routledge and Sons, 1876.

Bulwer Lytton, Edward. *Pelham*. London: Henry Colburn, 1828.

Bulwer Lytton, Edward. *A Strange Story*. 2 Vols. London: Sampson Low, Son, and Co., 1862.

Bulwer Lytton, Edward. *The Student: A Series of Papers*. London: Saunders and Otley, 1835.

Bulwer Lytton, Edward. *What Will He Do With It?* Edinburgh: William Blackwood and Sons, 1859.

Bulwer Lytton, Edward. *Zanoni* (1842). London: Routledge, Warne, and Routledge, 1864.

Bulwer Lytton, Edward. "*Zicci* (1838)." In *The Greatest Gothic Novels of Edward Bulwer-Lytton*, 1397–1512. Chicago, IL: OK Books, 2021. Kindle Edition.

Burroughs, William S. *The Adding Machine: Selected Essays*. New York: Seaver Books, 1986.

Butler, Alison. "Dion Fortune and the Society of the Inner Light." In *The Occult World*, edited by Christopher Partridge, 315–319. Abingdon: Routledge, 2015.

Caithness, Countess of [Marie Sinclair]. *A Midnight Visit to Holyrood*. London: C. L. H. Wallace, 1887.

Cantú, Keith A. "A Triangle of Art: The Relationship Between Aleister Crowley, Ananda Coomaraswamy, and Ratan Devi." *Religion and the Arts* 28 (2024): 89–106.

Carney, James. "Supernatural Intuition and Classic Detection: A Cognitivist Approach." *Style* 48, no. 2 (2014): 203–218.

Castex, Pierre Georges. *Le conte fantastique en France: de Nodier à Maupassant*. Paris: Librairie José Corti, 1951.

Cazotte, Jacques. *Le Diable Amoreux*. Paris, 1772.

Chajes, Julie. *Recycled Lives: A History of Reincarnation in Blavatsky's Theosophy*. Oxford: Oxford University Press, 2019.

BIBLIOGRAPHY 213

Christie, Agatha. *The Mysterious Affair at Styles* (1920). London: Pan Books, 1954.

Clark, David R. "'Metaphors for Poetry': W.B. Yeats and the Occult." In *The World of W.B. Yeats: Essays in Perspective*, edited by Robin Skelton and Ann Saddlemyer, 54–66. Victoria: Adelphi Bookshop, 1965.

Clarke, Clare. *British Detective Fiction, 1891–1901: The Successors to Sherlock Holmes.* London: Palgrave Macmillan, 2020.

Clarke, Clare. *Late Victorian Crime Fiction in the Shadows of Sherlock.* Basingstoke: Palgrave Macmillan, 2014.

Cohn, Elisha. *Still Life: Suspended Development in the Victorian Novel.* Oxford: Oxford University Press, 2015.

Collins, Mabel, and —. *The Blossom and the Fruit: A True Story of a Black Magician.* London: Published by the Authors, 1888.

Collins, Mabel. *The Idyll of the White Lotus.* London: Reeves and Turner, 1884.

Collins, Mabel. *Light on the Path.* London: Reeves and Turner, 1885.

Collins, Mabel. *Morial the Mahatma.* New York: United States Book Company, 1891.

Collins, Mortimer. *The Secret of Long Life.* 1871.

Collins, Mortimer. *Transmigration.* 3 Vols. London: Hurst & Blackett, 1874.

Collins, Wilkie. *The Moonstone: A Romance.* London: Tinsley Brothers, 1868.

Cook, Michael. *Detective Fiction and the Ghost Story.* Cham: Palgrave Macmillan, 2014.

Corelli, Marie. *Ardath: The Story of a Dead Self.* London: Richard Bentley & Co., 1889.

Corelli, Marie. *The Life Everlasting: A Reality of Romance.* New York: A. L. Burt, 1911.

Corelli, Marie. *A Romance of Two Worlds* (1886). London: Methuen and Co., 1922.

Corelli, Marie. *The Sorrows of Satan.* London: Methuen & Co., 1895.

Corelli, Marie. *The Soul of Lilith.* London: Richard Bentley & Co., 1892.

Corelli, Marie. *Ziska: The Problem of a Wicked Soul.* New York: Frederick A. Stokes Company, 1897.

Crowley, Aleister. "The Artistic Temperament." In *The Simon Iff Stories & Other Works*, by Aleister Crowley, edited by William Breeze, 44–60. Ware: Wordsworth Editions, 2012.

Crowley, Aleister. 1917. "The Big Game (1917)." In *The Simon Iff Stories & Other Works*, by Aleister Crowley, edited by William Breeze, 23–43. Ware: Wordsworth Editions, 2012.

Crowley, Aleister. *The Book of the Law.* London: O. T. O., BCM/ANKH, 1938.

Crowley, Aleister. *The Confessions of Aleister Crowley.* London: Mandrake Press, 1929.

Crowley, Aleister. *The Confessions of Aleister Crowley: An Autohagiography.* Edited by John Symonds and Kenneth Grant. London: Routledge & Kegan Paul, 1979.

Crowley, Aleister. "Ineligible (1918)." In *The Simon Iff Stories & Other Works*, by Aleister Crowley, edited by William Breeze, 100–116. Ware: Wordsworth Editions, 2012.

Crowley, Aleister. *The Law is For All: An Extended Commentary on The Book of the Law.* Edited by Israel Regardie. St Paul: Llewellyn Publications, 1975.

Crowley, Aleister. *Magick in Theory and Practice.* Edited by John Symonds and Kenneth Grant. London: Routledge & Kegan Paul, 1973.

Crowley, Aleister. "Not Good Enough (1918)." In *The Simon Iff Stories & Other Works*, by Aleister Crowley, edited by William Breeze, 100–116. Ware: Wordsworth Editions, 2012.

Crowley, Aleister. "Outside the Bank's Routine (1917)." In *The Simon Iff Stories & Other Works*, by Aleister Crowley, edited by William Breeze, 61–83. Ware: Wordsworth Editions, 2012.

Crowley, Aleister. *The Scrutinies of Simon Iff & Other Works.* Edited by William Breeze. Ware: Wordsworth Editions, 2012.

Crowley, Aleister. *The Scrutinies of Simon Iff.* Edited by Martin P. Starr. Chicago: Teitan Press, 1987.

Cusack, Carole. "A Magickal School in the Twenty-First Century: The Grey School of Wizardry and its Prehistory." In *Fictional Practice: Magic, Narration, and the Power of Imagination*, edited by Bernd-Christian Otto and Dirk Johanssen, 314–333. Leiden: Brill, 2021.

Davidsen, Markus Altena. "Fiction-Based Religion: Conceptualizing a New Category against History-Based Religion and Fandom." *Culture and Religion* 14, no. 4 (2013): 378–395.

214 BIBLIOGRAPHY

Davies, Owen. *Grimoires: A History of Magic Books.* Oxford: Oxford University Press, 2009.

Demarest, Marc. *Chasing Down Emma.* ehbritten.blogspot.com.

Demarest, Marc. "Introduction to the Annotated Edition." In *Art Magic*, by Emma Hardinge Britten, edited by Marc Demarest, iii–lvi. Forest Grove: Typhon Press, 2011.

Deveney, John Patrick. *Paschal Beverly Randolph: A Nineteenth-Century Black American Spiritualist, Rosicrucian, and Sex Magician.* Albany: State University of New York Press, 1997.

DiBernard, Barbara. *Alchemy and Finnegan's Wake.* Albany: State University of New York Press, 1980.

Dickens, Charles. *Bleak House.* London: Bradbury and Evans, 1853.

Dickens, Charles. *The Letters of Charles Dickens: Volume 7, 1853–57.* Edited by Graham Storey, Kathleen Tillotson, and Angus Easson. Oxford: Clarendon Press, 1993.

Dine, S. S. "Twenty Rules for Writing Detective Stories." *The American Magazine.* September 1928, 129–131.

Dixon, Joy. *Divine Feminine: Theosophy and Feminism in England.* Baltimore: Johns Hopkins University Press, 2001.

Dobson, Eleanor. *Victorian Alchemy: Science, Magic, and Ancient Egypt.* London: UCL Press, 2022.

Dobson, Eleanor, ed. *Victorian Literature Culture and Ancient Egypt.* Manchester: Manchester University Press, 2020.

Dobson, Eleanor. *Writing the Sphinx: Literature, Culture, and Egyptology.* Edinburgh: Edinburgh University Press, 2020.

Downing, Lisa. *Selfish Women.* London: Routledge, 2019.

Doyle, Arthur Conan. "The Blue Carbuncle (1892)." In *The Adventures of Sherlock Holmes*, by Arthur Conan Doyle, edited by Richard Lancelyn Green, 149–170. Oxford: Oxford University Press, 1993.

Doyle, Arthur Conan. "The Boscombe Valley Mystery (1891)." In *The Adventures of Sherlock Holmes*, by Arthur Conan Doyle, edited by Richard Lancelyn Green, 75–101. Oxford: Oxford University Press, 1993.

Doyle, Arthur Conan. *The Case-Book of Sherlock Holmes.* London: John Murray, 1927.

Doyle, Arthur Conan. "The Copper Beeches (1892)." In *The Adventures of Sherlock Holmes*, by Arthur Conan Doyle, edited by Richard Lancelyn Green, 270–296. Oxford: Oxford University Press, 1993.

Doyle, Arthur Conan. *The History of Spiritualism.* London: Cassell & Co., 1926.

Doyle, Arthur Conan. "Mr Hodgson: To the Editor of *Light*." August 28, 1887, 404.

Doyle, Arthur Conan. *The Land of Mist.* London: Hutchinson & Co., 1926.

Doyle, Arthur Conan. *The Parasite.* London: A. Constable & Co., 1984.

Doyle, Arthur Conan. "A Scandal in Bohemia (1891)." In *The Adventures of Sherlock Holmes*, by Arthur Conan Doyle, edited by Richard Lancelyn Green, 5–29. Oxford: Oxford University Press, 1993.

Doyle, Arthur Conan. *The Sign of Four.* Edited by Shafquat Towheed. Peterborough: Broadview Press, 2010.

Doyle, Arthur Conan. "Sir Arthur Conan Doyle's Resignation." *Journal for the Society for Psychical Research* (March 1930): 45–46.

Doyle, Arthur Conan. "The Speckled Band (1892)." In *The Adventures of Sherlock Holmes*, by Arthur Conan Doyle, edited by Richard Lancelyn Green, 171–197. Oxford: Oxford University Press, 1993.

Doyle, Arthur Conan. "A Study in Scarlet." In *The Complete Novels and Stories*, 1–120. New York: Bantam Dell, 1986.

Doyle, Arthur Conan. "A Test Séance." *Light.* July 2, 1887, 303.

Drazin, Adam. "The Object Biography." In *Lineages and Perspectives in Material Culture Studies: Perspectives from UCL Anthropology*, edited by Timothy Carroll, Antonia Walford, and Shireen Walton, 61–74. London: Routledge, 2020.

BIBLIOGRAPHY   215

Duguid, David. *Hafed, Prince of Persia: His Experiences in Earth-Life and Spirit-Life.* London: J. Burns, 1876.

Earle, David M. *Re-Covering Modernism: Modernism, Pulps, Paperbacks, and the Prejudice of Form.* Burlington: Ashgate, 2009.

E. C. "Problems of Popularity." *The Speaker: The Liberal Review* 5, no. 106 (October 12, 1901): 50–51.

"Editorial." *The Equinox: The Official Organ of the A∴A∴, The Review of Scientific Illuminism* 1, no. 1 (1909): 1–3.

"Editorial Notice." *Lucifer* 3, no. 14 (October 1888): 137.

Edwards, Paul. *Reincarnation: A Critical Examination.* Amherst: Prometheus Books, 2002.

Eldrige, Sarah Vandergrift, and C. Allen Speight. "Introduction." In *Wilhelm Meister's Apprenticeship and Philosophy*, edited by Sarah Vandergrift Eldrige and C. Allen Speight, 1–17. Oxford: Oxford University Press, 2020.

Ellis, Linda. *Appearing to Diminish: Female Development and the British Bildungsroman, 1750–1850.* Lewisburg: Bucknell University Press, 1999.

Eliot, T. S. "In Memoriam." In *In Memoriam, A.H.H.*, by Lord Alfred Tennyson, edited by Erik Gray, 135–139. London: W. W. Norton & Co., 2004.

"Esoteric Bosh." *Saturday Review of Politics, Literature, and Science* 58, no. 1499 (July 19, 1884): 70.

Ezra. "Haunted Houses 1: The Picture Spectres." *Spiritual Telegraph* 1, no. 30 (November 21, 1857): 233–234.

Fanger, Claire. "Mirror, Mask, and Anti-Self: Forces of Literary Creation in Dion Fortune and W.B. Yeats." In *Esotericism, Art, and Imagination*, edited by Arthur Versluis, Lee Irwin, John D. Richards, and Melinda Weinstein, 161–182. East Lansing: Michigan State University Press, 2008.

Farnell, Kim. *Mystical Vampire: The Life and Works of Mabel Collins.* Oxford: Mandrake, 2005.

Faxneld, Per. *Satanic Feminism: Lucifer as the Liberator of Women in Nineteenth-Century Culture.* Oxford: Oxford University Press, 2017.

Federico, Annette. *Idol of Suburbia: Marie Corelli and Late Victorian Literary Culture.* London: University of Virginia Press, 2000.

Felski, Rita. *The Gender of Modernity.* London: Harvard University Press, 1995.

Feraro, Shai. *Women and Gender Issues in British Paganism, 1945–1990.* London: Palgrave Macmillan, 2020.

Ferguson, Barbara. "'My Spook Writes in Steadese': Voice, Mediation, and the New Journalism in W.T. Stead's *Borderland*." *Victorian Review* 47, no. 1 (2021): 135–152.

Ferguson, Christine. "Beyond Belief: Literature, Esotericism Studies, and the Challenges of Biographical Reading in Arthur Conan Doyle's *The Land of Mist*." *Aries* 22, no. 1 (2021): 1–26.

Ferguson, Christine. "*Dracula* and the Occult." In *The Cambridge Companion to Dracula*, edited by Roger Luckhurst, 57–65. Cambridge: Cambridge University Press, 2017.

Ferguson, Christine. "The Luciferian Public Sphere: Theosophy and Editorial Seekership in the 1880s." *Victorian Periodicals Review* 53, no. 1 (Spring 2020): 76–101.

Fleischhack, Maria. *Narrating Ancient Egypt: The Representation of Ancient Egypt in Nineteenth-Century and Early Twentieth-Century Fiction.* Frankfurt: Peter Lang, 2015.

Fort, Charles. "*The Book of the Damned* (1919)." In *The Complete Books of Charles Fort*, edited by Damon Knight, 3–310. New York: Dover, 1974.

Fort, Charles. "*Wild Talents* (1932)." In *The Complete Books of Charles Fort*, edited by Damon Knight, 843–1062. New York: Dover, 1974.

Fortune, Dion. *The Demon Lover.* London: Noel Douglas, 1927.

Fortune, Dion. *The Goat-Foot God* (1936). York Beach: Weiser Books, 1999.

Fortune, Dion. *Moon Magic.* London: Aquarian Press, 1956.

Fortune, Dion. *The Mystical Qabbalah.* London: Williams & Norgate, 1935.

Fortune, Dion. *Psychic Self-Defence* (1930). London: Global Grey, 2018. Kindle.

216 BIBLIOGRAPHY

Fortune, Dion. *Sane Occultism and Practical Occultism in Daily Life* (1929). Wellingborough: Aquarian Press, 1987.

Fortune, Dion. *The Sea Priestess* (1935). York Beach: Weiser Books, 2003.

Fortune, Dion. *The Secrets of Dr Taverner* (1926). York Beach: Weiser Books, 2011.

Fortune, Dion. *The Winged Bull*. London: Williams and Norgate, 1935.

Fraiman, Susan. *Unbecoming Women: British Women Writers and the Novel of Development*. New York: Columbia University Press, 1993.

Frank, Lawrence. *Victorian Detective Fiction and the Nature of Evidence: The Scientific Investigations of Poe, Dickens, and Doyle*. London: Palgrave Macmillan, 2003.

Franklin, J. Jeffrey. *Spirit Matters: Occult Beliefs, Alternative Religions, and the Crisis of Faith in Victorian Britain*. Ithaca: Cornell University Press, 2018.

Frazer, James George. *The Golden Bough: A Study in Comparative Religion*. London: Macmillan & Co., 1890.

Freeman, Nick. "The Black Magic Bogeyman, 1908–1935." In *The Occult Imagination in Britain, 1875–1947*, edited by Christine Ferguson and Andrew Radford, 94–109. London: Routledge, 2018.

Gange, David. *Dialogues with the Dead: Egyptology in British Culture and Religion, 1822–1922*. Oxford: Oxford University Press, 2013.

Gasperini, Anna. *Nineteenth-Century Popular Fiction, Medicine, and Anatomy: The Victorian Penny Blood and the 1832 Anatomy Act*. Cham: Palgrave Macmillan, 2019.

Gekle, William Francis. *Arthur Machen: Weaver of Fantasy*. Millbrook, NY: Round Table Press, 1949.

Gelder, Ken. *Popular Fiction: The Logics and Practices of a Literary Field*. London: Routledge, 2004.

Gilbert, R. A. *A.E. Waite: A Magician of Many Parts*. Wellingborough: Crucible, 1987.

Gilbert, Robert. "The Great Chain of Unreason: The Publication and Distribution of the Literature of Rejected Knowledge in England During the Victorian Era." PhD diss., University of London, 2009.

Godwin, Joscelyn. *The Theosophical Enlightenment*. Albany: State University of New York Press, 1994.

Goethe, Johann Wolfgang von. *Wilhelm Meister's Apprenticeship*. 3 Vols. Translated by Thomas Carlyle. Edinburgh: Oliver & Boyd, 1894.

Goethe, Johann Wolfgang von. *Wilhelm Meister's Lehrjahre, oder die entsagenden*. Stuttgart: Cotta'sche Buchhandlung, 1821.

Goodrick-Clarke, Nicholas. *The Western Esoteric Traditions: A Historical Introduction*. Oxford: Oxford University Press, 2008.

Goulet, Andrea. "Crime Fiction and Modern Science." In *The Routledge Companion to Crime Fiction*, edited by Janice Allan, Jesper Guiddal, Stewart King, and Andrew Pepper, 291–300. Milton Keynes: Routledge, 2020.

Green, Paul. *Encyclopedia of Weird Detectives: Supernatural and Paranormal Elements in Novels, Pulps, Comics, Film, Television, Games, and Other Media*. Jefferson, NC: McFarland & Company, 2019.

Haggard, H. Rider. "About Fiction." *Contemporary Review* 51 (February 1887): 172–180.

Haggard, H. Rider. *Ayesha: The Return of She*. London: Ward, Lock, and Co., 1905.

Haggard, H. Rider. *King Solomon's Mines*. London: Cassell & Company, 1885.

Haggard, H. Rider. *She: A History of Adventure* (1887). London: Oxford World's Classics, 1989.

Haggard, H. Rider. *She and Allan*. London: Hutchinson & Co., 1921.

Haggard, H. Rider. *Wisdom's Daughter*. London: Hutchinson & Co., 1923.

Hammer, Olav. *Claiming Knowledge: Strategies of Epistemology from Theosophy to the New Age*. Leiden: Brill, 2004.

Hamnett, Nina. *Laughing Torso: Reminiscences of Nina Hamnett*. London: Constable & Co., 1932.

BIBLIOGRAPHY 217

Hanegraaff, Wouter. *Esotericism and the Academy: Rejected Knowledge in Western Culture*. Oxford: Oxford University Press, 2012.

Hanegraaff, Wouter. *Western Esotericism: A Guide for the Perplexed.* London: Bloomsbury, 2013.

Hardy, Thomas. *Tess of the d'Urbervilles* (1891). New York: W. W. Norton and Co., 1991.

Hardy, Thomas. *The Well-Beloved and Alicia's Diary.* Paris: Zulma Classics, 2005.

Harper, George Mills, ed. *Yeats and the Occult.* New York: Macmillan, 1975.

Heady, Chense. "Father Brown, Labour Priest: G.K. Chesterton and the Class Politics of Golden Age Detective Fiction." *Journal of Popular Fiction* 53, no. 4 (Autumn 2020): 865–885.

Hirst, Sam. *Theology in Early British and Irish Gothic, 1764–1834.* London: Anthem Press, 2023.

Hoffman, Megan. *Gender and Representation in British "Golden Age" Crime Fiction: Women Writing Women.* London: Palgrave Macmillan, 2016.

"Hornsey Spirit Mystery." *Daily News.* April 11, 1921.

Horsely, Lee. *Twentieth-Century Crime Fiction.* Oxford: Oxford University Press, 2005.

Hodgson, W. H. "The Gateway of the Monster (1910)." In *Supernatural Sleuths: Stories from the Golden Age of the Occult Detective*, edited by Nick Rennison, 137–159. Harpenden: No Exit Press, 2017.

Howe, Suzanne. *Wilhelm Meister and his English Kinsmen: Apprentices to Life.* New York: Columbia University Press, 1930.

Howitt, William. "Spiritualist Idiosyncrasies in the Goethe Family." *The Spiritual Magazine* New Series 1, no. 9 (September 1866): 416–426.

Huckvale, David. *A Dark and Stormy Oeuvre: Crime, Magic, and Power in the Novels of Edward Bulwer Lytton.* Jefferson, NC: McFarland and Co., 2015.

Hull, Edith Maude. *The Sheik.* London: E. Nast & Grayson, 1919.

Hulme, Fergus. *The Mystery of a Hansom Cab.* London: The Hansom Cab Publishing Company, 1887.

Hultgren, Neil. *Melodramatic Imperial Writing from the Sepoy Rebellion to Cecil Rhodes.* Athens: Ohio University Press, 2014.

Hunter, Jack, ed. *Damned Facts: Fortean Essays on Religion, Folklore, and the Paranormal.* Paphos: Aporeitic Press, 2016.

Hunter, Jack. "Intermediatism and the Study of Religion." *Paranthropology: Journal of Anthropological Approaches to the Paranormal* 7, no. 1 (July 2016): 51–56.

Huysmans, J. K. *The Damned.* Translated by Terry Hale. London: Penguin, 2001.

Huyssen, Andreas. *After the Great Divide: Modernism, Mass Culture, Postmodernism.* Bloomington: Indiana University Press, 1986.

Jackson, Kate. *George Newnes and the New Journalism, 1880–1910: Culture and Profit.* Aldershot: Ashgate, 2001.

Jeffers, Thomas. *Apprenticeships: The Bildungsroman from Goethe to Santanyana.* New York: Palgrave Macmillan, 2005.

Jones, Anna Maria. "Inductive Science, Literary Theory, and the Occult in Edward Bulwer-Lytton's 'Suggestive System.'" In *Strange Science: Investigating the Limits of Knowledge in the Victorian Age*, edited by Lara Karpenko and Shalyn Claggett, 215–235. Ann Arbor: University of Michigan Press, 2017.

Josephson-Storm, Jason Ananda. *The Myth of Disenchantment: Magic, Modernity, and the Birth of the Human Sciences.* Chicago: University of Chicago Press, 2017.

Joshi, Priti. *In Another Country: Colonialism, Culture, and the English Novel in India.* New York: Columbia University Press, 2002.

Killeen, Jarlath. *Gothic Literature, 1825–1914.* Cardiff: University of Wales Press, 2009.

Killeen, Jarlath. "Victorian Gothic Pulp Fiction." In *The Victorian Gothic: An Edinburgh Companion*, edited by Andrew Smith and William Hughes, 43–56. Edinburgh: Edinburgh University Press, 2012.

"The King of Depravity." *John Bull.* March 10, 1923.

"The King of Depravity Arrives." *John Bull.* March 14, 1923.

218   BIBLIOGRAPHY

Kipling, Rudyard. "The Mark of the Beast." In *Life's Handicap*, 240–259. London: Macmillan & Co., 1891.

Knight, Damon. *Charles Fort: Prophet of the Unexplained* (1971). Golden, CO: Reanimus Press, 2021.

Knight, Gareth. *Dion Fortune and the Inner Light*. Loughborough: Thoth, 2000.

Knight, Mark. "The Limits of Orthodoxy in a Secular Age: The Strange Case of Marie Corelli." *Nineteenth-Century Literature* 73, no. 3 (2018): 379–398.

Knight, Mark, and Charles LaPorte. "Talking about Religion in Eighteenth- and Nineteenth-Century Literature." *Modern Language Quarterly* 83, no. 4 (2022): 367–372.

Knight, Stephen. *Crime Fiction, 1800–2000: Detection, Death, Diversity*. Basingstoke: Palgrave Macmillan, 2004.

Knox, Ronald. "Ten Rules for a Good Detective Story." *Publisher's Weekly*. October 5, 1929, 1729.

Kripal, Jeffrey J. *Authors of the Impossible: The Paranormal and the Sacred*. London: University of Chicago Press, 2010.

Lang, Andrew. "Realism and Romance." *Contemporary Review* 52 (November 1887): 683–693.

La Porte, Charles. "Victorian Literature, Religion, and Secularization." *Literature Compass* 10, no. 3 (March 2013): 277–287.

LaPorte, Charles, and Sebastian Lecourt. "Nineteenth-Century Literature, New Religious Movements, and Secularization." *Nineteenth-Century Literature* 73, no. 2 (2018): 147–160.

Lee, Susanna. "Crime Fiction and Theories of Justice." In *The Routledge Companion to Crime Fiction*, edited by Janice Allan, Jesper Guiddal Stewart, and Andrew Penner, 282–290. Milton Keynes: Routledge, 2020.

Le Fanu, Sheridan. "Green Tea." In *In a Glass Darkly* (1872), 5–40. Oxford: Oxford World's Classics, 1993.

Le Sage, Alain-René. *Le Diable bôiteaux*. Paris: Chez la veuve Barbin, 1707.

Lewis, Matthew. *The Monk: A Romance*. Waterford: J. Saunders, 1796.

Levine, Caroline. *Forms: Whole, Rhythm, Hierarchy, Network*. Princeton: Princeton University Press, 2015.

Lingan, Edward. *The Theatre of the Occult Revival: Alternative Spiritual Performance from 1875 to the Present*. New York: Palgrave Macmillan, 2014.

"Literature." *Caledonian Mercury*. April 4, 1842.

"Literature." *Morning Post*. June 16, 1843.

Lord, Evelyn. *The Hell-Fire Clubs: Sex, Satanism, and Secret Societies*. New Haven: Yale University Press, 2010.

Luckhurst, Roger. *The Invention of Telepathy: 1870–1901*. Oxford: Oxford University Press, 2002.

Luckhurst, Roger. *The Mummy's Curse: The True History of a Dark Fantasy*. Oxford: Oxford University Press, 2012.

Luckhurst, Roger. "W.T. Stead's Occult Economies." In *Culture and Science in the Nineteenth-Century Media*, edited by Louise Henson, Geoffrey Cantor, Gowan Dawson, Richard Noakes, Sally Shuttleworth, and Jonathan R. Topham, 125–135. Aldershot: Ashgate, 2004.

Lynch, Deidre. "Keeping Faith with Literature." *Modern Language Quarterly* 83, no. 2 (2022): 539–547.

Lyons, Sara. "Recent Developments in Victorian Studies and the *Bildungsroman*." *Literature Compass* 15, no. 4 (April 2018): 1–12.

Lyons, Sara. "Secularism and Secularization at the *Fin de Siècle*." In *The Edinburgh Companion to the Fin de Siècle: Literature, Culture, and Arts*, edited by Josephine Guy, 124–145. Edinburgh: Edinburgh University Press, 2018.

Machen, Arthur. *Dr Stiggins: His Views and His Principles*. Westminster: Francis Griffiths, 1906.

Machen, Arthur. *Far Off Things*. London: Martin Secker, 1922.

Machen, Arthur. "*The Great God Pan* (1894)." In *The Great God Pan and Other Horror Stories*, by Arthur Machen, edited by Aaron Worth, 9–54. Oxford: Oxford University Press, 2018.

BIBLIOGRAPHY 219

Machen, Arthur. "*The Green Round* (1933)." In *Delphi Complete Works of Arthur Machen*, 584–706. Hastings: Delphi Classics, 2013.

Machen, Arthur. "The Inmost Light (1894)." In *The Great God Pan and Other Horror Stories*, by Arthur Machen, edited by Aaron Worth, 55–78. Oxford: Oxford University Press, 2018.

Machen, Arthur. *The London Adventure* (1924). Newport, South Wales: Three Imposters, 2014.

Machen, Arthur. "The Lost Club (1890)." In *The Great God Pan and Other Horror Stories*, by Arthur Machen, edited by Aaron Worth, 3–8. Oxford: Oxford University Press, 2018.

Machen, Arthur. *Notes and Queries*. London: Spurr and Swift, 1926.

Machen, Arthur. "The Ready Reporter." In *The Book of Fleet Street*, edited by T. Michael Pope, 143–153. London: Cassell & Company, 1930.

Machen, Arthur. "Ritual (1937)." In *The Great God Pan and Other Horror Stories*, by Arthur Machen, edited by Aaron Worth, 347–350. Oxford: Oxford University Press, 2018.

Machen, Arthur. "The Shining Pyramid (1895)." In *The Great God Pan and Other Horror Stories*, by Arthur Machen, edited by Aaron Worth, 222–241. Oxford: Oxford University Press, 2018.

Machen, Hilary. "Foreword." In *Arthur Machen: Selected Letters*, edited by Roger Dobson, Godfrey Brangham, and R. A. Gilbert, 13–17. Wellingborough: Aquarian Press, 1988.

Machin, James. *Weird Fiction in Britain, 1880–1939*. Cham: Palgrave Macmillan, 2018.

Maitland, Edward. *Anna Kingsford: Her Life, Letters, Diary, and Work*. 2 Vols. London: George Redway, 1896.

[Martineau, Harriet]. "Zanoni Explained." In *Zanoni*, by Edward Bulwer Lytton, 302–303. London: Routledge, Warne, and Routledge, 1864.

Mason, A. E. W. *The Prisoner in the Opal* (1928). Kelly Bray, Cornwall: House of Stratus Books, 2009.

Masuzawa, Tomoko. *The Invention of World Religions; or, How European Universalism was Preserved in the Language of Pluralism*. Chicago: University of Chicago Press, 2005.

Mathiesen, Robert. "Britten, Emma [Floyd] Hardinge." In *Dictionary of Gnosis and Western Esotericism*, edited by Wouter Hanegraaff, 202–206. Leiden: Brill, 2006.

Mathiesen, Robert. *The Unseen Worlds of Emma Hardinge Britten: Some Chapters in the History of Western Occultism*. New York: Camberton, 2001.

Maturin, Charles. *Melmoth the Wanderer: A Tale*. 4 Vols. Edinburgh: Archibald Constable and Company, 1820.

McClintock, Anne. *Imperial Leather: Race, Gender, and Sexuality in the Imperial Contest*. London: Routledge, 1995.

"That Mischievous Spirit." *Nottingham Evening Post*. February 23, 1921.

Mitchell, Leslie. *Bulwer Lytton: The Rise and Fall of a Victorian Man of Letters*. London: Hambledon, 2003.

Mitchison, Naomi. *The Corn King and the Spring Queen* (1931). Edinburgh: Canongate, 1990.

Moretti, Franco. *The Way of the World: The Bildungsroman in European Culture*. London: Verso, 1987.

Morrison, Van. *Beautiful Vision*. Mercury Records, 1982. Vinyl.

Morrisson, Mark S. "The Periodical Culture of the Occult Revival: Esoteric Wisdom, Modernity, and Counter-Public Spheres." *Journal of Modern Literature* 31, no. 2 (2008): 1–22.

Morrisson, Mark S. "Women, Periodicals, and Esotericism in Modernist-Era Culture." In *Women, Periodicals, and Print Culture in Britain, 1880s–1920s: The Modernist Era*, edited by Faith Binckes and Carey Snyder, 374–388. Edinburgh: Edinburgh University Press, 2019.

"More Alchemy." *Household Words* 11, no. 276 (July 7, 1855): 540–543.

Morse, J. J. "Preface." In *Autobiography of Emma Hardinge Britten*, by Emma Hardinge Britten, edited by Mrs. Margaret Wilkinson, v–ix. Manchester: John Heywood, 1900.

Mücke, Dorothea E. von. *The Seduction of the Occult and the Rise of the Fantastic Tale*. Stanford: Stanford University Press, 2003.

Mulpetre, Owen. "W.T. Stead and the New Journalism." M.Phil, University of Teesside, 2010.

220 BIBLIOGRAPHY

Mulvey-Roberts, Marie. "Edward Bulwer-Lytton and Poisoned Prose." In *The Palgrave Book of Steam Age Gothic*, edited by Clive Bloom, 91–112. Cham: Palgrave Macmillan, 2021.

Natale, Simone. *Supernatural Entertainments: Victorian Spiritualism and the Rise of Modern Media Culture*. University Park: Pennsylvania State University Press, 2016.

Nelson, Victoria. *Gothicka: Vampire Heroes, Human Gods, and the New Supernatural*. Cambridge: Harvard University Press, 2012.

Nelson, Victorian. *The Secret Life of Puppets*. Cambridge: Harvard University Press, 2001.

Neuman, Justin. *Fiction Beyond Secularism*. Evanston, IL: Northwestern University Press, 2014.

Newell, Stephanie. *Literary Culture in Colonial Ghana*. Manchester: Manchester University Press, 2002.

Noakes, Richard. *Physics and Psychics: The Occult and the Sciences in Modern Britain*. Cambridge: Cambridge University Press, 2019.

Northcliffe, Lord [Alfred Harmsworth]. "An Appreciation by Lord Northcliffe." In *The Life Beyond the Veil: Book 1*, by George Vale Owen. New York: George H. Doran Company, 1921.

Olcott, Henry Steel. *Old Diary Leaves: The True Story of the Theosophical Society*. London: G. P. Putnam's Sons, 1895.

Oppenheim, Janet. *The Other World: Spiritualism and Psychical Research in England, 1850–1914*. Cambridge: Cambridge University Press, 1985.

Owen, Alex. *The Darkened Room: Women, Power, and Spiritualism in Late Victorian England*. Chicago: University of Chicago Press, 1989.

Owen, Alex. *The Place of Enchantment: British Occultism and the Culture of the Modern*. Chicago: University of Chicago Press, 2004.

Paige, Norman." "Permanent Re-Enchantments: On Some Literary Uses of the Supernatural from Early Empiricism to Modern Aesthetics." In *The Re-Enchantment of the World: Secular Magic in a Rational Age*, edited by Joshua Landy and Michael Saler, 157–180. Stanford: Stanford University Press, 2009.

Parker-Perkola, Anne. "Dion Fortune and the Temples of the Numinous." In *Essays on Women in Western Esotericism*, edited by Amy Hale, 357–373. Cham: Springer International, 2022.

Partridge, Christopher. "Occulture is Ordinary." In *Contemporary Esotericism*, edited by Egil Asprem and Kennet Granholm, 113–133. Sheffield: Equinox, 2013.

Pasi, Marco. *Aleister Crowley and the Temptation of Politics*. Durham: Acumen Press, 2014.

Pasi, Marco. "Arthur Machen's Panic Fears: Western Esotericism and the Irruption of Negative Epistemology." *Aries* 7 (2007): 63–83.

Pécastaing-Boissière, Muriel. *Annie Besant: Struggles and Quest*. London: Theosophical Publishing House, 2017.

Pittard, Christopher. *Purity and Contamination in Late Victorian Detective Fiction*. London: Routledge, 2016.

Poe, Edgar Allan. "The Murders in the Rue Morgue." In *Complete Tales and Poems of Edgar Allan Poe*, 141–168. New York: Vintage Books, 1975.

Porter, Katherine H. *Through a Glass Darkly: Spiritualism in the Browning Circle*. New York: Octagon Books, 1972.

Poston, Laurence. "1832." In *A New Companion to Victorian Literature and Culture*, edited by Herbert Tucker, 1–18. Oxford: John Wiley & Sons, 2014.

Praed, Rosa Campbell. *Nyria*. London: T. Fisher Unwin, 1904.

Prichard, Kate, and Hesketh Prichard. "The Story of the Moor Road (1898)." In *The Ghost Slayers: Thrilling Tales of Occult Detection*, edited by Mike Ashley, 11–29. London: British Library, 2022.

Prothero, Stephen. *The White Buddhist: The Asian Odyssey of Henry Steel Olcott*. Bloomington: Indiana University Press, 1996.

"The Quest of *The Well-Beloved*." *Review of Reviews* 15 (April 1897): 394.

Quinn, Patrick J. *Aleister Crowley, Sylvester Viereck, Literature, Lust, and the Great War*. Newcastle-Upon-Tyne: Cambridge Scholars Publishing, 2021.

BIBLIOGRAPHY 221

Ramaswamy, Sumathi. *The Lost Land of Lemuria: Fabulous Geographies, Catastrophic Histories*. Berkeley: University of California Press, 2004.

Radford, Andrew. "What Lies Below the Horizon of Life: The Occult Fiction of Dion Fortune." In *Modernist Women Writers and Spirituality*, edited by Elizabeth Anderson, Andrew Radford, and Heather Walton, 201–218. London: Macmillan, 2016.

Randolph, Paschal Beverly. *The Wonderful Story of Ravalette. Also, Tom Clark and His Wife, The Double Dreams and the Curious Things that Befell them Therein; or, The Rosicrucian's Story*. New York: Sinclair Tousey, 1863.

Regardie, Israel. *The Golden Daw: A Complete Course in Ceremonial Magic*. Woodbury: Llewellyn Publication, 1989.

Rennison, Nick. "Introduction." In *Supernatural Sherlocks: Stories from the Golden Age of the Occult Detective*, edited by Nick Rennison, 7–13. Harpenden: No Exit Press, 2017.

Renton, David. *Horatio Bottomley and the Far Right Before Fascism*. London: Routledge 2022.

Reynolds, Aidan, and William Charlton. *Arthur Machen*. Oxford: Caermaen Books, 1988.

Reynolds, G. W. M. *Wagner the Werewolf* (1847–1847). Ware: Wordsworth Editions, 2006.

Richet, Charles. *Thirty Years of Psychical Research, Being a Treatise on Metapsychics*. Translated by Stanley de Brath. London: Macmillan & Co., 1923.

Ritschel, Nelson O'Ceallaigh. *Bernard Shaw, W.T. Stead, and the New Journalism: Whitechapel, Parnell, Titanic and the Great War*. Cham: Springer International, 2017.

Roberts, Marie. *Gothic Immortals: The Fiction of the Brotherhood of the Rosy Cross*. London: Routledge, 1990.

"A Romance of Two Worlds." *Quarterly Review* 188, no. 376 (October 1898): 306–337.

Rosenthal, Jesse. *Good Form: The Ethical Experience of the Victorian Novel*. Princeton: Princeton University Press, 2016.

Roukema, Aren. "Naturalists in *Ghost Land*: Victorian Occultism and Science Fiction." In *The Occult Imagination in Britain, 1875–1947*, edited by Christine Ferguson and Andrew Radford, 183–205. London: Routledge, 2018.

Rowland, Susan. "The 'Classical' Model of the Golden Age." In *A Companion to Crime Fiction*, edited by Charles J. Rzepka and Lee Horsley, 117–127. Oxford: Blackwell Wiley, 2010.

Rubery, Matthew. "Journalism." In *The Cambridge Companion to Victorian Culture*, edited by Francis O'Gorman, 177–194. Cambridge: Cambridge University Press, 2010.

Saler, Michael. *As If: Modern Enchantment and the Literary Prehistory of Virtual Reality*. Oxford: Oxford University Press, 2012.

Salmon, Richard. "The English Bildungsroman." In *The Oxford History of the Novel in English: Volume 3: The Nineteenth-Century Novel, 1820–1880*, edited by John Kucich and Jenny Bourne Taylor, 90–105. Oxford: Oxford University Press, 2012.

Salmon, Richard. "The Genealogy of the Literary *Bildungsroman*: Edward Bulwer-Lytton and W.M. Thackeray." *Studies in the Novel* 36, no. 1 (Spring 2004): 41–55.

Sambrooke, Jerilyn. "Secularism, Religion, and the 20th-21st-Century Novel." *Literature Compass* 15, no. 1 (2018): 1–13.

Sankey, James. "Realism and the Epistemic Objectivity of Science." *Kriterion* 35, no. 1 (2021): 5–20.

Santucci, James. "The Notion of Race in Theosophy." *Nova Religio: The Journal of Alternative and Emergent Religions* 11, no. 3 (February 2008): 37–63.

Santucci, James. "Theosophy." In *The Cambridge Companion to New Religious Movements*, edited by Olav Hammer, 231–246. Cambridge: Cambridge University Press, 2012.

Schaffer, Talia. "Canon." *Victorian Literature and Culture* 46, no. 3/4 (2018): 594–597.

Senior, John. *The Way Down and Out: The Occult in Symbolist Literature*. Ithaca: Cornell University Press, 1959.

Serafini, Stefano. "The Gothic Side of Golden Age Detective Fiction." In *Gothic Metamorphoses Across the Century: Contexts, Legacies, Media*, edited by Maurizio Ascari, Serena Baiesi, and David Levente Palatinus, 117–130. Bern: Peter Lang, 2020.

222 BIBLIOGRAPHY

Sharma, Niyati. "Race and the Entranced Mind in Late Victorian Popular Fiction." D.Phil, University of Oxford, 2018.

Shelley, Mary. *Frankenstein; or, the Modern Prometheus*. London: Lackington, Hughes, Harding, Mavor & Jones, 1818.

Shelley, Percy Bysshe. *St Irvynne; or, the Rosicrucian*. London: John Joseph Stockell, 1811.

Sidgwick, Henry. "Address of the President at the First General Meeting." In *The Fin de Siècle: A Reader in Cultural History, c. 1880–1914*, edited by Sally Ledger and Roger Luckhurst, 273–274. Oxford: Oxford University Press, 2000.

Sinnett, A. P. *Esoteric Buddhism*. London: Trübner & Co., 1883.

Sinnett, A. P. *Karma*. London: Chapman and Hall, 1886.

Smajíc, Srdjan. *Ghost-Seers, Detectives, and Spiritualists: Theories of Vision in Victorian Literature and Science*. Cambridge: Cambridge University Press, 2010.

"Specimens of Alchemists." *Household Words* 11, no. 273 (June 16, 1855): 457–465.

Spivak, Gayatri Chakravorty. "Can the Subaltern Speak?" In *Marxism and the Interpretation of Culture*, edited by Cary Nelson and Lawrence Grossberg, 271–313. Basingstoke: Macmillan, 1988.

Spooner, Catherine. "Crime and the Gothic." In *A Companion to Crime Fiction*, edited by Charles J. Rzepka and Lee Horsely, 245–257. Oxford: Blackwell Wiley, 2010.

Spooner, Catherine. *Post-Millenial Gothic: Comedy, Romance, and the Rise of Happy Gothic*. London: Bloomsbury, 2017.

Starr, Martin P. "Introduction." In *The Scrutinies of Simon Iff*, by Aleister Crowley, edited by Martin P. Starr, ix–xvii. Chicago: Teitan Press, 1987.

Stead, W. T. *After Death; or, Letters from Julia*. Chicago: The Progressive Thinker Publishing House, 1910.

Stead, W. T. "The Future of Journalism." *The Contemporary Review* 50 (November 1886): 663–679.

Stead, W. T. "How We Intend to Study the Borderland." *Borderland* 1, no. 1 (July 1893): 4–26.

Stead, W. T. "My Experience of Automatic Writing." *Borderland* 1, no. 1 (July 1893): 39–49.

Stead, W. T. "The Study of Psychical Phenomena." *Borderland* 1, no. 1 (July 1893): 3–6.

Steiner, Rudolf. *Four Mystery Dramas: The Portal of Initiation, The Soul's Probation, The Guardian of the Threshold, The Soul's Awakening*. Translated by Ruth Pusch and Hans Pusch. Hudson, NY: Steiner Books, 2007.

Steiner, Rudolf. *Nature's Open Secret: Introduction to Goethe's Scientific Writings*. Translated by John Barnes and Mado Spiegler. New York: Anthroposophic Press, 2000.

Steiner, Rudolf. *An Outline of Occult Science*. Translated by Max Gysi. London: Theosophical Publishing Society, 1914.

Stevenson, Robert Louis. *The Strange Case of Dr Jekyll and Mr Hyde* (1886). Edited by Martin Danahay. Peterborough, ON: Broadview, 2005.

"A Strange Story." *The Saturday Review* 13, no. 332 (March 8, 1862), 273–275.

Strube, Julian. "Towards the Study of Esotericism without the 'Western': Esotericism from the Perspective of a Global Religious History." In *New Approaches to the Study of Esotericism*, edited by Egil Asprem and Julian Strube, 45–66. Leiden: Brill, 2021.

Stuckrad, Kocku Von. "Western Esotericism: Towards an Integrative Model of Interpretation." *Religion* 35, no. 2 (2005): 78–97.

Surette, Leon. *The Birth of Modernism: Ezra Pound, T.S. Eliot, W.B. Yeats, and the Occult*. Montreal: McGill-Queens University Press, 1993.

Sutin, Lawrence. *Do What Thou Wilt: A Life of Aleister Crowley*. New York: St. Martin's Press, 2014.

Swaffer, Hannen. *Northcliffe's Return* (1925). London: Psychic Press, 1939.

Sweetser, Wesley D. *Arthur Machen*. London: Arthur Machen Society, 1960.

Sword, Helen. *Ghostwriting Modernism*. Ithaca: Cornell University Press, 2002.

Tennyson, Alfred, Lord. *In Memoriam, A.H.H.* London: Edward Moxon, 1850.

Taylor, Charles. *A Secular Age* (2007). Cambridge: Harvard University Press, 2018.

BIBLIOGRAPHY 223

Thomas, Ronald R. *Detective Fiction and the Rise of Forensic Science*. Cambridge: Cambridge University Press, 1999.

Thurschwell, Pamela. *Literature, Technology, and Magical Thinking, 1880–1920*. Cambridge: Cambridge University Press, 2001.

Tibet, David. "Foreword." In *The Drug and Other Stories* by Aleister Crowley, edited by William Breeze, vii-viii. Ware: Wordsworth Editions, 2010.

Tillotson, Kathleen. *Novels of the Eighteen-Forties*. Oxford: Clarendon, 1954.

"Transmigration." *British Quarterly Review* 59, no. 118 (April 1874): 574–575.

Tromp, Marlene. *Altered States: Sex, Nation, Drugs, and Self-Transformation in Victorian Spiritualism*. Albany: State University of New York Press, 2006.

Turner, Mark. "Seriality, Miscellaneity, and Compression in Nineteenth-Century Print." *Victorian Studies* 62, no. 2 (2020): 283–294.

The Unseen Universe 1, no. 1 (April 1892).

Urban, Hugh. *Magia Sexualis: Sex, Magic, and Liberation in Modern Western Esotericism*. Berkeley: University of California Press, 2006.

Urban, Hugh. *Secrecy: Silence, Power, and Religion*. Chicago: University of Chicago Press, 2022.

Versluis, Arthur. *Restoring Paradise: Western Esotericism, Literature, Art, and Consciousness*. Albany: State University of New York Press, 2004.

Villars, Nicolas de Montaucon de. *Le Comte de Gabalis, ou entretiens sur les sciences secretes*. Cologne: Pierre Marteau, 1670.

Viswanathan, Gauri. *Outside the Fold: Conversion, Modernity, and Belief*. Princeton: Princeton University Press, 1998.

Walker, E. D. *Reincarnation: A Study of Forgotten Truth*. New York: John W. Lovell, 1888.

Wallraven, Miriam. *Women Writers and the Occult in Literature and Culture: Female Lucifers, Priestesses, and Witches*. London: Routledge, 2015.

Walpole, Horace. *The Castle of Otranto*. London: William Bathoe, 1764.

Walton, Samantha. *Guilty but Insane: Mind and Law in Golden Age Detective Fiction*. Oxford: Oxford University Press, 2015.

Warren, Samuel. "The Spectral Dog." In *Passages from the Diary of a Late Physician*, 84–87. London: Routledge, 1832.

Warren, Samuel. "The Spectre Smitten." In *Passages from the Diary of a Late Physician*, 149–165. London: Routledge, 1832.

Warwick, Alexandra. "Feeling Gothicky." *Gothic Studies* 9, no. 1 (May 2007): 5–15.

"The Well-Beloved." *Academy and Literature* 1300 (April 3, 1897): 381.

"The Well-Beloved." *Athenaeum* 3624 (April 10, 1897): 471.

"The West End Palmistry Case." *Civil and Military Gazette*. October 27, 1904.

"A Wizard of Wickedness." *John Bull*. March 17, 1923.

Wolff, Robert Lee. *Strange Stories and Other Explorations in Victorian Fiction*. Boston: Gambit Press, 1971.

Woodman, Justin. "'Cthulhu Gnosis': Monstrosity, Selfhood, and Secular Re-Enchantment in Lovecraftian Occult Practice." In *Fictional Practice: Magic, Narration, and the Power of Imagination*, edited by Bernd-Christian Otto and Dirk Johanssen, 289–313. Leiden: Brill, 2021.

Wordsworth, William. "Ode: Intimations of Immortality." In *Poems, In Two Volumes*. London: Longman, Hurst, Rees, and Orme, 1807.

Worth, Aaron. "Introduction." In *The Great God Pan and Other Horror Stories*, by Arthur Machen, edited by Aaron Worth, ix-xxx. Oxford: Oxford University Press, 2018.

Youngkin, Molly. "A 'Duty' to 'Tabulate and Record': Emma Hardinge Britten as Periodical Editor and Spiritualist Historian." *Victorian Periodicals Review* 49, no. 1 (Spring 2016): 49–76.

"Zanoni." *Literary Gazette* 1310 (February 26, 1842): 4.

"Zanoni: by the Author of 'Night and Morning,' 'Rienzi,' etc." *The Metropolitan Magazine* 33, no. 132 (April 1842): 354–355.

224 BIBLIOGRAPHY

"Zanoni." *Sheffield Independent.* January 2, 1847.

Ziolkowski, Theodore. *The Lure of the Arcane: The Literature of Cult and Conspiracy.* Baltimore: Johns Hopkins University Press, 2013.

Zorya, Kateryna. "If One Knows Where to Look, Fiction is Magic: Reading Fictional Texts as Manuals of Magic in Post-Soviet Ukraine, Russia, and Belarus." In *Fictional Practice: Magic, Narration, and the Power of Imagination*, edited by Bernd-Christian Otto and Dirk Johanssen, 261–288. Leiden: Brill, 2021.

Index

For the benefit of digital users, indexed terms that span two pages (e.g., 52–53) may, on occasion, appear on only one of those pages.

Aeon of Horus, 152–53
Ainsworth, William Harrison
   Auriol; or the Elixir of Life, 23–24, 25–26
Aiwass, 152–53, 156. *See also* Crowley, Aleister
Alchemy, 5–6, 200n.80, *See also* Machen, Arthur
Algeo, John, 171–72
All the Year Round, 55–56, 122. *See also*
   Dickens, Charles
Ames, Julia, 109–10. *See also* Stead, W.T.
Angel of Mons, 115–16, 199n.53, *See also*,
   Machen, Arthur
Arnold, Matthew, 106–7, 197n.10
Asad, Talal, 180
Askew, Claude and Alice
   "The Fear," 147–48
Asprem, Egil, 7–8, 184n.23
Atlantis Bookshop, 170–71
Auden, W.H., 147–48
"Austria". *See* Britten, Emma Hardinge
*Authors Take Sides on the Spanish Civil
   War*, 121–22

Babylonian Empire, First, 195–96n.53
Bakhtin, Mikhail, 42–43
Baldick, Chris, 17–18
Ball, Michael, 47
Barrie, J.M.
   Peter Pan, 56–57
Beetham, Margaret, 135
Beilis, Menahim Mendel, 205n.92
Bergunder, Michael, 6–7
Bertillonage, 144–45
Besant, Annie, 73–75, 78–79, 106, 194n.9,
   194n.14, 197n.7
bibliocentrism (within occult revival), 37–38,
   103–4, 135, 136–37
bibliotherapy, 171–72
Bildungsroman, 4–5, 36–37, 41–71, 190n.12
   contrasting plots of male and female
     Bildungshelden, 41–42, 189n.6
   temporality within, 42–43, 56–57 (*see also*
     father figures in fiction)

biographical approaches to occult fiction, 4–5,
   21–22, 35–36, 150–51, 176–77, 203n.48
Black Mass in fiction, 170–71, 174. *See also*
   Satanism in fiction
Blackwood, Algernon.
   "John Silence" literary character, 38, 142–43
   "A Psychical Invasion," 146, 202n.13
Blavatsky, H.P., 106, 197n.7, 197n.102
   influence by Allan Kardec, 73–75, 194n.10
   Isis Unveiled, 34–35, 73–75, 103–4
   on Paschal Beverly Randolph, 78–79,
     195n.32
   on reincarnation, 73–76
   relationship to Mabel Collins, 91–92, 93–94,
     196n.73
   The Secret Doctrine, 73–75
   and *Zanoni*, 1–2, 34–35
blood libel, 160–61, 205n.92
Bogdan, Henrik, 152–53, 161–62, 205n.96
Book of Genesis, 138–39
Book of John, 205–6n.99
Bookshops, Occult, 2–3, 38–39, 170–71
Borderland. *See* Stead, W.T.
Botting, Fred, 18, 19–21
Bottomley, Horatio, 168
Bourdieu, Pierre, 177–78
Braddon, Mary Elizabeth, 144–45
Bradley, Dennis, 111–12
Braidotti, Rosa, 90
Brantlinger, Patrick, 15–16, 25–26, 187n.87
Breeze, William, 148–49, 203n.48
Britten, Emma Hardinge, 1–2, 40, 58–63, 109–
   10, 177–78
   Art Magic, 62–64
   "Austria," as pseudonym, 63–64
   Autobiography of Emma Hardinge Britten,
     58–60, 62–63, 192n.75
   Chevalier Louis de B__ as pseudonym,
     58–59, 62–63, 191–92n.72, 192n.73,
     193n.90, 193n.111
   "Extracts from 'Ghostland,' Volume II,"
     62–65, 68–69, 192n.78

226 INDEX

Britten, Emma Hardinge (*cont.*)
  "Ezra" as pseudonym, 59–60
  Ghost Land; Or Researches into the Mysteries of Occultism, 36–37, 40–41, 48, 63–71, 138–39, 178–79
  The Mystery of No. 9 Stanhope Street, 61–64
  The Unseen Universe, 61, 63–64, 192n.78
  The Western Star, 63–64
  The Wildfire Club, 59–61, 62–63
Brodie-Innes, J.W.
  The Devil's Mistress, 174–76
Brooks, Peter, 28–29
Brown, Andrew, 48–49, 50–51
Brown, Callum, 180
Brown, Julia Prewitt, 42–43
Brown, Stewart J., 110–11
Bulwer, Lytton, Edward, 27–39, 40, 177–78, 187n.80, 190–91n.35
  Asmodeus at Large, 27–32, 34–35, 49–50, 188n.99
  attitude to literary serialization, 25–26
  Falkland, 27–28, 49–50
  literary reputation of, 25–26, 34–35, 48–49, 57–58, 183n.5, 183n.9
  New Monthly Magazine, 27–28, 188n.96
  participation in occult revival, 19–21, 22, 63, 186n.74, 187n.83
  political career, 25–26, 48–49, 187n.93
  A Strange Story, 36–37, 64–65, 70, 138–39, 191n.42, 191n.44
    as occult *bildungsroman* 40–41, 48–58, 63, 69–70, 98–99, 178–79
  "The Tale of Kosem Kesamim the Magician," 27–28, 30–31, 188n.97
  Zanoni, 1–5, 22–27, 49–50, 63, 170–71, 178–79
    French Revolution in, 25, 30–31, 33–34, 178–79, 188n.123
    influence on the occult revival, 22, 91–92, 183n.3
    treatment of occultism in, 19, 23–25, 31–36
  "Zanoni Explained," 34–35
  Zicci, 30–32, 188nn.108–9
  See also Dweller in the Threshold

Caithness, Countess of [Marie Sinclair], 73–77
  A Midnight Visit to Holyrood, 75–76, 194n.16
Campo Tosto inheritance case, 124, 125–26, 133
Carlyle, Thomas, 43–44, 190n.13
Carnacki the Ghost-Finder (character). *See* W.H. Hodgson
Castex, Pierre Georges, 8–9, 184n.29

Cazotte, Jacques, 17–18
Chajes, Julie, 73–75, 193n.2, 194n.7
Chambers's Journal, 122
chaos magic, 179–80
Chesterton, G.K.
  Father Brown, 141–42, 156–57
Chevalier Louis de B_. *See* Britten, Emma Hardinge
Christian Spiritualist, 59–60, 192n.78
Christie, Agatha, 140, 141–42, 163–64
  The Mysterious Affair at Styles, 140–41
Cohn, Elisha, 69–70
Collins, Mabel, 37, 40, 73–75, 80, 106, 177–78, 197n.7, 197n.102
  authorship, controversies around, 91–94
  The Blossom and the Fruit, 23–24, 31–32, 37, 41–42, 80, 91–102, 178–79
  The Idyll of the White Lotus, 92–93
  An Innocent Sinner, 92–93
  Libel action against Blavatsky, 93–94
  Light on the Path, 92–93, 97–98
  Morial the Mahatma, 104–5
  The Prettiest Woman in Warsaw, 92–93
  Theosophical Society, involvement in, 91–94
Collins, Mortimer, 80
  The Secret of Long Life, 80
  Transmigration, 80–82, 195n.34
Collins, Wilkie, 144–45
  The Moonstone, 204n.52
Coomaraswamy, Ananda Kentish, 150–51, 161–62, 205n.95, 206n.119
Corelli, Marie, 37, 40, 73–75, 177–78
  Ardath, 86–88, 100, 195–96n.53, 196n.57
  and Christianity, 86–87
  colonial reception of, 195n.51
  The Life Everlasting, 86–87, 100
  popularity of, 85–86, 187n.80
  relationship to the occult revival, 86–87
  A Romance of Two Worlds, 22, 86–87, 197n.104
  The Sorrows of Satan, 43–44, 85–86, 104–5
  The Soul of Lilith, 104–5
  women's suffrage, opposition to, 87–88, 196n.56
  Ziska: The Problem of a Wicked Soul, 37, 41–42, 87–91, 94, 95–96, 100, 101–2, 138–39, 178–79
Coues, Elliott, 93, 196n.74
Crofton, Sarah, 109–11, 114–15, 198n.20
Crowley, Aleister, 4–5, 21–22, 148–69, 177–78, 203n.40, 205n.95, 205n.96, 206n.119
  Abbey of Thelema, Cefalù, 156, 204n.52
  antisemitism, 160–61, 205n.92

INDEX 227

"The Artistic Temperament," 160–61,
204n.52, 205n.92
"The Big Game," 156–60, 163–64
The Book of the Law, 38, 88, 91–92,
139, 152–56
The Butterfly Net, 148–49
"The Conduct of John Briggs," 159–60
The Confessions of Aleister Crowley, 151–52,
153–54, 162–63
as counter-cultural figure, 148–49
and daoism, 156–57, 204n.76
and detective fiction, 38, 142–43, 151–52,
204n.52
"Edward Kelly" as pseudonym of, 148–49
The Equinox, 150
Frazer, J.G., influence by, 205n.87
Golden Twigs, 205n.87
"Ineligible," 161–63, 168, 205–6n.99
and *The International*, 148–49, 203n.40,
205n.87
law, concept of, 152–56, 160, 162–63, 205n.86
The Law is for All, 154–56
Libel suit against Constable & Co., 204n.64
Magick, definition of, 204n.53
Magick in Theory and Practice, 91–92
And misogyny, 166, 167–68
Moonchild, 148–49
"Not Good Enough," 159–60, 161–63, 165–68
"Outside the Bank's Routine," 162, 163–66,
204n.52, 206n.106
political attitudes of, 38, 139, 162–63, 167–69
and race, 161–62, 165–68, 205n.92
on rape, 155
The Scrutinies of Simon Iff, 38, 139, 141–42,
145–46, 147–52, 156–69, 178–79, 181–82
Simon Iff as self-portrait of, 150–51, 203n.48
Simon Iff Abroad, 148–49
Simon Iff in America, 148–49
Simon Iff, Psychoanalyst, 148–49
will, theorization of, 152–54, 162–63, 168–
69, 205n.86

Daily Mail. See Northcliffe, Lord
Davies, Owen, 185n.42
Demarest, Marc, 62–63, 191–92n.72
Democrat (Albany), 129–30
Denley, John, 2–3
Detection Club, 143–44
detective fiction, 4–5, 138–48, 156–69
class dimensions of, 139–40, 141–42, 201n.4,
202n.11
formal features, 140–41, 201n.4
gender roles in, 141–42, 202n.12

golden age, 41–42, 139–42, 157, 201n.3,
201n.4, 201n.8
politics of, 139, 140, 141–42, 161–62
supernaturalism, attitude towards, 143–44
and gothic, 202n.20, 202n.24
occult detection, 38, 138–40, 142–48, 156–69
racial politics of, 141–42
and religion, 138–40, 144–46
science, relationship to, 144–46
supernaturalism, rejection of, 143–44
Devachan, 194n.13
Devi, Ratan, 150–51, 161–62, 205n.95, 206n.119
Dickens, Charles, 1–2, 59–60, 63, 192n.80
and *All the Year Round*, 48–49, 50–51
Great Expectations, 48, 50–51, 69, 191n.42
Dine, S.S., 143–44, 146
Diogenes Club, 204n.75
Dixon, Joy, 72–73, 196n.85
Downing, Lisa, 97
Doyle, Arthur Conan, 19–21, 58–59, 113–14,
144–45, 187n.78, 201n.113
The Adventures of Sherlock Holmes, 145
"The Blue Carbuncle," 145
"The Boscombe Valley Mystery," 145
"The Five Orange Pips," 145–46
The Hound of the Baskervilles, 144–45
The Land of Mist, 104–5, 111–12
"A Scandal in Bohemia," 146
"The Speckled Band," 145–46
A Study in Scarlet, 145, 151–52
Drazin, Adam, 10–11
Duguid, David, 40
Dweller in the Threshold, 1–2, 30–33, 34–35,
183n.6, 189n.132, *See also* Bulwer
Lytton, Edward

Eagleton, Terry, 10–11
Earle, David M., 21
"Edward Kelly". *See* Crowley, Aleister
Egypt, Ancient in Late Victorian Culture, 73–
75, 194n.8
Eldrige, Sarah Vandergrift, 43–44
Eliot, T.S., 180–81
epistemic objectivity, 201n.117
esotericism studies, 5–14, 184n.19, 184n.23
approaches to literature, 3–5, 7–14, 35–36,
69–70, 184n.26
rejected knowledge paradigm within, 6–8, 15
Evening News. See Machen, Arthur
"Ezra". *See* Britten, Emma Hardinge

Fanger, Claire, 171–72
Farnell, Kim, 93–94

228   INDEX

Father Brown (fictional character). *See*
    Chesterton, G.K.
father figures in fiction, 40–41, 43–45, 54–56,
    65, 66–69
Faustian themes in literature, 22–27. *See also*
    Goethe, Johann Wilhelm von
Faxneld, Per, 10–11, 185n.49
Felski, Rita, 85–86, 87–88, 90–91
feminism
    imperial, 90
    and occultism, 37, 72–73, 101–2
fiction-based religions, 207–8n.31
Flaxman Low (fictional character). *See*
    Prichard, Kate and Hesketh
Fort, Charles, 13–14, 103–4, 106–7, 114–15,
    127–37, 177–78, 200n.93
    The Book of the Damned, 127, 131, 132–33, 134
    "damned data," 127–28, 131
    As fiction writer, 129–30
    and Fortean style, 127, 133, 134, 135
    "Fryhusen's Colony," 129–30, 200n.101
    "Glencliff's Mysterious Burglar," 129–30,
        200n.101
    "I Meddled," 129–30, 200n.101
    "In a Newspaper Office," 129–30, 200n.101
    intermediatism, 131
    journalistic career of, 37–38, 127, 129–30
    Lo! 127
    New Lands, 127
    Wild Talents, 127, 128–30, 132–34
    "With the Assistance of Fryhusen," 129–30,
        200n.101
Fortean Times, 127, 135
Fortune, Dion, 1–2, 21–22, 142–43, 197n.102,
    202n.15
    The Demon Lover, 206n.4
    *The Esoteric Philosophy of Love and
        Marriage*, 207n.20
    The Goat-Foot God, 4–5, 31–32, 38–39, 170–
        73, 174–77, 206n.4
    Moon Magic, 206n.4
    "The Novels of Dion Fortune," 171–72, 207n.10
    Psychic Self-Defence, 207n.8
    Sane Occultism, 207n.20
    "The Scent of Poppies," 202n.13
    The Sea Priestess, 171–72, 206n.4
    The Secrets of Dr Taverner, 171–72, 202n.15,
        206n.4, 207n.8
    and sexual polarity, 100, 171–72, 197n.111,
        206–7n.6, 207n.20
    Society of the Inner Light, 171–72, 179–80,
        207n.10
    The Winged Bull, 206n.4
Foster, Jeanne Robert, 150–51, 206n.106

Frankenstein. See Shelley, Mary
Frazer, J.G.
    The Golden Bough, 160, 205n.87, 205n.92
Freemasonry, 124–25
French Revolution, 160–61. *See also* Edward
    Bulwer Lytton, *Zanoni*

Gekle, William Francis, 116
Gelder, Ken, 21
Gender. *See* detective fiction, gender roles in;
    initiation and gender; masculinity;
    reincarnation and gender mutability;
    romance revival, gender coordinates of;
    violence, gender-based; women writers
    as romance revivalists
ghosts in fiction, 44–46, 47–48, 142–43
Gilbert, R.A., 2–3
Godwin, Joscelyn, 1–2, 27–28, 63
Goethe, Johann Wilhelm von
    Faust, Part One, 43–44
    The Sorrows of Young Werther, 64–65
    Spiritualist and Occult receptions of, 43–44,
        50–51, 190n.14
    Wilhelm Meisters Apprenticeship, 40, 43–48,
        49–50, 54–55, 56, 189n.1, 190n.20
Golden Age Detective Fiction. *See* detective
    fiction
Goodrick-Clarke, Nicholas, 9–10
gothic
    literary conventions of, 2–3, 60–61
    as negative aesthetics, 18–21, 23–24, 33–34
    and religion, 15–16, 17–18, 23–24, 186n.55
gothic studies, 4–6, 10–11, 14–22, 35–36, 181,
    185n.50, 185n.52
    and anxiety thesis, 15–16, 17
    and hauntology, 15–16, 17
    psychoanalytic approaches within, 5–6, 15–
        16, 17, 184n.26, 184n.34
Goulet, Andrea, 144–45
Grey School of Wizardry, 179–80

Hadit, 152–53
Haggard, H. Rider, 73–75
    "About Fiction," 77–78
    Ayesha: The Return of She, 75
    King Solomon's Mines, 78
    She and Allan, 75
    She: A History of Adventure, 26–27, 51–52,
        72–73, 75, 94
    gender roles in, 78, 82–83, 101–2
    Wisdom's Daughter, 75
Hall, Edith Maude
    The Sheik, 90–91
Hammer, Olav, 73–75, 76, 193n.2, 194n.7

INDEX 229

Hanegraaff, Wouter, 6–8, 15
Hardy, Thomas
  Tess of the d'Urbervilles, 83–84
  The Well-Beloved, 83–85
Harmsworth, Alfred. *See* Northcliffe, Lord
Hauntology. *See* Gothic studies
Hell-Fire Club, 192n.83
Hermetic Order of the Golden Dawn, 114–16,
    123–24, 142–43, 150, 170–72, 206n.3
Hiram Abiff, 156–57
Hirst, Sam, 15–16
Hodgson, W.H.
  Carnacki the Ghost-Finder, 142–43
  "The Gateway of the Monster," 202n.13
Hornsey Poltergeist, 116–17, 124–25
Household Words, 122, 200n.80
Howe, Suzanne, 49–50
Howitt, William, 43–44
Huckvale, David, 34–35
Hulme, Fergus
  The Mystery of a Hansom Cab, 151–52
Hunter, Jack, 131, 200n.93
Huysmans, J[oris-].K[arl]
  The Damned, 174–75
Huyssen, Andreas, 150

imperial romance, 37, 78–79, 88, 90. *See also*
    Romance Revival
imperialism. *See* feminism; imperial romance;
    Theosophy
Independent (Queens, NY), 129–30
initiation
  in fiction, 32–33, 38–39, 171–73, 178
  and gender, 197n.104
intermediatism. *See* Fort, Charles
The International. See Crowley, Aleister

John Bull, 113–14, 156, 167–68
John Silence (character). *See* Blackwood,
    Algernon
Jones, Anna Maria, 34–35
Jones, Tim, 17–18
journoccultism, 29–30, 37–38, 103–37
  informational mode of, 103–4, 107–
    15, 136–37
  mystical mode of, 103–4, 121–37, 181–82
Joyce, James
  Finnegan's Wake, 154–55, 171–72
Julia's Bureau. *See* Stead, W.T.

Kabbalah, 5–6, 73–75
Kaczynski, Richard, 154–55, 205n.86
Kant, Immanuel, 73–75
Kardec, Allan, 8–9, 73–75, 194n.10

Karma, 37, 72–75, 80, 82–83, 84–85, 86–
    87, 90, 91
Keely, John Worrell, 135–36
Keightley, Bertram and Archibald, 93–94
Keiro (Charles Stephenson), 198n.33
Kelly, Rose, 150–51, 152–53, 206n.106
Killeen, Jarlath, 15, 19–21
King, Stephen, 179–80
Kingsford, Anna, 73–77, 106, 197n.7, 197n.102
Kipling, Rudyard
  "The Mark of the Beast," 204n.52
Knight, Damon, 127–29
Knight, Gareth, 171–72, 206–7n.6, 207n.10
Knight, Mark, 181
Knox, Ronald, 143–44
Koot Hoomi, 93
Kripal, Jeffrey J., 13–14, 127–28, 199n.47,
    200n.93

Lang, Andrew, 77–78
LaPorte, Charles, 180–81, 208n.41
Lazarus, 205–6n.99
Leadbeater, C[harles].W[ebster], 194n.14,
    196n.85
Lecourt, Sebastian, 180–81
Lees, Robert James, 106, 197n.7
Le Fanu, Sheridan, 38, 146–47
  "Green Tea," 147–48
Leonard, Gladys Osborne, 111–12, 113–14
Le Sage, Alain-René
  Le Diable Boiteux, 28–29, 188n.102
Leslie, Robert Murray, 150–51
Lessing, Gottfried Ephraim, 73–75
Lévi, Éliphas, 8–9, 160
Levine, Caroline, 172–73
Lewis, Matthew, 23
Light, 43–44
Literature, 115–16
Loveday, Raoul, 156
Lucifer, 60–61, 91, 92–93, 192n.85, 196n.73
Luckhurst, Roger, 8–9, 108–9
Lynch, Deidre, 180
Lyons, Sara, 41–42

MacDonald, Ramsay, 168
Machen, Arthur, 38, 103–4, 106–7, 114–21,
    136–37, 142–43, 187n.80
  and alchemy, 122–23, 200n.80
  "The Bowmen," 115–16
  Dr Stiggins: His Views and Principles, 121–22
  employment at the *Evening News*, 115–16,
    122, 124–25
  Far Off Things, 121–22
  The Great God Pan, 97–98, 117–18

230   INDEX

Machen, Arthur (*cont.*)
  The Green Round, 117–21
  "The Inmost Light," 199n.67, 202n.13
  journalistic career of, 37–38, 115–17, 121–26,
      181–82, 199n.47, 199n.61
  The London Adventure, 116–17, 121–22,
      124–26
  "The Lost Club," 117
  "The Novel of the Black Seal," 117–18
  "Ritual," 199n.67
  "The Shining Pyramid," 202n.13
  Things Near and Far, 121–22, 123
Machen, Hilary, 116
Machin, James, 115–16
magick, definition of. *See* Crowley, Aleister
Maitland, Edward
  *Anna Kingsford: Her Life, Letters, Diary, and
      Work*, 194n.16
Marlowe, Christopher, 14–15, 22–23
Marryat, Florence
  The Blood of the Vampire, 88
Marsh, Richard
  The Beetle, 88
Martineau, Harriet, 34–35
masculinity, 36–37, 65–67, 70, 77–78. *See
      also* father figures in fiction; initiation
      and gender; romance revival, gender
      coordinates of
Mason, A.E.W.
  The Prisoner in the Opal, 170–71, 172–
      74, 176–77
Masuzawa, Tomoko, 167–68, 180
Maturin, Charles
  Melmoth the Wanderer, 22–24, 27, 187n.95
McClintock, Anne, 78
Medium (TV Show), 144–45
Merton, Jeanne, 150–51, 206n.106
mesmerism in fiction, 51–52, 65–66, 144–45,
      202n.23
metempsychosis, 73–75. *See also* reincarnation
Mighall, Robert, 17–18
misogyny in fiction, 78–79, 120–21, 166, 168
Miss Marple, 141–42. *See also*
      Christie, Agatha
Mitchell, Leslie, 25–26, 30–31
Mitchison, Naomi
  The Corn King and the Spring Queen, 174–75
modernism, 150, 203n.45
Moretti, Franco, 41–43, 48, 69
Moriarty, Theodore, 202n.15, 207n.8
Morris Klaw (character). *See* Rohmer, Sax
Morrison, Steinie, 116–17
Morrisson, Mark S., 92–93, 106

Mozart, Wolfgang Amadeus, 46

Nelson, Victoria, 11–13, 184–85n.38, 185n.39,
      185n.43, 185n.44
Neo-Platonism, 73–75
Neuman, Justin, 180–81
new journalism, 4–5, 37–38, 103–4, 106–7,
      136–37. *See also* Stead, W.T.
newspapers, 37–38, 103–4, 132–33, 136–37
  visual style and typography, 104–5,
      106–7 (*see also* journoccultism; new
      journalism; periodicals; reporters,
      spiritualists and occultists as)
New York Herald, 133
Northcliffe, Lord, 111–12
  and the *Daily Mail*, 111–12, 198n.33
  as spirit, 112–15, 134 (*see also* Swaffer,
      Hannen)
Nuit, 152–53

occult detection. *See* detective fiction
occult revival, definition of, 4–5
occulture, as concept, 15
Olcott, Henry Steel, 63, 73–75, 106, 197n.7
  Esoteric Buddhism, 75, 194n.10
Orphic Circle, 63, 192n.73, 192n.86
Otto, Rudolf. *See* Sacred, the
Owen, Alex, 70, 203n.45
Owen, Reverend George Vale, 198n.33

Paige, Norman, 17–18
Partridge, Christopher. *See* occulture
Pasi, Marco, 19, 121–22, 162–63
paternal relationships. *See* father figures in
      fiction
Penny Blood, 187n.94
periodicals, 103–4, 131–32, 135. *See also* new
      journalism
Peters, Albert Vout, 111–12, 113–14
Poe, Edgar Allan, 144–45
politics of occult fiction, 3–4, 9–11, 178–79. *See
      also* Bulwer Lytton, Edward; Corelli,
      Marie; Crowley, Aleister
poltergeists, 119, 132–33. *See also* Hornsey
      poltergeist
popular fiction
  definitions of, 21, 177–78
  didactic uses of, 35–36
  market for, 4
popular sublime, 85–86, 88
Potter, Clifford, 111–12, 113–14
Potter, J.W., 111–12
Powell, Evan, 111–12

INDEX 231

Praed, Rosa Campbell, 73–75
Pratchett, Terry, 179–80
Prichard, Kate and Hesketh
    Flaxman Low (character), 142–43
    "The Story of the Moor Road," 146, 147–48,
        202n.13
publishing industry in Victorian period, 25

race
    Theosophical understandings of, 78–79,
        195n.31 (*see also* Crowley, Aleister,
        race; detective fiction, racial politics of;
        romance revival, ideas of race within;
        Theosophy, and race)
Radcliffe, Anne, 47–48
Ra-Hoor-Khuit, 152–53, 154–55, 168, 204n.64
Ramaswamy, Sumathi, 78–79
Randolph, Paschal Beverly, 40, 78–79, 195n.32
rape, 94–97. *See also* Crowley, Aleister;
    violence, gender-based
realism, literary, 28–29, 33–34, 40, 48, 77–78,
    187n.89
Regardie, Israel, 151–52, 206n.3
reincarnation
    in fiction, 37, 70–71, 72–73, 75, 76–
        77, 80–102
    and gender mutability, 196n.85
    occult revival popularization of, 37, 72, 73–
        77, 101–2, 193n.2
    See also Karma
rejected knowledge. *See* esotericism studies
Renoir, Katherine Mary Dalton
    "The Case of the Fortunate Youth," 147–48
reporters, spiritualists and occultists as, 103–4
Reynolds, G.W.M.
    Wagner the Wehr-Wolf, 23–24, 26–27
Richet, Charles, 201n.113
Roberts, Marie Mulvey, 8–9, 19–21, 27–28
Rohmer, Sax
    Morris Klaw, the Dream Detective
        (character), 142–43
romance revival, 4–5, 37, 77–79, 101–2
    gender coordinates of, 37, 72–73, 77–
        79, 85–86
    ideas of race within, 77–78
Rosenthal, Jesse, 43–44, 69–70
Rosicrucianism, 5–6
    in fiction (*see* Bulwer Lytton, *Zanoni*;
        Reynolds, G.W.M., *Wagner the
        Wehr-Wolf*)
Roukema, Aren, 62–63

Sacred, the, 11–13, 127–28

Said, Edward, 167–68
Salmon, Richard, 41–42, 49–50
Sambrooke, Jerilyn, 180–81
Satanism, in fiction, 17–18
Sayers, Dorothy, 143–44, 163–64
Scarlet Woman, 164–65
Schauerroman, 43–44
secrecy in occult fiction, 3–5, 33
secret societies in fiction 46–47
secularity and secularization, 11–13, 180–82,
    185n.42
    relationship to literary studies, 7–8, 40, 49–
        50, 69–70, 180–82, 208n.41
Seddon, Frederick, 116–17
selfishness as gendered attribute, 97
sex magic, 101–2, 171–72, 207n.23
sexual polarity. *See* Fortune, Dion
Shakespeare, William, 14–15
    Hamlet, 44–46, 54–55
Shelley, Mary
    *Frankenstein; or, the Modern
        Prometheus*, 67–68
Shelley, Percy Bysshe
    St Irvynne; or, The Rosicrucian, 23–24
Sherlock Holmes (character), 138–39, 141–43,
    145–46, 148–49, 156–57, 158–59,
    203n.29, *See also* Doyle, Arthur Conan
Sidgwick, Henry, 186n.76
Sidney Street, Battle of, 116–17
Simon Iff (character). *See* Crowley, Aleister
Sinclair, Marie. *See* Caithness, Countess of
Sinnett, A.P., 73–76, 106, 197n.7
    Karma, 72, 75, 82–84, 104–5
Societas Rosicruciana in Anglia, 19–21,
    48–49
Society for the Diffusion of Spiritual
    Knowledge, 59–60, 109–10
Society of the Inner Light. *See* Fortune, Dion
Society for Psychical Research, 19–21, 142–43,
    175–76, 184n.26, 186n.76, 186n.77
Speight, C. Allen, 43–44
Spiritisme, 73–75
Spiritual Age, 59–60, 190n.14
Spiritual Telegraph, 59–60
spiritualism, movement, 5–6, 25, 60–61, 109–
    10, 179–80
    relationship to mass media, 187n.88
    spirit mediumship, 107, 108–11, 113–14,
        132–33
    spirit photography, 132–33
    women's participation in, 40–41, 70
Spiritualist Magazine, 43–44
Spivak, Gayatri, 90

232 INDEX

Spooner, Catherine, 17
Starr, Martin P., 148–49, 150, 162–63, 167–68,
    203n.48, 206n.106
Stead, Estelle, 110–11
Stead, W.T., 37–38, 103–4, 106–15, 136–37,
    197n.10
    After Death; or Letters from Julia, 109–
        10, 114–15
    Borderland, 108–9, 198n.19
    "The Future of Journalism," 107–8
    introduction to spiritualism, 108–9
    journalistic career, 106–15
    Julia's Bureau, 108–11, 198n.29
    *Letters from Julia; or, Light from the
        Borderland*, 109–10, 111–12, 134
    "The Maiden Tribute of Modern Babylon,"
        106–7, 108, 198n.15
    and *Pall Mall Gazette*, 106–7
    as religious reformer, 107, 108
    as spirit, 112
    W.T. Stead Borderland Library, 110–11
Steiner, Rudolf, 1–2, 43–44
Stevenson, Robert Louis, 77–78
    The Strange Case of Dr Jekyll and Mr Hyde,
        51, 191n.47
    "The Suicide Club," 117
St James Gazette, 115–16
Stoker, Bram
    Dracula, 10–11, 23, 38, 51–52, 88, 97–98,
        186n.56
Strube, Julian, 7–8, 10–11
Stuart, Mary [Queen of Scots], 75–76
Stuckrad, Kocku von, 6–7
Summers, Montague, 17–18
Supernatural (TV show), 144–45
Sutin, Lawrence, 167–68
Swaffer, Hannen, 37–38, 103–4, 111–15,
    136–37
    Northcliffe's Return, 111–16
Sweetser, Wesley, 116

Tabloid. *See* newspaper
Tappan, Cora Scott, 194n.9
Taylor, Charles, 180
Tennyson, Alfred, 17–18, 180–81

Thelema, 38, 91–92, 96, 152–53, 179–80
    crime and, 156, 159–61, 162–63, 168–69
    meaning, 152–53
Thelemic philosophy, 152–56, 159–61, 162–63,
    165–66, 205n.86
Theosophical Society, 58–59, 73–75, 78–79
Theosophy, 5–6, 37, 72–73, 77–79, 80, 91, 142–
    43, 179–80
    and race, 78–79, 195n.31, 195n.32
    relationship to imperialism, 78–79
Tibet, David, 150–51
T.P.'s Weekly, 115–16
transmigration. *See* reincarnation

Urban, Hugh, 4–5

Vanity Fair, 115–16
Varma, Devendra, 17–18
Versluis, Arthur, 13–14, 185n.49
Viereck, Sylvester, 168, 203n.40
Villars, Abbé de, 183n.1
violence, gender-based, 37, 70–71, 72–73, 78–
    79, 94–95, 96, 97, 100–1
Viswanathan, Gauri, 78–79

Waite, A.E., 115–16
Walker, E.D., 73–75
Wallraven, Miriam, 7–8
Warren, Samuel
    Diary of a Late Physician, 146–47
Warwick, Alexandra, 16
Watkins Books, 170–71
Welcome Guest, 122
The Whirlwind, 115–16
will, in magical practice. *See* Crowley, Aleister
Wolfreys, Julian, 16
women writers as romance revivalists, 85–91
Woolf, Virginia
    The Years, 171–72
Wordsworth, William, 73–75
World (Brooklyn), 129–30

The X-Files (TV show), 144–45

Ziolkowski, Theodor, 46